# The Family System Test F

## Theory and Application

The *Family System Test FAST*, developed by Thomas M. Gehring, is an important new tool for investigating family relations. Based on the structural–systemic theory of families, it is a figural technique for representing emotional bonds (cohesion) and hierarchical structures in the family or similar social systems. In this unique volume, the editors draw on current theory and research in family psychology, together with a variety of empirical studies that have used the FAST, to provide a comprehensive overview and assessment of the test and its use in various clinical research contexts.

The book is divided into five sections, the first four of which each focus on a different aspect of the FAST. Part I describes the methodological concepts and psychometric properties of the FAST within the context of theoretically and empirically relevant aspects of the field of family psychology as a whole. Special emphasis is given to structural–systemic approaches to assessing individual and family functioning. Part II focuses on the use of the FAST in developmental research. For example, the FAST has been used to show how family constructs are influenced by age, and type of family and situation. Part III deals with cross-cultural issues and compares the interpersonal constructs of Japanese and Chinese families to those of Western families. Part IV addresses the applications of the FAST in a clinical setting – in diagnosis of biopsychosocial problems and planning and evaluation of clinical interventions. Finally, Part V looks at possible future directions and uses for the FAST.

**Thomas M. Gehring** is Senior Lecturer for Clinical Psychology at the University of Basle and Head of the Section of Methodology and Evaluation at the Department of Social and Preventive Medicine, University of Zurich. He is the author of the Family System Test (FAST). **Marianne Debry** is a Professor at the University of Liège and Head of the Department of Child and Adolescent Psychology. She has translated the FAST manual into French. **Peter K. Smith** is Professor of Psychology at Goldsmiths College, University of London, and Head of the Unit for School and Family Studies.

# The Family System Test FAST

Theory and Application

**Thomas M. Gehring, Marianne Debry and Peter K. Smith**

**Routledge**
Taylor & Francis Group

LONDON AND NEW YORK

First published 2001
by Brunner-Routledge

2 Park Square, Milton Park, Abingdon, Oxon OX14 4RN
711 Third Avenue, New York, NY 10017, USA

*Routledge is an imprint of the Taylor & Francis Group, an informa business*

First issued in paperback 2016

Typeset in Times by Keystroke, Jacaranda Lodge, Wolverhampton

*British Library Cataloguing in Publication Data*
A catalogue record for this book is available from the British Library

*Library of Congress Cataloging in Publication Data*
The Family System Test (FAST) : theory and application / [edited by] Thomas M. Gehring,
Marianne Debry, and Peter K. Smith
    p. cm.
  Includes bibliographical references and index.
  ISBN 978-1-138-96959-9 (pbk)
  ISBN 978-0-415-21789-7 (hbk)
  1. Family System Test. 2. Family assessment. I. Gehring, Thomas M.,
1953– II. Debry, Marianne, 1952– III. Smith, Peter K.
HQ728 .F31443 2001
306.85—dc21                                     00–053013

# Contents

*List of figures and tables*                                    viii
*List of contributors*                                          xi
*Foreword*                                                      xv
*Preface*                                                       xix

**PART I**
**Understanding family structures: Theory, assessment and
methodology**                                                   **1**

1.  **Concept and psychometric properties of the FAST**          3
    THOMAS M. GEHRING AND DANIEL MARTI

2.  **The FAST at the crossroads of systemic theories**          28
    MARIANNE DEBRY

3.  **Comprehensive family evaluation**                          45
    LUCIANO L'ABATE AND DOUGLAS K. SNYDER

4.  **Relational diagnosis: An overview of methods**             58
    JAY LEBOW

**PART II**
**Interpersonal patterns in non-clinical family systems**        **69**

5.  **Investigation of family schemata of preschool children:
    Methodological and conceptual considerations**               71
    LUCY MORLEY-WILLIAMS AND HELEN COWIE

6.  **Family constructs of first graders: Different measurement approaches yield distinct outcomes**    92
    FLORENCE MEYER

7.  **Perception of internal and external family boundaries by well-adjusted children, bullies and victims**    107
    LUCIA BERDONDINI AND MARIA LUISA GENTA

8.  **Comparing parents' and children's perceptions of the family: Can the FAST be used as a measure of social cognition and theory of mind ability?**    118
    PETER K. SMITH, ROWAN MYRON-WILSON AND JON SUTTON

9.  **Single-parent families: How does the loss of the father influence the father image of mothers and daughters?**    133
    REGINA HUNTER AND IRENE VON BALLMOOS

10.  **Perceptions of mother–daughter relations and pubertal development**    149
    KENNETH KIM AND THANES WONGYANNAVA

11.  **Cohesion and relative power in family relationships and adolescent coping with a real-life stressful situation**    157
    OFRA MAYSELESS AND MIRI SCHARF

**PART III**
**The FAST in Asian cultures**    **177**

12.  **Perceptions of family structures by Japanese students**    179
    KAZUO IKEDA AND TAKESHI HATTA

13.  **Characteristics of three-generation Chinese families**    194
    SHU SHU AND PETER K. SMITH

**PART IV**
**Clinical issues: Diagnosis, intervention and evaluation**    **209**

14.  **The FAST: A therapeutic tool for interactive assessment and treatment in family psychotherapy**    211
    SANDRA A. RIGAZIO-DIGILIO

15. **Conceptualization of parental interventions in child psychiatry**   233

THOMAS M. GEHRING, JULIE PAGE AND DANIEL MARTI

16. **Supervision: Reflecting clinical practice and team development**   247

CHRISTOPH STEINEBACH

**PART V**
**Conclusions and recommendations**   **265**

17. **Future directions for FAST and family evaluation**   267

MARIANNE DEBRY, PETER K. SMITH AND THOMAS M. GEHRING

**Author index**   **279**
**Subject index**   **286**

# Figures and tables

## Figures

| | | |
|---|---|---|
| 1.1 | FAST representation of cohesion and hierarchy in a family of five | 10 |
| 1.2 | Protocol of a FAST representation of a family with five members | 10 |
| 1.3 | Types of family cohesion and hierarchy structures | 12 |
| 2.1 | Family members' height means | 31 |
| 2.2 | Percentages of coalitions and hierarchy reversals in the three FAST representations | 32 |
| 2.3 | Relational structures in the three FAST representations | 36 |
| 2.4 | Analysis of factorial correspondences in relational structures | 37 |
| 2.5 | Interpretation of the correspondences analysis | 38 |
| 2.6 | FAST performed by Claire | 40 |
| 5.1 | Drawing by a secure child | 80 |
| 5.2 | Drawing by a defended child | 81 |
| 5.3 | Drawing by a coercive child | 83 |
| 5.4 | Drawing by a defended child | 83 |
| 5.5 | FAST plot of a defended child | 84 |
| 5.6 | FAST plot of a secure child | 84 |
| 5.7 | FAST plot of a coercive child | 85 |
| 5.8 | FAST plot of a secure child | 85 |
| 5.9 | FAST plot of James | 86 |
| 5.10 | FAST plot of Toby | 87 |
| 7.1 | Case example from a control child | 111 |
| 7.2 | Case example from a victim child | 111 |
| 7.3 | Case example from a bully child | 112 |
| 8.1 | A set of four FAST plots (terminology standardized from child's point of view) | 122 |
| 8.2 | Scoring tables from three sets of four FAST plots | 127 |
| 11.1 | Distances between figures on the FAST as a function of perspective | 163 |
| 11.2 | Relative power on the FAST as a function of different perspectives | 163 |
| 12.1 | Classification of Japanese family structures in typical, ideal and conflict representation | 183 |
| 12.2 | Classification of family structures | 186 |
| 14.1 | Session one – intertypical and interideal representations | 219 |

14.2   Session two – father's ideal representation                                225
14.3   Mid-therapy session – intertypical and father conflict representations  227
14.4   Final therapy session – parents' typical and future typical
       representations                                                          229
15.1   Planning and evaluation of parent-oriented problem-solving
       processes                                                                240

## Tables

1.1    Fundamental concept of the Family System Test                              8
1.2    Types of relational structures in individual and group representations
       of typical relationships by members of the same family                   13
1.3    Types of relational structures in individual FAST representations of
       typical relationships by parents as a function of the clinical status
       of the child                                                             15
6.1    Cohesion scores in typical and ideal representations on different
       system levels                                                            97
6.2    Hierarchy scores in typical and ideal representations on different
       system levels                                                            98
6.3    Types of relational structures in typical and ideal representations
       on different system levels                                               99
9.1    Demographic data concerning the daughters and their mothers in the
       divorced group                                                           139
9.2    Demographic data concerning the semiorphans and their mothers           140
9.3    Classification of type of relational structures in typical representation 142
9.4    Classification of type of relational structures in ideal representation  142
9.5    Classification of type of relational structures of the triadic
       representation                                                           143
10.1   Summary of results for cohesion between mothers and daughters            151
10.2   Summary of results for power between mothers and daughters               152
11.1   Pearson correlations between portrayals of distances on the FAST
       and indices of general adjustment                                        164
11.2   Correlations between FAST power gap perceptions of sons, fathers
       and mothers, and indices of general adjustment                           166
11.3   Pearson correlations between portrayals of distances on the FAST
       and adjustment to basic training                                         167
11.4   Final cluster centres based on perceptions of cohesion and power
       by all family members                                                    169
11.5   Adjustment to basic training of adolescents from various family
       structures (clusters based on the perspectives of all family members)   170
11.6   Cluster centres based on perceptions of cohesion and power by the
       adolescent                                                               170
11.7   Adjustment to basic training of adolescents from various family
       structures (based on clusters derived from the adolescent's
       perspective)                                                             171

12.1  Perceptions of cohesion and hierarchy by all Japanese samples   182
12.2  Mean dyadic distances in Japanese families   184
12.3  Perceptions of cohesion and hierarchy by Japanese and Swiss
      respondents   185
12.4  Cohesion of parent subsystem   187
12.5  Hierarchy of parent subsystem   188
12.6  Cohesion of sibling subsystem   188
12.7  Hierarchy of sibling subsystem   188
13.1  Educational background and occupation of grandparents and parents   199
13.2  Mean distance scores for each dyad as represented by all family
      members   200
13.3  Mean number of power blocks received by each family member   201
13.4  Perceptions of types of family structures by adults and children   202
15.1  Parents' attempted changes as assessed by differences between
      typical and ideal FAST representations in individual and group
      settings at the onset of child psychiatric treatment   237
15.2  Items and time of data collection by the SOFA questionnaire   239
15.3  Changing constructs of parents across therapy and in the follow-up
      as assessed by SOFA and FAST   243
16.1  Psychological aspects of cohesion and power on various system
      levels   248
16.2  Types of family structure as a function of personal resources and
      partner and patient characteristics from the mothers' perspective   249
16.3  Correlations between mothers' representations of typical family
      relations and their expected and desired relations in the therapeutic
      system with the FAST   254
16.4  Comparison of cohesion and power in mono- and interdisciplinary
      teams in typical, ideal and conflict representations   256
16.5  Types of typical team structure as a function of personal resources
      for professional development and perception of colleagues   256
16.6  Changing cohesion and hierarchy in therapy and supervision
      using the FAST   258
17.1  Characteristics of empirical studies with the FAST represented in
      this book   271

# Contributors

**Lucia Berdondini**, PhD, works as a Post-doctoral Research Fellow at the School of Education, University of Brighton, UK. She also works in Italy, running training courses for teachers, children and parents on the quality of relational dynamics, on communication, on conflict solving and on antibullying strategies. She is very interested in the area of antibullying intervention in schools and is carrying out action research in this field, planning and applying different techniques. She explores the process of these intervention projects and their effectiveness using observational methodologies.

**Helen Cowie**, MA, MSc, PhD, Diploma in Psychotherapy, is Research Professor in the School of Psychology and Counselling at the University of Surrey, Roehampton, UK, where she is also Director of the Centre for Peer and Family Relationships. She has worked for many years in the research area of peer relationships, in particular in the field of bullying and social exclusion. She is a practising Chartered Counselling Psychologist with a particular interest in peer and family relationships. She is the author of a large number of books and articles in the field of child development, in particular on peer support against bullying, on counselling and supporting children in distress and on children's narratives.

**Marianne Debry**, Professor at the University of Liège (Belgium), is Head of the Department of Child and Adolescent Psychology. She is responsible for the outpatient clinic at the University of Liège, which works with children, adolescents and families and where she works as child and family psychotherapist. She translated the FAST manual into French and she trains clinicians in its application.

**Thomas M. Gehring**, PhD, Clinical Psychologist and Psychotherapist, is the author of the FAST. He is Lecturer for Clinical Psychology at the University of Basle, Switzerland and Head of the Section of Methodology and Evaluation at the Department of Social and Preventive Medicine, University of Zurich, Switzerland. He serves as Psychological Supervisor at the Intensive Care Unit of the University Children's Hospital, Zurich.

**Maria Luisa Genta** is Professor of Developmental Psychology at Bologna University, Italy, and researcher in developmental psychology at the Psychology Department of the same university. She has worked in the research area of infant studies with European and American teams, mainly on early mother–infant interactions and the development of intersubjectivity in the dyad. She is also contributing to the development of Italian studies on bullying in schools and to the research area of peer relationships, joining European teams and focusing on observational strategies in peer groups.

**Takeshi Hatta**, PhD, is currently Professor at Nagoya University, Unit of Human Behavior and Information Processing, School of Informatics and Sciences, Nagoya City, Japan. He is a member of the Japanese Psychological Association, Japanese Neuropsychological Society, Association of Japanese Educational Psychology. His main research areas are Cognitive Psychology and Neuropsychology.

**Regina Hunter**, MA, PhD, Clinical Psychologist and Social Worker (MSW). Formation in Couple and Family Therapy, in Person-centred Psychotherapy and in Psychoanalysis. She works as a psychoanalyst in her own practice in Schaffhausen, Switzerland.

**Kazuo Ikeda**, MEd, is Associate Professor, Kochi University Faculty of Humanities, Department of Human Culture, Kochi City, Japan. His main research areas are cognitive psychology and social cognition.

**Kenneth Kim**, BA, BA, PhD, is a Lecturer at the School of Social Work, University of East Anglia, Norwich, UK, whose first degrees were in sociology (1988) and anthropology and psychology (1991) at York University, Canada, and whose PhD was in psychology (1997) at the University of Sheffield, UK. Research interests are in crossnational developmental psychology, particularly in the areas of family life, puberty and adolescence.

**Luciano L'Abate**, PhD, is Professor Emeritus of Psychology at Georgia State University, USA, where he served as Director of the Family Psychology Training Center and the Family Study Center. He is internationally known as a teacher, lecturer and clinician. Among his many professional affiliations, he is Diplomate and Examiner of the American Board of Professional Psychology; Fellow and Approved Supervisor of the American Association for Marriage and Family Therapy (AAMFT); Fellow of Divisions 12 and 43 of the American Psychological Association (APA); Charter Member of the American Family Therapy Academy; and Cofounder and Past President of the International Academy of Family Psychology.

**Jay Lebow**, PhD, is a Senior Therapist and Research Consultant at The Family Institute, Chicago, and Adjunct Associate Professor in the School of Education and Social Policy, Northwestern University, Chicago, IL, USA. He is involved in the ongoing treatment research at The Family Institute, teaches in various Institute programmes, and maintains a clinical practice. Among his many professional affiliations, he is a clinical member and an approved supervisor of the American Association of Marriage and Family Therapy, a member of the Board of Directors of the American Board of Family Psychology, a committee chair of the Board of Directors of the American Family Therapy Academy, and a member and Fellow of the American Psychological Association and its Divisions of Clinical and Family Psychology.

**Daniel Marti**, MD, MS, Child and Adolescent Psychiatrist, is Head of the Department of Psychosomatics and Psychiatry at the University Children's Hospital Zurich, Switzerland.

**Ofra Mayseless**, PhD, Clinical Psychologist and Researcher, is Associate Professor at the Faculty of Education at the University of Haifa, Israel. Her main research areas are attachment, parental caregiving and the transition from adolescence to adulthood.

**Florence Meyer**, PhD, Senior Lecturer at the Institute of Psychology of the University of Lausanne, Switzerland, is Clinical Psychologist at the Consultation Service for Children and Adolescents of the same University. Her main research areas are projective tests and techniques for child psychology (in particular drawings and FAST) and clinical consultation procedures (in particular the analysis of the request for help).

**Lucy Morley-Williams**, PhD, is a Graduate Assistant at the School of Psychology and Counselling, University of Surrey, Roehampton, London, UK. She currently works with adults with learning disabilities, focusing upon the assessment of quality of life and service provision. Her original research explored the association between attachment theory and the development of a theory of mind in the preschool child. She was also involved in the TMR bullying research projects.

**Rowan Myron-Wilson**, PhD, is a Lecturer at the University of Hull, UK. Her research interests include bullying, attachment, parent–child relationships and parental influence on antisocial behaviour.

**Julie Page**, MA, is a Research Associate at the Department of Social and Preventive Medicine, University of Zurich, Switzerland. Her main research areas are quality of life, social support and health-related interventions.

**Sandra Rigazio-DiGilio**, PhD, is Associate Professor in the COAMFTE-accredited masters and doctoral marriage and family therapy programs at the University of Connecticut, Storrs, USA. She is a Licensed Psychologist, a Licensed Marriage and Family Therapist, and an AAMFT Approved Supervisor. Her main research areas are focused on advancing a model of therapy (Systemic Cognitive–Developmental Therapy) and an accompanying supervisory model (Systemic Cognitive–Developmental Supervision) that both serve to advance an integrative, co-constructive and developmental framework.

**Miri Scharf**, PhD, Psychotherapist and Researcher, is Assistant Professor at the Faculty of Education at the University of Haifa, Israel. Her main research areas are attachment, parenting and friendship in middle childhood and in adolescence.

**Shu Shu** is a Research Assistant and Postgraduate Student at the Department of Psychology, Goldsmiths College, University of London, UK. She is interested in three-generation families in China and in life history narrative approaches to understanding development.

**Peter K. Smith** is Professor of Psychology and Head of the Unit of School and Family Studies at Goldsmiths College, University of London, UK. He is interested in many aspects of social development, including grandparenting, conflict and bullying in school, and social uses of theory of mind.

**Douglas K. Snyder**, PhD, is Professor and Director of Clinical Psychology Training at Texas A&M University, USA. He previously served on the faculty at Wayne State University and as Professor and Associate Dean of Arts and Sciences at the University of Kentucky. Professor Snyder is a Fellow of Divisions 5, 12, 29 and 43 of the APA and a Fellow of the Society for Personality Assessment. He has served as Editor of the *Clinician's Research Digest*, published monthly by the APA, as Associate Editor of the *Journal of Consulting and Clinical Psychology*, and on the editorial boards of numerous journals in marital and family therapy. Professor Snyder is author of the widely used Marital Satisfaction Inventory. He received the AAMFT's 1992 Outstanding Marriage and Family Therapy Research Award for his 4-year follow-up study comparing insight-oriented and behavioural marital therapy.

**Christoph Steinebach**, PhD, Clinical Psychologist, Psychotherapist, Supervisor and Consultant, is Professor of Developmental and Educational Psychology at the Catholic University of Applied Sciences, Freiburg, Germany.

**Jon Sutton**, PhD, worked until recently as a Research Lecturer at Glasgow Caledonian University, UK; he is now editor of *Psychologist*. His interests in the field of social development include bullying and theory of mind, disruptive behaviour and avoidance of responsibility, competition and Machiavellianism.

**Irene von Ballmoos**, MA, is a Clinical Psychologist in the Outpatient Clinic for Children and Adolescents of the Psychiatric Department of the City of Weinfelden, Switzerland, where she works with children, adolescents, their families and systems. Her main work is psychoanalytical, family, and group psychotherapy.

**Thanes Wongyannava**, BA, MSc, MPhil, is a Lecturer at the Faculty of Political Science, Thammasat University, Bangkok, Thailand. His first degree was in sociology and anthropology at Chulalongkorn University, Thailand, with postgraduate work in sociology at University of Wisconsin (Madison), USA, and Cambridge, UK. His research interests are in social theory and cross-cultural psychology, particularly in the area of gender and sexuality.

# Foreword

The contributors to this volume all share one basic assumption about the nature of family research and the practice of family therapy. That assumption is that both research and clinical practice should be guided by a clearly articulated theory of family behaviour. This theory should describe what is considered to be 'normal', 'healthy' or 'desirable' family functioning. It should also explain how dysfunctional family structures and faulty family processes develop, and why they remain stable over time and across generations. Implicit in this assumption is the belief that any instrument or procedure that is used for pretreatment assessment, to monitor the therapeutic process or to evaluate treatment outcomes must be a reliable and valid measure of the particular theoretical construct or constructs that are the focus of investigation or intervention.

All the contributors to this volume report their clinical and research experiences concerning the use of the Family System Test (FAST) in their work with family systems. The FAST is a projective measure designed to assess the respondent's perceptions of two key constructs derived from family systems theory, namely, cohesion and hierarchy. The FAST is unique in that this figure placement procedure enables the respondent to translate what are essentially symbolic, abstract, analogical and highly subjective internal representations of family dynamics into concrete and digital depictions of family structures and processes that can be used for both qualitative and quantitative analyses. When used in conjunction with questions specifically designed to elicit information concerning the development and evolution of family structures and processes over time and across the family lifecycle, the FAST becomes a very powerful clinical/research tool. For example, an individual can be asked to depict changes in group dynamics in his/her family of origin by responding to a few systems-oriented questions, such as the ones developed by Bagarozzi and Anderson (1989). Examples of questions designed to highlight changing patterns of cohesion include:

'In your family of origin, when you were (a child, teenager, young adult, etc.), to whom were you the closest?'
'Which person did you like the most?'
'Which person did you like the least?'

'Who owned you emotionally and what was the nature of the emotional attachment?'

'Which person did you fear?'

To learn about how hierarchical arrangements are perceived to have changed over time, a respondent is asked:

'When you were (a child, teenager, young adult, etc.), who had the most power in your family of origin?'

'What type of power was it?'

'How and when was this power used?'

'What type of power did each member of your family have?'

'How and when did he/she use it?'

Observing the changes in figure placements in response to these various questions about cohesion and hierarchy enables a dynamic picture of family systems development to emerge. In the same vein, respondents can be asked to arrange FAST figures as they were perceived to have behaved during important life events (e.g. family crises, family transitional stages and family celebrations).

As I read through this volume, I found myself thinking of ways that the FAST might be used to answer some difficult research questions and respond to a number of clinical challenges that confront therapists who engage in family diagnostic testing (Bagarozzi, 1989). For example, when children are asked to depict relationships between and among other family members it is important to consider how the validity and reliability of their responses are affected by limitations in their capacity for role taking and perspective reversal. A child's egocentrism (as conceptualized by cognitive developmentalists such as Piaget) must be taken into account, especially when children's arrangements are used to set treatment goals and evaluate therapeutic outcomes.

I believe that the FAST can be used to help the clinician unearth and assess family myths (Anderson and Bagarozzi, 1989; Bagarozzi and Anderson, 1989; Ferreira, 1963, 1966). For example, when a family group is asked to reach a consensus about figure placements and arrangements, the agreed-upon constellation can be thought of as representing a family myth, i.e. the way the family would like to be perceived by outsiders. When a family is asked to reach a consensus about ideal family functioning, the spectre of experimenter effects emerges and poses a challenge to clinicians and researchers alike.

Each chapter in this volume stimulated my thinking. Each contributor to this work offers something new. Few research-based texts, in my opinion, can appeal to both researchers and clinicians. Gehring, Debry and Smith, however, seem to have accomplished this difficult editorial feat with relative ease – no small accomplishment? I believe anyone who reads this volume will come away not only with a wealth of knowledge but with a greater appreciation for the complementary relationship between empirical research and clinical practice.

Dennis A. Bagarozzi

# References

Anderson, S.A. and Bagarozzi, D.A. (eds) (1989) *Family Myths: Psychotherapy Implications*, New York: Haworth.

Bagarozzi, D.A. (1989) 'Family diagnostic testing: A neglected area of expertise for the family psychologist', *The American Journal of Family Therapy* 17: 261–74.

—— and Anderson, S.A. (1989) *Personal, Marital and Family Myths: Theoretical Formulations and Clinical Strategies*, New York: W.W. Norton.

Ferreira, A. (1963) 'Family myths and homeostasis', *Archives of General Psychiatry* 9: 457–63.

—— (1966) 'Family myths', *Psychiatric Research Reports of the American Psychiatric Association*, 20: 85–90.

# Preface

Families are important systems with regard to the physical and psychosocial development of their members and thus deserve the attention and involvement of researchers, as well as of professionals who work either therapeutically or in the prevention of psychological and health-related problems. Families can be described as open and dynamic systems consisting of members with reciprocal relationships. The latter are characterized by features such as intimacy, generational differentiation and continuity. Family structures are involved in internal and environmental changes that occur in relation to time and thus have a past, a present and a future. Therefore, an important parameter for understanding family systems is the flexibility of interpersonal patterns. This can be defined as the ability to adapt relational structures to contextually and developmentally determined demands across the lifecycle.

Comprehensive family assessment calls for a particular set of foci and techniques that enable the integration of developmental and phenomenological aspects into a systemic perspective on the basis of the hypothesized networks of family structures. However, there is still a paucity of psychometrically validated instruments that meet the distinct requirements of systemic theories, as well as of clinical practice and research. Evaluation of family systems requires user-friendly and economical diagnostic tools that allow descriptions of the family from the perspective of parents and children of various age groups as derived from individual and interactive settings. Family measures should consider normative aspects and, at the same time, be appropriate for each case in its particular circumstances. In addition, they should be able to illuminate past and current interpersonal patterns to anticipate future family developments.

Clinicians and researchers from various fields agree that cohesion and hierarchy are two key dimensions that describe family structures. Cohesion is generally defined as emotional bonding or attachment between family members. It includes the regulation of closeness and remoteness between family members. Hierarchy refers to authority, dominance, decision-making power or the amount of influence exercised by one family member over another. An additional issue for the evaluation of family structures is the concept of boundaries. It is used to describe relationships between families and their social environment, as well as relationships between various subsystems within the family (e.g. parents and children).

ʋo most commonly used methods for analysing family relationships focus
the individual or observations of interactions. These two approaches
e different aspects of the family and neither of them yields a complete
picture of the complex family dynamics. Interaction tasks provide data from an
outside perspective. As systematic analyses of interactions are time-consuming,
these observation methods are not standard in clinical practice and in research. For
economic reasons, questionnaires that provide subjective information from a
family insider perspective are more frequently used. In general, these questionnaires
focus either solely on the family as a whole or on selected dyads and, therefore, yield
limited information on family structures. In addition, questionnaires cannot be used
with preschool children because they require reading skills.

The increased recognition of figure placement techniques represents an important
advance in family assessment. These tools allow us to measure family structures in
individual settings, and to include small children in the measure, and they can also
be administered as an interactive task. The use of this method in individual and
group settings provides information on the respondents' individual and shared
family constructs, as well as on communication patterns while they are working on
their joint representation. Yet, despite their versatility and their three-decade history,
figure placement techniques have only recently been systematically used as
diagnostic, therapeutic, supervisory and research instruments. Reasons for this
delayed acceptance include imprecise description of clinical procedures and the
relatively few reliability and validity studies.

The present book provides a comprehensive description of the practical and
research-oriented importance of the Family System Test, hereafter referred to as the
FAST.[1] This clinically derived figure placement technique was designed to assess
individual and joint perceptions of the structure of cohesion and hierarchy governing
family relationships in typical, conflict and ideal situations. The goal of the FAST
is to determine psychosocial and health-related issues in system-oriented terms, to
facilitate the analysis of family patterns in various research settings and to enable
the planning and evaluation of therapeutic and preventive interventions. On the
basis of structural family systems theory, the test attempts to create an instrument
that is both economic and flexible in its application.

The first pilot studies with the FAST were performed with patients and their
families at the Department of Child and Adolescent Psychiatry, University of
Zurich, in the early 1980s. In the initial phase, application and scoring of the test
were not standardized, as it was more important at the time to explore the range of
clinical uses for the FAST and its relevance for the conceptualization of therapeutic
interventions. The preliminary evaluation indicated that the FAST was a versatile
and flexible tool that facilitates systemic exploration and the development of family-
oriented hypotheses. Furthermore, it was shown that children from the age of 6
years understood the principle of the test and that it also worked well with people
suffering from serious mental disorders.

The FAST subsequently underwent systematic validation with various samples,
and a standardized procedure, including a semistructured follow-up interview, was
introduced. The psychometric properties of the FAST were established at the

Department of Psychology, Stanford University, California, and a number of studies with non-clinical families were conducted. The Stanford studies were then replicated with Swiss samples. The results showed that family representations of the two groups did not differ significantly. The same holds true for FAST representations of English and Italian adolescents. However, recent research including some by Asian respondents has proved that FAST representations are able to capture culture-specific structural differences between Asian and Western families. For example, it has been shown that in non-clinical Japanese families, mother–child relationships are perceived as highly cohesive whereas fathers are relatively centrifugal. Therefore, in contrast to Western societies, the existence of 'unclear cross-generational boundaries' is not indicative of dysfunctional family structures in this culture.

Based on the predictions of the structural family theory and the results of Western studies with clinical and non-clinical samples, patterns of family functioning were defined by combining the dimensions of cohesion and hierarchy. This categorical scoring procedure of the FAST saves time-consuming calculations and allows an initial evaluation of family structures as soon as the representations are completed. This is particularly helpful in clinical practice because it promotes the ad hoc use of participative–discoursive problem-solving strategies.

Our book consists of four parts that focus on different aspects of the FAST as a clinical and research tool; a fifth part contains conclusions and recommendations. The theoretical contributions and studies document the current knowledge drawn from international projects conducted in the past decade and attempt to improve the use of comprehensive systemic procedures for the evaluation and to develop human relationships in the context of the family and other social systems such as clinical teams. The structure of the book allows selected chapters to be read separately.

Part I of this work introduces theoretically and empirically relevant aspects of the field of family psychology, with special emphasis on systemic–structural approaches to assess individual and family functioning in clinical and research settings. The methodological concept of the FAST and its psychometric properties are described, followed by an outline of the significance of systems theory in order to gain insight into the complex organization of family development. Based on this, an overview of widely used, well-validated and conceptually sound family measurement approaches focusing on the interdependence between interpersonal structures and health-related outcomes is presented.

Part II focuses on the application of the FAST in developmental research, including data from non-clinical members of various family constellations (e.g. two- and single-parent families). Using samples of preschoolers, first graders, preadolescents, adolescents and young adults, it shows how family constructs are influenced by the age and gender of respondents, the type of family constellation and the represented situation. For example, the correspondence between perceptions of family structures and offspring's adjustment, and coping with military service, is studied. Using multirespondent research designs, this Part explores how parents and children of the same family view their relational structures.

Part III describes interpersonal constructs of members of modern Japanese families and three-generation Chinese families. Results of the two studies are compared with those derived from Western samples, and suggestions for an adaptation of the FAST procedure for its use with Asian families are made.

Part IV moves from the more general aspects of individual and family development to specific topics such as assignments of the systematic planning and evaluation of family-oriented interventions in clinical practice. The three contributions delineate the relevance of the FAST for relational diagnosis as well as the conceptualization of systemic problem-solving processes. Empirical data and a case example demonstrate the significance of a participative–discoursive use of this tool in planning, evaluation and supervision of therapy. Suggestions are made as to how the FAST might favour the emergence of high standards in interpersonal treatment approaches for psychological and medical problems.

Part V draws conclusions and makes recommendations for the future use of the FAST in family evaluation.

This book is planned to be an authoritative and innovative guide for system-oriented researchers, practitioners and students from various disciplines who work with children, adolescents and adults in clinical and non-clinical settings. It is our hope that the versatility of the ideas and findings presented will stimulate a creative application and further development of the FAST in different fields of public health, education and social welfare.

Thomas M. Gehring, Marianne Debry and Peter K. Smith

## Note

1    The extracts from the Family System Test (FAST), © 1998 Hogrefe & Huber Publishers, appear with permission of the publisher.

The FAST is a semi-quantitative figural technique for representing the bonds (cohesion) and hierarchical structures within families and similar social systems. It can be used qualitatively or semi-quantitatively in exploring, forming hypotheses about, and interpreting clinical findings, and is based on the structural-systemic theory of families.

For more details, please see the description at http://www.hhpub.com/catalogue/Gehring.html and at http://www.fast-test.com. In addition to the English-language version, the test is also available in German and various other languages. The complete English test kit (order #01 262 01; US ¢298.00 / DM 548.00) and the individual components (test forms, test materials, manual) can be obtained from Hogrefe & Huber Publishers at the following addresses:

**Europe & Rest of the World:**
Hogrefe & Huber Publishers
Rohnsweg 25
D-37085 Göttingen
Germany
Tel: +49 551 496090
Fax: +49 551 4960988
E-mail: custserv@hogrefe.de

**North America:**
Hogrefe & Huber Publishers
PO Box 388
Ashland, OH 44805
Tel: (800) 228-3749
Fax: (419) 281-6883
E-mail: hh@hhpub.com

# Part I

# Understanding family structures: Theory, assessment and methodology

# 1 Concept and psychometric properties of the FAST

*Thomas M. Gehring and Daniel Marti*

## Introduction

The consideration of the family is a crucial addition to the well-recognized notions of individual and environmental risk factors and resources of human development. Undoubtedly, there is still a great need for further development of comprehensive concepts for family diagnosis as it applies to health promotion and to the prevention and therapy of biopsychosocial problems. Suitable family assessment calls for a particular set of methodological techniques that allows the integration of individual, interpersonal and contextual parameters into a systemic perspective based on our current knowledge of the organization of family structures.

Any test reduces the complexity of human systems to a few parameters, a simplification required by working models. Moreover, the structure of a family system cannot be fully derived from the reports of its individual members, just as it is not possible to determine the characteristics of the family members solely by analysing their interactions. According to Jameson and Alexander (1994), family measures should consider normative aspects and, at the same time, be appropriate for each case in its particular circumstances. Comprehensive family evaluation, therefore, requires standardized test procedures that allow a quantitative and qualitative analysis of interpersonal constructs as well as of the interactional patterns of parents and children in various settings (L'Abate, 1994; Wilkinson, 1998; Werner-Wilson *et al.*, 1999).

This chapter describes the fundamental concept of the *Family System Test* FAST (Gehring, 1998, 2000), a clinically derived figure placement technique for the assessment of family cohesion and hierarchy structures in individual and joint settings. First, important aspects of family psychology are summarized, with emphasis being placed on well-adjusted and problematic relational structures. Second, psychometric properties of the FAST and its use to evaluate family functioning in research and clinical practice are described.

## Describing family structures

Systemic approaches provide a comprehensive framework for describing the relational structure of families on different levels such as dyads, triads or the family

as a unit (Ackerman, 1985; Minuchin, 1985; Kaslow, 1996). Families are characterized by features such as intimacy, generational differentiation and continuity.
They are organized systems that are conditioned by their environment, which, in
turn, receives inputs from these systems. These interdependent changes always
occur in relation to time. Therefore, the interpretation of respective processes should
include the past and the present, as well as the future.

### Cohesion and hierarchy

It is well known that cohesion and hierarchy are two fundamental dimensions that
describe the interpersonal structure of family systems. Cohesion is generally defined
as emotional bonding or attachment between family members (Bowen, 1960;
Stierlin, 1974). The structure of cohesion includes the regulation of closeness and
distance between family members and their respect of personal privacy. In reference
to family systems, cohesion is defined as the extent to which the family members
are organized as a coherent whole. Hierarchy covers several theoretical assumptions
and cannot be attached to a single definition (Kranichfeld, 1987). It can be referred
to authority, decision-making power or the amount of influence exercised by one
family member over another. The concept of hierarchy has also been used to study
the flexibility of roles and rules within the family (Olson, 1986).

### Family boundaries

One of the major issues for the description of family structures is the concept of
boundaries, and this is pertinent to the understanding of the family as an organized
system. The construct of boundaries is used to describe relations between families
and their social environment, as well as relations between various subsystems within
the family (e.g. individuals, dyads or triads). Family boundaries can be defined by
the rules that determine who belongs to a given system or subsystem (Minuchin,
1974). External family boundaries manifest themselves by the fact that family
members behave differently towards each other than they do towards people outside
their community of life. Internal family boundaries are marked by differences in the
behaviour among members of distinct subsystems. Studies of dyads and triads,
including parent, parent–child and sibling relations, demonstrate that interactions
among family members and the way relations are perceived differ according to type
and size of the subsystem (Rabinowitz and Eldan, 1984). The construct of generational boundaries refers to the fact that patterns of cohesion and hierarchy are
influenced by whether a subsystem consists of members of the same or different
generations (Beavers, 1985; Wood, 1985).

## Family stress and interpersonal structures

Research, including various methodological approaches, has shown that well-
adjusted and troubled families display different relational structures (Lebow and
Gurman, 1995). Using self-report or observation methods, it has been demonstrated

that members of non-clinical families are emotionally close to one another and that the relationships between the generations are neither egalitarian nor very hierarchical. The structure of such family relations is flexible in response to situational and developmental demands (Minuchin, 1985). Furthermore, depending on their age or specific roles, family members perceive their relations differently and are able to express their views coherently, as well as to work towards a consensus based on common goals (Oliveri and Reiss, 1982; Feldman and Gehring, 1988).

In contrast, troubled families often display centrifugal patterns. Their ties are disengaged, with few reciprocal relationships and an atmosphere of remoteness, which may lead to the expulsion of a family member (Minuchin and Fishman, 1981; Beavers and Voeller, 1983). In addition it has been reported that their structures are likely to be either rigid or chaotic (Green *et al.*, 1985; Selvini-Palazzoli, 1986). Such patterns are reflected in the difficulties that family members have in communicating their needs adequately and this, in turn, limits healthy individual and family development. Research that determined types of family structures on the basis of both cohesion and hierarchy dimensions showed that while cohesion is generally low in distressed families, the dimension of hierarchy tends to be either high or low (Friedman *et al.*, 1987; Preli and Protinsky, 1988; Anderson and Gavazzi, 1990; Green *et al.*, 1991). Therefore, on the basis of studies comparing distressed and non-distressed samples, it can be concluded that there is evidence for a linear relation between cohesion and family functioning, while no such relation exists with hierarchy.

Structural family theory predicts that in well-functioning families the rules governing interactions between parents differ from those in parent–child subsystems; a fact that is reflected by clear cross-generational boundaries. In other words, father–mother relationships generally display a higher degree of cohesion than parent–offspring relationships. There are also clear generational boundaries regarding hierarchy, in that parents have a relatively large voice in decision-making because of their experience and material resources. Distressed families, in contrast, display unclear generational boundaries (Haley, 1973; Wood and Talmon, 1983). This becomes manifest in cross-generational coalitions where cohesion between a parent and child is stronger than between the parents. Moreover, there are hierarchy reversals, where the power or influence of a child exceeds that of the parents.

## Spatial representations of family relationships

The first attempts at spatial representation of interpersonal structures were sociograms that quantified and visualized emotional bonding and hierarchical structures in social groups (Chapin, 1953). Spatial representations of family relations in clinical practice were introduced on the basis of 'human sculptures' (Satir, 1967; Simon, 1972; Duhl *et al.*, 1974). These techniques, however, have the potential to trigger strong emotional reactions in patients with serious psychological disorders and can therefore be used only by experienced therapists. Further limitations lie in their inability to quantify relational patterns or to allow independent studies of individual perceptions of family relations. Figure placement techniques involve figures that respondents arrange on a board to depict dyadic, triadic or larger subgroupings in order to operationalize their perceptions of emotional bonding. These techniques represent an advance because they can be used with parents and children in both individual and interactive settings, and therefore provide a standardized evaluation of the family members' interpersonal constructs as well as of their interaction.

The use of figure placement techniques in clinical practice and research has many advantages. These techniques are very versatile and fulfil the basic requirements of comprehensive family evaluation (Rigazio-DiGilio, 1993). For example, they can be applied with preschool children because they do not require reading or writing skills. As representations of family constructs are language independent, these tools are also well suited for cross-cultural research. Furthermore, they are simple to administer and the representations are easy to analyse both quantitatively (e.g. types of family structure) and qualitatively (e.g. follow-up interview). The family can be portrayed under various conditions (e.g. in a conflict situation), and family members unavailable for the study (e.g. grandparents) or significant persons outside the family (e.g. teachers) can also be included in the portrayals. An individual representation of the family takes only 5 minutes, or between 10 and 30 minutes when carried out in a group setting. This economic method elicits the family members' perceptions of structural patterns within the family, including all of its subsystems. When used as an interactive task, figure placement techniques provide information derived from standardized observation about how family members negotiate when attempting to reach a consensus.

Using figure placement techniques, scoring of cohesion is based on assessment of distances between figures. The construct of hierarchy is operationalized in different ways. For example, it has been measured by comparing the extent to which individual representations of cohesion agreed with the representation produced by the same family members in a group setting (Russell, 1980) or, in the case of figure schemata, by interpreting a horizontal line-up to indicate egalitarian relations and a vertical line-up to represent extremely hierarchical relations (Madanes *et al.*, 1980). Numerous research projects investigating cohesion in the family as a unit and also as distinct dyads yielded results that were convergent with structural theory. It has been shown that distances between figures vary as a function of the respondents' age, psychological problems and cultural background, as well as of the situation and dyad depicted (Gehring and Schultheiss, 1987; Gehring and Marti, 1993a). However, research attempting to measure both cohesion and hierarchy yielded only partially valid results because these two dimensions could not be determined simultaneously and independently. As a consequence the FAST, which overcomes this conceptual limitation, was introduced.

## Family System Test[1]

The FAST was designed for professionals who are interested in a systemic approach to individual and family development. The goal of this assessment device is to determine health-related developmental and psychosocial issues in family-oriented terms and at the same time to facilitate conceptualization and evaluation of clinical interventions. On the basis of structural family systems theory, this test attempts to create an instrument that is both economic and flexible in its application. The FAST can be used to represent family relationships in various situations by one or several family members individually, as a family task or in any combination thereof. In the following sections the fundamental concept and test procedure of the FAST, as well as its psychometric properties, are described, including clinical and non-clinical samples. Table 1.1 provides an overview of the test concept, focusing on the basic theoretical assumptions, procedure and scoring, as well as on qualitative evaluation.

### Test procedure

Before carrying out the FAST, the evaluator familiarizes the respondents with the test procedure. The evaluator presents the test materials and emphasizes that the portrayal of family cohesion and hierarchy reflects subjective perceptions.

### Test materials

The test materials for the family members consists of three parts:

1   A monochromatic square board (45 cm × 45 cm) divided into eighty-one squares (5 cm × 5 cm), with each square assigned to a coordinate (1/1 to 9/9).
2   Six male and six female figures (8 cm high).
3   Eighteen cylindrical blocks of three different heights (1.5 cm, 3 cm and 4.5 cm). Figure 1.1 shows a FAST representation of a family of five.

The test materials for the evaluator include a four-part test form to document anamnestic data concerning the family; the configuration of typical, ideal and conflict representations; the corresponding follow-up interviews; and a scoring sheet to determine types of family structures represented.[2]

### Test instructions

To explain to the family members how cohesion is portrayed, the evaluator first places several figures close to one another and then places them farther apart, while explaining that these patterns represent different degrees of cohesion among family members. The evaluator then elevates the figures with blocks of various sizes and explains that the differences in the vertical position correspond to levels of hierarchy within the family.[3]

Family members are first asked to represent their current relations (i.e. the typical representation). When they have completed the representation, the evaluator ascertains which family members are represented by the figures and then records the location and height of each figure in the FAST protocol (Figure 1.2). The family

*Table 1.1* Fundamental concept of the Family System Test

| | |
|---|---|
| **Application** | In research and in clinical practice as an individual test (with respondents aged 6 and over) and as a group test |
| | Analysis of family structures (perception and interaction) |
| | Diagnosis of psychological, social and health-related problems |
| | Planning and evaluation of preventive and therapeutic interventions |
| | In therapy training and in clinical supervision |
| **Theoretical basis** | Structural family systems theory |
| | Developmental family psychology |
| | Family psychopathology |
| **Underlying assumptions** | Healthy family functioning is characterized by balanced interpersonal structures (cohesive and moderately hierarchical), clear generational boundaries and flexible roles and rules |
| **Test dimensions** | Cohesion and hierarchy in the family and its subsystems |
| | Quality of generational boundaries |
| | Flexibility of interpersonal structures |
| **Test materials** | |
| *For the tester* | FAST manual including test instructions and guidelines for the scoring and interpretation of the representations |
| | Four-part test form |
| *For the respondents* | Monochromatic board (45 cm × 45 cm) with 81 squares (5 cm × 5 cm) |
| | Schematic male and female figures (8 cm) |
| | Cylindrical blocks of 3 different heights (1.5 cm, 3.0 cm, 4.5 cm) |
| **Length of test** | Individual test: 5 to 10 minutes |
| | Group test: 10 to 30 minutes |
| **Quantitative evaluation** | |
| *Cohesion* | Calculation based on distances between figures on the board. Figures positioned on directly adjacent squares score maximum cohesion while larger distances reflect less cohesive relations |
| *Cross-generational coalition* | A parent–child dyad is more cohesive than the parental dyad |
| *Hierarchy* | Calculation based on number and height of blocks used to elevate the figures. Same height of figures indicates egalitarian power structure. The greater the difference in height, the more hierarchical the relationship. |

*Table 1.1 continued*

| | |
|---|---|
| *Hierarchy reversal* | The elevation of a child figure surpasses that of a parent figure |
| *Types of family structures* | Classification of family structures is based on a combination of cohesion and hierarchy. Both dimensions are scored as either high, medium or low. A balanced structure refers to relations with medium or high cohesion and medium hierarchy. The other family configurations are called either labile–balanced or unbalanced |
| **Levels of analysis** | |
| *Perception of the family* | Interpersonal structures in typical, ideal and conflict representations<br>Changes from typical to ideal representation<br>Changes from typical to conflict representation |
| *Differences in perception* | Comparison of individual representations of different family members<br>Comparison of individual representations with the group representation |
| **Qualitative evaluation** | |
| *Test behaviour* | Order in which figures are positioned<br>Changes made in the positions of the figures<br>Spontaneous remarks uttered while setting up family portrayals<br>Representation of persons outside the family<br>Omission of family members |
| *Interaction* | Observation of the family during group test (Systemic Performance Roles in Interaction; SPRINT) |
| *Follow-up interview* | Exploration of subjective meaning of typical representation<br>Hypothetical questions about ideal family constructs (e.g. attempted changes to reach a particular goal)<br>Evaluation of conflict patterns (e.g. family members involved in the conflict)<br>Exploration of differences between individual representations of family members (e.g. father vs mother) and between individuals and their joint representations |

relations portrayed are explored in a semistructured follow-up interview. The evaluator then places the figures next to the board, puts the blocks away and asks the respondents to picture their desired family structures by placing the figures and the blocks on the board (i.e. the ideal representation). After the evaluator has recorded the family configuration and completed the follow-up interview, he or she clears the board. Respondents are then asked to portray the family in an important

*Figure 1.1* FAST representation of cohesion and hierarchy in a family of five.

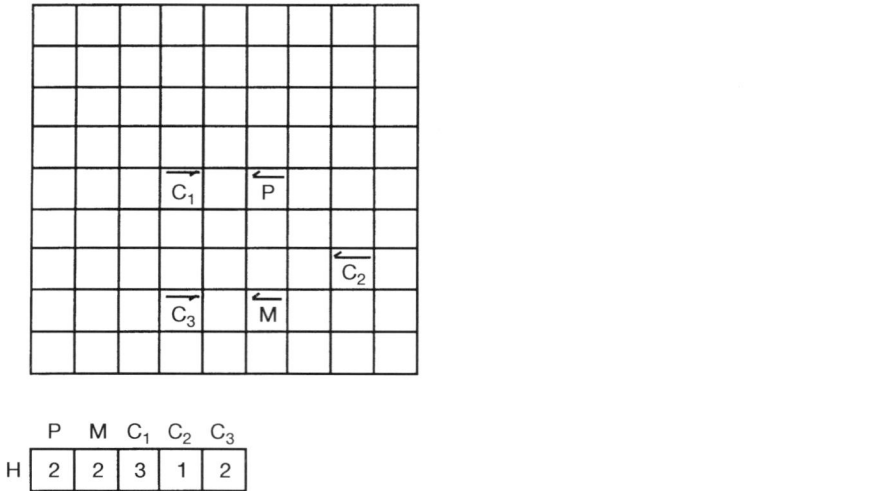

|   | P | M | $C_1$ | $C_2$ | $C_3$ |
|---|---|---|---|---|---|
| H | 2 | 2 | 3 | 1 | 2 |

*Figure 1.2* Protocol of a FAST representation of a family with five members.
C, child figure (number indicates birth order); H, height of figures; M, mother figure; P, father figure; 1, low hierarchy; 2, medium hierarchy; 3, high hierarchy; → direction in which figures are facing.

conflict. Following the recording of the conflict representation, the situation is explored.

## Scoring the FAST

Cohesion scores are derived from distances between figures and hierarchy scores from differences between the elevation of figures. Cohesion and hierarchy scores can be calculated for the family as a unit, as well as for its subsystems, on the basis of either an arithmetical or a categorical procedure.

The arithmetical evaluation of cohesion is based on Pythagoras' theorem. Thus, the distance between figures on adjacent squares is scored 1 and on diagonally adjacent squares 1.4. The maximum dyadic distance score is 11.3. In this case the two figures are positioned on diagonal corner squares. To generate cohesion scores, each of the distance scores is subtracted from 12. Cohesion scores thus range from 0.7 to 11, with the higher scores indicating increased cohesiveness.

Hierarchy scores are derived from the height of the blocks used to elevate the figures, with growing differences indicating increasingly marked hierarchies. A height difference of zero between two figures means that the relationship is perceived as egalitarian. For cross-generational dyads the height of the child figures is subtracted from the height of each parent figure.

Using categorical evaluation, cohesion and hierarchy are classified according to three categories, namely, low, medium or high. Family cohesion is scored high if all figures are placed in adjacent squares and medium if they are located within a 3 × 3 square area. Family cohesion is scored low if one or more figures are placed outside a 3 × 3 square area. A 'cross-generational coalition' is indicated if the parent relationship is less cohesive than any one of the parent–child dyads.

Evaluation of family hierarchy is based on the height difference between the less elevated parent figure and the most elevated child figure. It is scored low if the difference is less than a small block, medium if it is a small or middle-sized block, and high if it is a large block or more. The constellation of a child figure being higher than a parent figure is called 'reverse hierarchy'.

Patterns of cohesion and hierarchy scores can be grouped into three types of family structure (Figure 1.3). 'Balanced' indicates a family structure that is medium or highly cohesive and medium hierarchical. A structure with medium-level cohesion and low or high-level hierarchy, or with low cohesion and medium hierarchy, is considered 'labile–balanced'. A family structure is called 'unbalanced' if both dimensions show extreme values.

## Interpretation

The interpretation of test behaviour includes recording the order in which the figures are positioned and subsequent changes thereof, as well as the spontanous remarks of the respondents while setting up the representations. When one is interpreting test results, the quantitative–structural information from the representations should be linked to the qualitative–subjective responses provided by the family members

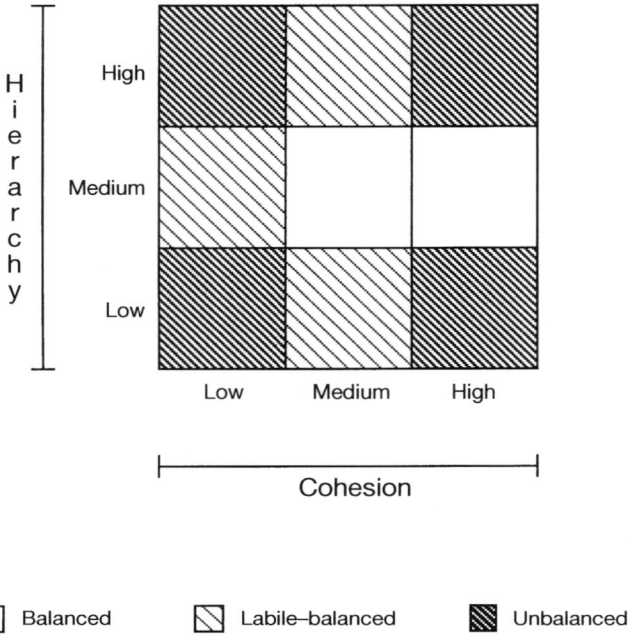

*Figure 1.3* Types of family cohesion and hierarchy structures.

in the follow-up interviews. This is based on a participative–discoursive process, which requires a consensus-oriented communication between family members and evaluator.

## Psychometric properties of the FAST

Psychometric properties of the FAST were established with healthy and troubled families from the San Francisco Bay area and the City of Zurich (for a review see Gehring and Page, 2000). Evaluation included the following aspects:

- independence of cohesion and hierarchy dimensions
- test–retest reliability
- external validity of family representations as assessed by family questionnaires and behavioural observation
- within-family comparisons, including correlations between individual representations of different family members and between individual and their joint representations
- relationship between family members' interpersonal constructs and their psychosocial wellbeing
- differences between family representations of clinical and non-clinical samples
- the influence of specific disorders on the portrayal of family structures.

In the following sections, data for non-clinical samples are briefly summarized. Cohesion and hierarchy scores of the FAST did not correlate and, therefore, these two dimensions are independent of one another. Test–retest stability of typical FAST scores was $r = 0.75$ for cohesion and $r = 0.73$ for hierarchy over a 1-week period. These coefficients were equivalent to those of the widely used Family Cohesion and Adaptability Scale (FACES III; Olson *et al.*, 1985) and the Family Environment Scale (FES; Moos and Moos, 1974). Furthermore, cohesion and hierarchy scores from the FAST representations were significantly correlated ($r = 0.21 - 0.49$, respectively) with comparable dimensions of the FACES and FES. Additional evidence for convergent validity was provided by the finding that the representation of cohesion with the FAST correlated ($r = 0.30$) with observed family functioning (Feldman *et al.*, 1989).

There were no significant correlations between FAST representations of members from the same family. This indicates that information from one family member cannot be used as a proxy for the interpersonal constructs of another family member. Furthermore, comparisons between the family members' individual and their joint representations revealed that fathers' typical portrayals were significantly related to those depicted by the family as a group (see Table 1.2). In other words, two-thirds of the fathers portrayed the same structure as the family collectively. This indicates that those members who experience the family most positively have a tendency to influence significantly the interactive representation (Gehring *et al.*, 1996).

Construct validity of the FAST was supported by the fact that, convergent with structural theory, family members in general depicted their typical relationships as balanced and with clear generational boundaries. In particular, the father–mother dyad was portrayed as very cohesive and near egalitarian, whereas parent–offspring dyads were characterized as less cohesive and with parents more powerful than

*Table 1.2* Types of relational structures in individual and group representations of typical relationships by members of the same family

| Family member and type of relational structure | Group representation | | |
|---|---|---|---|
| | *Balanced* ($n = 44$) | *Unbalanced* ($n = 26$) | *Chi-square* (df = 1) |
| Mother | | | |
| balanced ($n = 39$) | 39 | 17 | |
| unbalanced ($n = 31$) | 24 | 20 | ns |
| Father | | | |
| balanced ($n = 53$) | 53 | 23 | |
| unbalanced ($n = 17$) | 10 | 14 | 4.5* |
| Child | | | |
| balanced ($n = 45$) | 43 | 21 | |
| unbalanced ($n = 25$) | 20 | 16 | ns |

*$p < 0.05$; ns, not significant. Data in percentages.

their children. Moreover, family portrayals varied according to the age of children and the situation depicted (Gehring and Feldman, 1988). For example, typical portrayals of parent–offspring dyads including older adolescents displayed less cohesion and less hierarchy than those including younger adolescents. These show that the FAST is a valid tool for the description of the quality of generational boundaries. Compared with typical representations, the portrayal of ideal situations showed stronger cohesion and fewer hierarchical structures. Conflict representations were generally characterized by low cohesion and unclear generational boundaries in terms of cross-generational coalitions and reverse hierarchies.

Analysis of the correlations between FAST representations and self-reports on psychosocial wellbeing revealed many clinically relevant results. For example, parents' representations of cohesion in the marital dyad correlated ($r = 0.38$) with marital satisfaction as measured by the 'Locke–Wallace Adjustment Test' (Locke and Wallace, 1959). There was also a positive correlation ($r = 0.48$) between adolescents' representation of cohesion in parent–child dyads and the reported quality of communication with their parents as measured by the 'Parent–Adolescent Communication Questionnaire' (Barnes and Olson, 1985). A comparison of children's FAST representations with their responses to clinical questionnaires on depression (Beck *et al.*, 1961), anxiety (Spielberger, 1973) and behaviour problems (Achenbach and Edelbrock, 1987) showed a consistent pattern of correlation. For example, the less cohesive the family was portrayed, the greater was the number of reported psychological problems ($r = 0.25 - 0.51$). Furthermore, children who represented cross-generational coalitions or hierarchy reversals were more likely than others to report that they suffered from psychological problems.

## Clinical discriminant validity

This section presents the main findings on differences between FAST representations of non-clinical respondents and members of families attending medical or psychological treatment (Gehring and Marti, 1993b; Gehring *et al.*, 1996; Real del Sartre *et al.*, 1998). Evaluation was based on comparisons of typical, ideal and conflict representations by parents and children of the two groups and focused on the family as a whole, as well as on its subsystems.

The FAST demonstrated clinical discriminant validity for typical representations of families with a child psychiatric patient. Psychiatric and non-clinical samples differed significantly in their family constructs, the only exception being mothers with healthy children, as well as those with a disturbed offspring, who were both likely to show comparatively low cohesion. In other words, convergent with predictions from structural family theory, members of families with a mentally ill child were more likely than their counterparts to report unbalanced family structures (75 per cent vs 35 per cent) and to display unclear generational boundaries (i.e. cross-generational coalitions and reverse hierarchies). Analysis of representations of members of the same family (i.e. within-family comparisons) revealed that members of troubled families, unlike those with healthy children, perceived their current relationships similarly. The fact that parents as well as siblings of psychiatric patients were likely to represent unbalanced relational structures provides further evidence for the systemic approach, which emphasizes an interdependence between individual and family-related outcomes. The ideal family representations yielded only one significant difference between the two groups. Fewer child psychiatric patients portrayed their desired family relations as cohesive than their healthy counterparts. The conflict representations of both groups were characterized by unbalanced family structures with unclear generational boundaries.

We next investigated whether family constructs varied according to different clinical diagnoses of its members. Table 1.3 shows that typical FAST representations of mothers and fathers of healthy offspring and those of children who had physical or psychological problems displayed distinct patterns. It is noteworthy that the type of children's mental disorder as assessed by ICD 10 (World Health Organisation, 1989) was unrelated to the portrayal of family structures by parents, a finding that also holds true for the patients and their siblings. Members of families with an anorectic, as well as those with a behaviourally disturbed offspring, reported that their relationships were unbalanced and, thus, it can be hypothesized that distinct child psychiatric diagnoses do not necessarily yield different family outcomes. Somewhat surprisingly, almost two-thirds of parents of children suffering from cancer represented the family structures as balanced. However, in contrast to non-clinical families, mothers of cancer patients not only displayed balanced structures more often than fathers, but also had a pervasive influence on the joint representation. This finding reflects the fact that physical problems of children might affect mothers and fathers differently and that the parent who judges the relationships more positively contributes significantly to the consensus about family functioning. Finally, a pilot study in progress suggests that well-adjusted

*Table 1.3* Types of relational structures in individual FAST representations of typical relationships by parents as a function of the clinical status of the child ($n = 120$)

| Clinical status of child and family member | Type of relational structure | | Parental agreement (%) |
|---|---|---|---|
| | Balanced (%) | Unbalanced (%) | |
| Healthy | | | |
| mother | 56 | 44 | |
| father | 76 | 24 | 53 |
| Cancer | | | |
| mother | 73 | 27 | |
| father | 53 | 47 | 50 |
| Anorexia | | | |
| mother | 31 | 69 | |
| father | 23 | 77 | 92 |
| Behavioural disorder | | | |
| mother | 17 | 83 | |
| father | 17 | 83 | 100 |

offspring whose parents were in treatment because of the father's alcohol abuse were likely to represent problematic family structures. Therefore, it can be assumed that children's interpersonal constructs are related to the clinical status of their parents.

## Concluding comments

Family tests, like all psychological measurement techniques, always reduce a complex reality to a small number of dimensions. It is well known that the paradigms on which tests are based reflect zeitgeist, and there is also agreement that families represent dynamic organizations that evolve and develop within a sociocultural context. Therefore, an exclusive application of the FAST as a normative assessment of family functioning yields only limited information. However, this tool promotes reflection about family structures and, when applied in a participative–discoursive manner (including quantitative and qualitative data), it can contribute to an increased understanding of individual and interpersonal development.

The FAST demonstrated good psychometric properties, which were similar to those of commonly used family assessment devices. Construct validity of the FAST was established by the finding that studies with non-clinical samples yielded results that were consistent with structural family theory as well as with developmental and clinical psychology. Members of well-functioning families generally portrayed their typical relations as balanced and as displaying clear generational boundaries. Furthermore, portrayal of cross-generational dyads varied as a function of offspring's age, with relationships including older adolescents showing decreased cohesion and power differences. It is notable, however, that mothers were less likely than fathers to represent the family with balanced patterns. We assume that this difference is a result of the traditional role allocation, which forces mothers to be focused on the intrafamily context. As a consequence, they are more exposed to family-related hassles. This suggests that a comprehensive evaluation of non-clinical family structures should consider both parents in order to reveal gender-specific patterns.

Evidence for clinical discriminant validity of the FAST has been supplied by comparing portrayals of well-adjusted and troubled families. Interpersonal constructs of members of families with mentally disturbed offspring clearly differed from those of non-clinical families. Convergent with structural theory, patients, as well as their parents and siblings, characterized their typical relationships predominantly as unbalanced and as indicating more cross-generational coalitions and reverse hierarchies than their non-clinical counterparts. Accordingly, members of families with an alcoholic parent represented their family structures in the context of the drinking problem as unbalanced and as displaying unclear generational boundaries. Thus, it can be supposed that family members' interpersonal constructs are similarly affected by psychiatric problems of children and those of parents (Madanes *et al.*, 1980; Preli and Protinsky, 1988). The finding that mothers with a child suffering from cancer, in contrast to those with healthy or mentally disturbed children, characterized their family structures as predominantly balanced needs further explanation. We assume that, because of the child's severe physical illness, mothers are very engaged in the child's care as well as in providing emotional support (Landau-Hurtig, 1994; Filipp and Ferring, 1995). As a consequence, they might experience the family as a protective context for the patient and their great involvement as an important and satisfying task.

Comparisons of conflict representations did not reveal differences between untroubled families and those under health-related stress. In other words, healthy families, as well as those with members suffering from various clinical problems, represented their relations in conflict mostly as unbalanced. This indicates that conflict and the accompanying stress are perceived similarly by the two groups. However, families with a psychiatrically ill member perceive their relationships as relatively unflexible in response to conflict situations. The fact that they display similar patterns in typical and in conflict portrayals suggests that these families experience their current relations as strained too. Thus, it can be argued that unbalanced structures in typical representations are a reliable indicator of family problems.

Ideal representations were generally characterized by high cohesion and clear generational boundaries. Somewhat surprisingly, a majority of child psychiatric patients represented their ideal family relations as marked by relatively little cohesion. However, as numerous research projects have shown a positive correlation between family cohesion and individual wellbeing, it could be argued that a rejection of close relationships has detrimental effects on individuation and the development of autonomy. Because parents of disturbed children indicated a clear desire for an increased level of cohesion, it is likely that, compared with their offspring, they are more motivated for clinical interventions on the family level (see Chapter 15).

Although our research has shown that patterns of FAST representations are related to individual or family problems and resources, there are some drawbacks. For example, configurations that are dysfunctional according to the structural family theory are not a priori associated with individual or family disorders, or vice versa. Thus, a suitable evaluation of FAST representations in clinical practice should always consider additional individual and family-related data. It is also not possible with the FAST to reveal a relation between types of family structures and psychiatric categories according to ICD 10 because the two sources of information represent conceptually different perspectives (Jenkins, 1990). However, based on cross- and intrafamily analyses of parents' and children's relational constructs as assessed in different settings, the FAST allows the discrimination of non-clinical families from those with patients who have physical or psychological problems. Undoubtedly, our findings show that further cross-sectional and longitudinal research, including in-depth inverview and interactional observation, are necessary to clarify the distinct role of family structures for the onset and course of biopsychosocial problems (Reiss, 1989; Cicchetti, 1990).

Depending on the issues at hand, the FAST can be used with one or more family members individually, as an interactive task or in any combination thereof. The use of this tool in individual and group settings allows a comparison of the respondents' individual and shared family constructs, as well as of the interactive patterns while they are working on their joint representation. Because members of well-functioning families perceive their relationships differently, a comprehensive insight into their family dynamics requires application of the FAST with several members in various settings. An important advantage of the FAST is that it makes possible the study of a large number of different situations. For example, the test procedure can include past, current or anticipated events, and the figures need not be limited to the members of the respondents' nuclear families. In addition, the FAST can be used by experts to explain their own perceptions of the family structure as well as clinically relevant options for change. Such procedures improve effective conceptualization of therapeutic interventions and are also applicable to therapist training and in supervision.

In summary, the FAST is a versatile and economic tool with good psychometric properties, which can contribute towards an increased rapprochement between science and practice. As a consequence, it has the potential to promote a more comprehensive knowledge of the complex relation between individual and interpersonal aspects of family development across the lifespan.

## Notes

1. The FAST can be ordered from Hogrefe & Huber Publishers, P.O. Box 2487, Kirkland, WA 98083–2487, USA; phone (800) 228 3749, fax (425) 823 8324, e-mail hh@hhpub.com
2. The FAST test form for administering and scoring the typical, ideal, and conflict representations, and the use of abbreviations, are shown in the Appendix on pages 23–25 and 26–27, respectively. The cover page of the test form is used to document information on the client family including anamnestic data. The section 'Family representations' is used to enter data concerning: (i) persons to be included in the representations; (ii) family members' behaviour during the test; (iii) positions of figures on the board including direction in which they are facing and heights of figures; and (iv) characteristics of the represented situations as derived from the follow-up interview. Categorical evaluation of relational structures in the FAST is recorded in the section 'Evaluation of relational structures'. It includes: (i) type of relational structures in the representations (i.e. balanced, labile–balanced or unbalanced); (ii) differences between individual representations of different family members and between individual and group representations; (iii) flexibility of family structures (e.g. changes from typical to conflict representations); and (iv) the quality of generational boundaries.
3. A detailed description of the FAST test instructions and follow-up interviews to the typical, ideal and conflict representations are provided in the Appendix on pages 21–22 and page 26, respectively.

## References

Achenbach, T.M. and Edelbrock, C. (1987) 'Manual for the youth self-report and profile', Burlington: University of Vermont, Department of Psychiatry.

Ackerman, N. (1985) *A Theory of Family Systems*, New York: Gardner.

Anderson, S.A. and Gavazzi, S.M. (1990) 'A test of the Olson circumplex model: Examining its curvilinear assumption and the presence of extreme types', *Family Process* 29: 309–24.

Barnes, H.L. and Olson, D.H. (1985) 'Parent–adolescent communication and the circumplex model', *Child Development* 56: 438–47.

Beavers, R.W. (1985) *Successful Marriage*, New York: Norton.

—— and Voeller, M.N. (1983) 'Family models: Comparing and contrasting the Olson circumplex model with the Beavers systems model', *Family Process* 22: 85–98.

Beck, A.T., Ward, C.H., Mendelson, M., Mock, J. and Erbaugh, J. (1961) 'An inventory for measuring depression', *Archives of General Psychiatry* 4: 53–63.

Bowen, M. (1960) 'The family as the unit of study and treatment', *American Journal of Orthopsychiatry* 31: 40–60.

Chapin, F.S. (1953) 'A three-dimensional model for visual analysis of group structures', *Social Forces* 31: 20–25.

Cicchetti, D. (1990) 'A historical perspective on the discipline of developmental psychopathology', in J. Rolf, A.S. Masten, D. Cicchetti, K.H. Nuechterlein and S. Weintraub (eds) *Risk and Protective Factors in the Development of Psychopathology*, New York: Cambridge University Press.

Duhl, F., Kantor, D. and Duhl, B. (1974) 'Learning space and action', in A.D. Bloch (ed.) *Technique of Family Psychotherapy*, New York: Grune and Stratton.

Feldman, S.S. and Gehring, T.M. (1988) 'Changing perceptions of family cohesion and power across adolescence', *Child Development* 59: 1034–45.

—— Wentzel, K.R. and Gehring, T.M. (1989) 'A comparison of the views of mothers, fathers and preadolescents about family cohesion and power', *Journal of Family Psychology* 3: 39–60.

Filipp, S.H. and Ferring, D. (1995) 'Semantic differentiation of "cancer" from various perspectives', in B. Boothe, R. Hirsig, A. Helminger, B. Meier and R. Volkart (eds) *Perception – Evaluation – Interpretation*, Seattle, WA: Hogrefe and Huber Publishers.

Friedman, A.S., Utada, A. and Morrissey, M.R. (1987) 'Families of adolescent drug abusers are "rigid": Are these families either "disengaged" or "enmeshed", or both?', *Family Process* 26: 131–48.

Gehring, T.M. (1998) *The Family System Test*, Seattle, WA: Hogrefe and Huber Publishers.

—— (2000) *Family System Test (FAST)*, Zurich: University of Zurich. Online. Available at: http://www.fast-test.com

—— Feldman, S.S. (1988) 'Adolescents' perceptions of family cohesion and power: A methodological study of the Family System Test', *Journal of Adolescent Research* 3: 33–52.

—— Marti, D. (1993a) 'The architecture of family structures: Toward a spatial concept for measuring cohesion and hierarchy', *Family Process* 32: 135–39.

—— Marti, D. (1993b) 'The Family System Test: Differences in perception of family structures between nonclinical and clinical children', *Journal of Child Psychology and Psychiatry and Allied Disciplines* 34: 363–77.

—— Page, J. (2000) 'Family System Test (FAST): A systemic approach for family evaluation in clinical practice and research', in K. Gitlin-Weiner, A. Sandgrund and C.E. Schaefer (eds) *Play Diagnosis and Assessment*, New York: Wiley.

—— Schultheiss, R.B. (1987) 'Spatial representations and assessment of family relationships', *The American Journal of Family Therapy* 5: 261–4.

—— Candrian, M., Marti, D. and Real del Sartre, O. (1996) 'Family System Test (FAST): The relevance of parental family constructs for clinical intervention', *Child Psychiatry and Human Development* 27: 55–65.

Green, R.J., Kolevzon, M.S. and Vosler, N.R. (1985) 'The Beavers–Timberlawn model of family competence and the circumplex model of family adaptability and cohesion: Are they separate, but equal?', *Family Process* 24: 385–98.

—— Harris, R.N., Forte, J.A. and Robinson, M. (1991) 'Evaluating FACES III and the circumplex model: 2440 families', *Family Process* 30: 55–73.

Haley, J. (1973) 'Strategic therapy when a child is presented as the problem', *Journal of the American Academy of Child and Adolescent Psychiatry* 12: 641–59.

Jameson, P.B. and Alexander, J.F. (1994) 'Implications of a developmental family systems model for clinical practice', in L. L'Abate (ed.) *Handbook of Developmental Psychology and Psychopathology*, New York: Wiley.

Jenkins, H. (1990) 'Annotation: Family therapy – developments in thinking and practice', *Journal of Child Psychology and Psychiatry and Allied Disciplines* 31: 1015–26.

Kaslow, F.W. (ed.) (1996) *Handbook of Relational Diagnosis and Dysfunctional Family Patterns*, New York: Wiley.

Kranichfeld, M.L. (1987) 'Rethinking family power', *Journal of Family Issues* 8: 42–56.

L'Abate, L. (1994) *Family Evaluation*, London: Sage.

Landau-Hurtig, A. (1994) 'Chronic illness and developmental family psychology', in L. L'Abate (ed.) *Handbook of Developmental Psychology and Psychopathology*, New York: Wiley.

Lebow, J.L. and Gurman, A.S. (1995) 'Research assessing couple and family therapy', *Annual Review of Psychology* 46: 27–57.

Locke, H.J. and Wallace, K.M. (1959) 'Short marital-adjustment and prediction tests: Their reliability', *Marriage and Family Living*, August, 251–5.

Madanes, C., Dukes, J. and Harbin, H. (1980) 'Family ties of heroin addicts', *Archives of General Psychiatry* 37: 889–94.

Minuchin, P. (1985) 'Families and individual development: Provocations from the field of family therapy', *Child Development* 56: 289–302.

Minuchin, S. (1974) *Families and Family Therapy*, Cambridge, MA: Harvard University Press.

Minuchin, S. and Fishman, H.C. (1981) *Family Therapy Techniques*, Cambridge, MA: Harvard University Press.

Moos, R. and Moos, B.S. (1974) *Family Environment Scale (FES)*, Palo Alto, CA: Consulting Psychologists Press.

Oliveri, M.E. and Reiss, D. (1982) 'Families' schemata of social relationships', *Family Process* 21: 295–311.

Olson, D.H. (1986) 'Circumplex Model VII: Validation studies and FACES III', *Family Process* 25: 337–51.

—— Portner, J. and Lavee, Y. (1985) 'FACES III', in D.H. Olson, H.I. McCubbin, H. Barnes, A. Larsen, M. Muxen and M. Wilson (eds) *Family Inventories*, St. Paul, MN: Family Social Science, University of Minnesota.

Preli, R. and Protinsky, H. (1988) 'Aspects of family structures in alcoholic, recovered and nonalcoholic families', *Journal of Marital and Family Therapy* 14: 311–14.

Rabinowitz, A. and Eldan, Z. (1984) 'Social schemata of Israeli children on measures of distance and height in dyad and family placements', *The Psychological Record* 34: 343–51.

Real del Sartre, O., Stiefel, F., Leyvraz, S., Bauer, J., Gehring, T.M. and Guex, P. (1998) 'The Family System Test (FAST): A pilot study in families with a young adult member with cancer', *Support Care Cancer* 6: 416–20.

Reiss, D. (1989) 'The represented and practicing family: Contrasting visi
continuity', in A.J. Sameroff and R.N. Emde (eds) *Relationship Disturb
Childhood: A Developmental Approach*, New York: Basic Books.

Rigazio-DiGilio, S.A. (1993) 'The Family System Test (FAST): A spatial
of family structure and flexibility', *The American Journal of Fami.,* ...
369–75.

Russell, C.S. (1980) 'A methodological study of family cohesion and adaptability',
*Journal of Marital and Family Therapy* 6: 459–70.

Satir, V. (1967) *Conjoint Family Therapy*, Palo Alto, CA: Science and Behavior Books.

Selvini-Palazzoli, M. (1986) 'Toward a general model of psychotic family games', *Journal
of Marital and Family Therapy* 12: 339–49.

Simon, R.M. (1972) 'Sculpting the family', *Family Process* 11: 49–57.

Spielberger, C. (1973) *State–Trait Anxiety for Children: Preliminary Manual*, Palo Alto,
CA: Consulting Psychologists Press.

Stierlin, H. (1974) *Separating Parents and Adolescents*, New York: Quadrangle.

Werner-Wilson, R.J., Schindler Zimmerman, T. and Price, S.J. (1999) 'Are goals and
topics influenced by gender and modality in the initial marriage and family therapy
session?', *Journal of Marital and Family Therapy* 25: 253–62.

Wilkinson, I. (1998) *Child and Family Assessment: Clinical Guidelines for Practitioners*,
London: Routledge.

Wood, B. (1985) 'Proximity and hierarchy: Orthogonal dimensions of family inter-
connectedness', *Family Process* 24: 497–507.

—— Talmon, M. (1983) 'Family boundaries in transition: A search for alternatives',
*Family Process* 22: 347–57.

World Health Organisation (WHO) Division of Mental Health (1989) *Mental and
Behavioural Disorders, ICD-10*, Geneva: World Health Organisation.

# Appendix

## *FAST Test Instructions*

The experimenter (E) demonstrates the test materials and introduces the FAST to
the family members taking the test, with the following remarks:

> I would now like to explain a procedure we use for representing family
> relations. With this board and these figures and blocks [*E shows the test
> material*] you can show how close the members of your family are to one
> another and how much power or influence each member has in the family.
> Members of the same family usually evaluate their relations differently.

E now explains the representation of cohesion:

> Here are male and female figures representing the members of your family.
> By arranging the figures on the board, you can show how close the members
> of your family are to each other. You can use any of the spaces on the
> board.

E then places a pair of figures side-by-side on two adjacent squares on the board (minimum distance) and says:

> This means that these two members of the family have a very close relationship.

E now places the same two figures on two diagonally adjacent squares (second closest distance) and then moves them apart to two diagonally opposed corners of the board (maximum distance), and says:

> The further apart you place two figures, the more emotionally distant they are to each other. Placing the figures on diagonally opposite corners of the board means that you think the relationship between these two family members is not at all close.

E now explains the way hierarchy is represented using the two figures already positioned on the board:

> Here are blocks of three different sizes that you can use to elevate the figures. You can use these blocks to represent the power or influence that each member has in the family. The higher a figure is placed, the more power or influence that person has in the family. You can use any number of different blocks to elevate the figures.

E demonstrates this by elevating one of the figures with the smallest block (minimum increase, smallest difference in height) and says:

> This means that both family members have relatively little power or influence, although this one has slightly more than the other [*points to the respective figures*]. In other words there is little difference in hierarchy between the two.

E demonstrates varying differences in height between the two figures by using the different-sized blocks, and says:

> The greater the difference in height between the two figures, the more hierarchical their relation is.

E raises both figures to equal height with two of the same-sized blocks and says:

> If you place two figures at the same height, it means that their power or influence is balanced or equal.

E can now answer any questions the family members might have about the FAST.

# FAST Family System Test

Institution/Experimenter _____

Family _____

Patient/Position in family_____

Reason for consultation _____

Consultations to date: Number _____ Persons present _____

Type of sessions _____

|  | | P | M | C1 | C2 | C3 | | |
|---|---|---|---|---|---|---|---|---|
| R Individual test | | | | | | | | |
| R Group test | | | | | | | | |

## Anamnestic data on persons living in patient's household (FM/HH)

| FM | Date of birth | School/Profession | Specific illnesses | Additional information |
|---|---|---|---|---|
| | | | | |
| | | | | |
| | | | | |
| | | | | |
| | | | | |
| | | | | |

## Family members not living in patient's household (FM/RH)

| FM | Date of birth | School/Profession | Specific illnesses | Additional information |
|---|---|---|---|---|
| | | | | |
| | | | | |
| | | | | |
| | | | | |

## Psychological problems treated at other institutions

| FM | Date | Institution | Diagnosis | Therapy |
|---|---|---|---|---|
| | | | | |
| | | | | |
| | | | | |

Interpretation of test results

© 1998 Hogrefe & Huber Publishers

Order # 01 262 03

## Family Representations

Name _____

Date _____

P  M  C1 C2 C3

Figures
RPat
Age
Gender
R

### Typical representation (TR)

9
8
7
6
5
4
3
2
1
1 2 3 4 5 6 7 8 9

H
Co

Stability  ☐ low   ☐ high

Differences  ☐ small   ☐ large

BO/SPRINT _____

### Ideal representation (IR)

9
8
7
6
5
4
3
2
1
1 2 3 4 5 6 7 8 9

*SAMPLE*

H
Co

Situation  ☐ routine   ☐ special

Frequency  ☐ often   ☐ seldom

BO/SPRINT _____

### Conflict representation (CR)

9
8
7
6
5
4
3
2
1
1 2 3 4 5 6 7 8 9

H
Co

Type of conflict  ☐ parent   ☐ parent-child
                  ☐ sibling   ☐ other

Situation  ☐ routine   ☐ special

Frequency  ☐ often   ☐ seldom

BO/SPRINT _____

Comments

## Evaluation of Relational Structures

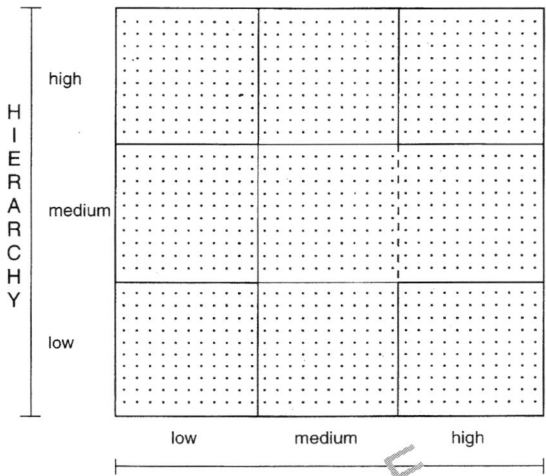

HIERARCHY

high

medium

low

low   medium   high

COHESION

SAMPLE

| | FaT B L U | PaT B L U | SiT B L U | FaI B L U | PaI B L U | SiI B L U | FaC B L U | PaC B L U | SiC B L U |
|---|---|---|---|---|---|---|---|---|---|
| TRS | | | | | | | | | |
| P | | | | | | | | | |
| M | | | | | | | | | |
| C | | | | | | | | | |
| InteR | | | | | | | | | |

DP

1 2 3  1 2 3  1 2 3  1 2 3  1 2 3  1 2 3  1 2 3  1 2 3  1 2 3

P/M
P/C
M/C
P/InteR
M/InteR
C/InteR

Typical to ideal | Typical to conflict | Comments

Fa 1 2 3   Pa 1 2 3   Si 1 2 3   Fa 1 2 3   Pa 1 2 3   Si 1 2 3

FLEX
P
M
C
InteR

Cross-generational coalition | Hierarchy reversals

TR yes no   IR yes no   CR yes no   TR yes no   IR yes no   CR yes no

GB
P
M
C
InteR

## Follow-up interview to FAST representations

The exploration of the typical representation includes the following four questions:

1   'Does this representation show a specific situation? If so, which one?'
2   'How long have the relations been the way that you have shown them here?'
3   'How are the relations here different from the way they used to be?'
4   'What is the reason that the relations have become the way you show them here?'

The exploration of the ideal representation includes the following five questions:

1   'Does this representation show a situation that has occurred at some point? If yes, what was the situation?' (If the answer is No, omit questions 2 and 3)
2   'How often does this situation occur and how long does it last when it does occur?'
3   'When did this situation first occur and when was the last time it happened?'
4   'What would have to happen (outside event, change in behaviour, etc.) to make typical relations correspond to how you wish they were ideally?'
5   'How important would this be for you and the other family members?'

The exploration of the conflict representation includes the following six questions:

1   'Who is involved in this conflict?'
2   'What is this conflict about?'
3   'How often does this conflict occur and how long does it last each time it does occur?'
4   'When did this situation first occur and when was the last time it happened?'
5   'How important is this conflict for you and the other family members?'
6   'What roles do the different family members have in solving this conflict?'

## Abbreviations

B       Balanced
BO      Behavioural observation
C(1)    Child figure, child or sibling (number indicates birth order in family or household)
CC      Cross-generational coalition
CLS     Common-law spouse (unmarried)
CN      Non-biologically related child or sibling (e.g. foster or adopted child)
Co      Cohesion
CR      Conflict representation
DD      Dyad distance
DP      Difference in perception
F       Figure

| | |
|---|---|
| Fa(T,I,C) | Family level (T = typical, I = ideal, C = conflict) |
| FI | Follow-up interview |
| FLEX | Flexibility |
| FM | Family member |
| FM(HH) | Member(s) of the patient's or respondent's household |
| FM(NHH) | Family member(s) of the patient or respondent not living in the same household |
| GB | Generational boundary |
| GM(M,P) | Grandmother (M = maternal, P = paternal) |
| GP(M,P) | Grandfather (M = maternal, P = paternal) |
| H | Height of figure |
| HD | Height difference |
| HH | Household |
| HR | Hierarchy reversal |
| IN | Important person not in the family |
| InteR | Interactive representation (consensus representation of two or more family members) |
| IR | Ideal representation |
| L | Labile–balanced |
| M | Mother figure, mother, maternal |
| N(M,P) | Adult living in the same household as the patient or respondent but who is not related to any of the family members (M = assumes function of mother, P = assumes function of father) |
| P | Father figure, father, paternal |
| Pa(T,I,C) | Parent level (T = typical, I = ideal, C = conflict) |
| Pat | (Index) Patient |
| R | Respondent |
| RPat | Relation to patient |
| SC(M,P) | Stepchild or sibling (M = maternal, P = paternal) |
| Si(T,I,C) | Sibling level (T = typical, I = ideal, C = conflict) |
| Sp | Spouse |
| SPRINT | Systemic performance roles in interaction (patterns of interaction during group test) |
| StM | Stepmother |
| StP | Stepfather |
| TR | Typical representation |
| TRS | Type of relational structure |
| U | Unbalanced |
| → | Direction in which figure is facing |

# 2 The FAST at the crossroads of systemic theories

*Marianne Debry*

A family is in the waiting room, and we invite its members to come into our office. This is our first encounter. We take, each time, a leap in the dark. Once again, we feel that each family has its own style. From the first glance, the first hello, we have an impression. They sat down as they liked; they explained their request in their own words; they brought their universe into our workplace.

Each family is a mystery, and the clinician sets off to discover its architecture, its dynamics, its history and its culture. Through the interview, the clinician has the opportunity to analyse *in vivo* family relationships. However, to get free from a merely impressionistic approach, the clinician needs specific means to delineate the family's functioning, both in the explanatory phase (systemic diagnosis and indications) and at the therapeutic level (assessment of the family evolution).

In fact, until recently, questionnaires (Olson and McCubbin, 1983; Beavers, 1993; Epstein *et al.*, 1993) were the only available tools. Although they proved to be useful their limitations are well known: tiresome administrative tasks, cultural biases and acquaintance with the written language.

The assessment of family functioning lags slightly behind the analysis of an individual personality. If it is true that a wide range of well-validated objective and projective tests is available to explore the individual affective dynamics, the situation is different when one seeks to assess the various aspects of the family system.

This situation results from the rather recent emergence of systemic theories and from the fact that the leaders of systemic schools were primarily therapists who developed concepts and intervention procedures, rather than assessment tools.

As a figure placement test, the FAST appeared just at the right moment to fill the gap: it is a test whose psychometric properties have been demonstrated, and an outstanding medium for people from various age groups and with different cultural and social backgrounds.

Assessment tools cannot be separated from theoretical references. They are founded on the concepts and processes they try to make operational. The purpose of this chapter is to consider the FAST from two systemic perspectives: structural and economic.

The FAST is entirely in line with the structural school, led by Minuchin. The test makes the disclosure of the inner structure of the family possible. It proposes a topographical representation of the boundaries around as well as inside the family system.

However, from some other points of view, the FAST is close to a dynamic perspective, i.e. the balance between forces that are present in the system. Through relational structures, cohesion and hierarchy levels are put in equation.

Our argument will be based on two types of data:

- Empirical data: both perspectives will be illustrated by the results from research performed with the FAST on non-clinical Belgian early adolescents (Gehring and Debry, 1995; Debry, 1997).
- Clinical data: each systemic perspective will be illustrated by a clinical example.

## Structural perspective

In the Freudian model, behaviours are the products of the psychic apparatus described in the two topics. In the structural systemic model, family transactions are also determined by a structure. This internal configuration of the family cannot be observed directly: it has to be inferred from the interactions between its members. The structure is characterized by inertia: it is steady. But it is also endowed with plasticity because it changes according to needs and stage of development.

The family system is surrounded by a boundary with the external environment. Inside the family, other boundaries delineate the marital subsystem, the child subsystem (singleton or siblings) as well as each person.

The boundaries of a subsystem are 'the rules which define who participates and how' (Minuchin, 1974: 69). The boundaries must be sufficiently clear and permeable. Diffuse boundaries generate enmeshed systems that do not warrant sufficient differentiation between the family members. At the opposite end, rigid boundaries reflect disengaged systems where the feeling of belonging is insufficient.

The concepts 'disengagement' and 'enmeshment' do not relate to a pathology but rather to a transactional style. According to Minuchin, most of the families are, at a given moment in their development, either enmeshed or disengaged subsystems. Consequently, these concepts are more descriptive than diagnostic and have to be nuanced as a function of the subsystems involved and the period in the lifecycle. The cross-generational boundary evolves in relation to the child's development. The older the child, the more parents ask the child's opinion and involve the child in the decisions and activities of the family.

The leaders of the structural movement emphasized the importance of clarity and permeability of boundaries in the family system. Minuchin conceptualized their possible disturbances and proposed two specific phenomena: hierarchy reversals and cross-generational coalitions.

1. A hierarchy reversal appears when a child takes more power than one of her/his parents, or than both. The adult relies on the child, occasionally or permanently, for decision making.

2.  There is a cross-generational coalition when a parent becomes closer to one of her/his children than to her/his spouse. The positive or negative character of this type of alliance depends on the age of the child and on the quality of the marital relation. For instance, a high degree of proximity between parent and child before and after birth is necessary. The situation is entirely different if the child, after an acute marital conflict, is taken hostage against the other parent, or if this kind of proximity has an incestuous flavour.

Several authors have described pathological forms of cross-generational coalitions. Haley (1979) called this kind of coalition a 'perverse triangle'. Three criteria must be met to create such a triangle:

1.  there must be at least two persons belonging to different generations
2.  third person must be the target of the coalition
3.  this coalition is denied or actively hidden.

### The FAST and the structural perspective

Minuchin proposed a 'family map', i.e. a pattern established by the therapist from observation of the family including types of boundaries (diffuse, clear, rigid), conflicts and coalitions.

The FAST is derived from the principle of the family map: to create a visual representation of the inner structure of the family, with few differences. It is a person or a family who produces the representation. The final product is three-dimensional and is realized by using small wooden figures. Three different representations are proposed: typical, ideal and conflictual. The representations are described at three levels: family, parents and siblings. The boundaries are assessed as follows: the boundary surrounding the family by the level of global cohesion and the cross-generational boundary or by the position of parents and children in terms of cohesion and hierarchy.

Results from research on Belgian preadolescents are presented to illustrate their family constructs. Participants are 167 early adolescents (age range 10 to 12 years) coming from intact families, each of them with two children. The most common structure is one where generations are differentiated on the basis of the order of placement, of the cohesion inside the subsystems and of the hierarchy between parents and children.

### Placement order

The order of figures placement significantly differs according to family members ($F = 86.91$, $p < 0.0001$). Father and mother are usually placed sooner than the children, particularly in the typical version.

*Cohesion inside the subsystem*

The members of a subsystem (parents or siblings) are significantly closer to one another than parents are to their children (global cohesion) ($F = 38$, $p < 0.0001$).

*Hierarchy*

The participant gives the wooden figures a height by elevating them with blocks of 1.5 cm, 3.0 cm or 4.5 cm, depending on the power they attribute to the various family members.

In the three versions, parents have a size that is significantly higher than that of the children. The differences in height are more obvious in the typical and conflictual versions (Figure 2.1). The average of the global hierarchy levels (between parents and children) considerably exceeds the average hierarchy between father and mother on the one hand, and between children on the other.

In their family representations early adolescents use different cues to show the cross-generational boundaries:

•   order of figures: parents are placed sooner than their children
•   a parent is placed closer to another parent than to the children; a child is nearer to her/his mother or sister than to her/his parents
•   parents are given more power than children.

*Disturbances of boundaries*

Disturbed boundaries can be detected in the representations. A cross-generational coalition is registered whenever the distance between a parent and a child is smaller than the distance between spouses. There is a hierarchy reversal whenever a child is higher than one of his/her parents.

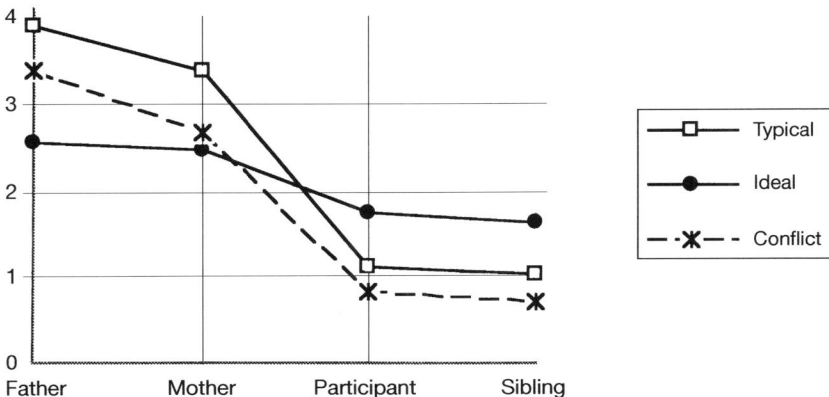

*Figure 2.1* Family members' height means.

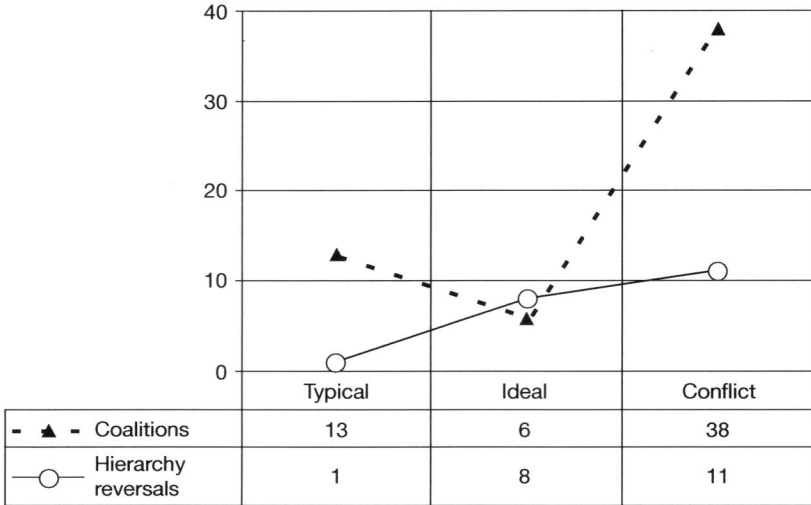

|  | Typical | Ideal | Conflict |
|---|---|---|---|
| - ▲ -  Coalitions | 13 | 6 | 38 |
| ─○─  Hierarchy reversals | 1 | 8 | 11 |

*Figure 2.2*  Percentages of coalitions and hierarchy reversals in the three FAST representations.

Figure 2.2 shows the average percentage of youngsters who represented their family by including cross-generational coalitions or hierarchy reversals. In the typical and conflictual versions, cross-generational coalitions clearly occupy the first place.

CROSS-GENERATIONAL COALITIONS

The distribution of coalitions between parents and children depends on the versions of the FAST. They are more frequent in the conflictual context and less so in the ideal one ($\chi^2 = 63.47$, $p < 0.0001$). This observation supports what Gehring *et al.* (1990) found. Compared with the typical situation, the number of cross-generational coalitions is twice as high as in conflict situations (15 and 30 per cent); ($n = 174$ non-clinical subjects, mean age: 11 years 6 months, US).

HIERARCHY REVERSALS

By representing a hierarchy reversal, the early adolescent gives herself/himself more power than allowed by her/his status. Hierarchy reversals are considerably less frequent in the typical version and more frequent in the conflictual context ($\chi^2 = 13.04$, $p < 0.001$). In the same study, Gehring *et al.* (1990) found similar results (0 per cent hierarchy reversals in the typical version compared with 11 per cent in the conflictual representation).

It is precisely in conflictual situations that boundaries get tangled to the utmost. Distributions are not spread at random across the types of conflicts and the boundary problems ($\chi^2 = 63.47$, $p < 0.0001$).

Cross-generational coalitions predominate in the case of conflicts between parents. In our sample a conflict between parents was the most frequent (56 per cent). In all the coalitions, the mother was more often involved with one or two children, than was the father ($\chi^2 = 16$, $p < 0.0001$).

Therefore, coalitions and hierarchy reversals are seldom observed in a non-clinical population: less than 15 per cent – with the exception of coalitions in the conflictual version of the FAST (38 per cent). Moreover, they rarely appear simultaneously in several versions of the FAST. From one version to another, only 9 per cent of preadolescents repeat a cross-generational coalition, and 1 per cent a hierarchy reversal. The simultaneous presence of cross-generational coalitions and hierarchy reversals is observed in only 10 per cent of the cases.

One may thus conclude that in our non-clinical population of early adolescents, boundary disturbances seem more reactional than structural. It is during the reaction to the stress produced by a conflict that cross-generational alliances and reversals of authority take place. Nevertheless, they must be considered in that conflictual context.

The assumption of a pathological structural boundary can only be made when data are redundant through several tests (the FAST, the family drawing) and the family interview. In this case, the dynamics of the parental couple will be worth studying. The following clinical example reveals a father–son pathological boundary in association with marital problems.

### Clinical example

Marc, aged 4 years, came to us for school problems. His fits of anger and refusals to obey were making him less and less adapted to his class. Marc lives with his mother during the week. His father works abroad and is with his family only at the weekend.

The mother does not appreciate the way they spend the weekends. She seldom sees her husband, who shares his time between visiting his parents and playing with Marc. Father and son are always together. The father says he tries to compensate for his absence by looking after his son. The mother blames him for not helping her to discipline Marc, who is overexcited in the presence of his father. She says there is a considerable difference in Marc's behaviour when he is alone with her to when his father is present.

The parents are invited to represent on the square board the relationships in the family during the week or during the weekend. Asked to begin, the mother gives herself a height of 3 cm and places Marc at a distance of 1 square, with a height equal to zero. Therefore, it seems that during the week, cohesion and hierarchy are well managed in the relationships between mother and son. The structure is well balanced, at least in the representation of the mother.

The father does not change the pattern put on the board by the mother, but he adds a figure that represents himself in the cell next to his son's. Both figures have the same height; they face each other, as if they were glued together.

The scene is highly suggestive: the mother, the only one who assumes the parental function, and, in front of her, two children looking like twin brothers or, even more, like siamese twins. The boundary between Marc and his father is extremely diffuse and the system 'father/son' is enmeshed. Furthermore, the father describes many traits he shares with his son, to such a degree that one wonders who is who. He shows an extreme fondness for his son, whom he strongly idealizes.

He explains his difficulty to fulfil a function of authority both in his family and at his work. He is even more reluctant to impose rules on Marc because he does not see him frequently. A cross-generational coalition has developed between father and son. They are like two overexcited children who undermine their mother's authority. We heard later that the paternal grandfather openly encouraged Marc to adopt behaviours that were forbidden by his mother.

On the other hand, the couple seem to avoid any intimacy, and Marc is used as a kind of shield. Marc's symptom (insubordination towards his teacher) serves several functions. As a little man of paternal lineage, he can only obey his mother when his father or grandfather is absent. He breaks the rule out of male loyalty. He behaves in the same way at school. This depreciates his mother, who is taken by the teacher to be incompetent in that role. She is therefore disqualified on both fronts: inside and outside the family.

By merging with his father and being as it were his 'alter ego', Marc is an object of admiration for his father. Moreover, provocative and dependent, he focuses his parents' attention on his person and gives them the opportunity to avoid what they so much fear: the confrontation with each other.

For Marc a therapy was proposed that aimed to make him able to grow up and to differentiate himself. Through parental counselling the parents realized that they idealized Marc in order to restore their own poor self-concept.

Progressively, Marc broke away and developed relationships outside the family and the parents learned to live more for themselves without asking Marc to be the sole meaning to their existence. In this therapy, the FAST revealed the inner structure of the family with two and three persons. A restructuring of the boundaries progressively took place thanks to the evolution of the parents as individuals and as partners.

## Dynamic perspective

While the structural approach gives us a static representation of the family, the dynamic approach reveals the field of the internal forces of the family system.

There are many conceptualizations of family functioning and a certain degree of convergence exists between them. The family is an open system, constantly seeking equilibrium. Fontaine (1988) identifies two axes that determine its functioning:

- a synchronic axis related to cohesion
- a diachronic axis associated with adaptability.

## Synchronic axis

In a cohesive family, members see themselves as forming a consistent entity. Cohesion represents the emotional links of each family member with the other ones. Also, cohesion reveals the degree of autonomy reached by each member in relation to the system (Day *et al.*, 1995).

Many concepts have been proposed: enmeshment/disengagement (Minuchin, 1974); centrifugal/centripetal functioning (Stierlin, 1973; Beavers, 1993); affect (Kantor and Lehr, 1975), differentiation of the family ego (Bowen, 1978); cohesion (Olson and McCubbin, 1983); affective resonance (Epstein *et al.*, 1993).

## Diachronic axis

The family must adapt itself to both circumstantial and developmental stress; to the events of daily life as well as to the various stages of its lifecycle. To that effect, structures of power, roles and rules pertaining to intrafamily relationships must inevitably be modified. Several authors suggest the following concepts: power (Kantor and Lehr, 1975), adaptability (Olson and McCubbin, 1993), capacity to change (Beavers, 1993), behaviour control (Epstein *et al.*, 1993).

The extreme poles on the adaptability axis are: the rigid mode (excessive resistance to change) and the chaotic one (chronic instability).

## The FAST and the dynamic perspective

Based on cohesion and hierarchy, the FAST is clearly in line with the tradition of research. The question is: to what extent do these dimensions overlap? In our study, we tested the independence of cohesion and hierarchy.

### Relation between cohesion and hierarchy

In general, correlation analyses showed that cohesion and hierarchy are virtually independent.

Only three coefficients reached a sufficient level of significance ($p < 0.001$): FAST ideal subsystem siblings ($-0.39$) and FAST conflict: subsystem parents ($-0.25$). The relation is always negative. The closer the relation, the weaker the hierarchy, at least between spouses and, particularly, between brothers.

This demonstrates that preadolescents differentiate very well between the two kinds of instructions, first about distances, then about heights. They have therefore integrated the concepts cohesion and hierarchy.

Finally, the independence of the two dimensions supports the psychometric properties of the test in terms of validity.

*Relational structures*

The relation between cohesion and hierarchy appears even more clearly when they are combined. Labelled 'relational structures', they are obtained by crossing the levels (low, medium, high) recorded in cohesion and hierarchy.

On the basis of the literature, Gehring states that relations in dysfunctional families are either extremely low or extremely high for both dimensions (Gehring *et al.*, 1995). Cohesion is sometimes weak (disengaged families), sometimes excessive (enmeshed families). Hierarchical relations fluctuate from abdication to bossiness. Gehring distinguishes three types of structures: balanced, labile–balanced and unbalanced.[1]

Our findings about structures are rather unexpected. Our non-clinical sample should have presented a majority of balanced structures. However, the predominance of unbalanced structures (57 per cent) and the deficit of balanced ones (9 per cent) for the three versions of the FAST are obvious ($\chi^2 = 35.09$, $p < 0.001$).

Why have the preadolescents from our sample such a preference for unbalanced structures? Figure 2.3 shows the distribution of structures inside the three categories (balanced, labile–balanced, unbalanced). Thus, 34 per cent of children represented the structure co3hi1, characterized by an upper cohesion (co) and a lower hierarchy (h) (for the three FAST versions and for the three levels: family, parents, siblings).

More than in other studies, our preadolescents privileged unbalanced structures (57 per cent for the three versions of the FAST). Reluctance towards authority and proneness to cohesion explain this finding. There is an overload in extreme structures with maximal cohesion and minimal hierarchy.

These respondents view cohesion and hierarchy as diametrically opposed. The more they are eager for cohesion, the more they reject hierarchy: 47 per cent of relational structures show a superior cohesion and 60 per cent a low hierarchy.

These early adolescents (10 to 12 years) have a hybrid profile that is perhaps typical of preadolescence. Like children, they still need support, warmth and

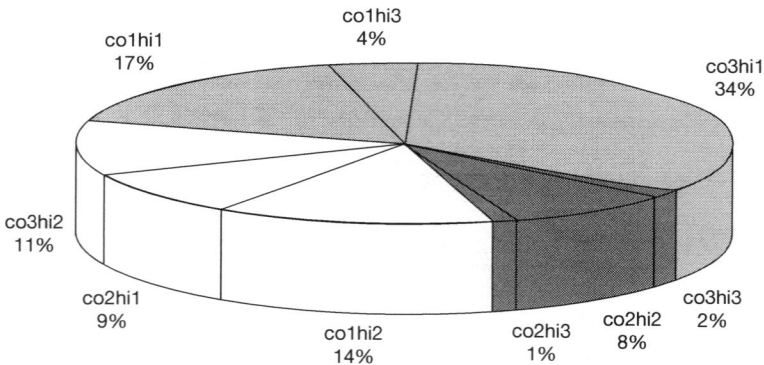

*Figure 2.3* Relational structures in the three FAST representations.
co, cohesion; hi, hierarchy; 1, low level; 2, medium level; 3, high level.

**Realistic pole**          Typical family .

               .

            **BALANCED**

             • Ideal family

                      **LABILE–BALANCED**
                         •

Typical parents •

Axis 2 ——————————————— Typical siblings    Conflict family
                 **UNBALANCED**     • Conflict parents
Ideal parents • •     •       •
        Ideal siblings    Conflict siblings

**Idyllic pole**          Axis 1          **Conflictual pole**

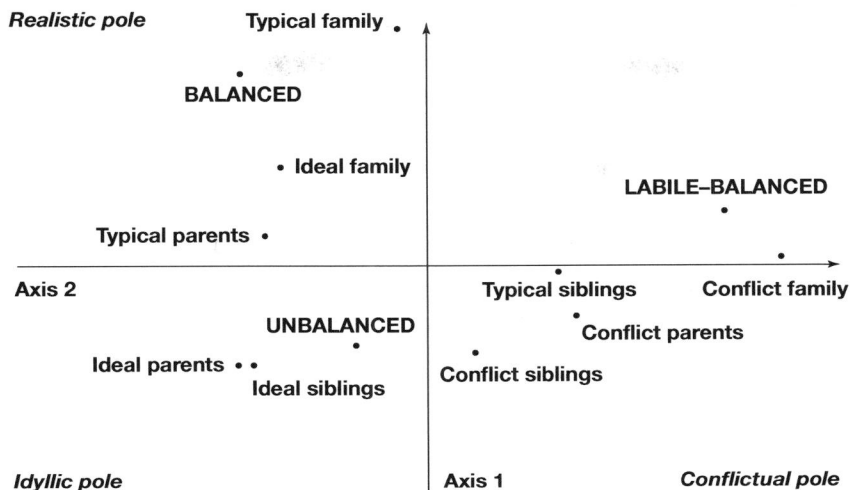

*Figure 2.4* Analysis of factorial correspondences in relational structures.

harmony. But, like teenagers, they already want to assert themselves and to become autonomous.

A factorial correspondences analysis has been carried out on the relational structures, on cohesion as well as on hierarchy levels (Figure 2.4).

The first factor explains 82 per cent of the variance, the second 18 per cent. For the first dimension, balanced structures are opposed to unbalanced ones; labile–balanced structures are located between the two. The higher the variables along axis 1, the more the hierarchy increases. In the second dimension, conflictual situations are opposed to typical and ideal ones. The further to the right a variable is located, the weaker is the cohesion.

The correspondences analysis gives a triangular structure, in which three centres of gravity are the relational structures.

IDYLLIC POLE: LOWER LEFT QUADRANT

This is the pole where maximal cohesion and minimal hierarchy are combined. These are the relations to which early adolescents aspire for the cross-generational subsystems (FAST ideal: subsystem parents and FAST ideal: subsystem siblings). Between the parents, as well as between the siblings, the respondents imagine a narrow and egalitarian relation.

CONFLICTUAL POLE: LOWER RIGHT QUADRANT

The three levels of the conflictual version are present (family, parents and siblings). There is a weak cohesion in the relational structures. The hierarchy is low (conflict between parents or siblings) or average (conflict between parents and children). In order to emphasize this conflict, children reduce cohesion more than they increase hierarchy.

In this cluster, hierarchy is average and linked to various degrees of cohesion. It is a more realistic pole, well represented by a typical global picture: the whole family in its daily life. Preadolescents are aware of the differences of power between parents and themselves. This explains why hierarchy is more stressed.

The farther we go along the horizontal axis towards the unbalanced pole, the more cohesion increases and the more hierarchy becomes weak. Here we find the points representing the variables 'FAST ideal: level family' and 'FAST typical: subsystem parents'. Therefore these two variables are contaminated by a wish for cohesion from the idyllic cluster, while keeping the cross-generational boundary present in the realistic cluster. This leads us to assume that the typical version would already contain a certain degree of idealization.

The analysis of correspondences could be interpreted as the crossing of two dimensions: merging (or fusion) and differentiation (Figure 2.5). This ideal cross-generational merging subsystem (parents or siblings) is represented by welded and egalitarian ties. More than 80 per cent of these structures have a maximal cohesion and a minimal hierarchy.

At the same time, partners of the same generation are opposed in 85 per cent of the conflicts. Conflict seems to be an attempt to introduce a differentiation in the subsystem, where partners could be at risk of being confused. To avoid merging, early adolescents would therefore protect themselves by resorting to conflict.

Cross-generational relations represent another means of differentiation. Our findings show how the dividing lines between generations are already known at that age. Distance and hierarchy are present between parents and children. We might

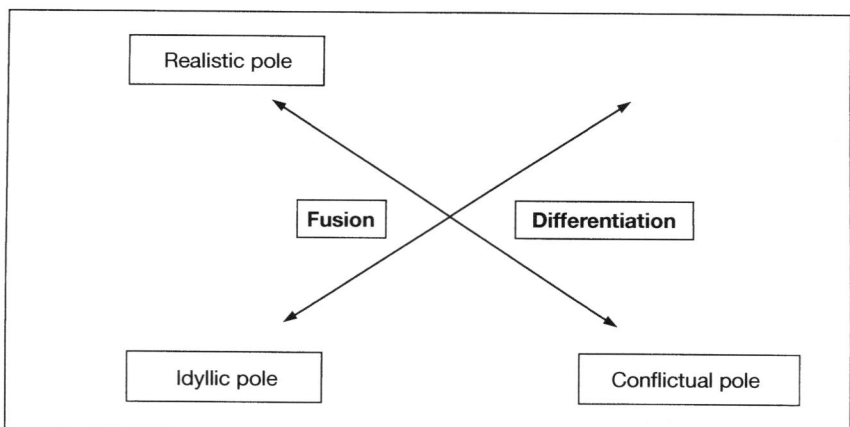

*Figure 2.5* Interpretation of the correspondences analysis.

explain the weak presence of cross-generational conflicts (15 per cent) by the fact that differentiation between parents and children is more easily integrated and that conflict is less necessary to preserve one's identity.

All these observations could be summed up in a single metaphor. The pre-adolescent is like a tightrope walker. He leaves the universe of childhood and goes ahead towards adolescence. His feet are riveted to the rope of family cohesion, the very foundation of his development. In his hands, he holds a long pole, to keep his precarious equilibrium. If the balancing pole draws him towards merging, there is a risk of falling into non-existence. The preadolescent restores his balance by leaning on what enables him to define his identity: distance by conflict and differentiation by generational status. The procedure of recoursing to conflict in order to differentiate oneself will be illustrated by Claire's example.

### Clinical example

Claire, 17 years old, seeks advice after several school failures. She repeated her class, 1 year ago, and she is now experiencing a new setback. She is the elder of two children; her brother is 13 years old.

Claire is in permanent conflict with her father about her school failures and the way she spends the evenings with her friends. During the family interview she left the room and slammed the door because her father expressed a negative opinion about her.

The FAST (Figure 2.6) was performed during an interview with Claire alone.

From a structural point of view, the typical and ideal versions of the FAST reveal a trio and an isolated member, the father. In these two representations there is a cross-generational coalition between mother and her two children. In the conflictual version, one observes a hierarchy reversal between mother and daughter in favour of the latter. Father's hierarchical status is considered to be superior to mother's.

The comments made by Claire are interesting:

- Typical FAST: 'My father is very much authoritarian. When I ask him if I can go out, he never gives me his permission wholeheartedly. Of course, I ask that more often than my brother.'
- Ideal FAST: 'This is when I can talk with my father and when he agrees to listen to me.'
- Conflict FAST: 'On that occasion, I told my father that I wanted to leave the house. He answered that I was dependent on them since I did not earn my living. I slammed the door and I only came back in the evening.'

Oedipal ties are very powerful. Claire talks only about her father. The ideal family is one where father and daughter understand each other. The other members have secondary roles. Furthermore, mother and son remain very close to each other in the three representations.

The dynamics between cohesion and hierarchy shift from a labile–balanced structure (typical FAST) to a balanced structure (ideal FAST), then to an unbalanced

**Typical representation**

| | F | M | C | B |
|---|---|---|---|---|
| Height | 6 | 4.5 | 3 | 3 |
| Order | 4 | 3 | 1 | 2 |

| | Relational structures | |
|---|---|---|
| Family | Co1Hi2 | labile–balanced |
| Parent | Co1Hi2 | labile–balanced |
| Sibling | Co3Hi1 | unbalanced |

**Ideal representation**

| | F | M | C | B |
|---|---|---|---|---|
| Height | 1.5 | 1.5 | 0 | 0 |
| Order | 4 | 2 | 1 | 3 |

| | Relational structures | |
|---|---|---|
| Family | Co2Hi2 | balanced |
| Parent | Co1Hi1 | unbalanced |
| Sibling | Co3Hi1 | unbalanced |

**Conflict representation**

| | F | M | C | B |
|---|---|---|---|---|
| Height | 4.5 | 3 | 4.5 | 0 |
| Order | 1 | 3 | 2 | 4 |

| | Relational structures | |
|---|---|---|
| Family | Co1Hi1 | unbalanced |
| Parent | Co1Hi2 | labile–balanced |
| Sibling | Co1Hi3 | unbalanced |

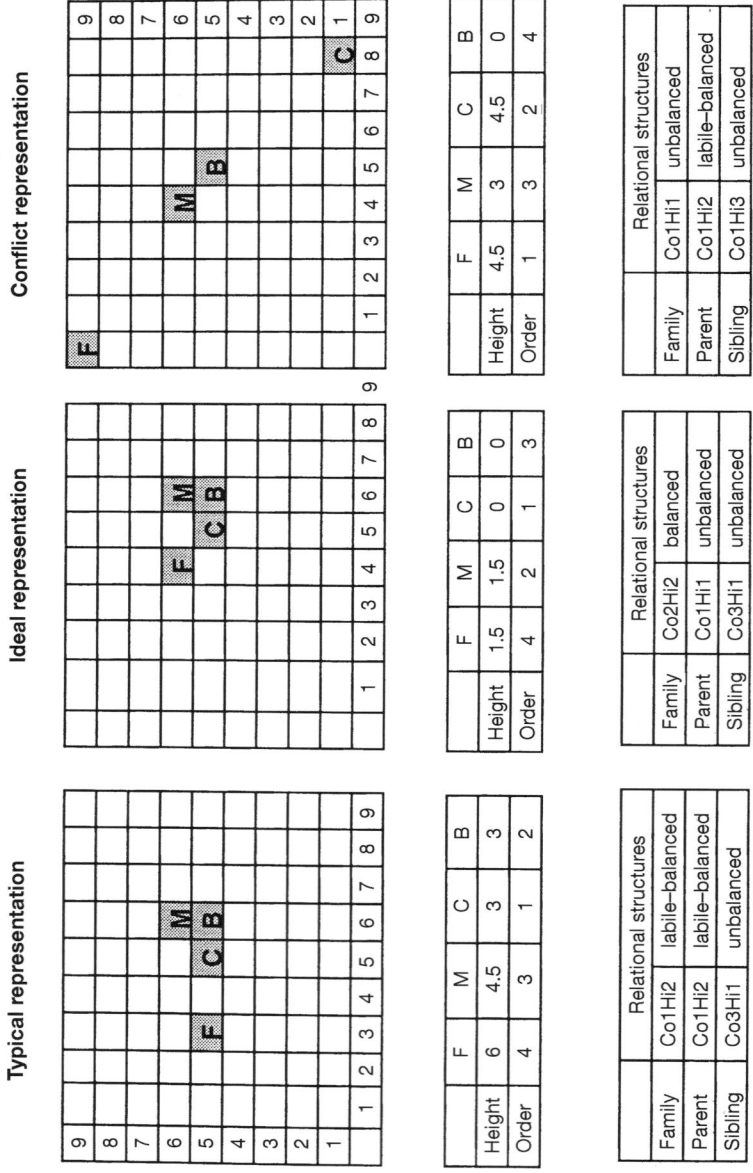

*Figure 2.6* FAST performed by Claire.
B, brother; C, Claire; Co, cohesion; F, father; Hi, hierarchy; 1, low level; 2, medium level; 3, high level.

one (conflict FAST). This FAST sounds like the family interview: communication full of emotions, confrontation between father and daughter and sudden exit of the latter.

The cocoon protecting mother and children could be the idyllic pole; a mother who is rather permissive and cordial. Both the mother and the brother treat Claire tactfully because they know how emotional she is.

The father personifies the conflictual pole. He is the only person who sets limits for Claire. He is sometimes peremptory, even more because he does not feel supported by his wife. Father and daughter form a passionate couple. Father's rigidity and Claire's uncompromising character give rise to explosive symmetrical escalations.

Cohesion and hierarchy fluctuate from a regressive position predominantly marked by harmony without differentiation, towards a 'teenage' position characterized by conflict and desire for more autonomy. This might lead to equilibrium if the positions were not split to that extent. Claire undermines the parental cohesion; she is a bone of contention between her parents.

The symptom of failure at school is a neurotic compromise that permits both parties to postpone Claire's departure from the family and challenge father's considerable ambition with regard to school proficiency.

During family therapy, Claire progressively learned to communicate more quietly and to assert herself in a more constructive way. The parents reinforced their cohesion: the father became more flexible and the mother more resolute.

## Conclusion

### *Some salient findings of our study*

- The children from our non-clinical sample are able clearly to differentiate between generations, particularly in the typical version.
- It is confirmed that cohesion and hierarchy are perceived as distinct dimensions.
- Disturbed boundaries are rather rare. They are significantly more frequent in the conflictual representation.
- Unbalanced structures, massively present in the representations of preadolescents, do not necessarily reflect a family dysfunctioning. They may reflect specific aspirations at a given age. It is preferable to give these categories a descriptive function, rather than a normative one.

### *The FAST at the crossroads of systemic theories*

We located the FAST at the crossroads of a structural and a dynamic perspective. Their contributions are complementary. As a structural tool, the FAST gives us the map of the family structure, in three different contexts. These three pictures have to be compared. The whole system is scanned, but so are the subsystems and their connections.

But how does the family function with that structure? What are its dynamics? The family is a field of contradictory forces: centrifugal and centripetal ones; belonging and individualization; merging and differentiation; homeostasis and change.

One variable is essential for the equilibrium of the system: the cross-generational boundary. Some properties are required: clarity, permeability and capacity to evolve. Given these preconditions, the cross-generational boundary will represent an interface open to the multiple regulations required in daily life.

This cross-generational boundary is connected with parental cohesion and marital understanding. Our study shows that boundary disturbances occur much more frequently in marital conflicts. Furthermore, Marc and Claire were able to find a right way as soon as their parents recovered enough consistency, at least in their roles of educators.

### A *third perspective: time*

The developmental aspect appears behind the concepts 'boundary' and 'adaptability'. The system must be modified in function in different stages of the lifecycle. Young people from our sample have paradoxical representations, which superpose those of children and adolescents. The two clinical examples (Marc and Claire) are also illustrations of difficult transitions: a toddler becoming a single child; an adolescent who is the eldest becoming autonomous.

The cross-generational aspect is another manifestation of the importance of time. Similar transactions are repeated through generations. Family members can get entangled in loyalty conflicts (Boszormenyi-Nagy and Spark, 1973). Consequently, it seems that Marc and his father had to be loyal to Marc's paternal grandfather by rejecting any authority, particularly from the mother.

The lifecycle is therefore like a frame into which the FAST must be incorporated to find its full meaning. I would even dare to say that time is the fourth dimension of the FAST, the hidden one.

Nevertheless, it is possible to incorporate a time dimension into the FAST by slightly changing the instructions. For example, two representations could be asked for: the original family and the current one. If the family is undergoing a major developmental transition or a traumatic life event, representations of the relationships before and after the event are worthwhile. Respondents can use several sets of the test to enable comparison of the family patterns. Therefore, the FAST must be relocated in the history of the nuclear family and, beyond this point, in the history of the ascending lineages.

The family sitting in the waiting room is often ensnared in repetitive frustrating transactions. Its members find it difficult to describe their internal functioning to a stranger. Tests like the FAST enable them to represent family relations in their structures, their dynamics and also their history. The square board and its figures propose an easy symbolism portraying hierarchy and cohesion, the boundaries and their disturbances.

When a working alliance is established, the family is ready for a long trip: from experience to representation; from meaning to change. Symptom repetition is progressively wearing off and there is room for insight. The family becomes able, at the end of the day, to go alone its own way.

## Notes

1.  Balanced structures: average level of hierarchy with average or superior cohesion
    Labile–balanced structures: lower hierarchy + average cohesion; average hierarchy + lower cohesion; superior hierarchy + average cohesion
    Unbalanced structures: lower or superior hierarchy and cohesion.

## References

Beavers, R.W. (1993) 'Measuring family competence: The Beavers systems model', in F. Walsh (ed.) *Normal Family Processes*, 2nd ed., New York: Guilford Press.

Boszormenyi-Nagy, I. and Spark, G. (1973) *Invisible Loyalties*, New York: Harper and Row.

Bowen, M. (1978) *Family Therapy in Clinical Practice*, New York: Jason Aronson.

Day, R.D., Gilbert, K.R., Settles, B.H. and Burr, W.R. (1995) *Research and Theory in Family Science*, Pacific Grove: Brooks/Cole.

Debry, M. (1997) 'Approche systémique du dessin de famille, sa validation par le Test du Système Familial (FAST)', *Revue de Psychologie et Psychométrie* 18(1): 7–22.

Epstein, N.B., Bishop, D., Ryan, C., Miller, I. and Keitner, D. (1993) 'The McMaster Model: View of healthy family functioning', in F. Walsh (ed.) *Normal Family Processes*, 2nd ed., New York: Guilford Press.

Feldman, S.S. and Gehring, T.M. (1998) 'Changing perception of family cohesion and power across adolescence', *Child Development* 59: 1034–45.

—— Wentzel, K.R. and Gehring, T.M. (1989) 'A comparison of the views of mothers, fathers and preadolescents about the family cohesion and power', *Journal of Family Psychology* 3: 39–60.

Fontaine, P. (1988) 'Evaluation de familles: modèles et échelles', in J.C. Benoit, J.A. Malarewicz, J. Beaujean, Y. Colas and S. Kannas (eds) *Dictionnaire clinique des thérapies familiales systémiques*, Paris: ESF.

Gehring, T.M. and Debry, M. (1995) *L'évaluation du système familial: le FAST*, Braine-le-Château: ATM.

—— Feldman, S.S. (1988) 'Adolescents' perceptions of family cohesion and power: A methodological study of the Family System Test', *Journal of Adolescent Research* 3(1): 33–52.

—— Marti, D. (1990) 'Der Familiensystemtest. Typen familiärer Beziehungsstrukturen', *Bulletin der Schweizer Psychologen* 11: 13–19.

—— Marti, D. (1993a) 'The Family System Test: Differences in perception of family structures between non-clinical and clinical children', *Journal of Child Psychology and Psychiatry* 34(3): 363–77.

—— Marti, D. (1993b) 'The architecture of family structures: Toward a spatial conception for measuring cohesion and hierarchy', *Family Process* 32: 135–9.

—— Marti, D. (1993c) 'Debate and argument: Children's family constructs and classification of mental disorders: Different measurement approaches may yield different results', *Journal of Child Psychology and Psychiatry* 35(3): 551–3.

——, Wentzel, K.R., Feldman, S.S. and Munson, J. (1990) 'Conflicts in families of adolescents', *Journal of Family Psychology* 3: 290–309.

—— Marti, M.S. and Sidler, A. (1994) 'Family System Test (FAST): Are parents and children's family constructs either different or similar?', *Child Psychiatry and Human Development* 25(2): 125–38.

Haley, J. (1979) *Nouvelles stratégies en thérapie familiale*, Paris: Delarge.

Kantor, D. and Lehr, W. (1975) *Inside the Family*, San Francisco, CA: Jossey Bass.

Marti, M.S. and Gehring, T.M (1992) 'Is there a relationship between children's mental disorders and their ideal family constructs?', *Journal of the American Academy of Child and Adolescent Psychiatry* 31(3): 490–4.

Minuchin, S. (1974) *Familles en thérapie*, Paris: Editions Universitaires.

Olson, D.H. and McCubbin, H.I. (1983) *What Makes Them Work?*, Beverly Hills, CA: Sage.

Pretzer, J., Epstein, N., and Fleming, B. (1991) The Marital Attitude Survey: A measure of dysfunctional attributions and expectancies. *Journal of Cognitive Psychotherapy: An International Quarterly*, 5, 131–148.

Stierlin, H. (1973) 'Group fantasies and family myths – some theoretical and practical aspects', *Family Process* 12(2): 111–25.

# 3 Comprehensive family evaluation

*Luciano L'Abate and Douglas K. Snyder*

The purposes of this chapter are to:

- link the practice of family evaluation to family theory and to the interface between individual–family relationships
- provide an overview of the status of family evaluation in clinical practice and in research
- consider professional and scientific issues related to family assessment
- suggest changes in the delivery of mental health services that will affect how family evaluation will be conducted in the future.

## Theoretical foundations

The practice of family evaluation suffers from inadequate theoretical foundations because very few instruments have been derived directly from theory. By 'family evaluation' we mean a comprehensive process of assessment and appraisal that extends beyond the systematic gathering of both quantitative and qualitative data (be they from structured or non-structured tasks) to include the interpretation and synthesis of these data into an integrated formulation of the family's current functioning, as well as an articulation of appropriate interventions for facilitating the family's wellbeing – an ambitious undertaking! Furthermore, with the exception of the Circumplex FACES III (Olson *et al.*, 1989), the Family Environment Scale (Moos and Moos, 1994), and the Family System Test (FAST) (Gehring, 1993), few empirically derived tests have been used to direct preventive or therapeutic inter-ventions. Fincham *et al.* (1997) reached a similar conclusion regarding measures of marital quality, noting that:

> the relative absence of adequate theory is reflected in the disjuncture that exists between theoretical statements and measures of marital quality. There are many measures of marital quality available, but few appear to be derived from theory. Moreover, where there is a theoretical foundation, the link between the theory and the measure is often tenuous.
>
> (Fincham *et al.*, 1997: 277)

Ideally, family theory should direct us nomothetically towards relevant constructs and their dynamics within families, dyads and individuals. However, there cannot be a theory of families that does not include dyads, or a theory of dyads that does not include individuals. Hence, given the difficulties of defining what a 'family' is, a relevant theory should be concerned with a science of intimate relationships rather than only families, couples or individuals (L'Abate, 1997; L'Abate 1998a, b). Additionally, family evaluation should direct us idiographically in how to intervene with specific problems within each specific family. This specificity, however, is difficult to achieve when discourse remains the only medium of communication and intervention (L'Abate, 1999). Alternative (non-verbal) techniques of family assessment and intervention warrant careful development – a point we will expand on later in this chapter.

## The importance of family evaluation

Family evaluation is not yet in the mainstream of clinical practice, no matter how important such evaluation may be viewed by a handful of researchers. Although many sourcebooks have been compiled concerning marital and family evaluation (Holman, 1983; Karpel and Strauss, 1983; Bloom, 1985; Jacob and Tennenbaum, 1988; Grotevant and Carlson, 1989; Touliatos *et al.*, 1990; L'Abate and Bagarozzi, 1993; L'Abate, 1994b), a mere 39 per cent of marital and family therapists report using any standardized measures regularly (Boughner *et al.*, 1994). That is, objective evaluation in mental health still remains in the hands (and heads) of academicians and researchers, not in the general practice of most clinicians (Wynne, 1983; Dell, 1986).

Ideally, family evaluation that is both valid and relevant should provide the critical link between family theory and family intervention. Furthermore, it should facilitate a determination of whether preventive, psychotherapeutic, and rehabilitative interventions have been efficacious and cost-effective. Hence, initial evaluation for its own sake, without further evaluation following some intervention, may have limited utility. Certainly from a clinical perspective, systematic family assessment is necessary to provide an objective check against therapists' own subjective appraisals of any treatment gains and consideration of termination or additional interventions from an alternative approach. For example, Kochalka *et al.* (1987) found that after an initial crisis had subsided and therapy terminated, many families seemed to profit from an objective evaluation and further structured enrichment training in the hands of paraprofessionals. In the US, where managed care requires greater accountability from mental health professionals than it does in the UK, comprehensive family evaluation may be necessary to document objectively whatever outcome professionals cannot substantiate solely on the basis of their own subjective impressions.

However, if most family assessment instruments are not theory driven, how can the field ever fulfil an ideal of linking theory with practice? Most instruments developed for family evaluation are of limited relevance for evaluating theory because they were not derived from theory in the first place. At best, such instruments have been empirically derived from constructs that may or may not have theoretical relevance. Thus, either our theories have been inadequate in generating test instruments or the test instruments themselves may be theoretically barren, if not psychometrically inadequate. To wit, many of the theoretical approaches to family therapy exercising hegemony on clinical practice in the past few decades have done little to generate relevant techniques for objectively evaluating either family systems or the family theories themselves (Fisher, 1982; O'Sullivan *et al.*, 1984; Fisher *et al.*, 1985). It often seems that the only family 'evaluation' that counts is the subjective assessment of the therapist treating the family. We would demand better evidence from the veterinarians who treat our pets!

## Empirical foundations

The inadequate linkage of family theory and family evaluation techniques is compounded by deficient attention to psychometric properties underlying most family assessment methods. Although most family therapists have neglected the use of standardized techniques to evaluate families, family evaluation measures began to proliferate in the late 1960s. Unfortunately, many instruments suffered woefully from inattention to basic psychometric properties (see Snyder and Rice, 1996). For example, many tests were based on inappropriate standardization and clinical samples – rendering meaningless nomothetic comparisons of data obtained from clinical families with data obtained from community samples.

Moreover, the most fundamental issues of reliability have often received scant attention. Indicators of reliability for self-report measures, if reported at all, have typically been restricted to indices of internal consistency. Measures of temporal stability are infrequent; without documenting the consistency of scores across time in the absence of intervention, interpreting changes in scores following treatment is not possible. In addition, the collection of observations from multiple persons within the family system regarding both their own and their family members' behaviour makes it possible to delineate the stability of family constructs across multiple observers. Despite this opportunity, test developers have rarely examined the stability of observations across family members as an important facet of reliability. Finally, although potential inconsistency in ratings of family members' interactions, as well as of individual members' behaviour on various performance tasks (including figure placement tasks such as the FAST), renders indicators of interrater reliability critical, such reliability indices are frequently absent.

For most family evaluation methods, data bearing on validity are also sparse or lacking entirely. At a minimum, theory-relevant measures should be expected to distinguish reliably between clinical and non-clinical samples. Statistical significance of group discrimination is not sufficient; calculation of the effect size (e.g. Cohen, 1988) is critical to evaluating the magnitude of group differences. Similarly, convergence of family measures with independent measures of similar constructs, although desirable, is not sufficient evidence of construct validity; also important is evidence that the measure in question demonstrates little or no convergence with measures of unrelated or dissimilar constructs (Cronbach and Meehl, 1955).

Changes in family evaluation data following relevant clinical interventions also comprise a critical source of evidence for a measure's construct validity.

Finally, beyond issues of reliability and validity are those related to clinical utility. To what extent does a given family evaluation method contribute incrementally to clinical decisions promoting effective intervention (Hayes *et al.*, 1987)? Implications of family evaluation data for clinical intervention must often be accrued over lengthy clinical trials across multiple settings and practitioners with diverse theoretical orientations. Unfortunately, very few family evaluation methods have had specific clinical implications articulated in any structured or standardized form.

In a significant departure from the discouraging status of many existing approaches to family evaluation, the present text offers a promising step towards the ambitious goal of linking theory with practice. The FAST comprises an assessment technique with rich potential for both clinical and research applications across diverse cultures. Since its initial development in the early 1980s, considerable work has been done to document the theoretical and empirical underpinnings of the FAST. Whether these efforts will extend beyond the research setting to broadly influence clinical practice remains to be seen.

## The FAST: promise and prospect

The authors of this chapter have previously proposed multifaceted, multilevel models for comprehensive family evaluation (L'Abate, 1994a; Snyder *et al.*, 1995; Heffer and Snyder, 1998). These models articulate relevant constructs of functioning across multiple system levels (individuals, couples, nuclear and extended family systems, as well as the broader community and culture). Underlying these models are basic assumptions regarding ideal characteristics and processes of family evaluation. We briefly summarize those assumptions here and comment on their relevance to appraising the FAST for both its inherent promise for evaluating families as well as its prospects reflected in empirical findings accrued to date.

1. *Assessment is a continual hypothesis-testing process.* Family evaluation proceeds best when specific questions and hypotheses are generated, data gathered and evaluated in light of existing theory, and further interventions conducted. Repeated evaluation is essential, not only within each family and professional, but also across different professionals.

The FAST lends itself readily to repeated assessments, in part because administration time is relatively brief (about 5–10 minutes for individual representations and about 10–30 minutes for collaborative family representations). Research by Gehring *et al.* (1996) indicates that family representations on the FAST from parents of child psychiatric patients shift towards a healthier balance of cohesion and family hierarchy following treatment, supporting repeated administrations of this measure to evaluate treatment efficacy.

2. *Family evaluation is distinct from individual assessment.* It requires evaluation of structural elements of the family system that are not captured by multiple assessment of individual family members. From a family systems perspective, the 'whole' of the family is greater than the sum of its parts.

The FAST elicits both quantitative and qualitative data from individual family members as well as from the family interacting collaboratively. Comparisons of the interactive family representation with individual data facilitate interpretations of family hierarchy and decision-making processes. The level of cohesion characterizing any dyad within the family can be appraised not only by comparing representations of the two members comprising that dyad but also by evaluating representations of that dyad by other members of the family.

3. *Family evaluation should be driven by theory.* In turn, such theory must define the dimensions to be measured and link observations to specific interventions that are tailored idiographically for each family.

The FAST is based on a structural–systemic theory of families and explicitly assumes that healthy families are characterized by:

- a balanced relationship structure reflecting medium to high cohesion and moderate levels of hierarchy
- clear generational boundaries
- flexible organization.

Cohesion is assessed quantitatively by the distance between figures positioned on a 45 cm × 45 cm board partitioned into 81 squares. Hierarchy is assessed quantitatively by the number and height of blocks (ranging from 1.5 cm to 4.5 cm) used to elevate figures, although some research (Gehring and Wyler, 1986) indicates that the meaning of heights is not uniform across family members (Rigazio-DiGilio, 1993). Both cohesion and hierarchy can also be inferred from comparisons of individual family members' representations and comparisons of these with the family collaborative representation. Moreover, inferences regarding these constructs can be derived from the rich observational data accrued during family members' interactions – either appraised impressionistically or subjected to a more formal rating system such as the FAST developers' Systemic Performance Roles in Interaction (SPRINT) coding scheme. In keeping with the premise that assessment itself comprises an intervention (Tomm, 1988), evaluations derived from the FAST can be shared with family members in developing a collaborative formulation regarding current family functioning as well as treatment objectives and strategy.

4. *Family evaluation should also be driven by empiricism.* Family assessment methods should reflect constructs that can be defined operationally and modified on the basis of empirical findings concerning the reliability and validity of each construct.

Gehring and colleagues have conducted considerable research examining the psychometric characteristics of quantitative indices derived from the FAST.

Regarding reliability, Gehring and Feldman (1988) obtained 1-week test–retest correlations ranging from 0.63 to 0.87 in a sample of 137 sixth-graders and 130 ninth to twelfth graders. Longer-term (4-month) test–retest correlations for a subset of twenty ninth to twelfth graders were somewhat lower (0.59 for cohesion and 0.42 for hierarchy). In examining consistency of FAST scores across family members in seventy intact families with preadolescent offspring, Gehring et al. (1994) found that:

- fathers represented typical family relations as balanced more often than mothers
- children were more likely than fathers to portray the family as unbalanced in conflict representations
- fathers' typical portrayals most often showed the same structure as those done by the family members as a group.

It should be noted, however, that variations in family members' FAST representations may reflect effects of family hierarchy rather than inherent unreliability of the measure itself.

Validity data regarding the FAST have derived from three sources:

1   group differences between clinical and non-clinical samples
2   changes in FAST scores following clinical intervention
3   correlations of FAST scores with alternative measures of family functioning.

Regarding group differences, Gehring and Marti (1993) contrasted Swiss samples of 280 non-clinical and 120 outpatients comprising first to twelfth graders from intact families. Clinical respondents showed higher rates of representations indicating low family cohesion (52 vs 24 per cent) and cross-generational coalitions (38 vs 28 per cent) than non-clinical participants. Clinical respondents were also less likely to represent their families with medium levels of hierarchy (53 vs 77 per cent), more likely to portray reverse hierarchies (18 vs 3 per cent) and less likely to depict balanced family structures (28 vs 60 per cent). Similarly, Gehring et al. (1996) compared parents' family representations for mothers and fathers of non-clinical children, cancer patients and child psychiatric patients; they found that parents of psychiatric patients were more likely to show their families to have low cohesion and hierarchically unclear generational boundaries (i.e. unbalanced structure) than were parents in the other two samples. Gehring et al. (1996) also found that the family patterns depicted by parents in the psychiatric sample following completion of treatment reflected a change towards a more balanced family system. Finally, in their sample of 267 adolescents and preadolescents, Gehring and Feldman (1988) found scores on the FAST to correlate with corresponding measures derived from the Family Environment Scale (FES; Moos and Moos, 1994); specifically, correlations between the FAST and FES cohesion scales ranged from 0.43 to 0.57; correlations between the FAST hierarchy index and FES control scale ranged from 0.20 to 0.30.

5. *Family evaluation must address socioecological and developmental contexts.* Assessment techniques should allow generalizability across cultures and facilitate observations along similar dimensions across the developmental continuum.

As the FAST is a figure placement technique, performance is relatively independent of language. Although family patterns of interaction are clearly influenced by culture, the test authors have undertaken a series of investigations to amass representative data from families of different nationalities. Less clear is the effect of culture and related sociodemographic moderators on FAST scores within a given country; to date, much of the research with the FAST has drawn on middle-class intact families (Rigazio-DiGilio, 1993). Its relative independence from language also facilitates comparisons of family representations from family members across the developmental continuum; the test authors assert that the FAST can be used with children as young as 6 years old.

6. *Family evaluation should include multiple levels and perspectives.* Measures should facilitate comparison of data from multiple family members across multiple situations.

In addition to facilitating comparisons of family representations across different family members, the FAST administration procedures explicitly elicit perspectives on different family contexts (i.e. interactions in typical, ideal and conflict situations). Moreover, the flexible assignment of identities to different wooden figures permits the inclusion of individuals outside the immediate family. To date, relatively little research has been reported on use of the FAST for depicting extended family systems comprising former spouses, siblings of various orders (e.g. half-siblings, step-siblings) living outside the home, or significant individuals outside the family system (e.g. school or medical personnel).

Additional advantages and potential limitations of the FAST as a family evaluation technique bear noting. First, as a figure placement task, the FAST shares certain features of other projective performance techniques (Anastasi and Urbina, 1997). Because there is no obvious 'right' or 'wrong' response, the FAST poses relatively little threat and may be less susceptible to social desirability biases than alternative measures. The FAST comprises a non-verbal expressive technique that may assist family members in communicating important features of the family system and patterns of interaction that they have difficulty articulating verbally.

At the same time, measures such as the FAST are often highly susceptible to effects of the clinician and other situational variables, including subtle differences in the phrasing or tone of verbal instructions and features of the client–therapist relationship. Objective coding of qualitative data and translation of these data to relevant family constructs and interventions may depend on the skill and experience of the clinician. Thus, as with similar assessment techniques, the FAST may 'serve best in sequential decisions by suggesting leads for further exploration or hypotheses about the individual [or family] for subsequent verification' (Anastasi and Urbina, 1997: 442; material in brackets added).

## Discussion

Evaluation of the FAST cannot be divorced from the overall context of prevailing family evaluation practices, including political, economic and professional dynamics. Given the less than ideal status of family evaluation noted earlier in this chapter we need to ask: 'Why does family evaluation often occupy such low status?' One response is that most family therapists find evaluation either irrelevant to treatment goals or distracting and potentially interfering with these goals. However, this response stands in stark contrast to a growing trend by managed care companies to require and mandate greater accountability and use of objective measures to document treatment efficacy.

A second response is that most family therapists have not been adequately trained in family evaluation. Years ago, when the first author had to justify developing a family evaluation course within a curriculum of family psychology, a survey of extant family therapy programmes failed to indicate that such a course existed. (The sole exception occurred in a training programme where a former doctoral student of the first author had developed such a course!) Hence, from the very beginning of training, most family therapists are led to believe that family evaluation is not important.

In addition, the apparent irrelevance of objective evaluation in family therapy reflects an extension of negative attitudes of many mental health practitioners towards perceived intrusions into their 'private' practices. Compounding these negative attitudes is a common misperception that 'any good history' will suffice (Melchert, 1998). Add to this background the anti-empirical stance of many family therapy orientations (Wynne, 1983; Dell, 1986) and one can readily understand why objective assessment, and family evaluation in particular, are often held in such low regard.

Consequently, we can: (i) do away with family evaluation altogether, which would be an irresponsible and unacceptable choice; (ii) mandate family evaluation – a choice that might take decisions regarding the nature of evaluation away from the various family therapy professions (psychology, psychiatry, social work, and nursing) and turn them over to third parties such as managed care or insurance companies; or (iii) improve the status of family evaluation by making it more relevant to the treatment process. It is to a consideration of this last alternative that we now turn our attention.

### *How can comprehensive family evaluation be improved?*

Previous attempts to streamline family evaluation have not received endorsements from many sources. Shorter tests or test-batteries will not resolve the issue of making family evaluation relevant to the treatment process. Instead, to make family evaluation relevant to treatment, the first author has argued that we need to change the medium of intervention from verbal to visual and written (L'Abate, 1999). As drastic as this conclusion may be, nothing less will produce changes in how therapists view family evaluation. As long as talk remains the major means of communication and intervention, little progress in linking evaluation with treatment will be made. The status quo in mental health reflects the paradox that we try to help people change their own lives but we find it very difficult to change our own professional practices (L'Abate, 1997).

With the dramatic expansion of the Internet, a veritable revolution in mental health practices is taking place. If they want to survive in an increasingly competitive enterprise, mental health professionals will need to rely on the visual and written media even more than they have relied on verbal discourse in the past. They must learn to help distressed families at a distance without face-to-face contact (L'Abate, 1999). For example, teleconferencing will allow us to evaluate families at a distance without ever seeing them in person. Of course, the implications of this for family evaluation are enormous (L'Abate, 2001) and controversial (Lebow, 1998; Miller and Gergen, 1998), and raise a host of ethical and professional issues (L'Abate, in press).

Current research on the beneficial uses of writing (Esterling *et al.*, 1999) indicates that significant physical and psychological changes can take place when individuals write about their emotional hurts for only 20 minutes a day for four consecutive days. Distance writing could then become the prelude to computer-assisted interventions varying in structure to include:

- open-ended techniques such as diaries and journals
- focused interventions such as asking families to write about specific hurts
- guided techniques such as having family members answer questions prepared by a professional in response to previous homework assignments
- programmed writing comprising a series of homework assignments concerning a specific topic and presented in mental health workbooks.

The first author and his colleagues at the Workbooks for Better Living have developed a broad array of workbooks tailored to clinical interventions with couples and families (L'Abate, in press; L'Abate *et al.*, 1998).[1] Workbooks can be selected and administered based on the recipient of interventions (e.g. couples or families) and source of assessment data (e.g. referral question or evaluation data from objective measures). Detailed writing assignments provided in each workbook range in number from three to fifteen. Workbooks tailored to findings from objective measures include those based on the Marital Satisfaction Inventory – Revised (Snyder, 1997) and the Family Environment Scale (FES; Moos and Moos, 1994). Topics addressed by workbooks developed for couples include:

- examining motivations for getting married
- improving relationship intimacy
- reducing marital unhappiness and conflict
- developing improved methods of negotiation
- eliminating relationship violence
- forgiving relationship injuries and developing trust
- recognizing positive features of one's partner and sharing joy

- challenging interpersonal patterns contributing to depression
- asserting relationship wishes and needs in a constructive manner.

Similarly, topics addressed by workbooks developed for families include:

- dealing with sibling rivalry
- reducing arguments between parent and child
- dealing with temper tantrums more constructively
- using time-out procedures effectively
- reducing arguments between parents
- recognizing and expressing feelings more effectively
- identifying relationship styles
- promoting cohesion and balance of power in the family
- meeting unique challenges of foster and adoptive families.

Many of the workbooks already developed are relevant to constructs assessed by the FAST; indeed, we can anticipate when a workbook facilitating programmed writing and clinical interventions in other than a face-to-face verbal modality will be available specifically for use with the FAST.

Workbooks offering structured non-verbal exercises can often link intervention with evaluation in a manner that is difficult and expensive to achieve through face-to-face discourse. Moreover, the visual modality available through workbooks (as with figure placement tasks) can facilitate use of these media with young children. For example, L'Abate and Wagner (1985) developed a theory-derived battery of four tests based completely on figures that could be administered to entire families including children as young as 5 years of age.

More recently, L'Abate (1992) developed a Self–Other Profile Test (SOPT) derived from a developmental and contextual theory of relational competence to evaluate individuals' perceptions of 'self' and 'intimate others'. The psychometric properties of this brief measure (which takes only 2 minutes to administer and 1 minute to score) appear adequate (L'Abate, 1997). This test leads directly to preventive interventions prescribed through workbooks related to characterizations both of oneself and of significant others. In turn, characterizations of self and others are linked directly to relevant therapeutic interventions. Research is under way to evaluate the concurrent validity of this evaluation procedure in its various age-related forms with families of handicapped and non-handicapped children from various Italian institutions (Eleonora Maino, personal communication, 5 October 1998).

In a related vein, Cusinato (1997) has developed a verbal–visual test based on L'Abate's selfhood model using vignettes composed by drawings of persons and written questions for seven stages of the lifecycle. Preliminary evidence supports the psychometric properties of this technique as a measure of the selfhood model. The visual components of Cusinato's technique also suggest the usefulness of examining the congruence of clinical interpretations derived from this evaluation procedure and those obtained from the FAST.

# Conclusions

In this chapter we have summarized the current status of family evaluation and placed the FAST within a comprehensive family evaluation model based on both theoretical and empirical considerations. In addition, we suggest that dramatic changes must be undertaken in the delivery of mental health services that will affect how family evaluation will be conducted in the future.

Whether practitioners feel prepared for these changes or not, we assert that family evaluation methods will need to incorporate new distance practices that include theoretically relevant and psychometrically sound techniques that are quick to administer and easy to score. In the competitive world of family evaluation, the FAST will need to demonstrate its superiority in ease of administration and scoring, superior concurrent and construct validity, derivation from valid theory, and explicit implications for family interventions. We also argue that clinical interventions must respond to emerging technologies enabling relevant and effective interventions to be conducted in non-traditional modalities such as programmed distance writing. In developing new evaluation and intervention technologies, family therapists should embrace the opportunity to lead the mental health professions boldly to new frontiers.

## Notes

1. Readers interested in pursuing these materials should visit the first author's website at http://www.mentalhealthhelp.com

## References

Anastasi, A. and Urbina, S. (1997) *Psychological Testing* (7th ed.), Upper Saddle River, NJ: Prentice Hall.

Bloom, B.L. (1985) 'A factor analysis of self-report measures of family functioning', *Family Process* 24, 225–39.

Boughner, S.R., Hayes, S.F., Bubenzer, D.L. and West, J.D. (1994) 'Use of standardized assessment instruments by marital and family therapists: A survey', *Journal of Marital and Family Therapy* 20: 69–75.

Cohen, J. (1988) *Statistical Power Analysis for the Behavioral Sciences* (2nd ed.), New York: Academic Press.

Cronbach, L.J. and Meehl, P.E. (1955) 'Construct validity in psychological tests', *Psychological Bulletin* 52: 281–302.

Cusinato, M. (1997) *TRD: Test di relazione diadica*. Treviso, Italy: Edizioni Centro della Famiglia.

Dell, P.F. (1986) 'Can the family therapy field be rigorous?', *Journal of Marital and Family Therapy* 12: 37–8.

Esterling, B.A., L'Abate, L., Murray, E. and Pennebaker, J. (1999) 'Empirical foundations for writing in prevention and psychotherapy: Mental and physical outcomes', *Clinical Psychology Review* 19: 79–96.

Fincham, F.D., Beach, S.R.H. and Kemp-Fincham, S.I. (1997) 'Marital quality: A new theoretical perspective', in R.J. Sternberg and M. Hojjat (eds) *Satisfaction in Close Relationships*, New York: Guilford.

Fisher, L. (1982) 'Transactional theories but individual assessment: A frequent discrepancy in family research', *Family Process* 21: 313–20.

—— Kokes, R.F., Ransom, D.C., Phillips, S.L. and Rudd, P. (1985) 'Alternative strategies for creating "relational" family data', *Family Process* 24: 213–24.

Gehring, T.M. (1993) *Familiensystemtest (FAST)* (Handbook of Family System Test), Weinheim: Beltz.

—— Feldman, S.S. (1988) 'Adolescents' perceptions of family cohesion and power: A methodological study of the Family System Test', *Journal of Adolescent Research* 3: 33–52.

—— Marti, D. (1993) 'The Family System Test: Differences in perception of family structures between non-clinical and clinical children', *Journal of Child Psychology and Psychiatry and Allied Disciplines* 34: 363–77.

—— Wyler, I.L. (1986) 'Family System Test (FAST): A three-dimensional approach to investigate family relationships', *Child Psychiatry and Human Development* 16: 235–48.

—— Marti, D. and Sidler, A. (1994) 'Family System Test (FAST): Are parents' and children's family constructs either different or similar, or both?', *Child Psychiatry and Human Development* 25: 125–38.

—— Candrian, M., Marti, D. and Real del Sarte, O. (1996) 'Family System Test (FAST): The relevance of parental family constructs for clinical intervention', *Child Psychiatry and Human Development* 27: 55–65.

Grotevant, H.D. and Carlson, C.I. (1989) *Family Assessment: A Guide to Methods and Measures*, New York: Guilford.

Hayes, S.C., Nelson, R.O and Jarrett, R.B. (1987) 'The treatment utility of assessment: A functional approach to evaluating assessment quality', *American Psychologist* 42: 963–74.

Heffer, R.W. and Snyder, D.K. (1998) 'Comprehensive assessment of family functioning', in L. L'Abate (ed.) *Handbook of Family Psychopathology*, New York: Guilford Press.

Holman, A. (1983) *Family Assessment: Tools for Understanding and Intervention*, Beverly Hills, CA: Sage.

Jacob, T. and Tennenbaum, D.L. (1988) *Family Assessment: Rationale, Methods, and Future Directions*, New York: Plenum.

Karpel, M.A. and Strauss, E.S. (1983) *Family Evaluation*, New York: Gardner.

Kochalka, J., Buzas, H., L'Abate, L., McHenry, S. and Gibson, E. (1987) 'Structured enrichment: Training and implementation with paraprofessionals', in L. L'Abate (ed.) *Family Psychology II: Theory, Therapy, Enrichment and Training*, Lanham, MD: University Press of America.

L'Abate, L. (1992) *Programmed Writing: A Self-administered Approach for Interventions with Individuals, Couples, and Families*, Pacific Grove, CA: Brooks/Cole.

—— (1994a) *A Theory of Personality Development*, New York: Wiley.

—— (1994b) *Family Evaluation: A Psychological Approach*, Thousand Oaks, CA: Sage.

—— (1997) *The Self in the Family: A Classification of Personality, Criminality, and Psychopathology*, New York: Wiley.

—— (1998a) 'Discovery of the family: From the inside to the outside', *American Journal of Family Therapy* 26: 265–80.

—— (1998b) 'How should a theory of personality socialization in the family be evaluated? Strategies of theory testing', *Famiglia, Interdisciplinarita', Ricerca: Rivista di Studi Familiari* 3: 5–32.

—— (1999) 'Taking the bull by the horns: Beyond talk in psychological interventions', *The Family Journal Counseling and Therapy with Couples and Families* 7: 206–20.

—— (2001) *Distance Writing and Computer-assisted Interventions in Psychiatry and Mental Health*, Westport, CT: Ablex.

—— (in press) *Beyond Psychotherapy: Programmed Writing and Structured Computer-assisted Interventions*, Westport, CT: Greenwood.

—— Bagarozzi, D.A. (1993) *Handbook of Family Evaluation*, New York: Brunner/Mazel.

—— Wagner, V. (1985) 'Theory-derived, family-oriented test batteries', in L. L'Abate (ed.) *Handbook of Family Psychology and Therapy*. Pacific Grove, CA: Brooks/Cole.

—— Odell, M. and Medlock, A. (1998) *An Annotated Bibliography of Selected Self-help Workbooks*, Atlanta, GA: Workbooks for Better Living, LLC. Available at: http://www.mentalhealthhelp.com

Lebow, J. (1998) Commentary on Miller and Gergen: 'Not just talk, maybe some risk: The therapeutic potentials and pitfalls of computer-mediated conversation', *Journal of Marital and Family Therapy* 24: 203–6.

Melchert, T.P. (1998) 'A review of instruments for assessing family history', *Clinical Psychology Review* 18: 163–88.

Miller, J.K. and Gergen, K.J. (1998) 'The therapeutic potentials of computer mediated conversation', *Journal of Marital and Family Therapy* 24: 189–202.

Moos, R.H. and Moos, B.S. (1994) *Family Environment Scale Manual: Development, Application, and Research*, Palo Alto, CA: Consulting Psychologists Press.

Olson, D.H., Russell, C.S. and Sprenkle, D.H. (eds) (1989) *Circumplex Model: Systematic Assessment and Treatment of Families*, New York: Haworth.

O'Sullivan, S., Berger, M. and Foster, M. (1984) 'The utility of structural family therapy nomenclature: Between clinician agreement in the conjoint family assessment interview', *Journal of Marital and Family Therapy* 10: 179–84.

Rigazio-DiGilio, S.A. (1993) 'The Family System Test (FAST): A spatial representation of family structure and flexibility', *American Journal of Family Therapy* 21: 369–75.

Snyder, D.K. (1997) *Manual for the Marital Satisfaction Inventory – Revised*, Los Angeles, CA: Western Psychological Services.

Snyder, D.K. and Rice, J.L. (1996) 'Methodological issues and strategies in scale development', in D.H. Sprenkle and S.M. Moon (eds) *Research Methods in Family Therapy*, New York: Guilford Press.

Snyder, D.K., Cavell, T.A., Heffer, R.W. and Mangrum, L.F. (1995) 'Marital and family assessment: A multifaceted, multilevel approach', in R.H. Mikesell, D.D. Lusterman and S.H. McDaniel (eds) *Integrating Family Therapy: Handbook of Family Psychology and Systems Theory*, Washington, DC: American Psychological Association.

Tomm, K. (1988) 'Interventive interviewing: Part III. Intending to ask lineal, circular, strategic, or reflexive questions?', *Family Process* 27: 1–15.

Touliatos, J., Perlmutter, B.F. and Straus, M.A. (eds) (1990) *Handbook of Family Measurement Techniques*, Newbury Park, CA: Sage.

Wynne, L.C. (1983) 'Family research and family therapy: A reunion?', *Journal of Marital and Family Therapy* 9: 113–17.

# 4 Relational diagnosis: An overview of methods

*Jay Lebow*

During the 1990s there was a significant breakthrough in relational diagnosis and assessment. Prior to this time, flowing from an ideology focused on the individual, the tradition of assessment in mental health concentrated almost exclusively on describing disorders and personality characteristics within individuals. Both systems assessing disorders, such as the DSM IV of the American Psychiatric Association and the ICD 9, and systems assessing dimensions of pathology and personality, such as the Minnesota Multiphasic Personality Inventory-R and Thematic Apperception Test, have been predicated on the assumption that description is best offered at the level of the person in isolation.

A relational viewpoint contrasts with this view. While allowing that description at the level of the individual may assume importance, relational diagnosis emphasizes the dimensions of interaction that emerge across individuals. A relational viewpoint suggests that much of what is most essential is manifested in the ongoing processes between people.

## Development of the relational view

There are both a broader and a more limited version of the relational viewpoint. In the broader versions of the relational viewpoint, which were most prominent early in the history of family therapy, the relational perspective was offered as a radical contrast to the individual view. The first generation of family therapists pictured the systems in which people lived as having such powerful properties that they could be viewed as the essential determinant of individual thoughts, feelings and behaviour. From this vantage point, what was occurring at the level of the individual was insignificant, and therefore clinicians did not need to be concerned with whether an individual was depressed, anxious or schizophrenic. Individual personality and disturbance, and therefore individual assessment, were seen as of little use. What mattered from this view were the roles individuals filled and how their behaviour played out in interactional cycles, which could best be addressed through assessment of interactions.

These bold thoughts of a new paradigm helped move attention towards relational assessment and diagnosis. However, the complete rejection of individual assessment was not warranted. The radical position taken stemmed from ideology, not the data about families. Indeed, the brilliant ideas about systemic impacts were developed without a well-validated method for assessing interactional processes. Assessment had to depend on the eye of the observer and therefore remained subject to considerable bias. Those who could not see the presence of powerful individual factors did not notice their impact. But what remained was the brilliant insight of the incredible impact and importance of relationships. Many years of family research has confirmed and reconfirmed the power of this influence.

More recently, a more mature science-based view of relational diagnosis presents systems assessment not as a complete rejection of individual assessment but as an additional dimension for assessment, and one that is just as important as individual assessment. A complete understanding must consider both interactional factors and family and other system processes. This vantage point is now most common among family psychologists and marriage and family therapists, with the more radical position, which rejects individual diagnosis and assessment, falling into disfavour. The present vantage point allows that individual functioning does make a difference but believes that individual functioning is inevitably interwoven in a circular process with interactional processes.

From this perspective, interactional views and assessment should always be part of our diagnostic view, and our measures should always assess the interactional factors, regardless of the issue being assessed. We need to know both how individuals function and how the systems in which they live function, regardless of the problem under study. The present version of the relational viewpoint also suggests that there are a number of conditions and difficulties for which relational diagnosis assumes greater importance than individual diagnosis. For example, the evidence overwhelmingly suggests that couple satisfaction, and its flip-side, marital maladjustment, are far more a product of what occurs in the relationship process between individuals than of the particular characteristics of the individuals.

The development of the relational viewpoint has led to efforts to describe pathology from a relational perspective. At one level, this has led to the development of relational nomenclatures, describing interaction patterns that are problematic. Just as the DSM IV offers the criteria for individual diagnosis, a similar list of criteria can be offered for problematic relational patterns, be they marital difficulties, triangulation between parents and children, or family violence. Such criteria have been summarized in relation to a number of common interpersonal difficulties in a seminal book edited by Florence Kaslow (1996).

In parallel with this form of diagnosis has been the development of measures that tap interpersonal processes. The relational viewpoint has led to a series of methods for assessing relationships.

## Dimensions of relational measures

### *Sources of report*

Measures of interpersonal processes can be divided across three dimensions. There are measures in which clients report their own views of their interpersonal processes, termed self-report measures. Self-report measures have the strength of including the individual's views of their experiences and of being based on all the information about family life available to the individual. They are clearly the best route to assessing the inner experience of those involved in an interaction or interactional pattern. However, self-report measures also offer the distinct possibility for considerable distortion of the processes that are occurring. For example, a depressed spouse may label and rate all the processes in a marriage with an overly negative viewpoint, providing a distorted view of what is occurring in the relationship.

An alternative source of data is to have family members rate one another. Here, bias about self may be removed, but bias towards others and towards family processes remains a distinct possibility.

A third source of ratings comes from more objective raters who have less stake in the labelling of ongoing family processes. Such raters can be expected to be less affected by bias. However, these individuals must inevitably base ratings on small samples of observed behaviour, and research has shown some bias occurs even with little in the way of connection. Thus, each of these methods for rating interactional processes has benefits and liabilities.

Another set of methods moves away from ratings and towards more objective counts of behaviour. These methods are typically invoked in laboratory interactional tasks, where families are observed and their processes rated on various indices. The most elaborate versions of these methods, such as those invoked in the marital studies of John Gottman (1999), include videotaping interactional sequences and microencoding the behaviour on various dimensions on a second-by-second basis. These methods have the advantage of great objectivity and therefore valid internal validity in terms of the accuracy of the ratings. However, they carry the disadvantage of having to be based on small samples of interaction created in atypical settings, most often laboratories. No matter how much effort is made to make these settings like settings in which behaviour is not observed, the results remain susceptible to subject reactivity to the study environment, which may cause the subjects to alter their behaviour in subtle ways. The small timeframe during which the information is acquired to be rated in these efforts also creates the distinct possibility that we may capture atypical patterns. Therefore, this source of information offers unique data but cannot replace self-report, family member reports and observer reports on client behaviour in natural environments.

### Range of focus

Another important distinction across relational measures is by their range of focus. Some interactional measures aim at whole-family processes and limit themselves to attempting to describe the whole family. Such measures capture the big picture but also carry the disadvantage that they must be some average of the processes studied within smaller units within the family. Thus, a 'disengaged' family may actually include two members who are quite close. Other measures focus more specifically on subsystems. For example, measures may focus on the couple relationship or only on parent–child dyads. These measures can tap a dimension of family experience more precisely but are more limited in scope.

### Naturalistic vs laboratory measures

Measures can also be differentiated between those that examine family systems in the context of situations specially created to assess interactions and naturalistic observation of families in their native contexts. Measures that are predicated on specially created interaction tasks have the advantage of pulling for precisely the patterns that one is looking to examine. Along with ensuring the presence of the phenomenon of interest, these assessment devices also are very efficient in the use of client and observer time. In contrast, naturalistic measures offer a view of the family in its own environment and are therefore less likely to be altered by the research but they necessitate longer periods to study interaction, far more searching for the kind of phenomenon under study and much greater expense.

### Levels of abstraction

Measures also differ in the complexity of the construct that they are designed to address. Some measures are designed to assess simple concepts, while others are designed to assess the most complex concepts. This dimension has assumed particular importance among relational measures because of the innate complexity of many systems concepts. This has often produced a forced choice between measures that could easily be validated assessing constructs of little interest (for example, how much individuals in a family talk) and measures assessing very complex variables that had low reliability and validity (for example, family structure). Fortunately, recent measure development has struck a constructive balance that has allowed for complexity of constructs and construct validation of instruments.

## An overview of measures

There clearly is no one best set of measurement techniques. Instead, we have a range of measures that assess interaction from different perspectives. To arrive at a full picture of interaction, there is a need for what Campbell and Fiske (1959) termed a multitrait multimethod matrix, including various types of measures from various sources to assess various aspects of interaction. In research and clinical work, careful instrument selection becomes vital to ensure that the measure (or measures) that taps the aspects of interaction of greatest interest in a particular endeavour is utilized. In these choices, selecting a reliable and valid measure is especially important. In the history of relational diagnosis, measures have varied considerably in their validation.

Today, we are most fortunate to have many fine measures for assessing relational process. Below, I present a number of these measures. This list is not intended to be comprehensive in including all the measures that have good reliability and validity for measuring relational processes, but instead it is constructed to point the reader to the most widely used instruments, along with others that are new and exciting.

## Couple measures

### The Locke–Wallace Marital Adjustment Test

This instrument, developed in 1959, is a short self-report questionnaire consisting of fifteen items asking couples about areas of agreement and disagreement, followed by a series of items asking about diverse aspects of the relationship, such as whether they would marry again or confide in their partner (Locke and Wallace, 1959). The Locke–Wallace remains among the most widely used measures for assessing marital quality.

### The Weiss–Cerreto Marital Status Inventory

This brief self-report instrument measures the extent to which a married individual is considering dissolution of the marriage or has taken action towards obtaining a divorce (Weiss and Cerreto, 1980).

### The Dyadic Adjustment Scale

The Dyadic Adjustment Scale (Spanier, 1976) is a thirty-two-item self-report inventory designed to measure the severity of relationship discord in couples. Scores range from 0 to 151, with higher values indicating more favourable adjustment. Items load on four factors: dyadic consensus, dyadic cohesion, dyadic satisfaction and affectional expression. Much like the Locke–Wallace, this scale was designed to assess both married and unmarried couples.

### The Marital Satisfaction Inventory

Like the Locke-Wallace and Dyadic Adjustment Scale, this couple self-report instrument is intended to provide an overall indication of relationship satisfaction (Snyder, 1979). Additionally, subscales tap a range of specific dimensions of couple functioning. The MSI-R is a 150-item true–false self-report measure, including a global distress measure and subscales assessing affective communication, problem-solving communication, aggression, time together, disagreement about finances, sexual dissatisfaction, role orientation, family history of distress, dissatisfaction with children, and conflict over childrearing.

### The Positive and Negative Quality in Marriage Scale

This scale offers a simple measure for assessing positive and negative quality in marriage (Fincham and Linfield, 1997). Based on the theory that there are readily differentiated positive and negative aspects to couple relationships, this six-item scale inquires directly about these dimensions of relationship.

### The Areas of Change Questionnaire

The Areas of Change Questionnaire (Weiss *et al.*, 1973) is a self-report measure listing thirty-four specific areas of marital functioning and asking the degree to which change is desired from the respondent's partners in each area. It is the most widely used instrument for tapping areas in which couples desire change.

### The Marital Attitude Scale

The Marital Attitude Scale (Pretzer *et al.*, 1991) is a seventy-four-item self-report scale assessing dysfunctional thoughts and attributions associated with marital discord. Eight subscales address dimensions such as attribution of causality to behaviour and personality of the spouse.

### The Conflict Tactics Scale

The Conflict Tactics Scale (Strauss, 1979) is the most widely used instrument for assessing physical aggression in marriage and other acts of aggression. Of note here is the general tendency to underreport these behaviours.

### Instruments developed by John Gottman and colleagues

In the process of his intense study of marital process, John Gottman (1999) has developed a number of state-of-the-art instruments for assessing couples. Gottman began with the development of measures to encode microprocesses occurring between couples, subsequently added life story interviews, and, more recently, has assembled an impressive battery of self-report instruments designed to assess specific aspects of couple process.

Gottman has recently developed several self-report instruments. The Waltz–Rusher–Gottman Emotional Abuse Questionnaire assesses less tangible signs of abuse, such as social isolation, degradation, sexual coercion and the destruction of property. The Gottman Marital Style Questionnaire inquires about preferred styles of marriage. The Perceptual Issues Questionnaire, the Gottman Areas of Change Checklist, the Gottman Areas of Disagreement Scale, and the Solvable Problems Checklist all assess areas and attitudes towards change. The Gottman Love and Respect Scale inquires about love and respect, and the Distance and Isolation Scale about distance and isolation. The Krokoff–Gottman Enjoyable Conversations Scale inquires about conversations and the Gottman Areas of Strength Scale about strengths.

A series of self-report questionnaires called the Sound Marital Home Questionnaires include:

- Love Maps: a twenty-item questionnaire assessing views of love
- The Fondness and Admiration System: tracking fondness and admiration
- Turning Toward or Away: tracking moves towards and away from the partner
- Negative Perspective: a twenty-item questionnaire assessing negative sentiment override
- The Gottman 17 Areas Questionnaire: tracking areas of difficulty
- Start-up: a twenty-item questionnaire assessing the perception of harsh start-up by the partner
- Accepting Influence: a twenty-item questionnaire that assesses the extent to which both partners perceive they accept influence from their partner
- Repair Attempts: a twenty-item questionnaire assessing partners' perceptions of the success at attempts at repair
- Compromise: a twenty-item questionnaire that assesses partners' perceptions of their ability to compromise
- Gridlock: a twenty-item questionnaire assessing the presence of stuck conflicts
- The Four Horsemen: a thirty-three-item questionnaire assessing the presence of criticism, defensiveness, contempt and stonewalling
- Flooding: a fifteen-item questionnaire assessing the degree to which each person feels flooded in dealing with the other
- Emotional Disengagement and Loneliness: a twenty-item questionnaire assessing disengagement and loneliness
- Innocent Victim and Righteous Indignation Scale: a twenty-two-item questionnaire assessing the degree to which each partner sees self as innocent
- The Shared Meanings Questionnaire: eliciting shared meanings.

Gottman also pioneered the development of structured interviews designed to elaborate couple process. The Oral History interview asks couples about their history marriage and their philosophy of marriage. The Meta-emotion Interview inquires about the history of their relationship regarding the primary emotions and about their philosophy of emotion.

Gottman's best-known measure for encoding couples' verbal and non-verbal behaviour in the context of interaction tasks is called the Rapid Couples Interaction Scoring System (Krokoff *et al.*, 1989). The measure uses a checklist of thirteen behaviours that are scored for the speaker and nine behaviours that are scored for the listener on each turn at speech. The data are coded each turn at speech and later summarized into various scales: complain/criticize; defensiveness, contempt and stonewalling; positive presentation of issues, asset, humour and positive listener. The Category System for Partners Interaction also utilizes videotaped segments to code blocks of speech by partner, assessing communication and problem-solving skills. In the Specific Affect Coding System (Gottman and Krokoff, 1989), coders consider an informational gestalt consisting of verbal content, voice tone, context, facial expression, gestures and body movement. Coders classify each turn at speech as affectively neutral, as one of five negative affects (anger, disgust/contempt, sadness, fear, or whining), or as one of four positive affects (affection/caring, humour, interest/curiosity, or joy/enthusiasm).

## The Marital Interaction Coding System

The Marital Interaction Coding System (Weiss and Summers, 1983) is the oldest and most widely used system for encoding couple behaviour in interaction tasks. Included are a range of positive and negative behaviours.

## Family measures

### The Global Assessment of Relational Functioning

The Global Assessment of Relational Functioning, or GARF, is a simple rating scale on which any relational unit (i.e. family, couple or other grouping) can be rated for its functionality on a 100-point scale. The goal is to assign a number to the quality of functioning of the particular relationship. At ratings of 1–20, the relational unit is viewed as too dysfunctional to retain continuity of contact and attachment. At 21–40, the relational unit is obviously and seriously dysfunctional, and forms of satisfactory relating are rare. At 41–60, the relational unit has occasional times of satisfying and competent functioning together, but clearly dysfunctional, dissatisfying relationships tend to predominate. At 61–80, the functioning of the relational unit is somewhat unsatisfactory but, over a period of time, many if not all of the difficulties are resolved without complaints. At 81–99, the relational unit is functioning satisfactorily both from the self-report of participants and from reports of observers.

### The Beavers Scales

Robert Beavers and his colleagues have developed both observer rating and self-report measures of family interaction. The two key constructs in both types of measures are competence (operationalized as how well the family system interacts to nurture development of its members) and style (operationalized as the focus family members use to obtain nurturance and support). The Beavers–Timberlawn Family Evaluation Scales were developed in the 1970s to assess family functioning across a number of continuums of strengths and weaknesses. They have been revised and renamed the Beavers Interactional Competence Scale. On the version of these scales designed for assessment by raters, the observer bases ratings on 10-minute tapes of interactional tasks. The Family Competence Scale contains twelve subscale ratings and a global health–pathology rating. The Family Style scale includes seven subscale ratings as well as a global centripetal/centrifugal style rating. Family competence is rated on linear scales, on which the healthiest ratings are given the lowest scores, whereas on the style scales midrange scores are healthiest. The analogous self-report measure, the Beavers Self-report Instrument (SFI), features a global scale, much like that in the clinical rating scale, and four subscales: conflict, leadership, cohesion, and emotional expressiveness.

*The Circumplex Measures*

The Circumplex model of family functioning developed by David Olson and colleagues (Olson *et al.*, 1979, 1983) led to the development of both rater and self-report instruments. The model is based on placing interaction within the context of adaptability and cohesion. Extremes on adaptability and cohesion are viewed as problematic, whereas a range of midrange responses are viewed as functional. More recently, communication has been added as a third dimension to examine. In contrast to cohesion and adaptability, communication is viewed as a linear measure on which more is better. FACES III and IV measures these dimensions through a series of five-point Likert scales. In parallel, the Clinical Rating Scales are structured to assess the same constructs from a rater perspective.

*Family System Test (FAST)*

The Family System Test (Gehring, 1998) is an innovative technique that utilizes the generation of figures by family members to represent emotional bonds and hierarchical structures. Health is defined by a combination of cohesion and balanced hierarchy. The Family System Test is described throughout this volume.

*The McMaster Measures*

The McMaster model of family functioning developed by Epstein and colleagues (Epstein *et al.*, 1983) postulates six core areas of relational functioning: problem solving, communication, roles, affective responsiveness, affective involvement, and behaviour control. This model has led to three instruments. The Family Assessment Device is a sixty-item self-report inventory covering general functioning plus score for each of the six specific dimensions. The Family Assessment Device has been shown to distinguish between samples with and without psychopathology and between families that are healthy and unhealthy on each dimension of the McMaster model. The McMaster Structured Interview of Family Functioning is a 2-hour structured interview of all family members. The McMaster Clinical Rating Scales are utilized in the context of this interview to assess six areas of concern plus general functioning on seven-point Likert scales.

*The Family Environment Scale*

The Family Environment Scale (Moos and Moos, 1976, 1981) operationalizes the typology of family social environments through a self-report measure. The scale contains ninety true–false items assessing three domains: relationships, personal growth and system maintenance.

*Conclusion*

Clearly, relational diagnosis has advanced monumentally since the early 1980s. Progress is clear on two distinct fronts. First, relational diagnosis has moved from the realm of a brilliant global insight generated by pioneers with systemic vision to a much more fully articulated and operationalized viewpoint. Research has demonstrated on innumerable occasions the powerful effect of relationships and relational factors on behaviour, affects, cognitions, and even physiology. Theoretical frameworks have been advanced that suggest it is imperative to track factors across multiple systems, including the levels of individual, the couple, and the family. In so doing, relational diagnosis has achieved respect as an essential dimension to track.

Second, the technology and instrumentation for tracking relational variables has advanced incredibly. Whereas two decades ago there were few instruments, and those that existed were poorly validated, today's clinicians and researchers can draw from a wealth of instruments designed to assess a wide range of relational factors.

Given the advances in the clarity of the relational view, its acceptance and the advance in the technology to assess relationships, the first decade of the twenty-first century looks to be a time of far greater utilization of these instruments in clinical work, and the generation of a great deal of research to help us understand relationships better.

## References

Campbell, D.T. and Fiske, D.W. (1959) 'Convergent and discriminant validation by the multitrait–multimethod matrix', *Psychological Bulletin* 56: 81–105.

Epstein, N.B., Baldwin, L.M. and Bishop, D.S. (1983) 'The McMaster family assessment device', *Journal of Marital and Family Therapy* 9(2): 171–80.

Fincham, F.D. and Bradbury, T.N. (1992) 'Assessing attributions in marriage: The relationship attribution measure', *Journal of Personality and Social Psychology* 62: 457–68.

—— and Linfield, K.J. (1997) 'A new look at marital quality: Can spouses feel positive and negative about their marriage?', *Journal of Family Psychology* 11: 489–502.

Gehring, T.M. (1998) *The Family System Test*, Seattle, WA: Hogrefe and Huber Publishers.

Gottman, J.M. (1979) *Marital Interaction: Experimental Investigations*, San Diego, CA: Academic Press.

—— (1999) *The Marriage Clinic*, New York: Norton.

—— and Krokoff, L.J. (1989) 'The relationship between marital interaction and marital satisfaction: A longitudinal view', *Journal of Consulting and Clinical Psychology* 57: 47–52.

—— and Levenson, R.W. (1985) 'A valid procedure for obtaining self-report of affect in marital interaction', *Journal of Consulting and Clinical Psychology* 53: 151–60.

Kaslow, F. (1996) *Handbook of Relational Diagnosis*, New York: Wiley.

Krokoff, L.J., Gottman, J.M. and Haas, S.D. (1989) 'Validation of rapid couples interaction scoring system', *Behavioural Assessment* 11: 65–79.

Locke, H. and Wallace, K. (1959) 'Short marital-adjustment and prediction tests: Their reliability and validity', *Marriage and Family Living* 21: 251–5.

Miller, I.W., Epstein, N.B., Bishop, D.S. and Keitner, G.I. (1985) 'The McMaster family assessment device: Reliability and validity', *Journal of Marital and Family Therapy* 11(4): 345–56.

Moos, R.H. and Moos, B.S. (1976) 'A typology of family social environments', *Family Process* 15: 357–72.

—— Moos, B.S. (1981) *Family Environment Scale Manual*, Palo Alto, CA: Consulting Psychologists Press.

Olson, D.H., Sprenkle, D.H. and Russell, C.S. (1979) 'Circumplex model of marital and family systems: I. Cohesion and adaptability dimensions, family types, and clinical applications', *Family Process* 18: 3–28.

—— Russell, C.S. and Sprenkle, D.H. (1983) 'Circumplex model VI: Theoretical update', *Family Process* 22: 69–83.

Pretzer, J., Epstein, N., and Fleming, B. (1991) The Marital Attitude Survey: A measure of dysfunctional attributions and expectancies. *Journal of Cognitive Psychotherapy: An International Quarterly*, 5, 131–148.

Snyder, D.K. (1979) 'Multidimensional assessment of marital satisfaction', *Journal of Marriage and the Family* 41: 813–23.

Spanier, G.B. (1976) 'Measuring dyadic adjustment: New scales for assessing the quality of marriage and similar dyads', *Journal of Marriage and the Family* 38: 15–28.

Strauss, M.A. (1979) 'Measuring intrafamily conflict and violence: The Conflict Tactics (CT) Scales', *Journal of Marriage and the Family* 41: 75–88.

Weiss, R.L. and Cerreto, M.C. (1980) 'Development of a measure of dissolution potential', *American Journal of Family Therapy* 8: 80–5.

—— Heyman, R.E. (1990) 'Observation of marital interaction', in F.D. Fincham and T.N. Bradbury (eds) *The Psychology of Marriage: Basic Issues and Applications*, New York: Guilford Press.

—— Summers, K.J. (1983) 'Marital Interaction Coding System-III', in E.E. Filsinger (ed.) *A Sourcebook of Marriage and Family Assessment*, Beverly Hills, CA: Sage.

—— Hops, H. and Patterson, G.R. (1973) 'A framework for conceptualizing marital conflict: A technology for altering it, some data for evaluating it', in L.A. Hamerlynch, I.C. Handy and E.J. Mash (eds) *Behaviour Change: The Fourth Banff Conference on Behaviour Modification*, Champaign, IL: Research Press.

# Part II

# Interpersonal patterns in non-clinical family systems

# 5 Investigation of family schemata of preschool children: Methodological and conceptual considerations

*Lucy Morley-Williams and Helen Cowie*

## Preschoolers' representation of the family

Research indicates that preschool children can and do differentiate between relationships within their families (Dunn, 1988; Bretherton *et al.*, 1990; Reid *et al.*, 1990). In turn, these family factors play a key role in influencing the child's later capacity to form and maintain relationships outside the context of the family, for example peer relationships in school settings. A variety of instruments are available to access children's inner worlds in social, emotional and linguistic domains. Scarlett and Wolf (1979) provided preschool children with toy figures and props as a way to chart developmental changes in the way in which children tell stories. Theory of mind tasks, particularly those exploring false belief acquisition, often employ puppets and soft toys in familiar settings to ensure the test is accessible to young children (Bartsch and Wellman, 1989; Harris, 1989). Assessing children's drawings is another method that has been drawn upon to explore individual development through the child's representation of their experience (Freeman, 1980; Cox, 1991). The FAST as a figure placement method utilizes a technique that is frequently used in therapeutic settings as a reliable and informative means of entering the child's world and elucidating their understanding of close relationships (Sjolund and Schaefer, 1994).

Work by Bowers *et al.* (1992) indicated the role of the FAST as a useful tool in enhancing our understanding of family variables that interact with child personality. In this exploration of bully–victim relationships within schools, 9–11-year-old children were asked to place wooden figures on a large board divided into squares to 'make a picture' of their family, and then place the figures on 'power blocks' to indicate the perceived power of each member. Bowers *et al.* identified distinct patterns for bullies and victims in comparison with the control group in the ways in which they portrayed their families. The bully sample tended to have figures spread across the board, a disengaged family structure; particularly distinctive was the existence of one figure in a corner plot. Fathers were viewed as the most powerful figure, as were other members in comparison to the self. In contrast, the victims in this sample were unique in the lack of separation among family members. They tended to produce an enmeshed family structure; fathers were viewed by victims as being the most powerful. Other family members placed closest to self were considered equal, while those placed further away were perceived as more powerful. The control children presented a balance between cohesion and some distance, with power more equally delegated.

## Insights from attachment theory

Attachment theory as originated by Bowlby (1969, 1973, 1979, 1988) is also concerned with the study of relationships, concentrating upon the caregiver–child dyad as a focus of study rather than the family as a unit (Reiss, 1989). This perspective introduces the concept of the internal working model (IWM), which is the internalized relationship experienced by the infant during the first year. This model serves as a prototype for future relationships, providing the ground rules of how personal relationships are understood and organized.

From this perspective, maturation and developmental changes during the preschool years (Schneider-Rosen, 1990; Crittenden, 1995; Fagot and Pears, 1996) lead to a variety of changes in the overt displays of attachment behaviours; the advent of language, locomotion and the greater reliance on mental representations (i.e. the internal working model) reduces the need for behaviour directly to mirror the internal state. A good example of this is the behaviour of infants classified as 'avoidant' during the reunion episodes of the Strange Situation. This procedure, developed by Ainsworth *et al.* (1978), consists of a series of separations and reunions designed to activate the attachment system and reveal the infant's expectations regarding the caregiver's usual response. For the avoidant infant, to defend against the expectation of rejection of their need for support, the child physically turns away from the caregiver. By the preschool age, the same strategy is more subtle; with an awareness that such an action would possibly be perceived as unacceptable by the caregiver, the child instead focuses upon activity and inanimate objects as a form of displacement (Crittenden, 1995). Toddlers and preschoolers are able to implement distal behaviours to communicate with their caregiver and organize a greater range of strategies to negotiate proximity.

## Measures of attachment

Attachment for the preschool age range can be gauged by measures that recognize the inherent changes that have emerged since infancy. For example, the Separation Anxiety Test (SAT) is a projective test that includes a series of photographs depicting separations that would provoke both mild and severe anxiety (Slough and Greenberg, 1990). The nature of the children's responses to a series of questions asking them to describe their affective state, the justification for these feelings and their coping strategies differentiates among attachment patterns (Shouldice and Stevenson-Hinde, 1992; Wright *et al.*, 1995). Similarly, the Preschool Assessment of Attachment (PAA) (Crittenden, 1995) is based on the protocol of the Strange Situation but has expanded classification criteria and focuses upon the function rather than the existence of discrete behaviours. Within this system the avoidant child is termed 'defended', the secure becomes 'balanced' and the ambivalent infant is termed 'coercive'. In addition, each category has a number of subgroups that further underline the subtle variations of strategies utilized during this period.

These patterns of attachment, or distinct forms of representations of the relationship directly lived by the infant and child, are linked to developmental outcomes (Crowell and Feldman, 1988; Grossmann and Grossmann, 1991; Belsky *et al.*, 1996). Secure attachment is associated primarily with positive social and emotional development (Lieberman, 1977; Matas *et al.*, 1978; Grossmann *et al.*, 1988; Park and Waters, 1989; Youngblade *et al.*, 1993; Cassidy *et al.*, 1996). With the Adult Attachment Interview (AAI) (George *et al.*, 1985) comes greater understanding of the intergenerational transmission of attachment and the effect on child outcome (Ainsworth and Eichberg, 1991; Levine *et al.*, 1991; Benoit and Parker, 1994; Fonagy *et al.*, 1994).

Attachment theory has been criticized for its concentration on the caregiver–child dyad and for failing to recognize the relationship in the wider context of the family (Dunn, 1993). Several questions are currently the focus of research, particularly the nature of the child's attachment to the mother and father respectively, and how the child integrates or selects different patterns of attachment with each (Fonagy *et al.*, 1994). The role of siblings (Dunn and Munn, 1985; Dunn, 1993) has also been explored. With the recognition of many consistencies and similarities between family systems and attachment theory (Reiss, 1989; Marvin and Stewart, 1990; Cowan *et al.*, 1996), one further means of examining the links between these two perspectives is to assess how the child's attachment status influences the way in which they represent their family.

## Investigation

### *Rationale of the study*

The present study is part of a wider investigation into preschoolers' conceptions of peer and family relationships. The main emphasis of this pilot study was to see whether attachment status, using the broad categories of the Preschool Assessment of Attachment (PAA), would be reflected in the family plots produced by preschoolers using the FAST. This was based on the premise that the internal working model reflects the way in which the child views relationships dependent on the classification as 'defended', 'balanced' or 'coercive'.

These three categories are described below.

### *The defended child*

The defended child deflects attention away from the relationship, typically by redirecting the focus upon activities or objects, thus retaining some level of access and interaction, but lacking disclosure of feeling. These children infer the caregivers' intention by observations of their behaviour and adjust their plans and movements accordingly. On separation and reunion both child and caregiver are uncomfortable with closeness, there is little or no eye contact, attention is on the environment and decisions are made by the caregiver without mutual agreement. Often these children exhibit false positive affect, presenting the image that the relationship is happy, to ensure they remain appealing to the caregiver.

## The balanced child

The securely attached balanced preschooler demonstrates clear communication within the dyad. The balanced child is able to express openly their emotional state, and the relationship is characterized by 'psychological intimacy' (Crittenden, 1995). This sense of stability and security allows the child a far greater range of emotional expression and behaviours. The relationship is not characterized by anxiety or unusual monitoring of the parent on the part of the child.

## The coercive child

The coercive child alternates between displays of anger and coy helplessness. For example, the child will whine and complain while the caregiver attempts to placate. At the first sign of annoyance from the caregiver, the child will make a display of coyness, as if to appease the parent, before returning to a show of annoyance. This fluctuating behaviour results in a pattern of unresolved conflict, where both parties are unable to divert their energies away from the relationship. Unlike the defended child, who inhibits her/his true affective state, the coercive child seems to abandon self-regulation of feeling and exaggerates her/his displays of anger or helplessness.

## Hypotheses

It was predicted that children classified as 'defended' would portray their families as disengaged, with low cohesion, which would capture the lack of psychological intimacy and absence of emotional connectedness typical of these children (Crittenden, 1995). Although the defended child may appear relatively self-reliant, this tends to be superficial and is not indicative of a solid sense of self-worth or competence. This display by the defended (or avoidant) infant/child of an appearance of competence that does not seem to reflect the child's real internal state has been noted by various researchers. Spangler and Grossmann (1993; cited in Lyons-Ruth, 1996) found that the heart rate of secure (balanced) and avoidant (defended) children was significantly raised during the second separation of the Strange Situation, although only the secure child expressed this anxiety through openly demonstrating their felt self. After reunion, when the child was free to explore, the secure infant's heart rate reduced to the preseparation rate: Whereas, belying their calm appearance attending to play resources, the avoidant infant's heart rate remained elevated. Similarly, recording the observations of avoidant children working on a problem-solving task with their mothers, Crowell and Feldman (1988, 1989) report that although the child was able to complete the activity, there was a lack of shared learning and intimacy, with the child appearing anxious throughout. Thus it was predicted that the FAST plots would indicate the child's perception that he or she was emotionally distant from family members and that he or she lacked power within the family as a whole.

The balanced child was expected to produce plots sharing the characteristics of the control group in the study by Bowers *et al.* (1992), where closeness represented shared intimacy, with some distancing indicating a recognition of individuality. The recognition of the child's individuality and the provision of opportunities to develop a sense of self as a competent, thinking individual has been noted as a characteristic of the secure parent–child dyad (Matas *et al.*, 1978; George and Solomon, 1989; Meins, 1997).

The coercive preschooler was predicted to view the family as enmeshed, based on the high levels of affect and conflict restricting the focus on the relationship at the expense of everything else. Commenting upon the interactional patterns of ambivalent/coercive children and their mothers, Crowell and Feldman (1988, 1989) highlight the existence of this pattern of enmeshment and focus upon the relationship at the expense of independence and exploration. The mothers had clear difficulties in organizing or structuring the task for their children, providing confusing and inconsistent information with a combination of positive and negative affect and coercion. These dyads were characterized by: (i) a lack of synchrony; (ii) the child's main focus being away from the activity and towards the mother; (iii) behaviours that were negative and controlling (that the parents needed to redirect attention back to their own needs was evident in the comments made during the course of the task; for example, 'Let's pretend it's mommy's birthday cake, make me a cake' or 'Do it for mom' (Crowell and Feldman, 1989)). The intermittent and inconsistent caregiving experienced by coercive children has been suggested by Cassidy and Berlin (1994) to be the optimal strategy (unconsciously practised by the parent) to ensure dependency in the child. Often these children are underestimated, with the parent placing limitations on the child's cognitive development, preferring to treat the child as younger than her/his actual chronological age (George and Solomon, 1989). As the child engages in coercion to control the unpredictable caregiver, it was predicted that this type of preschooler would view the self in the FAST plots as being powerful.

### *Procedure*

Extensive observations were conducted over a 3-month period of the participants' relationships and behaviour in everyday situations. Prior to the administration of the FAST, the children were asked to draw pictures of their families; the aim of this was to introduce them to working on a one-to-one basis with the researcher. However, these pictures proved to be illuminating in terms of differentiating between the three attachment groups and were subsequently analysed for the purposes of the present study. Following this, the FAST was undertaken individually with each child in a separate quiet area of the nursery.

*Sample*

The participants were twenty-four children, mean age 4.6 (with an age range of
4.0 to 5.1), twelve boys and twelve girls, eighteen white, four Afro-Caribbean,
one Chinese and one mixed race in a nursery attached to a school in a working-
class/lower middle-class area of south London. The nursery ran two sessions, one
in the morning and a second commencing in the early afternoon, with a break for
the staff during lunchtime. The children (fourteen from the morning session and ten
from the afternoon group) were selected on the basis of their willingness to do the
tasks. This self-selection ensured that no child was pressurized into undertaking
the experimental tests if they appeared reluctant.

*Observations*

Attachment status was determined by the major categories of the PAA based on
extensive observations of the children in the nursery. Although the PAA was
originally designed to be used in a laboratory setting, such as the Strange Situation,
a personal communication from P.M. Crittenden (April, 1996) suggested that the
classification system could be applied to naturalistic settings. On a rotating basis
each child was selected to be the focus of study and was observed across the distinct
episodes of the nursery session; for example, during separations and reunions, free
play and staff-led activities. Each child's behaviour and interaction with both adults
and peers was recorded in a narrative form. It is important to note that the
observations were exploratory and were included in the study to test the suitability
of utilizing the PAA in a naturalistic setting in order to determine attachment status.
Thus it is acknowledged that the generalizability of the results remains open and
further research needs to be undertaken to confirm the reliability of this
methodology.

   In the present study the three major patterns of defended (A), balanced (B) and
coercive (C) were assigned to the children, on the basis of the strategies employed
by the children in their daily interactions with one another (see earlier descriptions
on pages 73–74). The children's behaviour was coded by one of the authors (LMW),
who had been trained to administer and code preschoolers' behaviour through the
PAA by Crittenden in 1996.

*The FAST*

The FAST, designed by Gehring and Wyler (1986), consists of a large wooden
board divided into eighty-one squares, with wooden figures representing adult
females and males, girls and boys. In addition there are cylindrical blocks of three
heights measuring 1.5 cm, 3.0 cm and 4.5 cm, the 'power blocks'. Each child was
seen individually following the same protocol as described by Bowers *et al.* (1992).
The age of the sample meant that it was imperative that the procedure was as relaxed
and as like a game as possible. Initially, the children were allowed to play with a
tape recorder – recording and playing back their voices. Each child was asked to
look inside a large envelope that contained the figures and blocks, and was then

given the opportunity to play with the figures, with prompting as to which family members they could be.

The FAST cohesion scores were calculated by measuring the distance between various dyads, e.g. child to mother. Members on adjoining squares received a score of 1; for those on adjacent diagonal squares the score was 1.4. Thus the greatest difference between any two figures was 11.3. The cohesion score was obtained by subtracting the dyadic distance from a score of 12. To achieve a power score for each identified dyad the height of the 'other' figure was subtracted from the height of the 'self' figure. A negative score indicated that the child perceived the self figure as less powerful, a positive score indicated that the child perceived the self figure as more powerful, and a score of zero suggested that both parties were seen as being of equal power status.

## Results

Out of the twenty-four children, four were classified as defended, sixteen as balanced and four as coercive.

### Observations of balanced children

From the observations, balanced children experienced no difficulty in separations from their parent at the beginning of the nursery session. Behaviours exhibited by these dyads on departure were varied, from physical contact, hugs and kisses, pats on the head, slight touch, to more distal signals such as held eye contact, nods and smiles. Reunions were smooth and easy, usually accompanied by discussion of the child's time in the nursery, or of the plans for the rest of the day. The great variety of interactional styles displayed by this group confirmed Crittenden's (1995) findings that the balanced child has greater scope for expressing their individuality.

Within the broad range of behaviours exhibited by balanced children, common to all was co-operative play with peers and staff, and full participation in and enjoyment of organized educational activities. Although conflicts did arise, balanced children were noted for their ability to resolve disputes quickly with one another. Here is an example:

*Child 1*: It's my birthday!
*Child 2*: No it isn't!
*Child 1*: Yes it is.
*Child 2*: (Leans forward, face close) NO! It is not your birthday!
*Child 1*: I'm not your friend anymore, you're not coming to my birthday, my mum won't let you in the house.
*Child 2*: I don't want to, it's not your birthday.

Silence ensues for a couple of minutes, both deliberately focusing on the activity. Child 1 has difficulty in cutting out a shape, and glances at her companion:

*Child 1*:  I can't do it.
*Child 2*:  (Glances up and they look at each other)
*Child 1*:  I'm your friend now.

Silence for a few moments but with continued eye contact.

*Child 2*:  Can I come to your house?
*Child 1*:  Do you want to come to my party?
*Child 2*:  Yes.
*Child 1*:  Okay, Okay?
*Child 2*:  Yes!

Both commence singing 'Happy Birthday', giggling and laughing.

Pretend play and fantasy was another distinctive feature of the balanced children's interaction within the nursery, often centred in the home corner, which became a setting for various groups. For example, to a group of boys acting out the roles of mechanics, taking calls from customers and fixing cars, it was a garage. In contrast, for three girls it transformed into a school, with one child playing 'teacher', the others her 'pupils'. Although in these sessions some children were more dominant, balanced children were open to others' suggestions and were willing to extend play to include newcomers. Within this nursery, because there were few 'best friend' dyads, the children's relationships were fairly fluid and interchangeable. Balanced children were adept at adjusting their behaviour to that of a companion.

For example, one normally boisterous balanced child patiently guided a quieter child with a puzzle. On the whole, balanced children exhibited real enjoyment and pleasure when playing with others, or would often stop and smile or laugh at another group of children when they were having fun, even though they were not participating directly.

### Observations of coercive children

In contrast, both defended and coercive children were noted for their inability to engage in extended periods of co-operative play with others. Interactions involving these children had a markedly lower incidence of positive and constructive behaviours. There were considerably higher levels of expressed negative affect by coercive children. Disputes were often initiated by the coercive child, who typically blamed the other child, and, as a result, these disputes were often left unresolved.

For example, Charlotte, a coercive child, adopted different strategies for children and for adults: with peers she was awkward and destructive, averting her gaze as she snatched toys or interfered with others' play. With staff her non-compliance was less direct. She would smile coyly, head bowed, while ignoring instructions or requests. This helplessness was a common feature of all coercive children's behaviour with staff and appeared to be a strategy for getting attention.

Coercive children tended to read personal rejection into other children's neutral behaviour towards them. For example, Alan, a coercive child, tried to initiate contact with Jane, who was clearly engrossed in an activity with a friend. Jane declined the approach with a smile, commenting that she was busy. This resulted in a loud outburst of anger from Alan, stating that he didn't care because he didn't like her anyway. The vehemence of the response clearly startled Jane. Often, negative or destructive behaviour to peers followed separations from the parent, which tended to be drawn out and difficult, with both parties seemingly unable to separate. Children were at times clingy and coy, hanging on to the parent and becoming more helpless as the parent's anger and frustration grew. At other times, parent and child would engage in protracted arguments, with a strong theme of blame, which were left unfinished; both parent and child would appear unhappy as they separated. The coercive children thus took longer than any other group in settling down to the nursery routine. Reunions were characterized by similar alternation between clinginess and complaint.

### Observations of defended children

Defended children's play was dominated by concentration on activities. Their play was typically 'in parallel with' rather than 'in collaboration with' others, and they often spurned attempts by those around them to interact. All acts of physical aggression observed in this study were carried out by defended children, either in an attempt to prevent others joining in or in anger as another child interrupted them in solitary play. In two cases, there was unprovoked punching, pinching, and kicking.

There was marked insensitivity to other children's affective states by this group, either by being overtly rejecting or by ignoring others' distress. For example, David, a defended child, was working on a table with a group of children and a member of staff, when another child fell heavily and approached the staff member in distress. All the other children responded in some way, either by looks of concern or by commenting sympathetically. David continued to work, showing no sign that he was aware of anything happening.

Separation from the parent of the defended child was short and clinical. Typically, they started an activity without glancing at the parent, who left abruptly and without warning. Reunions had an equally empty quality.

### Interpretation of drawings

The children's drawings were included as a warm-up exercise and yet appeared to differentiate between the attachment categories and tied in with observational material, especially the child's behaviour while on task. Balanced children all seemed to derive enjoyment from the exercise, were happy and relaxed, often volunteering information about their family, or describing what they were doing.

In Figure 5.1, a drawing by a secure child, we see that family members are connected to each other; most are smiling and all have distinctive features

*Figure 5.1* Drawing by a secure child.

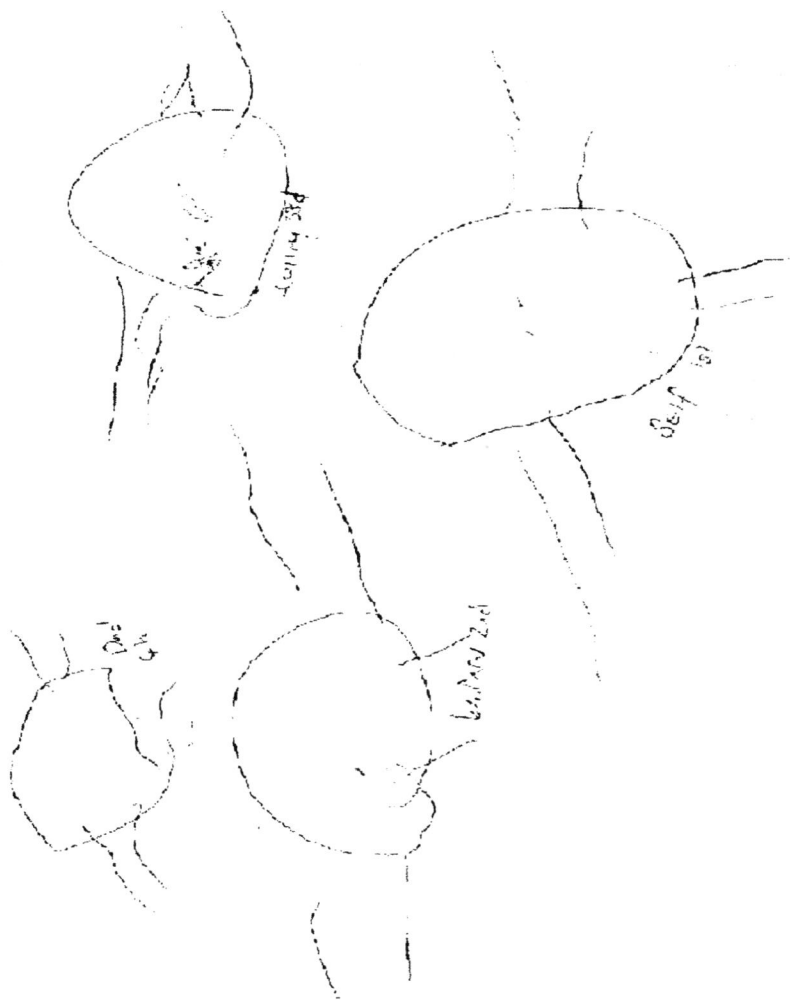

*Figure 5.2* Drawing by a defended child.

(for example, the child drew her father with a moustache and commented on the favourite clothes worn by other family members). The defended children, by contrast, drew their pictures in a perfunctory way and without any real interest. In Figure 5.2 (a drawing by a defended child) we see that there is scant detail, even of basic features such as eyes and mouths. It appeared that this style of drawing exhibited by the defended children revealed a lack of interest in focusing upon the family; possibly a defensive mechanism restricting the value attached to interpersonal relationships. The coercive children found it difficult to engage in the task, often scribbling and claiming that they were unable to draw. In some cases, they took time out from the task to disrupt other children. Their depictions were uniformly immature. It was apparent that the insecure children were uncomfortable with the drawing exercise and, as age was not a discriminatory factor, this revealed the inherent difficulties these children experienced in the context of the attachment relationship.

One coercive and one defended child had strong reactions to the picture-drawing task, and later to the FAST. James, the coercive child, was distracted and awkward as he drew his picture (Figure 5.3). There are few features, and the self was initially named as his father, before being named as James. When he was asked to redraw his father he became agitated and scribbled furiously. Obstructive behaviour, immature conduct and a failure to co-operate have all been considered to be a physical manifestation of the coercive strategy (Shouldice and Stevenson-Hinde, 1992) and feasibly were the underlying cause of the observed behaviour while the child was engaged in the drawing task. Furthermore, his on-task conduct had clear parallels to his behaviour within the nursery, as he was unpopular with other children and was constantly in trouble for being silly and creating disturbances.

In Figure 5.4 we see the picture drawn by Toby, another defended child. As he was drawing the features, he spoke in an artificially bright voice, saying, 'These are my legs, and arms, and eyes.' He then abruptly switched to the third person, saying, 'This little boy is really angry. Look he is really mad.' When he had completed the picture of himself, the researcher invited him to draw his mother. In response, he scribbled frantically and finally attempted to destroy the picture. It was notable that when Toby described the affective state of the self he distanced himself from the drawing, apparently unable to acknowledge his felt internal state or the conflicted feelings aroused by his insecure attachment.

## The FAST

Problems were immediately apparent with the administration of the FAST, as most of the children had difficulty in following the instructions, even after many prompts and demonstrations. Fifteen of the twenty-four children placed their families in either vertical or horizontal lines, with no discernible patterns to distinguish between the attachment categories. Seven children, in addition, used the whole board playfully but were not responding to the FAST instructions. Power also seemed to be a confusing concept, as many interpreted power in terms of age or height (see Figures 5.5–5.8). There were, however, two exceptional responses, performed by

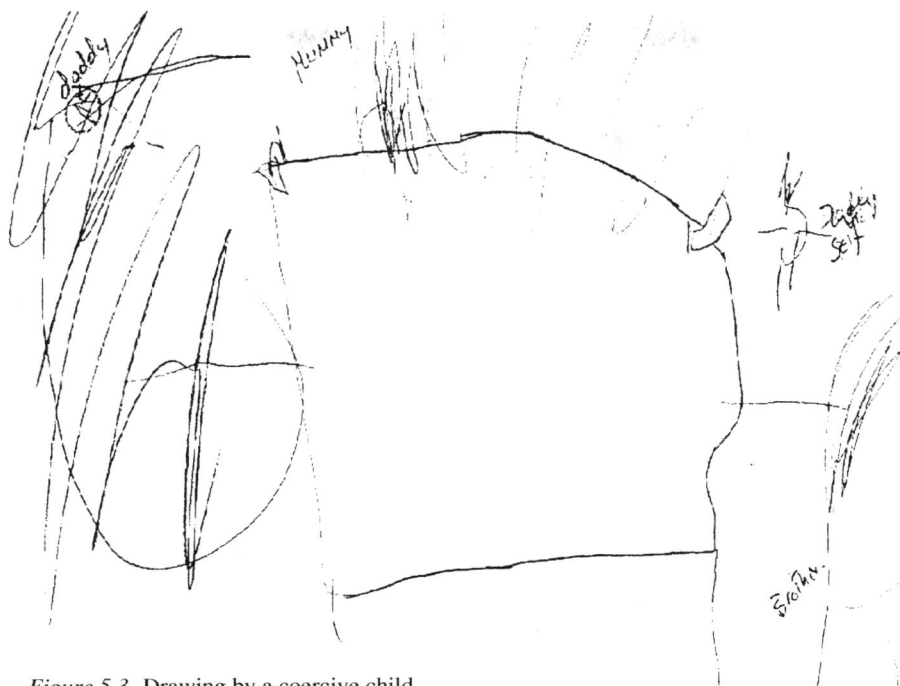

*Figure 5.3* Drawing by a coercive child.

*Figure 5.4* Drawing by a defended child.

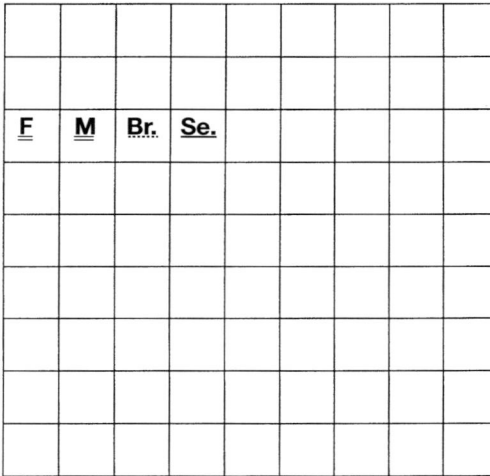

*Figure 5.5*  FAST plot of a defended child.
Br, brother (power block 1.5 cm); F, father (power block 4.5 cm); M, mother (power block 4.5 cm); Se, self (power block 3.0 cm).

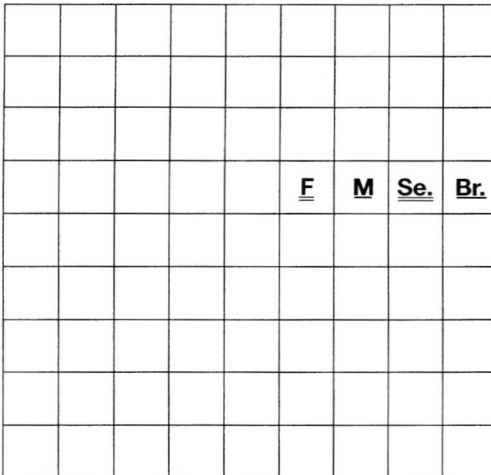

*Figure 5.6*  FAST plot of a secure child
Br, brother (power block 3.0 cm); F, father (power block 4.5 cm); M, mother (power block 3.0 cm); Se, self (power block 4.5 cm).

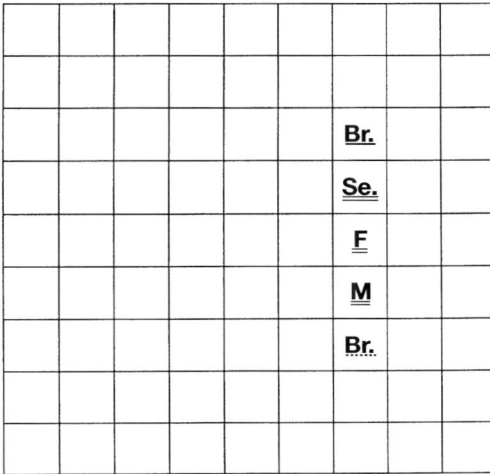

*Figure 5.7* FAST plot of a coercive child
Br, brother (power block 3.0 cm); Br, brother (power block 1.5 cm); F, father (power block 4.5 cm); M, mother (power block 4.5 cm); Se, self (power block 4.5 cm).

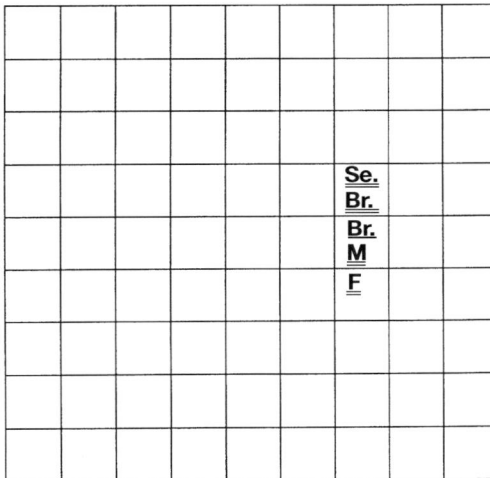

*Figure 5.8* FAST plot of a secure child
Br, brother (power block 3.0 cm); Br, brother (power block 4.5 cm); F, father (power block 4.5 cm); M, mother (power block 4.5 cm); Se, self (power block 4.5 cm).

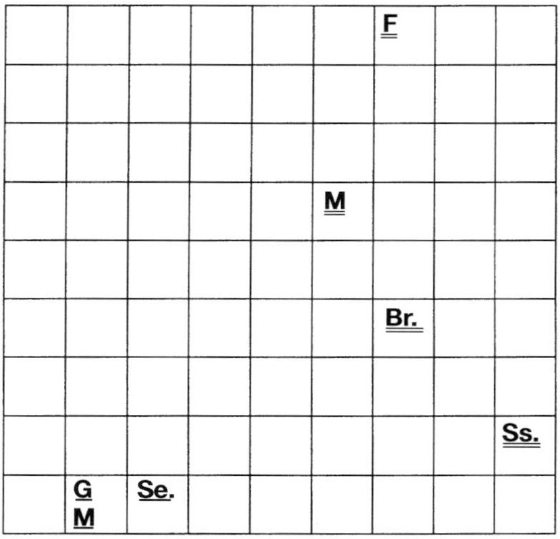

|  |  |  |  |  | **F̲** |  |  |  |
|--|--|--|--|--|--|--|--|--|
|  |  |  |  |  |  |  |  |  |
|  |  |  |  |  |  |  |  |  |
|  |  |  |  | **M̲** |  |  |  |  |
|  |  |  |  |  |  |  |  |  |
|  |  |  |  | **Br.** |  |  |  |  |
|  |  |  |  |  |  |  |  |  |
|  |  |  |  |  |  | **Ss.** |  |  |
|  | **G M** | **Se.** |  |  |  |  |  |  |

*Figure 5.9*  FAST plot of James

Br, brother (power block 4.5 cm); F, father (power block 4.5 cm); GM, grandmother (power block 3.0 cm); M, mother (power block 4.5 cm); Se, self (power block 3.0 cm); Ss, sister (power block 4.5 cm).

one coercive and one defended boy (the two who had strong reactions to the drawing task). James, the coercive child (Figure 5.9), was known for his inability to concentrate, yet with the FAST he was subdued and quiet, and placed the figures in a disengaged plot, with the self isolated from the others. Having completed the task he sat in silence observing the placements, and after a few minutes put a figure representing his grandmother next to the self. He remained quiet, and (uncharacteristically for him) offered to help tidy up.

Toby's response was very different, but as striking as the previous example (Figure 5.10). He placed the figure of self at the top of the board, and mother and father on the opposite side, directly below. He then enacted a fierce fight between these two figures, becoming totally engrossed with the action, introducing the self as another protagonist. This activity was abruptly cut off, and the figures dropped. Toby suddenly began chatting and smiling, picked up his doll and asked very politely if he could go, without any sign of the intense activity that had taken place. It seemed that for these two participants, when the focus of attention was directed upon their families, they reacted in a distinctive manner, indicative of the particular problems they faced in terms of their interpersonal relationships.

## Discussion

Prior to discussing the results it is important to acknowledge the limitations of the present study. First, as stated, the classification of the children's attachment status based upon the PAA was an exploratory methodology, and further replication

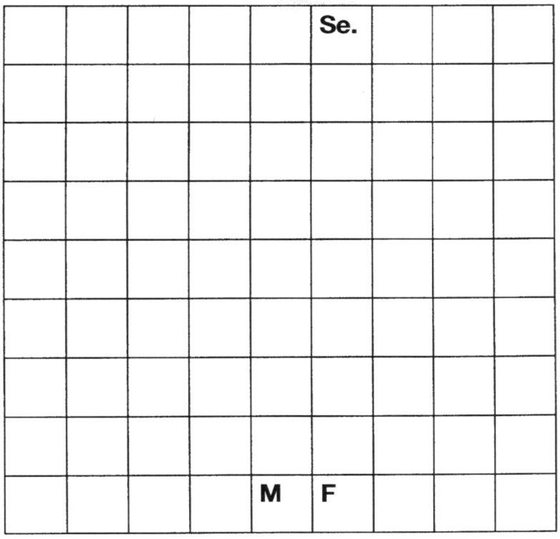

*Figure 5.10* FAST plot of Toby
F, father; M, mother; Se, self. *Note*: This child did not use the power blocks.

utilizing this coding system in a naturalistic setting is necessary. However, the results do indicate that it is possible to measure the quality of preschoolers' attachment relationships in a variety of ways; for example, through observations of reunions and separations and interactions with peers and adults in a familiar context. Second, the family drawings were included to ensure that the children were comfortable with working on a one-to-one basis with a researcher, thus the analysis of the portrayals is interpretative. Notwithstanding this fact, Kaplan and Main (1989, cited in Main, 1991) have developed a system that connects the portrayal of families in young children's drawings with attachment classification; this has been further developed as a useful tool in understanding how insecure attachment shapes the child's representation of their close relationships (Fury *et al.*, 1997). The lack of connectedness and personalized details in the pictures of defended children clearly parallels the findings in the above studies. For the coercive child, previous studies have noted how these children often display their interpersonal difficulties behaviourally through disruption and immature behaviour when on task (Shouldice and Stevenson-Hinde, 1992). This type of response was a characteristic of the coercive child in this study, both on task and evident in their conduct during observations. It could have been predicted on the basis of other studies that the FAST would also be an appropriate measure of family relationships.

In the present study, we can conclude that for the majority of preschool children the FAST in its present form did not prove to be an appropriate measure. However, for a small minority of insecure children, the FAST method was revealing because they were able to use the figures to reflect interpersonal problems that were confirmed through naturalistic observations and in their drawings. Perhaps for these children who are experiencing particular difficulties, any experimental test that probes into family relationships will result in a response where problems will be revealed. It further confirms the established use of such methods that employ figures and props to enable children to work through painful experiences. If the PAA had been used in the full version it is possible that more subtle differences might have been found between the rest of the children in the sample. However, these differences were more likely to be between observational material and family drawings rather than with the FAST. This does not in any way suggest that, as a projective test, the FAST does not have potential; in fact with school age children it seems to be a useful method for exploring children's representations of their families (Bowers *et al.*, 1992).

So what were its shortcomings in the present study? For the majority of the children the FAST lacked meaning and relevance. Perhaps preschoolers see their families as dynamic people in familiar contexts, and not as schematic wooden figures. To make the test more accessible it would be feasible to cover the board with a colourful cloth, to use well-known toy figures (for example, Play People) with a variety of facial expressions, to introduce props and a storyline, or a context such a living room, to create a more meaningful setting for the children. Such alterations would not necessarily alter the function of the test, and cohesion and power scores could still be calculated. Possibly, for children of this age group, the direction provided in this test of 'make a picture of your family' was too open and lacked sufficient guidance as to what was required. Indeed, revisions to traditional theory of mind tests measuring false belief indicate that younger children often need more explicit information to understand the nature of what is being asked. When changes are made, 3-year-olds reveal a capacity to understand false belief prior to the normal 4-year-old watershed for this type of reasoning (Lewis and Osborne, 1990; Siegal and Beattie, 1991; Mitchell, 1997). A similar process may have been at work in this study, with the children left with an unclear idea of how a 'picture' could be created with wooden figures and not on paper, thus at odds with their normal expectations. Once this instruction had been given, which may have seemed nonsensical, prompts and demonstrations would not necessarily clarify the procedure. The above changes could potentially make the test more 'user-friendly' and meaningful for this age group.

In conclusion, the present study does not confirm the suggestion that the FAST might be an effective tool in measuring perceived relationships for the majority of preschool children. The main explanation for this apparently lies in the age of the children and the present appearance of the test. However, in our view an imaginative adaptation of both design and administration of the FAST would allow it to be used as a means to gain insights in how young children represent their relationships with others.

## References

Ainsworth, M.D.S. and Eichberg, C. (1991) 'Effects on infant–mother attachment of mother's unresolved loss of an attachment figure, or other traumatic experience', in C. Murray Parkes, J. Stevenson-Hinde and P. Marris (eds) *Attachment across the Lifecycle*. London: Routledge.

Ainsworth, M.D.S., Blehar, M.C., Waters, E. and Wall, S. (1978) *Patterns of Attachment: A Psychological Study of the Strange Situation.* Hillsdale, NJ: Erlbaum.

Bartsch, K. and Wellman, H. (1989) 'Young children's attribution of action to beliefs and desires', *Child Development*, 60: 946–64.

Belsky, J., Spritz, B. and Crnic, K. (1996) 'Infant attachment and security and affective cognitive information processing at age 3', *Psychological Science*, 7: 111–14.

Benoit, D. and Parker, K.C.H. (1994) 'Stability and transmission of attachment across three generations', *Child Development*, 65: 1444–56.

Bowers, L., Smith, P.K. and Binney, V. (1992) 'Cohesion and power in the families of children involved in bully/victim problems at school', *Journal of Family Therapy*, 14: 371–87.

Bowlby, J. (1969) *Attachment and Loss, Vol. 1: Attachment.* London: Hogarth Press.

—— (1973) *Attachment and Loss, Vol. 2: Separation, Anger and Anxiety.* London: Hogarth Press.

—— (1979) *The Making and Breaking of Affectional Bonds.* London: Tavistock Publications.

—— (1988) *A Secure Base: Clinical Application of Attachment History.* London: Routledge.

Bretherton, I., Prentiss, C. and Ridgeway, D. (1990) 'Family relationships as represented in a story completion task at thirty-seven and fifty-four months of age', *New Directions for Child Development*, 48: 85–105.

Cassidy, J. and Berlin, L.J. (1994) 'The insecure/ambivalent pattern of attachment: Theory and research', *Child Development*, 65: 971–91.

—— Kirsh, S.J., Scolton, K.L. and Parke, K.D. (1996) 'Attachment representations of peer relationships', *Developmental Psychology*, 32: 892–904.

Cowan, P.A., Cohn, D.A., Pape Cowan, C. and Pearson, J.L. (1996) 'Parents' attachment histories and children's externalising and internalising behaviors: Exploring family systems models of linkage', *Journal of Consulting and Clinical Psychology*, 64: 53–63.

Cox, M.V. (1991) *The Child's Point of View* (2nd ed.). Hemel Hempstead, UK: Harvester Wheatsheaf.

Crittenden, P.M. (1995) *The Preschool Assessment of Attachment: Coding Manual.* Miami, FL: Family Relations Institute.

Crowell, J.A. and Feldman, S.S. (1988) 'Mother's internal models of relationships and children's behavioral and development status: A study in mother–child interaction', *Child Development*, 59: 1273–85.

—— Feldman, S.S. (1989) 'Assessment of mother's internal models of relationships: Some clinical implications', *Infant Mental Health Journal*, 10: 173–84.

Dunn, J. (1988) *The Beginnings of Social Understanding.* Oxford: Basil Blackwell.

—— (1993) *Young Children's Close Relationships: Beyond Attachment.* Beverly Hills, CA: Sage.

—— Munn, P. (1985) 'Becoming a family member: Family conflict and the development of social understanding in the second year', *Child Development*, 56: 480–92.

Fagot, B.I. and Pears, K.L. (1996) 'Changes in attachment during the third year: Consequences and predictions', *Development and Psychopathology*, 8: 325–44.

Fonagy, P., Steele, M., Steele, H., Higgitt, A. and Target, M. (1994) 'The Emanuel Miller memorial lecture: The theory and practice of resilience', *Journal of Child Psychology and Psychiatry*, 35: 231–57.

Freeman, N.H. (1980) *Strategies of Representation in Young Children: Analysis of Spatial Skills and Drawing Processes.* London: Academic Press.

Fury, G., Carlson, E.A. and Sroufe, A.L. (1997) 'Children's representation of attachment relationships in family drawings', *Child Development*, 68: 1154–64.

Gehring, T.M. and Wyler, I.L. (1986) 'Family systems test (FAST): A three dimensional approach to investigate family relationships', *Child Psychiatry and Human Development*, 16: 235–48.

George, C. and Solomon, J. (1989) 'Internal working models of caregiving and security of attachment at age six', *Infant Mental Health Journal*, 10: 222–37.

—— Kaplan, N. and Main, M. (1985) 'The Berkeley Adult Attachment Interview' (unpublished protocol), Berkeley, CA: Department of Psychology, University of California.

Grossmann, K.E. and Grossmann, K. (1991) 'Attachment as an organizer of emotional and behavioural responses in a longitudinal perspective', in C. Murray Parkes, J. Stevenson-Hinde and P. Marris (eds) *Attachment across the Lifecycle*. London: Routledge.

—— Fremmer-Bombik, E., Rudolf, J. and Grossmann, K.E. (1988) 'Maternal representations as related to patterns of infant-mother attachment and maternal care during the first year', in R.A. Hinde and J. Stevenson-Hinde (eds) *Relationships within Families: Mutual Influences*. Oxford: Clarendon Press.

Harris, P.L. (1989) *Children and Emotion: The Development of Psychological Understanding*. London: Basil Blackwell.

Kaplan, N. and Main, M. (1989) 'A system for the analysis of family drawings', Unpublished manuscript, Department of Psychology, University of California, Berkeley. Cited in Main, M. (1991) 'Metacognitive knowledge, metacognitive monitoring and singular (coherent) vs multiple (incoherent) model of attachment', in C. Murray Parkes, J. Stevenson-Hinde and P. Marris (eds) *Attachment across the Lifecycle*. London: Routledge.

Levine, L.V., Tuber, S.B., Slade, A. and Ward, J. (1991) 'Mothers' mental representations and their relationship to mother-infant attachment', *Bulletin of the Menninger Clinic*, 55: 454–469.

Lewis, C. and Osborne, A. (1990) 'Three year olds' problems with false belief: conceptual deficit or linguistic artifact', *Child Development*, 61: 1514–19.

Lieberman, A.L. (1977) 'Preschooler's competence with a peer: Relations with attachment and peer experience', *Child Development*, 48: 1277–87.

Marvin, R.S. and Stewart, R.B. (1990) 'A family systems framework for the study of attachment', in M.T. Greenberg, D. Cicchetti and E.M. Cummings (eds) *Attachment in the Preschool Years*. Chicago, IL: University of Chicago Press.

Matas, L., Arend, R.A. and Sroufe, L.A. (1978) 'Continuity of adaptation in the second year: The relationship between quality of attachment and later peer competence', *Child Development*, 49: 547–56.

Meins, E. (1997) 'Security of attachment and maternal tutoring strategies: Interaction within the zone of proximal development', *British Journal of Developmental Psychology*, 15, 129–44.

Mitchell, P. (1997) *Theory of Mind: Introduction to a Theory of Mind*. Cambridge, MA: Harvard University Press.

Park, K.A. and Waters, E. (1989) 'Security of attachment and preschool friendships', *Child Development*, 60: 1076–81.

Reid, M., Landesman Ramey, S. and Burchinal, M. (1990) 'Dialogues with children about their families', *New Directions for Child Development*, 48: 5–27.

Reiss, D. (1989) 'The represented and practising family: Contrasting visions of family continuity', in A.J. Sameroff and R.N. Emde (eds) *Relationship Disturbances in Early Childhood*. New York: Basic Books.

Scarlett, G. and Wolf, D. (1979) 'When it's only make believe: The construction of a boundary between fantasy and reality in story telling', in E. Winner and H. Gardener (eds) *Fact, Fiction and Fantasy in Childhood*. San Francisco, CA: Jossey-Bass.

Schneider-Rosen, K. (1990) 'The developmental reorganization of attachment relationships: Guidelines for classification beyond infancy', in M.T. Greenberg, D. Cicchetti and E.M. Cummings (eds) *Attachment in the Preschool Years*. Chicago, IL: University of Chicago Press.

Shouldice, A. and Stevenson-Hinde, J. (1992) 'Coping with security distress: The Separation Anxiety Test and attachment classification at 4.5 years', *Journal of Child Psychology and Psychiatry*, 33: 331–48.

Siegal, M. and Beattie, K. (1991) 'Where to look first for children's knowledge of false beliefs?', *Cognition*, 38: 1–12.

Sjolund, M. and Schaefer, C.E. (1994) 'The Erica sand method of play diagnosis and assessment', in K. O'Conner and C. Schaefer (eds) *Handbook of Play Therapy*. New York: Wiley.

Slough, N.M. and Greenberg, M.T. (1990) 'Five year olds' representations of separations from parents: Responses from the perspective of self and other', *New Directions for Child Development*, 48: 67–84.

Spangler, G. and Grossmann, K.E. (1993) 'Biobehavioral organization in securely and insecurely attached infants', *Child Development*, 64: 1439–50. Cited in Lyons-Ruth, K. (1996) 'Attachment relationships among children with aggressive behavior problems: The role of disorganized early attachment patterns', *Journal of Consulting and Clinical Psychology*, 64: 64–73.

Wright, J.C., Binney, V. and Smith, P.K. (1995) 'Security of attachment in 8–12 year olds: A revised version of the Separation Anxiety Test, its psychometric properties and clinical interpretation', *Journal of Child Psychology and Psychiatry*, 36: 757–74.

Youngblade, L.M., Oark, K. and Belsky, J. (1993) 'Measurement of children's close friendships: A comparison of 2 independent assessment systems and their associations with attachment security', *International Journal of Behavioral Development*, 16: 563–87.

# 6 Family constructs of first graders: Different measurement approaches yield distinct outcomes

*Florence Meyer*

## Introduction

This research focuses on the validity of two currently used tests for the clinical assessment of family constructs of children, adolescents and adults, namely the Family Drawing Test (FDT; Corman, 1961) and the Family System Test (FAST; Gehring and Debry, 1995). These family measurement techniques are often incorporated into the psychological evaluation that usually precedes therapy. They allow for the collation of various types of information that are then used in conjunction with the family's request for help.

Clinicians and researchers generally agree that planning and evaluation of psychological interventions should not be limited to individual test procedures with a single family member but should also include multirespondent data and behavioural observation. One must also take into consideration issues dealing with the sociofamilial context and the subject's position in his or her family. Owing to the increased interest in the process of child consultation through investigation of familial representations, there are numerous tools that allow for greater inquiry into this dimension. The manual for family evaluation techniques proposed by Touliatos *et al.* (1990) contains a number of such tools. It has therefore become necessary to augment practical experience with a more complete knowledge of the specificity and validity of each instrument so that clinicians will have precise references at their disposal to facilitate the choice of tools that are appropriate for specific objectives.

A review of the pertinent literature shows that the FDT has been widely used in Europe and the US since the 1950s. The publications of several authors confirm this (Hulse, 1952; Porot, 1952; Reznikoff and Reznikoff, 1956; Burns and Kaufman, 1970, 1972). The aim of this test is to evaluate intrapsychological factors and the respondent's mental processes. It is foremost the psychodynamic approach, in conjunction with psychoanalytical concepts, which serves as referent when interpreting the results of the test. However, even if the approaches applied in child developmental research have emphasized understanding specifically the cognitive aspects of graphism, it should be noted that the test lacks theoretical support and is often used in an intuitive and arbitrary manner. For example, there are numerous sets of instructions for the FDT, several scoring grids, and many possible interpretations of the data. Consequently, the question arises as to which set of instructions a clinician should choose to evaluate which dimensions? This research seeks to contribute towards a better understanding of this projective technique by comparing two different test instructions for the FDT, namely 'Draw your family' and 'Draw an imaginary family'.

'The present interest in systematic theories supports the practitioner in his or her desire to catch the child in the complex network of family relationships' (Cambier and Pham Hoang Quoc Vu, 1985: 217). While it is exactly this interest that justifies the use of the FDT, there is a divergence among clinicians about whether or not the FDT provides a valid picture of the family per se. On the contrary, the argument can be made that it provides only the intrapsychological perception of the respondent, without giving any information on the functioning of his or her own family. It is therefore important to evaluate the family drawings in conjunction with the representations that result from the FAST.

This research attempts to clarify whether or not a relation exists between the two different test instructions for the FDT and two types of representations from the collectively completed FAST (i.e. group representation), specifically, the typical representation (TR) and the ideal representation (IR). Therefore the goal of this research is to reveal similarities and differences between individual graphic family perception in the FDT and family constructs as derived from collective FAST representations.

## Method

### *Respondents*

The sample for this study were thirty-one first graders (twenty-one girls and ten boys) from 5.5 to 8.7 years of ages (average age 7 years), selected from eight primary schools in Lausanne, Switzerland. All the children came from non-clinical middle- and upper-class families with an average of 4.3 members (range from three to eight members).

Letters requesting participation in this project were distributed to eight classes of the Lausanne public school (approximately 160 children). Only those children whose parents agreed to come to the university for the family interview were selected; this turned out to be a significant factor.

### *Procedure*

During the first individual session at school, the children were asked to draw their own families, and then explain their drawings.

In the second individual session, these children were asked to draw an imaginary family. The order in which test instructions were completed was reversed for half of the sample participants.

In the third session, the whole family participated in a biographic interview at the university. Using the FAST as an interactive task, the family members were asked to reach a consensus on their family constructs. All of these sessions were videotaped.

### Scoring

To analyse the data obtained from the FDT (see Appendix A on page 105), a scoring grid of 175 graphic variables was composed. As there was no standardized procedure for tabulating these test results, and to ensure that the grid was as exhaustive as possible, the principal scoring methods found in pertinent literature were combined. The variables were grouped into two levels of analysis. The first examines graphic motor characteristics while the second focuses on physical structure attributes. Most of the variables are dichotomic (for example, the absence or presence of the father figure) while others are numeric in nature (for example, the number of figures represented). In addition, the scoring method from the 'Draw a Person Test' (Royer, 1977) was incorporated so as to procure a global evaluation score for the body structure of each figure in the FDT.

To analyse the data concerning the FAST (see Appendix B on pages 105–6), five dimensions were studied: cohesion, hierarchy, types of relational structures, family boundaries and flexibility. This analysis was based on the tabulating instructions in the FAST manual (Gehring and Debry, 1995). To calculate the scores for hierarchy, cohesion and the types of relational structures, the categorial procedure was used (scale of three categories: low, medium, and high). Flexibility, graded as low (1 point), medium (2 points) or high (3 points), was obtained by subtracting the categorial scores for cohesion and hierarchy in the ideal representation of the FAST from those in the typical representation. Finally, the three phenomena that affect the generational boundaries were studied: intergenerational coalitions, reversed hierarchies, and what is referred to in this work as 'symbiosis/amalgamations' (when at least two figures or the entire family are touching and are placed in the same square).

## Results

### Comparison of real and imaginary family drawings

To evaluate if there were significant differences between the two kinds of family drawings, and after assuring ourselves that the order in which the test instructions were given did not lead to any difference, Student's *t*-test was applied to the 175 variables of the scoring grid for family drawings. It is important to underline that the results differ, on the qualitative or quantitative levels, depending on whether one is interested in the graphic motor aspect of the drawings or in the physical structures of the figures.

### Graphic motor characteristics

*Interinstruction differences*

The results from Student's *t*-test demonstrate that of the twenty variables relating to this level, there is practically no significant difference. This indicates that the artist's personal style, or what Morval (1973) describes as 'the general characteristics of drawing', does not vary when the child is drawing the portrait of an imaginary family as opposed to the actual family.

*The graphic motor, standard profile of the family drawing*

From the graphic motor perspective, a generalized portrait of the family drawing emerges, regardless of the instructions given. This 'standard profile' summarizes the global group tendencies that were observed in more than half of the participants. This profile demonstrates that the FDT is a task that, contrary to its reputation and brief instructions, is not quickly executed. The average time devoted to the drawings themselves, excluding the interview that follows, was 17 minutes. It is necessary to point out, however, that this varied from one person to another and that the time ranged from 2 to 38 minutes.

The pressure applied when drawing lines is generally normal, neither too strong nor too weak. Neither the rectilinear style nor the curvilinear style dominates. However, we found the curvilinear style to be more specific to boys. This fact contrasts with prevailing literature on the subject, which attributes a more angular graphic style to boys rather than to girls.

The family group is drawn from left to right, with each figure being completely constructed from top to bottom before moving on to the next. The entire drawing usually takes up no more than half of the available surface. The real family takes up more space than the imaginary one. Finally, children use seven to eight different colours in each picture.

### Characteristics of physical structures: Individual figures and family group

*Interinstruction differences*

This analysis level consists of two parts. The seventy variables of the first part, which related to each individually evaluated figure, showed no significant difference (as measured by Student's *t*-test) between the two types of drawings. It can therefore be assumed that, in terms of the presence and absence of elements of the physical outline, the bodies of the figures are drawn in the same manner for the real and imaginary families.

The second part of this level of analysis deals with the formation of the family group. Here, there is an essential difference between the two types of drawings. The number of characters and the composition of the family changes depending on whether the child is asked to draw a real or an imaginary family.

*The physical structures of each figure*

Just as described in the literature on this topic for 7-year-old children, all of the figures are clearly recognizable and identifiable as human beings. In the two types of drawings, the body image is well defined and contains all of the details expected for this age group. These results are described at great length in studies on the drawing of the human figure, which can be done well by 7-year-old children. Yet it is not insignificant that this fact also holds true for the entire family drawing, even for the figures the child draws last.

While there are differences in the drawings of boys and girls, these differences are more clearly distinguished in the parental figures than the child figures. On the other hand, the generational difference is less defined and is not always identifiable by an observer who does not know the family in question. However, in general, the figures representing different family members vary in height in decreasing order. The father is the largest, the mother slightly smaller than the father, with the children shown as the smallest. In the same vein, the father is depicted to the left and first, the mother is in the middle and second in line, while the children come last and are placed at the right-hand side of the family group.

Any animals or people outside the nuclear family are systematically positioned on the right side of the page. One important indication to highlight for the projective value of this test is that when two children are drawn, in 80 per cent of the cases a child figure of the same sex as the respondent is placed in the first position, directly next to the parents.

*Physical structures of the family group: composition and positioning of the family*

The standard profile of family size differs between the two sets of test instructions. The real family consists of many more figures ($M = 4.12$) than the imaginary family ($M = 3.70$, $t = 2.53$, $p < 0.05$). The findings indicate that, when asked to draw his or her own family, the child depicts a number of figures corresponding to the actual family size. However, when inventing a family, the child reduces the number of figures. This confirms that the same family is not represented in the two types of drawings.

In terms of the composition of the family, the average portrait almost always contains parental figures, the father being omitted slightly more often than the mother in cases where one of the two parents is absent. The respondent consistently draws him- or herself in the picture and depicts at least one child in the imaginary family. Finally, it is rather rare for the number of family members to be augmented or for strangers and animals to be integrated into the two types of families.

*Physical structures of the family group: relationships between figures*

The physical indications of relationships are practically identical in the two types of drawings. Father and mother are next to each other, often as a couple alongside the children but never in the middle of them. Occasionally, mother/respondent (in the real family) or mother/child (in the imaginary family) may form a couple. This pairing occurs much more frequently than father/respondent or father/child. The mother and father are the two closest figures while the father and child are the most distanced in the family grouping. The figures are rarely shown touching each other. When this occurs, it is only in the real family. In general, the family is not depicted participating in a group activity that could unify the various members. Finally, when figures are depicted as smiling they are the parents, and only in the real, not the imaginary, family.

To summarize, the outcome of family drawings varies as a function of the test instruction. The differences are not on the graphic level but are a result of the number of family members represented and their symbolic relations in term of their spatial position.

### Comparison of typical and ideal FAST representations

For the intraFAST analysis, five dimensions were studied (see Scoring on pages 105–6) to compare the data obtained from the typical representation (TR) with that of the ideal representation (IR), both of which were completed by the family as an interactive task.

### Cohesion

Table 6.1 shows that in the TR a large majority of the sample portrayed high cohesion on the family system level and in the parental dyad. In contrast, cohesion in the sibling subsystem is less marked than on the other two system levels. The IR

*Table 6.1* Cohesion scores in typical and ideal representations on different system levels

| System level | Typical representation (TR) (n = 30) | | | Ideal representation (IR) (n = 30) | | |
| --- | --- | --- | --- | --- | --- | --- |
| | Low (%) | Medium (%) | High (%) | Low (%) | Medium (%) | High (%) |
| Family[a] | 6.6 | 16.7 | 76.7 | 6.7 | 30.0 | 63.3 |
| Parents[b] | 11.1 | 7.4 | 81.5 | 6.9 | 20.7 | 72.4 |
| Siblings[c] | 20.0 | 36.0 | 44.0 | 20.0 | 24.0 | 56.0 |
| Effect[d] | $F$ | | $p$ | | | |
| representation | 0.15 | | 0.705 | | | |
| system level | **10.73** | | **0.000** | | | |
| interaction | 0.76 | | 0.472 | | | |

[a]  TR: mean distance = 2.70, sd, 0.59, IR: mean distance = 2.56, sd = 0.62;
[b]  TR: mean distance = 2.70, sd = 0.66, IR: Mean distance = 2.65, SD = 0.61;
[c]  TR: mean distance = 2.24, sd = 0.77, IR: mean distance = 2.36, sd = 0.81;
[d]  two-way ANOVA.

showed structural patterns similar to those of the TR, yet there are fewer cases with high family and parental cohesion as moderate levels of cohesion take over. Compared with the TR, the IR cohesion within the sibling system level is quite often scored as high.

Using ANOVA, no significant difference was found between the IR and the TR. However, the differences between the global family system and the parent and sibling systems levels are significant, without being affected by interaction between the representation and system levels.

In short, whereas cohesion between siblings, especially in the TR, is often portrayed as low, cohesion on the family and the parental level in general is represented predominantly as high.

## Hierarchy

Table 6.2 shows the results for hierarchy on the three family system levels. In the TR, hierarchy on the family level was mostly represented as moderate. As one might expect, hierarchy in the one-generational subsystem was predominantly low or medium. A similar pattern was found in the IR. It is notable, however, that the parental and sibling system levels were represented in most cases as low. ANOVA revealed significant representation and system-level effects, but no interaction.

## Types of relational structures

As one would expect on the basis of the analysis of the cohesion and hierarchy dimensions, a large majority of the respondents represented the typical relations

*Table 6.2* Hierarchy scores in typical and ideal representations on different system levels

| System level | Typical representation (TR) (n = 30) | | | Ideal representation (IR) (n = 30) | | | |
|---|---|---|---|---|---|---|---|
| | Low (%) | Medium (%) | High (%) | Low (%) | Medium (%) | High (%) | (%) |
| Family[a] | 16.6 | 76.7 | 6.7 | 20.0 | 73.3 | 6.7 | |
| Parents[b] | 59.3 | 33.3 | 7.4 | 72.4 | 27.6 | 0.0 | |
| Siblings[c] | 52.0 | 44.0 | 4.0 | 84.0 | 16.0 | 0.0 | |
| Effect[d] | F | | p | | | | |
| representation | **14.14** | | **0.001** | | | | |
| system level | **9.65** | | **0.000** | | | | |
| interaction | 2.83 | | 0.070 | | | | |

[a]  TR: mean distance = 1.90, sd = 0.48; IR: mean distance = 1.86, sd = 0.50;
[b]  TR: mean distance = 1.48, sd = 0.64; IR: mean distance = 1.27, sd = 0.45;
[c]  TR: mean distance = 1.52, sd = 0.58; IR: mean distance = 1.16, sd = 0.37;
[d]  two-way ANOVA.

*Table 6.3* Types of relational structures in typical and ideal representations on different system levels

| Systems level | Typical representation (n = 30) | | | Ideal representation (n = 30) | | |
|---|---|---|---|---|---|---|
| | Balanced (%) | Labile–balanced (%) | Unbalanced (%) | Balanced (%) | Labile–balanced (%) | Unbalanced (%) |
| Family | 76.7 | 3.3 | 20.0 | 56.6 | 26.7 | 16.7 |
| Parents | 25.9 | 14.8 | 59.3 | 27.6 | 13.8 | 58.6 |
| Siblings | 36.0 | 24.0 | 40.0 | 12.0 | 24.0 | 64.0 |

within the family as balanced (Table 6.3). Furthermore, the parental and sibling system levels were often portrayed as having unbalanced stuctures. Similar patterns were found for the IR, but it is noteworthy that the sibling subsystem showed a marked increase of unbalanced structures.

*Family boundaries*

Families showed more cross-generational coalitions in the IR than in the TR (27 vs 18.5 per cent). As one would expect, a similar pattern was also found for amalgamation (10 vs 26.7 per cent). For hierarchy reversals, a reverse pattern was found. While 10 per cent of respondents showed unclear generational boundaries in TR, no such structure appeared in the IR.

*Flexibility of family structures*

Analysis of shifts from TR and IR showed that, in general, families demonstrated only slight change of the family structure on the three system levels. On average, 80 per cent of the respondents showed a low change and only 6.3 per cent manifested a high change score. These results were due to the fact that they already represented relatively cohesive and hierarchically balanced structures in their TR.

## Comparison of FDT and FAST

Is there a relation between children's family constructs as derived from their individual FDT and their family members' collective FAST representations? In order to respond to this question, two points of intertest comparison were developed for the whole of the sample. The following aspects were used to determine similarities and differences between the two measures:

• real and imaginary family (FDT)
• typical and ideal collective representations (FAST) including the family level as well as parental and sibling system levels.

For methodological purposes, I will not develop in this context an analysis of the processes involved in the drawing and the FAST. However, I will point out that the children's behaviour during the individual drawing and the collectively completed FAST demonstrates that the different levels of implication are mobilized in the two tests and that the 'weight' of the child differs in the two tasks. For example, the drawing session encouraged the child's verbal self-expression through numerous commentaries during and after the drawing. This test therefore produces ample instructive interaction with the psychologist. However, during the FAST, interaction took place between the family members themselves and the child's influence varied according to individual family functioning. Thus, certain parents gave a great deal of freedom to the child in question whereas others decided on a process of negotiation in order to obtain a final consensus concerning their family relationships. It should be noted that each child was at least able to handle and control the figurine that represented him or her, whereas the parents concentrated more on parental and intergenerational relationships. At this qualitative level, it is evident that the FDT and the collective FAST allow the psychologist to observe different levels of interaction according to the test and that the analysis of the processes confirms the intertest differences found in the products of such tests.

Concerning the products of the drawings and the FAST, Pearson's correlation coefficients ($p = 0.05$) for all variables of the two tests demonstrated that there is practically no relation between the individual drawing and the collective FAST. Nevertheless, four groups of results merit further investigation.

*Composition of figures in the FDT and FAST cohesion*

One might assume that when a child incorporates members of the extended family or strangers into his or her drawing, the familial cohesion determined by the FAST would be rather weak and without symbiosis. However, calculations show that there is no correlation between these two variables.

One might also suppose that the two types of drawings would register differently when compared to the FAST, as the differences between the two sets of instructions for the drawings are manifested in the composition of the members of the family. In fact, neither of the two drawings shows more correlation with the FAST than the other. Therefore, we are faced with two, totally different, conceptions of the family. It is important to note, however, that when children depict a half-brother or a half-sister in their family group, there is a significantly weak score of parental cohesion in the FAST, with the greatest presence of intergenerational coalitions.

*Order in which figures are drawn and FAST hierarchy*

Pertinent literature often describes the order in which figures are drawn as a signifier of the degree of importance the child attributes to family members, the first figure being the most important in the eyes of the child. If this is true, we could thus extrapolate the role of this dimension to be an indicator of the power the child attributes to each family member and expect correlations with the hierarchy indication in the FAST.

While no correlation appears with the hierarchy as measured in the FAST, it is important to underline one interesting fact: when a child draws him- or herself first, before the two parents, there is a significant manifestation of intergenerational coalitions in the FAST. This may suggest that when a child assumes greater power in the drawing, the generational boundaries represented by the family display stronger cohesion between one parent and a child than between the two parents. The interpretations of this research allow for the possibility that the child who draws him- or herself before an adult, thus appropriating the position normally occupied by the parent figures (see first part), occupies the function of one of the parents or the other in terms of cohesion. This supposition is confirmed by the presence of intergenerational coalition in the FAST. This variable therefore corresponds more to the indications of family boundaries than to hierarchy.

### Sexual and generational differences in the FDT and reversed hierarchies, coalitions or symbiosis in the FAST

It might be assumed that a child from a family where generational boundaries are not well defined would have increased difficulty in creating clear differentiation between the sexes. However, once again, none of the variables corresponding to these two dimensions demonstrate any interconnections. On the other hand, the hierarchy reversals indicators of the FAST, expressed by the fact that a child is placed higher than one of the parents, correlates to the sexual distinction in the drawing. In particular, where the FAST exhibits the least occurrence of children represented with the same or greater size than one of the parents, the less often the child will change his or her opinion on the sex of a figure while drawing. This assures a better construction of sexual differentiation. The results therefore suggest that the hierarchical differences between family members in the FAST are more sensitive indicators than other variables of the child's capacity to differentiate the sexes in the drawing. However, this is only true for the drawing of the real family and not the imaginary family.

### Spatial organization of figures in the FDT and FAST cohesion

The question arises whether or not the appearance of touching among the figures in the drawing, as well as of the presence of a unifying group activity, correlates to a strong family cohesion in the FAST or even the manifestation of symbiosis. The answer is negative, as the two sets of variables display no correlations. Nevertheless, when a child draws figures touching each other, which is quite rare, he or she comes from a family displaying balanced relational structures; in other words, with average or strong cohesion and average hierarchy. Correlations also exists between the appearance of subgroups, uniting one parent and the children, in the drawing and weak family cohesion in the FAST, whereas, when a child portrays the parents in a couple alongside the children, family cohesion in the FAST is strong. This tendency is found in the two types of drawings. This leads to the supposition that the presence of subgroups (at least two figures closer to each other than the rest of the group) accompanies weak cohesion and hierarchy.

To conclude this section of the analysis, it is helpful to review the two dimensions where one could expect to find correlations among the variables of the two tests: the two sets of drawing instructions and the two types of representations from the FAST, including the family level as well as parental and sibling system levels.

The study of all of the correlation coefficients determines that the two drawings show very few connections with the FAST. Still, interesting tendencies exist. For example, different variables from the two kinds of family drawings correlate with the FAST. In addition, the drawing of the imaginary family displays greater interaction with the FAST than that of the real family.

The two drawings converge the most often with the ideal representations in the FAST as opposed to the typical situations, especially where hierarchy is concerned, as it is weaker in the ideal representation.

Finally, the most striking result from this intertest comparison is that the FAST's strongest point of correlation with the drawings lies in its representation of relationships in the sibling subsystem. To summarize, while the FDT and the FAST demonstrate very few interconnections, the complete inventory of significant correlations confirms that the drawing of the imaginary family is the closest to the ideal representation presented in the FAST's sibling subsystem.

Suffice to say, without going into further depth, that the analysis of certain variables common to the two tests, for example to size relationships among family members, demonstrates much more equitable relationships in the FAST than in the drawings. This is because the child implements much stronger demarcation between generations and in the parental couple in the drawing. Thus we see 50 per cent of children drawing the father as the largest family figure, whereas only 30 per cent of the families allocate this much power to him!

## Discussion and conclusion

The tests presented here seek to evaluate family constructs. The results of this research show that the two tests, FDT and FAST, produce different constructs of the family, apart from a few rare similarities, which are discussed below. These two projective techniques assess distinct psychological dimensions and present different conceptual significations.

This divergence can be explained by highlighting several elements. First of all, the recorded differences can be attributed to the fact that the FDT focuses on the child's individual perception, while the FAST targets an interactive dimension. This therefore confirms the systemic principle of totality, 'the whole is not equal to the sum of its parts', meaning that individual vision is always on a different level from collective vision; the two produce very distinct constructs. A psychologist who considers the construct of each individual family member separately overlooks new information that is produced at the systemic level. When completing the interactive representation, family members are allowed to share or even confront their personal conceptions – the result being a collective, dynamic image of the family. This image is extremely useful for the clinician seeking to understand familial relationships. In this regard, the FAST presents a helpful tool, which complements the benefits of the FDT.

One could object to the above interpretation by arguing that the differences are not derived from the individual and collective points of view, but that the two tests use different techniques to determine expression: one being a graphic representation while the other uses figure placement technique. Thus, if the measurement approaches are different, the results will naturally differ. This argumentation is, however, disproved by the work of Debry (1997), who demonstrates that when FDT and FAST, both done individually by the child, are compared, the two types of family representations are similar, more so for cohesion than for hierarchy. It follows that the differences, as outlined in this research, are due not to the different modes of expression of the tests (graphic vs positioning of figures) but to the fact that whole-family point of view and individual perspective are not identical.

Finally, it is important to examine the rare similarities found in the results of the two tests as they allow for better understanding and identifying of certain inherent aspects of the FAST. The FDT produces an image that most closely resembles those of the FAST sibling system level and the FAST ideal representation. This leads to the deduction that, during FAST interactive negotiation, the parents have more influence on the typical representation than the children. Yet the ideal representation reflects the child's personal desires.

It can be concluded that the analysis of FAST's sibling system level serves also as an indicator of the child's individual perspective, even though the task is an interactive one. One can therefore assume that the child exerts an influence on the representation of sibling relationships.

In conclusion, several application points should be reviewed. We have seen that the clinician's objective is to investigate different familial representations through various tools at his or her disposal. How does this study facilitate the choice of instructions for FDT and FAST or, in other words, how does it help the clinician to adapt test and instruction choice to his or her precise objectives?

It is important to underline that the FAST is a standardized tool, easy to tabulate and interpret. However, the FDT currently remains the object of qualitative validation, which is psychodynamic in nature and is without standardized references. This means that, for the latter test, the clinician's experience is decisive. It is therefore imperative that validation studies for FDT be developed.

The contribution of this research is to demonstrate that, while the two sets of FDT instructions are interchangeable from a graphic motor perspective, the two drawings are clearly distinct in terms of family composition. Previous work (Meyer, 1998a, b) highlighted that the imaginary family instructions correspond more to the child's desires and idealized conception. This reflects intrapsychological dimensions that are deeper and more regressive in projection than the real family drawing. This latter resembles the characteristics of the child's biological family.

Therefore, one can conclude that even though the two sets of instructions can be used one after the other, the real family drawing more effectively measures the child's capacity to adapt to his or her family reality. It should be kept in mind, however, that there is always a discrepancy between graphic representation and the actual family. The imaginary family instructions should be used when the focus of the evaluation is on the intrapsychological and idealistic aspects of the subject's mental processes.

Moreover, whatever differences may exist between the two sets of instructions, it is noted that the FDT does not assess the functioning of the actual family but determines the child's perception of this same family. It would therefore be problematic to draw conclusions about family relationships based on the FDT. This is confirmed in the comparison between the drawing and the FAST, which shows that, apart from a few rare similarities, the systemic and individual points of view are practically dichotomized.

This clinical validation study demonstrates that the two FDT instructions and the two types of tests (FDT and FAST) are complementary and thus necessary for the clinician who seeks to widen the limited focus on the individual to a more extensive focus on interpersonal relationships existing within the family. Therefore, in order to obtain comprehensive information on family systems, it is important to use a multimethod and multisystem-level approach with various respondents in different settings.

## References

Burns, R.C. and Kaufman, S.H. (1970) *Kinetic Family Drawings: An Introduction to Understanding Children through Kinetic Drawing*, New York: Brunner/Mazel.

—— (1972) *Actions, Styles and Symbols in Kinetic Family Drawings (K–F–D): An Interpretative Manual*, New York: Brunner/Mazel.

Cambier, A. and Pham Hoang Quoc Vu (1985) 'Problématique oedipienne et représentation de la famille', *Bulletin de Psychologie* 38: 369 (217–29).

Corman, L. (1961) *Le Test du Dessin de Famille*, Paris: P. U. F.

Debry, M. (1997) 'Approche systémique du dessin de famille: Sa validation par le Test du Système Familial (FAST)', *Psychologie et Psychométrie* 18(1): 17–43.

Gehring, T.M. and Debry, M. (1995) *L'Evaluation du Système Familial: Le FAST*, Braines-le Château: Application des Techniques Modernes SPRL.

Hulse, W.C. (1952). 'Childhood conflict expressed through family drawings', *Journal of Projective Techniques* 16: 66–76.

Meyer, F. (1998a) 'Essai de validation clinique du dessin de famille', unpublished Psych.D. Thesis, University of Lausanne.

—— (1998b) 'Essai de validation clinique du dessin de famille', *Journal des Psychologues* 162: 64–5.

Morval, M. (1973) 'Etude du dessin de famille chez des écoliers Montréalais', *Revue de Psychologie Appliquée* 23: 67–89.

Porot, M. (1952) 'Le dessin de la famille: Exploration par le dessin de la situation affective de l'enfant dans sa famille', *Pédiatrie* 103: 359–81.

Reznikoff, M. and Reznikoff, H.R. (1956) 'The family drawing test: A comparative study of children drawing', *Journal of Clinical Psychology* 12: 167–9.

Royer, J. (1977) *La Personnalité de l'Enfant à travers le Dessin du Bonhomme*, Brussels: Editest.
Touliatos, J., Perlmutter, B.F. and Straus, M.A. (1990) *Handbook of Family Measurement Techniques*, Newbury Park, CA: Sage Publications.

# Appendix A

## *Scoring grids for the FDT drawings*

### *Graphic motor characteristics*

Time on task; line pressure; graphic style, rectilinear or curvilinear; direction in which group is drawn (i.e. left to right); direction in which characters are drawn (i.e. top to bottom); surface taken up by entire drawing; colours.

### *Physical structure characteristics*

PHYSICAL STRUCTURES OF EACH CHARACTER

Character's global score according to Royer's (1977) marking; missing aspects; physical abnormalities and oddities; character's position in group; order in which character is drawn; sexual and generational differences; size of figures.

PHYSICAL STRUCTURES OF THE GROUP

*a. The composition and position of the family.* Number of characters; presence of characters; surface occupied by group only; zone of page occupied by the group; setting; alignment of characters.

*b. Relationships among characters.* Places occupied by family members; space between figures; touching between characters; actions; smiles.

# Appendix B

## *Scoring grids for FAST*

### *Cohesion*

Family cohesion; parental cohesion; sibling cohesion.

### *Hierarchy*

Family hierarchy; parental hierarchy; sibling hierarchy.

*Types of relational structures (TRS)*

Family TRS; parental TRS; sibling TRS.

*Family boundaries*

Intergenerational coalitions; hierarchy reversals; symbiosis/amalgamations.

*Flexibility of family structures*

Subtraction of the scores for cohesion and hierarchy of the ideal representation (IR) from those of the typical representation (TR).

# 7 Perception of internal and external family boundaries by well-adjusted children, bullies and victims

*Lucia Berdondini and Maria Luisa Genta*

## The phenomenon of bullying

Bullying among children at school is a complex problem. Researchers have studied it from different points of view and tackled it with practical interventions for several years in many countries (Olweus, 1991; Smith, 1991; Rigby and Slee, 1993; Pepler and Craig, 1995; Genta *et al.*, 1996). The first studies of bullying were carried out in Scandinavia (Olweus, 1978) and were then extended to the UK (Smith, 1991); there are now many countries involved in the research (for example Italy, Spain, Portugal, Japan, Australia, Canada).

Bullying is usually defined as a form of aggressive behaviour that happens repeatedly. It is performed by one person or more another, and there is usually a difference of strength (physical or psychological) between the bully and the victim. Bullying others can be characterized by physical attacks but also by verbal aggressions or threats, rejection by peers and by indirect aggression such as spreading nasty rumours (Olweus, 1991).

Moreover, bullying is considered a social phenomenon (Salmivalli *et al.*, 1996; Sutton and Smith, 1999), and not only a dyadic problem, or concerning a relationship between the persons who are actively involved. Lagerspetz *et al.* (1982) have pointed out that bullying among schoolchildren is based on social relationships in the group. They suggest that aggression in a group can be studied by examining the relationship between people taking different roles, or having roles assigned to them.

Bullies and victims have been found to have typical characteristics: bullying children are aggressive to peers and to adults, they lack empathy to victims but they have average or even quite high self-esteem (Olweus, 1978, 1991, 1994; Bjorkqvist *et al.*, 1982; Lagerspetz *et al.*, 1982; Pulkkinen and Tremblay, 1992). They also have social perceptions that support their aggressive behaviours (Perry *et al.*, 1988).

In studies where sociometric status (Coie *et al.*, 1982) was assessed, bullying children were often seen by peers as controversial or rejected, but very often they have one or two follower friends (Cairns *et al.*, 1988; Boulton and Smith, 1993; Smith *et al.*, 1994).

From other studies we know that victimized children may be physically weak (Olweus, 1978; Stephenson and Smith, 1989) or timid and submissive (Schwartz *et al.*, 1993). Some researchers argue that they are not able to use efficient social tactics (Perry *et al.*, 1988; Pierce, 1990).

## Parenting and family structure as predictive of peer victimization

Smith and Myron-Wilson (1998) present an exhaustive review of studies in Europe, Australia, and the US that have linked parenting and different roles in the bullying phenomenon. They highlight that violent behaviour and harsh discipline in parents were found to be linked with bullying behaviour, and overprotectiveness in parents with victimization. They also discuss the complexity of such phenomena, analysing the differences between boys and girls, and the relations between different roles in bullying behaviour and particular dysfunctional parenting.

Schwartz *et al.* (1997) studied the early family experiences of boys who later emerged as aggressive victims, passive victims, non-victimized aggressors and normative boys. The aggressive victim group had experienced more punitive, hostile, and abusive family treatment than the other groups, whereas the non-victimized aggressive group had a history of greater exposure to adult aggression and conflict, but not victimization by adults, than did the normative group. The passive victim group did not differ from the normative group on any home environment variable.

Among preadolescents there may be sex-specific links between perceived family interaction and peer victimization. For boys, victimization was associated with perceived maternal overprotectiveness, especially when boys reported reacting with fear during mother–child conflict. For girls, victimization was associated with perceived maternal rejection and with girls' reports of aggressive coping during mother–child conflict (Finnegan *et al.*, 1998).

Rigby (1993) found that self-reported bullying correlated with poorer family functioning. Moreover, bullies reported poor relationships with fathers (boy bullies reported the same also with mothers), whereas among victims only data concerning girls were found to be significant. Girl victims, in fact, reported poor relationships with mothers, but not with fathers.

Another study concerning parenting was carried out on a sample of bullies, victims, and control children (primary and secondary schools, from 8 to 13 years old) (Fonzi *et al.*, 1996). A questionnaire focusing on possible parenting styles towards the issue of bullying was used. This measured the following possible parental attitudes: indifference towards the issue, delegation, reinforcement/retorsion, coercion– punishment. The results showed that bullies and victims perceived their parents as characterized by indifference towards the issue compared to uninvolved children. Control participants perceived their parents as supportive and available to talk with them about the issue of bullying (Fonzi *et al.*, 1996).

## The use of FAST in studies on bullying

The FAST has been used with samples of British and Italian children involved in bullying to measure their perception of family structure (Bowers *et al.*, 1992; Berdondini and Smith, 1996). These studies demonstrated that the perception of one's own family is different for bullies and victims respectively. They also confirm some of the findings about the child's perception of parenting and peer victimization (Finnegan *et al.*, 1998).

Working in the UK, Bowers *et al.* (1992) compared subgroups of bullies, victims and bully/victims (also called 'provocative victims' – children who are involved in both bullying others and being bullied themselves) with uninvolved children, in their representation of family structure using the FAST. They found that bullies often represented the family as a disintegrated group, particularly the parental dyad, and that often the biological father was absent from home; the bullies usually perceived fathers as more powerful than mothers and themselves as less powerful within the family. Victims perceived the family as a close and united group, with no separation of figures; they tended to have more powerful fathers than mothers but they did not perceive siblings and others family members as particularly powerful. Bully/victim children did not have cohesion scores as low as bullies, but were similar in relegating some family members from the rest of the group. Again, the father was seen as particularly powerful compared to the mother. Bully/victims tended to have the highest power scores for self. Finally, uninvolved children showed a representation of their family as moderately cohesive and with father and mother quite powerful but with near equality between them.

Many of these findings were replicated in Italy by Berdondini and Smith (1996). In this case, only bully, victim and uninvolved children participated. The results showed that, once again, bullies often had no biological father at home and that they generally represented their family as having a low cohesion, especially the mother– father dyad.

The results showing a much more united family in victims were also confirmed.

Another interesting aspect, not explored in these studies, is how the child represents the relationship between his/her own family and the external social dimension. This perspective can offer important information, especially in a study focused on children involved in aggressive episodes among peers. The present study explores this by adding two external figures not belonging to the family. Two typical representatives of our society were chosen for defining the boundaries between family and external world: a 'neutral' neighbour, and a drug addict.

### *Aims*

The main research aim is to use the FAST to explore the differences in bullies, victims and well-adjusted children in the perception of internal and external family boundaries.

A secondary aim is to check results from previous studies about different children's perception of their parental dyads.

## Method

### Sample

The study was carried out in four primary schools of a zone in Bologna, Italy. The total sample was 243 children (age range 8 to 11 years).

### Classification system

Peer nominations were used to identify bullies, victims, and control children. The procedure was as follows: the researcher presented to each class the issue of bullying, talking with children about it, and giving them a clear definition of what is considered 'to be a bully' and 'to be a victim'. At this point each child in the class was given a paper with this written definition and was asked to name in writing three bullies and three victims from their classmates. Children could also write their own name as bully or victim, if they wished. For each child the percentage of nominations as bully and as victim he/she received from the whole class was calculated.

We applied the methodology used by Bowers *et al.* (1992) – to fall into the 'bully' category, a child had to receive 50 per cent or more peer nominations as a bully and less than 33 per cent as a victim. To fall into the 'victim' category a child had to receive 50 per cent of peer nominations as victim and less than 33 per cent as bully. To be classed as bully/victim a child had to receive more than 33 per cent of both bully and victim nominations. To be classed as a 'control' a child had to receive less than 33 per cent of both bully and victim nominations.

In order to have a balanced sample, a smaller group of eighty-seven children (twenty-seven bullies, thirty victims, and thirty controls) was selected to be analysed through FAST. Control children were selected from the participants who received the lowest peer nominations as bullies and as victims (both under 15 per cent of peer nominations). Out of the whole sample only three children were nominated as bully/victims and so this category was not included in the sample.

### Instrument

The technique used for eliciting an individual's perceptions of power and cohesion within their family was the FAST. The material used was the same as that used by Gehring and Wyler (1986): a wooden board 45 cm × 45 cm divided into eighty-one squares each 5 cm × 5 cm, twenty wooden figures and some cylindrical wooden blocks of three different heights (1.5 cm, 3.0 cm and 4.5 cm).

Children were seen individually, and were asked to represent their families and, at the same time, the two additional figures using the FAST materials. In particular, they were asked to imagine two anonymous neighbours, one of whom is a drug addict, and to represent 'how close all these persons feel to each other' and who were the most powerful in the group. The group representation was then recorded on standard recording sheets. Three case examples of typical plots from one control, one victim, and one bully child are presented in Figures 7.1, 7.2, and 7.3.

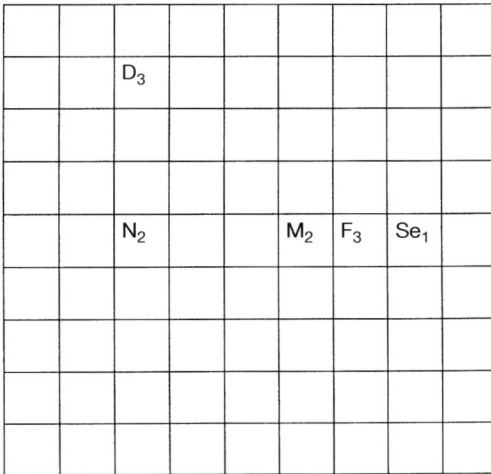

*Figure 7.1* Case example from a control child.
D, drug addict; F, father; M, mother; N, neighbour; Se, self. *Note*: the subscript indicates the elevation of the figure: 1, small block (1.5 cm); 2, medium block (3.0 cm); 3, large block (4.5 cm).

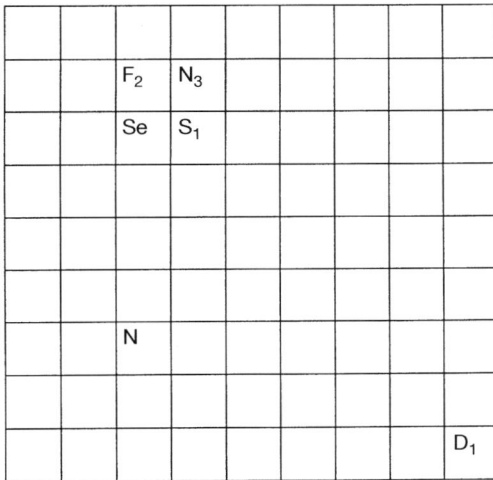

*Figure 7.2* Case example from a victim child.
D, drug addict; F, father; M, mother; N, neighbour; S, sister; Se, self. *Note*: the subscript indicates the elevation of the figure: 1, small block (1.5 cm); 2, medium block (3.0 cm); 3, large block (4.5 cm).

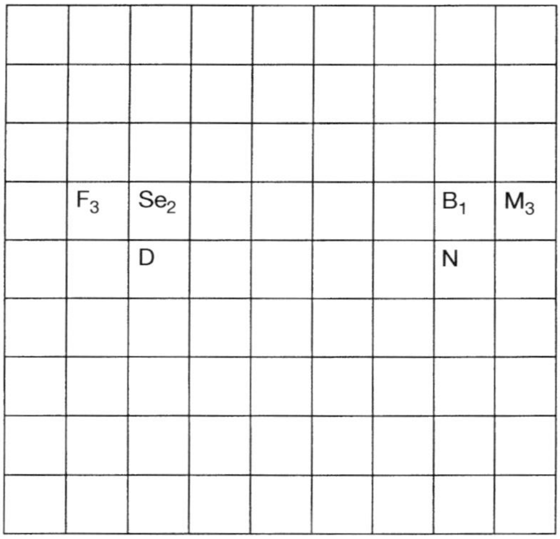

*Figure 7.3* Case example from a bully child.
B, brother; D, drug addict; F, father; M, mother; N, neighbour; Se, self. *Note*: the subscript indicates the elevation of the figure: 1, small block (1.5 cm); 2, medium block (3.0 cm); 3, large block (4.5 cm).

## Scoring procedure

Children's use of the FAST was scored considering first of all some 'spatial configurations'. 'No separation of figures' refers to those plots in which all the figures were connected into one group, including via diagonal connections. 'In a continuous line' is a subtype of the previous characteristic, in which all the figures are in a horizontal or vertical line. 'One corner' refers to plots with at least one corner square occupied (Figure 7.2). 'Two sides or corners' refers to plots with two different sides or corner squares occupied.

Following Gehring and Feldman (1988), cohesion was calculated by comparing distances between dyads. Only selected dyads were analysed, namely mother–father, self–father, self–mother, self–neighbour, self–addict, mother–neighbour, mother–addict, father–neighbour, father–addict, because the aim of this study was focused on children's perception of their family boundaries with the external world. Particular attention was devoted to parental figures, as it was felt that children perceive them as especially representative of the social contacts of the family.

Scores for power were calculated as follows: the adults' height was subtracted from the height of 'self', the mother's height was subtracted from father's and the neighbour's and addict's height were subtracted from father's and mother's. Scores ranged between +3 and –3. A negative score thus corresponds to an adult being more powerful than self, the mother more than the father, or the neighbour and the drug addict more than the mother or the father.

## Results

The main findings regarding the differences between the FAST representations for bullies, victims, and controls are reported first. The analyses of cohesion and power in the selected dyads were carried out using one-way ANOVAs, and the Fisher test was used to explore specific differences between groups.

### General characteristics of plots

There were no significant differences between the 'spatial configurations' of the three groups. One trend approaching significance was found: victims used the 'one corner' position for the drug addict more often than bullies and controls ($\chi^2_{(2)} = 5.17$; $p < 0.07$) (see Figure 7.2).

### Cohesion

Bullies showed lower cohesion in the mother–father dyad than both victim and control children ($F_{(2, 79)} = 2.63$, Fisher's $t = 0.98$, $p < 0.05$ bullies vs victims; $t = 0.76$, $p < 0.05$ bullies vs controls). The mean values for mother–father dyads were 9.62 for bullies (standard deviation (sd) = 2.12), 10.49 for victims (sd = 0.65) and 10.25 for controls (sd = 1.10). Victims and controls differed regarding the mother–addict relation, with victims showing less cohesion in this dyad than controls ($F_{(2,80)} = 2.38$, Fisher's $t = 1.02$, $p < 0.05$). The mean values were 6.74 (sd = 2.62) for victims and 7.85 (sd = 1.47) for controls.

### Power

Significant differences occurred in the power measures for dyads, including figures representing persons from outside the family. Compared to others, control children showed the drug addict as significantly more powerful than themselves ($F_{(2,84)} = 4.9$, $p < 0.01$), with the following mean values: –0.033 (sd = 1.07) for controls, 0.3 (sd = 0.75) for victims and 0.70 (sd = 0.78) for bullies. Compared to victims, bullies perceived themselves as more powerful than the neighbour ($F_{(2,84)} = 2.46$, Fisher's $t = 0.42$, $p < 0.05$), with mean values being 0.83 (sd = 0.83) for bullies and 0.59 (sd = 0.79) for victims. Finally, bullies also attributed more power to the mother than to the drug addict in comparison to control children ($F_{(2,80)} = 2.47$, Fisher's $t = 0.69$, $p < 0.05$), with mean values being 1.83 (sd = 1.12) for bullies and 1.07 (sd = 1.36) for controls.

## Conclusions

The present study demonstrates that the FAST can provide interesting information that would otherwise be difficult to collect. If we compare the results to the previous studies on bullying, only one is overtly relevant. This is the lower cohesion in bullies' parental dyads compared to the other two groups. In previous studies, bullies represented their own family as less cohesive than did other participants, especially in the mother–father dyad (Bowers *et al.*, 1992; Berdondini and Smith, 1996).

However, the addition of the two strangers changed the way the board was used: the corners, which in the previous studies were available for the family members, in the present study were often used for the external figures. For example, victims frequently put the drug addict on that part of the board. Otherwise, they generally put much more distance between their mother and the drug addict than bullies, and especially controls, did, as if to mark the separation between their highly cohesive family and strangers. Thus, this result might be seen as confirming the previous studies in which victims represented their families as overprotective (Bowers *et al.*, 1992; Berdondini and Smith, 1996).

With particular regard to the two external figures, and especially to the drug addict, it is interesting to notice how differently each group of children represented their relationship with them. Victims chose personal distance (cohesion), to isolate the drug addict. Bullies did not show any particular difference in the perception of their family members and the two strangers, apart from assigning more power to themselves than to the neighbour, as if this was not a particularly relevant person. Control children, by contrast, usually took distance from the external figures, and especially from the drug addict, through the measure of power. They assigned to this figure a very high power, equal to the parents'. The concept of power in this study was explained to children as the capacity to influence the others. Thus, it seems that in some cases children interpreted the stereotype of the drug addict as a person with a strongly influential role. This result evokes a familiar world of communication and discussion with children about their relationship with the external environment and all the risks and dangers that can be found within it. It seems that controls and victims have a clear representation of social stereotypes, neutral as well as negative, probably passed on by their family, even if they represented them through different indexes. With regard to this, it is quite interesting that bullies, who do not seem to have this strong differentiation between family and external world, seem to live in a more disorganized environment. It could be argued that, just for this reason, the communication between these children and their parents is probably different from that in the other two groups. Maybe in these families there are fewer, or at least different, conventional social stereotypes, just because there are fewer definite boundaries between internal and external environments.

From these data, and from what previous studies have revealed about family structures of bullies, victims, and controls, it seems possible to argue the following perspective. Generally, bullies have a less structured family, with not very clear boundaries between internal and external environments. Victims have a close family, perhaps overprotective, and are consequently isolated from external dimensions. Controls present a more flexible family structure than the other two groups, with a more intense communication with external figures, even if this highlights the possible negative influences of some social stereotypes.

In his study on familial dynamics, Reiss (1971, 1981) mentioned a similar perspective. He distinguished three types of family:

- 'Environment sensitive', which is balanced between the demands of internal cohesion, personal independence of individual members, availability to external changes and events.
- 'Consensus sensitive', which is distinguished by an internal dynamic based on closeness and cohesion among members but considering the external world as dangerous and threatening.
- 'Interpersonal distance sensitive', whose structure is disintegrated and the boundaries between internal group and external world are not really defined.

It is certainly too easy and schematic to interpret the present data only through this perspective, but the different attitudes towards external environment are fundamental variables of risk mechanisms linked to familial dynamics. The present study represents an attempt to explore this area and it seems very interesting to extend and deepen it in the future. Further research could be focused on the use of FAST on a larger sample, considering the presence of the two external figures but also considering the rest of the family members, in order to attain a real systemic perspective.

It would also be useful to explore in such samples the representation of the family in an 'ideal' and 'conflict' situation, besides the real one. The possibility of exploring these other two representations of family structure in the framework of research on bullying would be innovative. Moreover, it could provide more extended information about the perceptions by bullies, victims and controls of the educational style and communication within the family, offering the possibility of learning more about the link between personal background and interpersonal relationships.

## References

Berdondini, L. and Smith, P.K. (1996) 'Cohesion and power in the families of children involved in bully/victim problems at school: An Italian replication', *Journal of Family Therapy*, 18(1): 99–102.

Bjorkqvist, K., Ekman, K. and Lagerspetz, K.M.J. (1982) 'Bullies and victims: Their ego picture, ideal ego picture and normative ego picture', *Scandinavian Journal of Psychology*, 23: 307–13.

Boulton, M.J. and Smith, P.K. (1993) 'Ethnic, gender partner and activity preferences in mixed race schools in the UK: Playground observations', in C. Hart (ed.) *Children on Playgrounds*, New York: State University of New York Press.

Bowers, L., Smith, P.K. and Binney, V. (1992) 'Cohesion and power in the families of children involved in bully/victim problems at school', *Journal of Family Therapy*, 14(4): 371–87.

Cairns, R.B., Cairns, B.D., Neckerman, H.J., Gest, S.D. and Gariepy, J. (1988) 'Social networks and aggressive behavior: Peer support or peer rejection?', *Developmental Psychology*, 24: 815–23.

Coie, J.D., Dodge, K.A. and Coppotelli, H. (1982) 'Dimensions and types of social status: A cross-age perspective', *Developmental Psychology*, 18: 557–70.

Finnegan, R.A., Hodges, E.V.E. and Perry, D.G. (1998) 'Victimization by peers: Associations with children's reports of mother-child interaction', *Journal of Personality and Social Psychology*, 75(4): 1076–86.

Fonzi, A., Ciucci, E., Berti, C. and Brighi, A. (1996) 'Riconoscimento delle emozioni, stili educativi familiari e psizione nel gruppo di bambini che fanno e subiscono prepotenze', *Età Evolutiva*, 53: 81–9.

Gehring, T.M. and Feldman, S.S. (1988) 'Adolescents' perception of family cohesion and power: A methodological study of the Family System Test', *Journal of Adolescent Research*, 3: 33–52.

——— and Wyler, I.L. (1986) 'Family System Test (FAST): A three dimensional approach to investigate human relationships', *Child Psychiatry and Human Development*, 16: 235–48.

Genta, M.L., Menesini, E., Fonzi, A., Costabile, A. and Smith, P.K. (1996) 'Bullies and victims in schools in central and southern Italy', *European Journal of Psychology of Education*, 11: 97–110.

Hodges, E.V.E. and Perry, D.G. (1999) 'Personal and interpersonal antecedents and consequences of victimization by peers', *Journal of Personality and Social Psychology*, 76(4): 677–85.

Lagerspetz, K.M.J., Bjorkqvist, K., Berts, M. and King, E. (1982) 'Group aggression among school children in three schools', *Scandinavian Journal of Psychology*, 23: 45–52.

Olweus, D. (1978) *Aggression in the School: Bullies and Whipping Boys*, Washington, DC: Hemisphere.

——— (1991) 'Bully/victim problems among school children: Basic facts and effects of a school based intervention program', in D. Pepler and K. Rubin (eds) *The Development and Treatment of Childhood Aggression*, Hillsdale, NJ: Erlbaum.

——— (1994) 'Bullying at school: Basic facts and effects of a school based intervention program', *Journal of Child Psychology and Psychiatry and Allied Disciplines*, 35: 1171–90.

Pepler, D. and Craig, W.M. (1995) 'A peek behind the fence: Naturalistic observations of aggressive children with remote audiovisual recording', *Developmental Psychology*, 31: 548–53.

Perry, D.G., Kusel, S.J. and Perry, L.C. (1988) 'Victims of peer aggression', *Developmental Psychology*, 6: 807–14.

Pierce, S. (1990) 'The behavioral attributes of victimized children', unpublished master's thesis, Boca Raton, FL: Florida Atlantic University.

Pulkkinen, L. and Tremblay, R.E. (1992) 'Patterns of boys' social adjustment in two cultures and at different stages: A longitudinal perspective', *International Journal of Behavioural Development*, 15: 527–53.

Reiss, D. (1971) 'Varieties of consensual experience', *Family Process*, 10: 1–35.

——— (1981) *The Family's Construction of Reality*, Cambridge, MA: Harvard University Press.

Rigby, K. (1993) 'School children's perceptions of their families and parents as a function of peer-relations', *Journal of Genetic Psychology*, 154: 501–13.

——— and Slee, P.T. (1993) 'Dimensions of interpersonal relation among Australian children and implications for psychological well-being', *Journal of Social Psychology*, 133: 33–42.

Salmivalli, C., Lagerspetz, K.M.J., Bjorkqvist, K., Osterman, K. and Kaukiainen, A. (1996) 'Bullying as a group process: participant roles and their relations to social status within the group', *Aggressive Behavior*, 22: 1–15.

Schwartz, D., Dodge, K.A. and Coie, J.D. (1993) 'The emergence of chronic peer victimization in boys' play groups', *Child Development*, 64: 1755–72.

——, Dodge, K.A., Pettit, G.S. and Bates, J.E. (1997) 'The early socialization of aggressive victims of bullying', *Child Development*, 68: 665–75.
Smith, P.K. (1991) 'The silent nightmare: Bullying and victimization in school peer groups', *The Psychologist*, 4: 243–8.
—— and Myron-Wilson, R. (1998) 'Parenting and school bullying', *Clinical Child Psychology and Psychiatry*, 3: 405–17.
——, Cowie, H. and Berdondini, L. (1994) 'Co-operation and bullying', in P. Kutnick and C. Rogers (eds) *Groups in Schools*, London: Cassell Education.
Stephenson, P. and Smith, D. (1989) 'Bullying in the junior school', in D.P. Tattum and D.A. Lane (eds) *Bullying in Schools*, Stoke-on-Trent, UK: Trentham Books.
Sutton, J. and Smith, P.K. (1999) 'Bullying as a group process: An adaptation of the participant role approach', *Aggressive Behavior*, 25: 97–111.

# 8 Comparing parents' and children's perceptions of the family: Can the FAST be used as a measure of social cognition and theory of mind ability?

*Peter K. Smith, Rowan Myron-Wilson and Jon Sutton*

In this chapter we aim to:

- explore the associations between parents' and children's views of the family and how these views may differ
- examine methodological issues in comparing FAST plots in this way
- present case studies of the possible relevance of FAST to social cognition and theory of mind ability.

The FAST is traditionally used as a measure of the informant's perceptions of their family. In this, it is known to have good reliability and there is evidence for validity (Gehring, 1998). As part of validity assessment, it is possible to compare different informants' views of the same family. A few studies have done this and found significant levels of agreement. However, of interest here is that, superimposed on general levels of agreement, these studies also found some systematic differences. For example, Feldman *et al.* (1989) found systematic differences in perceptions of the family from fathers, mothers and their preadolescent children, with the children seeing less cohesion and more hierarchy in parent–child dyads. Gehring *et al.* (1994) looked at the perceptual differences of parents and children and found that, in a conflict representation, fathers portrayed family structures relatively frequently as balanced, whereas children were more likely to portray their family structure as unbalanced. Shu (1999) looked at differences in perceptions of grandparents, parents and children living together in three-generation families in Hefei, China. Individual respondents appeared to bias their perceptions so as to emphasize their own closeness to others (e.g. a grandparent might represent grandparent–grandchild cohesion as closer than the parents represented it).

The fact that different members of the same family may produce different FAST portrayals opens the possibility of another set of interesting comparisons. It would be possible to ask a family member not only to show their own representation of the family, but also to show the representation *as they think another family member would see it*. That is, given that members of the same family may have different representations of it, how much insight do they have into the representations that other family members have? Does the mother realize that her child may see the family differently from her? And does the child realize that the mother may see it differently? And how accurately do they perceive the differences?

In this chapter we discuss some exploratory work in this area, using a sample of mothers and middle-school-aged children from south-east London. We consider some of the methodological issues and difficulties involved in doing this. We also consider whether comparisons of this kind might enable a possible use of the FAST as a tool in assessing social cognitive skills in the area of family functioning.

## Social cognition and theory of mind

Social cognition refers to thinking about social relationships, and about the actions of others. Theory of mind refers more specifically to understanding that someone else may have different beliefs or knowledge about the world, from oneself (e.g. Premack and Woodruff, 1978; Mitchell, 1996). Theory of mind is thought to entail 'meta-representations', that is, representations of representations. A first-order representation is, for example, a mental state corresponding to a perception. I see a vase, and I have a first-order mental representation of that perception. Suppose I know that you see the vase too. Then I have a representation of 'your mental representation of the vase'. This is a metarepresentation, or a simple example of theory of mind ability.

It seems that children develop theory of mind ability between about 3 and 4 years of age. It is not always easy to tell if a child has a theory of mind. If you ask a child 'Can I see the vase?' they may correctly say 'Yes' simply because they can see the vase and they assume your knowledge or perception is the same as theirs. Therefore, the critical test has been to see if a child can understand and state someone else's knowledge or perception *even when it is different from their own*. This has become known as the false belief paradigm.

One paradigmatic task is the unexpected transfer task, of which Sally–Anne is the most usual form. The child is shown two dolls, Sally and Anne. Sally has a basket, Anne has a box. Sally puts a marble in her basket, then leaves. While she is away, Anne moves the marble into her box. Sally comes back. The child is asked, 'Where did Sally put her marble?' (control, memory question) and 'Where will Sally look for her marble now?' Usually, 3-year-olds say she will look in the box; 4-year-olds say she will look in the basket. The 4-year-olds can understand that Sally can have a false belief.

A similar task is the unexpected contents task, of which the 'Smarties' task is the usual form (Smarties being small chocolate buttons in a distinctive tubular container). The child is shown a closed tube of Smarties and asked what they think is in it. Then the top is taken off and they can see that, actually, it holds pencils. The top is put back on. Then the child is told that their friend X is coming in, and is asked 'What will X think is in the tube?' Four-year-olds, but not younger children, usually give the correct answer of 'Smarties'.

These tasks tend to be passed at around 4 years of age. However, theory of mind abilities clearly continue to develop. In fact, Happé *et al.* (1998) found evidence that theory of mind abilities continued to develop into old age, finding higher scores in elderly people than in young adults.

How can theory of mind be measured in older children and adults? One approach has been to develop more complicated false belief tasks. For example, Perner and Wimmer (1985) developed a second-order false belief task, which involves knowledge of the kind that 'X thinks that Y thinks that . . . '. These tasks tend to be passed at around 6–7 years of age.

Another approach has been to use understanding of stories that involve theory of mind elements such as deceit, double bluff, faux pas (Happé, 1994; Baron-Cohen *et al.*, 1999). These tend to be understood by middle childhood, but have also been used with adults. Yet another set of tasks used with adults have been the 'eyes' and 'faces' tests of Baron-Cohen (Baron-Cohen *et al.*, 1996, 1997), in which the emotion present in portraits or pictures of the eyes is surmised. There could, however, be doubts about whether these latter tests really assess theory of mind rather than just emotion recognition.

As yet, there is no theory of mind task that can be used across a wide age range from children to adults, and that could be confidently related to the ability to understand someone else's representations of knowledge and belief. We wondered whether we could use the FAST in this way. Would it be possible to use the FAST to look at a person's own representations, and also their knowledge of another person's representations, of the same stimulus (the family system)? Would this be a 'theory of mind' measure?

## Method

### Sample

We first collected data from 196 child participants, aged 7 to 10 years, from four schools in south-east London; they were an ethnically mixed sample and many came from quite poor or disadvantaged backgrounds characteristic of the area. Among a range of individual assessments made in school, these children were given the FAST, and also some theory of mind tests (such as Happé's short stories; see Sutton *et al.*, 1999).

We also invited the parents of these children to participate in some assessments, lasting about 1 hour and including the FAST. Only twenty-two parents were willing to take part. The data reported here are on these twenty-two parent–child pairs. Of the parents, twenty were mothers and two were fathers. Of the children, eleven were girls, eleven were boys. Twenty-one families were represented, as two boys were brothers. Of the twenty-one families, at least four were single parent (mother) families, two were single parent (father) families, and one was a stepfamily.

### Procedure

A standard FAST board was used with wooden figures representing children and adults, males and females (Gehring and Wyler, 1986). The children were given the

FAST materials and a standard explanation of how the position of the figures could represent closeness in the family, and of how the wooden power blocks could be placed under figures to represent power. They were then asked to make a normal representation of their family. Following this, they were asked to imagine how they thought their parent (the one who had volunteered to take part) would see the family, and to reposition the FAST figures to show this.

Similarly, the parents were given the FAST test and asked to show their family as they saw it; and then asked to imagine how their child (whom we had interviewed) would see the family and to reposition the FAST figures to show this.

In this way, we got four FAST plots and could compare:

- the child's own representation of the family; we called this $C_c$
- the child's representation of the mother's representation; we called this $C_m$ (as twenty of the twenty-two parents were mothers we will use this term generically)
- the mother's own representation of the family; we called this $M_m$
- the mother's representation of the child's representation; we called this $M_c$

*Practical difficulties in getting the plots*

We have found that practically all respondents enjoy the standard FAST procedure, and most give good plots quite readily. This was true of the present sample. In addition, in all twenty-two dyads, the child's own representation, $C_c$, did differ from the mother's own representation, $M_m$, on a number of aspects.

However, asking respondents to imagine the FAST plot of another (parent, child) was clearly more challenging. In fact, one mother absolutely refused to do it, saying that she thought it impossible to show what her child thought of the family. (This in itself is an interesting response, but we would not want to say she lacked a theory of mind.) This mother also gave a very minimal standard plot (omitting the father, whom the child included) and, in effect, results from this dyad could not be used, reducing the sample to twenty-one dyads. In addition, one of the twenty-one parents (the parent with two children in the sample) and two of the twenty-two children (one boy, one girl) made no changes in their representation. However, for twenty-one of the twenty-two dyads we obtained four usable plots. As an example, Figure 8.1 shows four plots from a boy and his mother.

*Comparison of the FAST plots*

We wished to measure the extent to which someone's own representation of the other's representation approaches the other's actual representation. This gives an operational definition that can be used to score the FAST plots to give a measure of child's theory of mind ability (how closely does his/her representation of the mother's plot approach the mother's actual plot?), and a measure of mother's theory of mind ability (how closely does her representation of the child's plot approach the child's actual plot?).

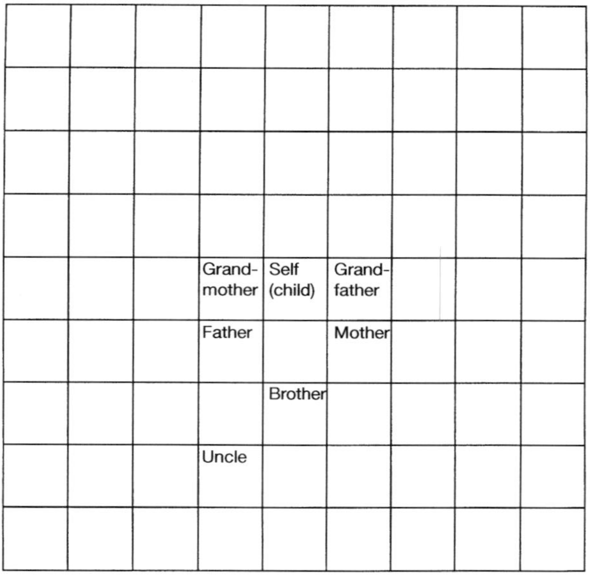

|  |  |  |  |  |  |  |  |  |
|---|---|---|---|---|---|---|---|---|
|  |  |  |  |  |  |  |  |  |
|  |  |  |  |  |  |  |  |  |
|  |  |  |  |  |  |  |  |  |
|  |  | Grand-mother | Self (child) | Grand-father |  |  |  |  |
|  |  | Father |  | Mother |  |  |  |  |
|  |  |  | Brother |  |  |  |  |  |
|  |  | Uncle |  |  |  |  |  |  |
|  |  |  |  |  |  |  |  |  |

(i)  Child's view of the family (as the child sees it): $C_c$

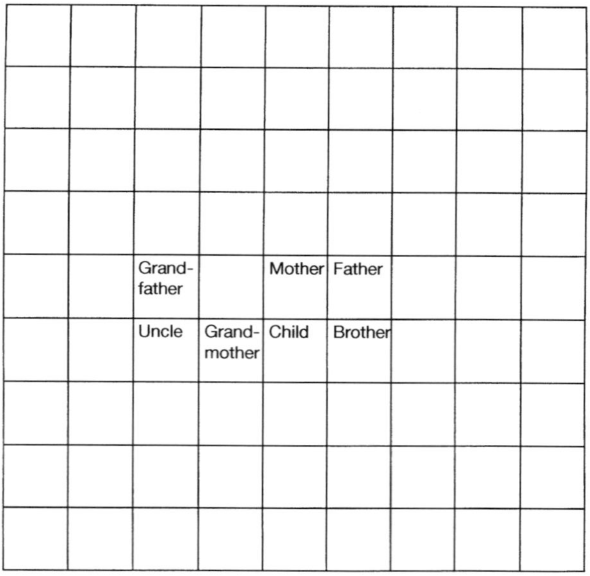

|  |  |  |  |  |  |  |  |  |
|---|---|---|---|---|---|---|---|---|
|  |  |  |  |  |  |  |  |  |
|  |  |  |  |  |  |  |  |  |
|  |  |  |  |  |  |  |  |  |
|  | Grand-father |  | Mother | Father |  |  |  |  |
|  | Uncle | Grand-mother | Child | Brother |  |  |  |  |
|  |  |  |  |  |  |  |  |  |
|  |  |  |  |  |  |  |  |  |
|  |  |  |  |  |  |  |  |  |

(ii)  Child's view of the family (as the mother sees it): $C_m$

*Figure 8.1* (above and opposite) A set of four FAST plots (terminology standardized from the child's point of view).

| | | | | | | | | |
|---|---|---|---|---|---|---|---|---|
| | | | | Uncle | | | | |
| | | | | | | | | |
| | | | | Brother₂ | | | | |
| | | | Father | Self₃ (mother) | Child₂ | | | |
| | | | | | | | | |
| | | | | | | | | |
| | | | | | | | | |
| | | | | | | | | |

(iii) Mother's view of the family (as the mother sees it): $M_m$

| | | | | | | | | |
|---|---|---|---|---|---|---|---|---|
| | | | | | | | | |
| | | | | | | | | |
| | | | | | | | | |
| | | | | Brother | | | | |
| | | | Father₂ | Child | Mother₃ | | | |
| | | | | | | | | |
| | | | | | | | | |
| | | | | | | | | |
| | | | | | | | | |

(iv) Mother's view of the family (as the child sees it): $M_c$

It is only possible to have such a measure if the other's representation is different from one's own representation. This is analogous to the false belief tasks described earlier, which create a situation in which someone's knowledge (about where the marble is, or what is in the Smarties tube) is 'out of date' or different from that of the person being questioned. In the case of the FAST plots, particular measures of the child's plot and the mother's plot are often different, but not necessarily or always so; however, it is only when the standard representations differ that we can hope to assess any theory of mind ability.

As mentioned above, we suppose that:

- $C_c$ = child's view of family (as the child sees it)
- $C_m$ = child's view of family (as the mother sees it)
- $M_m$ = mother's view of family (as the mother sees it)
- $M_c$ = mother's view of family (as the child sees it).

Thus, we can only measure any theory of mind ability in so far as $C_c$ is not equal to $M_m$.

## Measures

In comparing FAST plots, a number of possible measures could be used. For our purposes, we chose seven that might be considered central to the representation of the family, and which could be applied commonly across many (though not all) families.

As a first measure we took:

- the number of figures placed on the board.

As additional dyadic measures we took:

- mother–father distance
- mother–child distance
- father–child distance
- mother–father power
- mother–child power
- father–child power.

'Distance' (the inverse of cohesion) represents the diagonal distance between two figures, in square units (and using Pythagoras' theorem), and 'power' represents the difference in power blocks between the first labelled figure and the second labelled figure.

Most (not all) families had mother and father (or long-term partner), so many families had scores on all seven of these measures. In this exploratory work we did not score distance or power of other family members (siblings, grandparents, etc.) because of the great variability in the presence and number of these across families.

This complexity is only captured slightly by the first measure, of number of figures in the family.

*How much understanding does the child show of the mother's representation of the family?*

This is defined as the extent to which child's representation of the mother's representation, $C_m$, approaches the mother's actual representation $M_m$ (assuming the mother's representation $M_m$ is different from the child's representation $C_c$). Taking a particular measure (from those listed above), then we can consider a scale (for example, for the measure 'number of figures placed on board', this ranged from a minimum of three to a maximum of fifteen in our sample). The degree of understanding the child has of the mother's representation, which we call $C_{TOM}$ (child theory of mind index), can then be defined as

$C_{TOM} = 1 - |M_m - C_m| / |M_m - C_c|$. To help understand this, a schematic representation of these positions on the scale is given below:

For example, suppose $C_c = 3$ (the child places three figures in his/her own FAST representation), $C_m = 5$ (the child supposes the mother will place five figures), and $M_m = 8$ (the mother actually places eight figures). $|M_m - C_c|$ measures the difference between the standard child and mother representations; in this case 5. $|M_m - C_m|$ measures the difference between the mother's standard representation and the child's attempt to imagine that; in this case 3. Then $C_{TOM} = 1 - 3/5 = 2/5 = 0.40$. In other words, the child has moved 40 per cent of the way towards the mother's actual representation.

The modulus signs | | indicate that we ignore the positive or negative sign of the difference. What this means is that if the child 'overshoots', then this is also an error, of equivalent magnitude. Suppose $C_m = 11$ (the child supposes the mother will place eleven figures), then $|M_m - C_m|$ again equals 3 (actually –3, but with the negative sign removed), and this gets the same $C_{TOM}$ score of 0.40 as if $C_m = 5$.

Note that if $C_m = M_m$, then $C_{TOM} = 1$; that is, the child has perfectly represented the mother (on this measure). The greater the discrepancy between $C_m$ and $M_m$, the more that $C_{TOM}$ is reduced. If the child makes no movement in his/her representation, so that $C_c = C_m$, then $C_{TOM} = 0$; that is, the child shows no theory of mind ability.

Note also that if $C_m$ goes in the opposite direction to that predicted, away from $M_m$, then $C_{TOM}$ will become negative. This is realistic, as it means that the child's guess about the mother's representation is actually worse than if they just took their own representation:

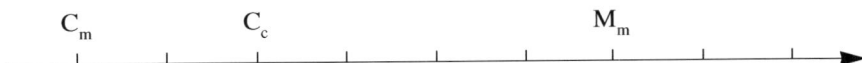

Finally, if $C_c = M_m$, so that there is no difference in the standard child and mother representations, then $C_{TOM}$ is an indefinite number; as mentioned earlier (and discussed further later), if there is no difference in the original representations, then we cannot estimate any theory of mind ability.

### How much understanding does the mother show of the child's representation of the family?

This is defined as the extent to which the mother's representation of the child's representation, $M_c$, approaches the child's actual representation $C_c$ (assuming the child's representation $C_c$ is different from the mother's representation $M_m$). The degree of understanding the mother has of the child's representation, which we call $M_{TOM}$ (mother theory of mind index), can then be defined as $M_{TOM} = 1 - |C_c - M_c| / |C_c - M_m|$. This formula corresponds exactly to that for the child measure, with a corresponding logic:

These two measures, $C_{TOM}$ and $M_{TOM}$, thus have sensible metric properties in relation to the qualities we are trying to assess. There is a possible exception to this, however, in the case of negatively scoring overshoots. For example, take the following situation regarding mother–father distance scores, which actually occurred in one dyad: $C_c = 1$ (the child places mother next to father), $C_m = 6.7$ (the child supposes the mother will place mother and father $3 \times 6$ squares away), and $M_m = 2.2$ (the mother places mother and father $2 \times 2$ squares away). Then $C_{TOM} = 1 - |M_m - C_m| / |M_m - C_c| = 1 - 4.5/1.2 = 1 - 3.75 = -2.75$. This is a large negative score. Yet, the child did at least guess correctly that the mother would place herself more distantly from the father than he himself did in his original plot.

Such a large negative score not only distorts averages but may also do injustice to the theory of mind measure being developed. To deal with this, it may be desirable (though arbitrary) to score overshoots like this (i.e. overshoots sufficiently large that the $C_{TOM}$ score becomes negative) as zero.

### Interpreting the results

An example of three coding summaries is given in Figure 8.2; the first of these provides the coding for the set of four FAST plots that was shown in Figure 8.1. All three are mother–son dyads. The scoring follows the formulae given above. The / lines indicate that $C_c = M_m$, so that no score can be given. The 0 scores indicate no movement, i.e. that $C_c = C_m$, or that $M_c = M_m$. An example of an 'extreme

| PC192 | n figs | MF dist | MC dist | FC dist | MF pow | MC pow | FC pow |
|-------|--------|---------|---------|---------|--------|--------|--------|
| $C_c$ | 8 | 2 | 1.4 | 1.4 | 0 | 0 | 0 |
| $C_m$ | 7 | 1 | 1 | 1.4 | 0 | 0 | 0 |
| $M_c$ | 4 | 2 | 1 | 1 | 1 | 3 | 2 |
| $M_m$ | 5 | 1 | 1 | 2 | 3 | 1 | −2 |
| $C_{TOM}$ | 33% | 100% | 100% | 0 | 0 | 0 | 0 |
| $M_{TOM}$ | −33% | 100% | 0 | 33% | 67% | −200% | 0 |

| PC193 | n figs | MF dist | MC dist | FC dist | MF pow | MC pow | FC pow |
|-------|--------|---------|---------|---------|--------|--------|--------|
| $C_c$ | 5 | 1.4 | 1 | 1 | 1 | 1 | 0 |
| $C_m$ | 5 | 1 | 1 | 1.4 | 0 | 1 | 1 |
| $M_c$ | 8 | 1.4 | 1 | 1 | 0 | 2 | 2 |
| $M_m$ | 10 | 1.4 | 1 | 1 | 1 | 2 | 1 |
| $C_{TOM}$ | 0 | / | / | / | / | 0 | 100% |
| $M_{TOM}$ | 40% | / | / | / | / | 0 | −100% |

| PC198 | n figs | MF dist | MC dist | FC dist | MF pow | MC pow | FC pow |
|-------|--------|---------|---------|---------|--------|--------|--------|
| $C_c$ | 5 | 1.4 | 1.4 | 2 | 0 | 2 | 2 |
| $C_m$ | 5 | 1.4 | 3.2 | 2 | 0 | 3 | 3 |
| $M_c$ | 5 | 1 | 3.6 | 4.2 | 0 | 3 | 3 |
| $M_m$ | 5 | 1.4 | 2 | 1.4 | 0 | 0 | 0 |
| $C_{TOM}$ | / | / | −100% | 0 | / | −50% | −50% |
| $M_{TOM}$ | / | / | −267% | −267%* | / | 50% | 50% |

*Figure 8.2* Scoring tables from three of four FAST plots. * = extreme overshoot; PC192 = parent/child dyad number 192; n figs = number of figures placed on board; dist = distance between figures ; pow = power difference between figures; M = mother; F = father; C = child; for abbreviations in left-hand columns see pp. 124–126.

overshoot' is present in the third coding set, for the mother's attempt to guess child's view of father–child distance.

To obtain final 'theory of mind' scores we needed to average over the seven measures. Given the provisional nature of this exploratory analysis, and the quite wide range of scores obtained, we decided to simplify this averaging by recoding as follows:

100% = 1
1 to 99% = 0.5
0 = 0
extreme overshoot = 0
−1 to −100% = −0.5
−101% or more = −1

The sum of all scores is then divided by the number of possible measures (this latter being seven for the first dyad, three for the second, and four for the third dyad in Figure 8.2).

Using this protocol, the scores for the dyads in Figure 8.2 are:

PC192:   $C_{TOM} = 0.36$, $M_{TOM} = 0.07$
PC193:   $C_{TOM} = 0.33$, $M_{TOM} = 0$
PC198:   $C_{TOM} = -0.38$, $M_{TOM} = 0$

## Findings

### Do child's and mother's own representations differ?

As a first step, we looked to see whether $C_c$ and $M_m$ were different, as if they were not, then no further 'theory of mind' exploration would be possible. In fact, $C_c$ and $M_m$ were different for 73 per cent of the eligible measures (non-eligible measures being mainly due to father absence). The only measure that fell markedly below this percentage was mother–child distance; seven of the twenty eligible dyads agreed at putting mother and child adjacent, and two more diagonally adjacent, so that overall only 55 per cent of dyads differed on this measure.

### Do children show any ability to assess the mother's representation?

Given that the mother's representation did often differ from the child's, did children show any ability to assess the mother's representation? As a first step, we looked at the proportion of child guesses that were in the correct direction; using the coding scheme above, just taking positive or negative signs. Overall, thirty-two guesses were in the correct direction and seventeen in the incorrect direction; this is 65 per cent correct where a guess was made different from one's own representation. Five of the correct guesses were extreme overshoots, but even ignoring these, twenty-seven correct gives a proportion of 61 per cent. The correct guesses were spread across all the measures, but were highest for mother–child power (six correct, two incorrect).

### To what extent can the child assess the mother's representation?

Using the coding scheme above over all eligible measures, the mean child score was $C_{TOM} = 0.11$. Of the twenty-one children, eleven had positive scores, six had zero scores and four had negative scores.

### Do mothers show any ability to assess the child's representation?

Given that the child's representation did often differ from the mother's (or father's), did mothers show any ability to assess the child's representation? As a first step, we looked at the proportion of mother guesses that were in the correct direction; using the coding scheme above, just taking positive or negative signs. Overall, thirty-eight guesses were in the correct direction and seventeen were in the incorrect direction; this is 69 per cent correct where a guess was made different from one's own representation. Three of the correct guesses were extreme overshoots, but even ignoring these, thirty-five correct gives a proportion of 67 per cent. The correct guesses were spread across all the measures, but were highest for mother–child power (six correct, one incorrect) and for number of figures (ten correct, four incorrect).

### To what extent does the mother assess the child's representation?

Using the coding scheme above over all eligible measures, the mean mother score was $M_{TOM} = 0.15$. Of the twenty-one mothers, twelve had positive scores, six had zero scores and three had negative scores.

### Are mother assessments any better than child assessments?

From the above, the proportion of guesses in the correct direction (69 vs 65 per cent) and the extent of correct guesses (0.15 vs 0.11) are slightly higher in mothers than children. However, these differences are not significant statistically so a larger sample would be needed to assess the generalizability of this trend.

### Does the success of children's assessments relate to other theory of mind measures?

For the children, we did have a separate theory of mind measure, based on the Happé short stories and recognition of emotion tasks (see Sutton *et al.*, 1999). We correlated these scores with the $C_{TOM}$ obtained from the FAST. However, the correlation was non-significant, and indeed slightly negative (–0.22); partial correlations controlling for age, and for verbal ability, made little difference.

## Discussion

This was very much an exploratory study; to our knowledge, no one has previously tried to use the FAST to ask respondents to guess someone else's representation of the same family. We feel the results are moderately encouraging, although certain difficulties also became evident in the course of the work.

It was possible to ask both mothers and children to do the task; that is, to represent the other's representation. Also, for many measures we found that not only were the original child and mother representations different (if they were not, we could not estimate the success of guessing the other's representation), but also, the majority of the assessments that ventured a different representation by the other were in the correct direction: 69 per cent for mothers and 65 per cent for children. There were certainly many guesses in the incorrect direction too, so it was not an easy task for people; but if the respondents had been guessing randomly we would not expect this success rate.

There were some methodological difficulties, which would need to be addressed in any further work along these lines. One relates to the number of figures placed on the plot; there was quite a lot of variation in this (and some success in assessing the others' representation), but clearly the actual instructions given will affect who is considered legitimate to put on the plot.

Another very practical difficulty relates to moving from the 'own' plot to 'other' plot representation. A 'clean sweep' of the board allows the respondent to start afresh (and use fewer or more figures as necessary) but, especially in large families, this means a relabelling of figures, which is time-consuming. However, if the figures were left and the respondent just asked to move them to the new representation, we found a rather conservative tendency to leave figures where they were.

A more conceptual difficulty concerns situations where $C_c = M_m$; there is no difference in the standard child and mother representations. As discussed, this means that no theory of mind score can be calculated. However, this does not mean that no theory of mind ability is present. For example, in a small, close family, all members might be clustered in the centre, and both mother and child might agree in representing this. They might also agree that the other sees things the same way. This could be argued to be a good theory of mind ability, but we can't usefully or reliably measure it. To some extent this is overcome by having a number of measures from the plots (it being unlikely that mother and child agree on all of them). It might also be possible to generate more variability by asking for conflict plots or ideal plots (and how the other would represent this, too) as well as standard plots. We did try this with a few children in our sample, but at this age it seemed to overload and confuse some of them.

Nevertheless, our results suggest that both mothers and children have some ability to assess the others' representation. There is also a trend for this ability to be greater in mothers than children, which might be expected given evidence that theory of mind abilities increase through the lifespan (Happé *et al.*, 1998). However, we did not succeed in finding a relationship, for children, with other theory of mind tasks suitable for this age. This finding might reflect one of a number of possible factors:

- despite the modest success of children on this FAST task, it is not measuring any kind of theory of mind ability on their part
- the methodology used to obtain the scores was inadequate
- the sample was too small to reach reliable conclusions
- the FAST task does measure some theory of mind ability, but one focused on a different area from the other tasks (knowledge of particular family relationships vs knowledge of general aspects of deceit, and emotions), and that there is little overlap of abilities in these two domains.

At present, we cannot tell which of the above explanations (or some other) is true. However, if some theory of mind or social cognitive measure could be developed using the FAST, it would have two distinct advantages. First, the measure could be the same across the age range, from middle childhood through to adult life. This could help in the task of finding comparable measures for (older) children and adults. The measure would of course be limited to the domain of knowledge of the family, but this is a highly salient domain for most persons through the lifespan. In fact, a second possible advantage of this measure is that it is a realistic domain for assessing such abilities, arguably more realistic than the artificial scenarios devised in conventional tests. However, there are also methodological problems to be addressed, which we have discussed above. We hope that this chapter contributes to opening up this new and innovative use of the FAST, and to providing some signposts for its future development.

# References

Baron-Cohen, S., Jolliffe, T., Mortimore, C. and Robertson, M. (1997) 'Another advanced test of theory of mind: Evidence from very high functioning adults with autism or Asperger syndrome', *Journal of Child Psychology and Psychiatry*, 38: 813–22.

—— O'Riordan, M., Jones, R., Stone, V. and Plaisted, K. (1999) 'A new test of social sensitivity: Detection of faux pas in normal children and children with Asperger syndrome', *Journal of Autism and Developmental Disorders*, 29, 407–18.

—— Riviere, A., Cross, P., Fukushima, M., Bryant, C., Sotillo, M., Hadwin, J. and French, D. (1996) 'Reading the mind in the face: A cross-cultural and developmental study', *Visual Cognition*, 3: 39–59.

Feldman, S.S., Wentzel, K.R. and Gehring, T.M. (1989) 'A comparison of the views of mothers, fathers, and pre-adolescents about family cohesion and power', *Journal of Family Psychology*, 3: 39–60.

Gehring, T.M. (1998) *The Family System Test*, Seattle, WA: Hogrefe and Huber Publishers.

—— and Wyler, I.L. (1986) 'Family System Test (FAST): A three dimensional approach to investigate family relationships', *Child Psychiatry and Human Development*, 16: 235–48.

——, Marti, D. and Sidler, A. (1994) 'Family System Test (FAST): Are parents' and children's family constructs either different or similar, or both?', *Child Psychiatry and Human Development*, 25: 125–38.

Happé, F.G.E. (1994) 'An advanced test of theory of mind: Understanding of story characters' thoughts and feelings by able autistic, mentally handicapped, and normal children and adults', *Journal of Autism and Developmental Disorders*, 24: 129–54.

Happé, F.G.E., Winner, E. and Brownell, H. (1998) 'The getting of wisdom: Theory of mind in old age', *Developmental Psychology*, 34: 358–62.

Mitchell, P. (1996) *Introduction to Theory of Mind*, London: Edward Arnold.

Perner, J. and Wimmer, H. (1985) '"John thinks that Mary thinks that . . . ": Attribution of second order beliefs by 5–10 year old children', *Journal of Experimental Child Psychology*, 39: 437–71.

Premack, D. and Woodruff, G. (1978) 'Does the chimpanzee have a theory of mind?', *Behavioral and Brain Sciences*, 1: 512–26.

Shu, S. (1999) 'Grandparents, parents and children: A study of three-generation family structure and intergenerational relationships in contemporary China'. Unpublished M.Phil. thesis, Goldsmiths College, University of London, UK.

Sutton, J., Smith, P.K. and Swettenham, J. (1999) 'Social cognition and bullying: Social inadequacy or skilled manipulation?', *British Journal of Developmental Psychology*, 17: 435–450.

# 9    Single-parent families: How does the loss of the father influence the father image of mothers and daughters?

*Regina Hunter and Irene von Ballmoos*

## Introduction

The goal of the research described below was to elucidate the father image of daughters after the loss of the father through divorce or death. In view of the differences in development depending on gender, the research was restricted to females. The father has the role of opening up the male world to the child. The assumption is that the way this relationship with the father is experienced gives a model for later life, relationships, sexuality, and structures of the personality like the ego-ideal, the super-ego and the position in triads. Social reality itself often creates situations where the father is missing either through divorce, death, work, war or for other reasons. In consequence, many children have to fill this void with an image of the father, who is such an important person for their development. With this growing interest in the relationship between the father and the family, triads became more significant (Fthenakis *et al.*, 1982). The mother nevertheless plays an important role in this process: her image of her partner and men in general is transferred to the daughter. This led to an investigation in which not only the daughters but also the mothers were the focus of interest.

## Theoretical background

### Father image

Girls use several sources to create a father image. This first is the actual father and his behaviour towards the girl. A second source is the mother, who serves the girl as a model for pictures and impressions about the father. Likewise, all the male figures the girl comes into touch with supply some impressions, memories and opportunities to create a particular father image by combining with each other. The father image grows in the course of time by a process of gradual internalization. Gill (1991) describes this mental representation of an object in three developmental levels:

- Incorporation is the earliest form of internalization and goes back to the time when an object is not seen as distinct from the self.

- Introjection is the process whereby the functions of an external object are taken over by its mental representation. The relationship with the object is replaced by one with an imagined object inside the subject's self (introject, internal object). The imagined object of the parents follows the same pattern, whereby some functions (introjection of the parental demands and prohibitions) enter into the super-ego of the child.
- Identification refers to the modification of the subject's self-representation in order to increase its resemblance to the object taken as a model. Identification with parental figures is a normal developmental process. They are focused on selected parts or qualities of the object and permit the continuation of the object relationship rather than replacing it. Conscious and unconscious fantasies are involved. An internal representation depends on the child's biological endowment and the quality of parent–child interaction. An individual representational world is the result of three interacting variables: the actual quality of interaction with the external object; the influence of the subject's physiological state and biological instincts, and the effect of the subject's internalized world. For girls who have lost their fathers it is more difficult to establish a differentiated perception of the father in this way than it is for girls of intact families. The mother takes on a great part of the task of conveying an image of the absent father.

### Death

The absence of the father influences the daughter in different ways. It is to be expected that orphans idealize their lost father because they have no chance to compare their images with the real father, and the unspoken rule has to be respected that nothing malicious should be said about the father. Mothers often support this attitude and idealize their relationship, as well as the image of their husbands.

The earlier in life the loss of the father took place, the more the life of the child is affected and the possibility of a strong mother identification increases (D'Andrade, 1973). The mother might overprotect her child and the emotional growth of the child can be retarded, and therefore dependence on the mother increases. In general, semiorphans show more introverted behaviour, e.g. retreat, shyness, and timidity (Hetherington, 1972, 1979). The relevant findings in the research into divorce and the loss of the father confirm that the loss of the father through death leads the daughter to exhibit more introvert behaviour and to identify herself with the mother.

### Divorce

Many authors describe a wide range of reactions of children after a divorce and its consequences for later life (e.g. Fthenakis *et al.*, 1982; Wallerstein and Blakeslee, 1989; Fassel, 1991). Children experience a divorce as a rejection of their personality (Beelmann and Schmidt-Denter, 1991). Often they have feelings of guilt and the idea that they are the reason for the divorce. Behind these feelings of guilt there are feelings of helplessness and unimportance, which are even more difficult to bear.

Children have the impression that they have no influence on an event that has changed their life so much. They feel lonely and often they get no support.

The child's relationship with the father changes after a divorce. The degree of care on the part of the father after the separation is often lowered and an emotional distance arises. The feelings of anger, guilt, and hurt caused by the separation and divorce are revived at the visitation weekends and therefore many men try to avoid them, so the closer father–child relationships are even more in danger. The prognoses are better when the children are younger than 8 years at the point of separation (Fthenakis *et al.*, 1982; Wallerstein and Blakeslee, 1989).

One of the problems a girl has to face after a divorce is that, according to our research, she has to fight with the confusing emotions of love and hate towards the father whom she needs but who has left. Children have to deal with these feelings of anger and betrayal in relation to their father. Most children do not give up their fathers, even if they show no interest in their daughters, or they are not much good, or they have left, or when step-fathers have come into the lives of the children. The father who has disappeared through divorce or death has not disappeared from the thoughts and feelings of the child. There is still a gap, which is filled by images. But in the absence of a shared daily life and arguments with the father, daughters have difficulties knowing how their fathers actually are as people and this makes it difficult for them to build a realistic image of their father and of men in general. These images and metaphors around the father create the realities for the daughters in their later dealings with men (Buchholz, 1991). Wallerstein and Blakeslee (1989) have found a double image of fathers after a divorce: like little detectives, the children know both sides of their father, the good and offending characteristics. They have a strong desire to create the image of a loving and caring father and at the same time they have a list of rejections. The ability to differentiate this image of the father is moreover seen as a parameter of development in general.

For the daughters of divorced families it is a big challenge to cope with this situation because they lack not only the presence of the father but also an image of a loving and caring father and of a relationship between their parents. Wallerstein and Blakeslee (1989) found that children who were sure of the love of their parents, or were the darling of one parent, could cope better with the situation of the divorce. A beloved child can maintain his/her self-esteem and hope. Concerning the coping, Kurdek *et al.* (1981) found that there was no correlation between the rational understanding of the reasons for the divorce and the emotional acceptance of this event. So it is possible to cope cognitively with the divorce of the parents, but this coping does not automatically find a correspondence in the emotional field. There are many new findings about the difficulties of grown-up children of divorced families (Parish, 1981; Parish and Wigle, 1985; Wallerstein and Blakeslee, 1989; Fassel, 1991). Fassel (1991) mentions particular difficulties for these adults in that they tend to take responsibility and position very fast, or they exhibit difficulties in establishing personal boundaries. Girls have to conform to their responsibilities and lose their childhood. This conformity often leads to depressive episodes during young adulthood and affects the choice of a partner and professional work. Another new research finding suggests that the younger the girl is at the time of the divorce, the less she seems to be affected (Fassel, 1991).

## Adaptations of the Family System Test (FAST)

Looking for a suitable research instrument to get more information on the influence of a father loss on daughters, we enlarged the FAST. In addition to the representations of the typical and the ideal family, two further representations (which are not part of the FAST as it was developed by Gehring) were done in this research. These additional representations were one of the family of origin and one showing a triad (a constellation of three persons).

The first addition, done by the mother only, asked for the representation of the mother's family of origin. The goal was to look for transgenerational aspects in creating an image of the father and of men in general. The idea of such a constellation is to be found in the theories of family therapy: many family therapy authors give the theoretical background that there is a transmission of psychodynamical aspects from one generation to the next (Minuchin, 1974; Hoffman, 1981; Sperling *et al.*, 1982; Satir, 1983). To give an example, there might be an exclusion of the male part and at the same time a coalition between mother and child, which can be traced back for generations. The work with the family of origin, and representing it visually, is an important part of therapeutic work, e.g. in the family sculptures of Satir and Baldwin (1983). The instruction for this representation of the family of origin was to show the family, with its members, as it was when the mother was a child herself. Emphasis was put on the question of whether there were similarities or differences between the family of origin and the current family. The mother was also asked if there were similarities or differences between her father and her former partner and, if possible, how these could be explained.

The second addition, labelled 'triadic representation', showed the triad as the basic constellation and the fundamental unit of relationship, with its three elements: father, mother, child. This constellation of the triad forms the basis of the findings of Buchholz (1990a, b). For a long time the dyad, i.e. the relation of two and the symbiosis between mother and child, was the theoretical basis for the explanation of many psychological phenomena. Since the results of family therapy, neonatological research data and psychoanalytic revisions have shown how important the influence of the father is for the child from the very beginning; the father has assumed more importance and an undeniable and independent function (Lichtenberg, 1983; Stern, 1986). Neonatological results have proved babies to be very capable of having different relationships and of initiating these relationships, and babies are no longer seen as passively receiving and fixed on only one person (the mother). Therefore the importance of the dyad with its symbol of the mother–child unit has been downgraded. Revisions of psychoanalytic theory take this new view of the baby into account and the notion of the father portrayed in the psychoanalytic theories as only playing his role in the oedipal phase is obsolete. The dyadic viewpoint in consequence was enlarged and the triad then postulated as the fundamental unit of relationship. The new concept of the triad assumes that the father has an autonomous function from the earliest stage in the life of the baby. So the father is already involved in the imaginary triad of fantasy to create together with the mother a fantasy around the future child.

The original position and scene as a child and third element in the relationship to mother and father is essential and formative for each individual. The interesting questions are the following: What place did the former child have? How did it deal with exclusion? Where were the boundaries blurred? And was there either the fear of being expelled or devoured? Even the methods of gaining this position in the triad are built into the relationship with the parents and are revived in later life. The fear of being too near or of being excluded is fundamental and every human being experiences it in his or her childhood to a greater or lesser extent. In the triad the child also has to learn to bear situations when the parents are together and the child is temporarily excluded. It is assumed that the healthy functioning of triads relies on the presence of a stable and loving relationship between the parents, or an equivalent of this relationship such as the image of the father can provide.

This theoretical background does not deny the existence of frequent dyads, but it postulates that these dyads are built through the exclusion of a third person or a third element. In this concept of the triad as a constellation of three elements potentially to be found everywhere, these triads are not tied to the presence of actual persons but can also be imagined as three positions in a field, which can manifest themselves as roles, fantasies, or as being missed out. The triad is seen as the 'smallest emotional unit' (Buchholz, 1991: 49, translation by the authors). Dyads are viewed as regressed triads and the third, excluded person in many families with pathological patterns is the father (Buchholz, 1991).

In our research, where single-parent families were the subject, this fact was no obstacle to taking the triadic aspect into account, for the functioning of the triad has more to do with the psychological capabilities of the persons involved than with actual persons (Rhode-Dachser, 1990). This means that a triad can be established when a single mother bringing up a child leaves room for a third, other person in reality, in her imagination or in a renouncement. It is suggested that in the place of the partner, a picture of the former partner and of men in general is replaced by the mother. This picture is also influenced by the family of origin, so that the results of the two added representations (triadic constellation and family of origin) could be evaluated in addition. It was expected that the representation of the triad would show constellations of relations in its most clear, reduced and fundamental form. Moreover, there was room for the influence of the father, who could have been missed out in the representations hitherto. Further, the psychological capacity to give room to a third, which is not attached to a personal presence, was expected to be seen. The instructions for the triadic representation were to show a constellation of the three figures – man, woman, and child. It was then asked whether the figures stood for particular persons and where the idea for this representation had come from.

The instructions and the questioning on these representations were developed by the authors and were reviewed by the author of the FAST, Gehring.

## Methods

### *Sample*

Designed as a pilot study, the sample consisted of nine daughters from 5.8 to 10.5 years of age (mean age 7.6) and their mothers with age ranging from 32 to 45 years (mean age 37). Four of the nine daughters had lost their father through an accident or because of a physical illness. The parents of the other respondents were divorced. The mean time of the marriage was 5 years and times ranged from less than 1 year to 9 years (see Tables 9.1 and 9.2 for an overview).

The daughters and their mothers were found through self-help groups, parish support groups and through friends. Mothers who were not a single parent, with a new partner living in the same household, and mothers with husbands who had committed suicide were excluded. In the current situation, all of the mothers lived alone with their children but some of them had a friend outside the family; none was remarried. All the widows came from an intact family. In the divorced sample, two of the five mothers had grown up themselves in a divorced family, whereas three of them had experienced an intact family.

### *Procedure*

After a short period of small talk and giving information about the study, mothers and daughters were separated to be examined.

#### *Testing the daughters*

Several projective tests were done by the daughters. They had to tell a short story to some selected pictures of the 'Thematische Gestaltungstest Salzburg' (TGT-(S)) (Revers and Allesch, 1985) and of the 'Columbus' pictures (Langeveld, 1969), which showed different situations of family life and father–daughter relations. Then they had to draw their family in the guise of animals (Brem-Gräser, 1986). Finally, we used the two known representations of the FAST – the typical and the ideal family (Gehring, 1993) – and the triadic representation. All the projective tests were carried out, analysed, and compared according to the methods proposed by the respective authors.

#### *Testing the mothers*

To verify the father image from another viewpoint, the mothers were questioned with a qualitative half-structured interview including the following topics: the procedure of the divorce/the form of death, changes in and support by the inner and outer family, the daughters' feelings of loss and reactions to the death/divorce, how they coped with the situation, the resources, the nature of the relationship between father and daughter, and the mother's attitude towards the fathers and towards the relationship between father and daughter. The interviews were analysed using the qualitative content-analysing methods of Mayring (1993). At the end of the

*Table 9.1* Demographic data concerning the daughters and their mothers in the divorced group

| | Age (years; months) | Reason for loss | Age at loss (years) | Siblings (age/gender) | Age of mother | Age of father | Duration of marriage (years) | Father contact | Status of the family of origin (mother) |
|---|---|---|---|---|---|---|---|---|---|
| 1 | 6;11 | fws | 4½ | 10/f, 7/f, 5/m, 3/m | 39 | 39 | 9 | Once a month, birthday, one-week holiday | Divorced family |
| 2 | 8;10 | mws | Before birth | Single child | 32 | 34 | ½ | None | Intact family |
| 3 | 7;11 | mws | 4 | 9/m, 8/f | 33 | 40 | 7 | Once a month | Intact family |
| 4 | 5;8 | mws | 4 | 7/f, 5/f | 34 | 33 | 6 | Once every 4 months | Divorced family |
| 5 | 5;11 | fws | 2 | 6/f, 4/m | 33 | 30 | 3 | Once in 1½ month | Intact family |

f, female; fws, father wanted separation; m, male; mws, mother wanted separation; tested daughter in italic.

Table 9.2 Demographic data concerning the semiorphans and their mothers

| | Age (years; month) | Reason for loss | Age at loss (years) | Siblings (age/gender) | Age of mother | Age of father at his death | Term of marriage (years) | Last contact with the father | Situation of the family of origin (mother) |
|---|---|---|---|---|---|---|---|---|---|
| 6a | 6;10 | Accident | 4 | Twins (first born) | 45 | 50 | 4 | 2½ years ago | Intact family |
| 6b | 6;10 | Accident | 4 | Twins (second born) | 45 | 50 | 4 | 2½ years ago | Intact family |
| 7 | 10;5 | Accident | 5 | 10/f, 8/m | 41 | 35 | 6½ | 5½ years ago | Intact family |
| 8 | 8;8 | Cardiac infarction | 5 | 8/f, 6/f | 32 | 39 | 7 | 1½ year ago | Intact family |

f, female; m, male; tested daughter in italic.

interview session, the FAST representations were done: the typical and the ideal representation, the family of origin and the triadic representation.

### *Scoring*

The different FAST representations done by the mothers and the daughters were compared. The main points of the general analysis were the depiction of the father and mother figure with respect to the distance between them and whether they were looking at each other; the identification (cohesion and hierarchy), the gender identification and the introduction of other figures as substitutes for the lost father. In the analysis of the FAST representations we looked at the cohesion and hierarchy (low, medium, or high), the classification of the structure of the family, the parental and the child system (balanced, unstable– balanced and unbalanced type), and the introduction of the father, a father figure or other figures. Concerning the qualitative approach to this study, the FAST representations were also analysed in a more qualitative way to give weight to the particular form of the familiy system. The results were combined in the two groups of daughters with divorced parents and dead father.

## Results

The results of all the tests, and especially of the FAST, were a valuable contribution to the questions of our research. We will concentrate on the results of the FAST.

### *The FAST representations of the daughters*

The father figure appears to an equal extent in both groups, and came up in the typical representation as well as in the ideal. Three out of five daughters with divorced parents and three out of four semiorphans introduced the father in the typical as well as in the ideal representation. Semiorphans did not introduce other figures or a father substitute. Two daughters of divorced parents put up other figures such as grandmother, godfather, godmother and cousins. Once these had been introduced in the typical representations, the daughters also put them up in the ideal representations.

In the typical representation, most of the daughters of divorced families showed an unbalanced family structure as well as an unbalanced structure in the parental system. This result was in contrast to the daughters of the widows, where more balanced family structures and a hierarchy inversion in the parental system were found (see Table 9.3 for an overview).

In the ideal representation it was striking that low hierarchy was shown in both family types. But they seemed to be more balanced than in the typical representation. The wish for an 'ideal' family seemed common to all the daughters, but was most desired by two daughters with divorced parents (extreme cohesion and low hierarchy). In the parental system as well as in the child system the semiorphans showed more unbalanced structures than daughters from divorced parents (see Table 9.4 for an overview).

*Table 9.3* Classification of type of relational structures in typical representation

| | Family level | | Parental subsystem | | Child subsystem | |
|---|---|---|---|---|---|---|
| * | *Daughter* | *Mother* | *Daughter* | *Mother* | *Daughter* | *Mother* |
| 1 | Balanced | Unbalanced | Unbalanced | Unbalanced | Balanced | Unstable–balanced |
| 2 | Unbalanced | Unbalanced | — | — | — | — |
| 3 | Unbalanced | Unbalanced | Unbalanced | Unbalanced | Unbalanced | Unbalanced |
| 4 | Unbalanced | Unstable–balanced | Balanced | Unstable–balanced | Balanced | Unbalanced |
| 5 | Unbalanced | Unstable–balanced | — | Unbalanced | Unbalanced | Balanced |
| 6a | Unstable–balanced | Unstable–balanced | Unstable–balanced | — | Unbalanced | Unbalanced |
| 6b | Unstable–balanced | Unstable–balanced | Unstable–balanced | — | Unbalanced | Unbalanced |
| 7 | Balanced | Unstable–balanced | — | — | Balanced | Unbalanced |
| 8 | Unbalanced | Unbalanced | Unbalanced | — | Unbalanced | Unbalanced |

* Divorced families: 1–5; widows/semiorphans: 6a–8.

*Table 9.4* Classification of type of relational structures in ideal representation

| | Family level | | Parental subsystem | | Child subsystem | |
|---|---|---|---|---|---|---|
| * | *Daughter* | *Mother* | *Daughter* | *Mother* | *Daughter* | *Mother* |
| 1 | Unbalanced | Unbalanced | Unbalanced | Unbalanced | Balanced | Unbalanced |
| 2 | — | Unbalanced | – | Unbalanced | — | — |
| 3 | Unbalanced | Unstable–balanced | Unbalanced | Unbalanced | Unbalanced | Unbalanced |
| 4 | Balanced | Unstable–balanced | Balanced | Unbalanced | Balanced | Unstable–balanced |
| 5 | Balanced | Unbalanced | — | Unbalanced | Balanced | Unstable–balanced |
| 6a | Unbalanced | Unstable–balanced | Unbalanced | Unbalanced | Unbalanced | Unbalanced |
| 6b | Balanced | Unstable–balanced | Unbalanced | Unbalanced | Unbalanced | Unbalanced |
| 7 | Balanced | Unstable–balanced | — | Unbalanced | Balanced | Unbalanced |
| 8 | Unstable–balanced | Unbalanced | Unbalanced | Unstable–balanced | Unbalanced | Unbalanced |

* Divorced families: 1–5; widows/semiorphans: 6a–8.

*Table 9.5* Classification of type of relational structures of the triadic representation

| * | Family level | | Parental subsystem | |
|---|---|---|---|---|
| | *Daughter* | *Mother* | *Daughter* | *Mother* |
| 1 | Balanced | Unbalanced | Balanced | Unbalanced |
| 2 | Unbalanced | Unbalanced | Unbalanced | Unbalanced |
| 3 | Unbalanced | Unbalanced | Unbalanced | Unbalanced |
| 4 | Balanced | Unbalanced | Unbalanced | Unstable–balanced |
| 5 | Unbalanced | Unbalanced | Unbalanced | Unbalanced |
| 6a | Unbalanced | Unbalanced | Unbalanced | Unbalanced |
| 6b | Unstable–balanced | Unbalanced | Balanced | Unbalanced |
| 7 | Balanced | Unbalanced | Balanced | Unbalanced |
| 8 | Balanced | Unbalanced | Balanced | Unbalanced |

* Divorced families: 1–5; widows/semiorphans: 6a–8. Triadic representation with only one child-figure, therefore no data for child subsystem.

These results of the typical representation were repeated in the triadic representation. The daughters with divorced parents showed more unbalanced family structures than the semiorphans. Regarding the parental system, the daughters with divorced parents showed an unbalanced system (four out of five), while every semiorphan showed a balanced structure (see Table 9.5 for an overview).

### The FAST representation of the mothers

Only one of the divorced mothers introduced the father in any of the FAST representations; that one mother put up the father in the typical representation. However, many other persons were introduced, not always as a father substitute but often as a further emotionally close person. Frequently there were more than three new figures on the board, e.g. grandparents, new partners, foster-parents with their children, and the sisters and brothers of the mother with their spouses and children. In the ideal representation, two out of five divorced mothers reduced the tall figure of other persons down to the new partner. The widows took persons from the closer family as new introduced figures, like grandparents, or sisters and brothers of the mother or father. They had a clear idea of the ideal representation: the remaining family (mother and children) and the death father or a new partner.

In the typical representation, the mothers of both groups showed more unbalanced structures in the family and the child system. In the widows group, no result was found in the parental system because they did not introduce the father or a new partner (see Table 9.3).

The results of the typical representation were repeated in the ideal representation, where more unbalanced structures in the family, the parental and the child systems were shown. All the divorced mothers had an unbalanced structure in the parental system, whereas the widows had an unstable–balanced one (see Table 9.4).

In the triad representation, all the mothers showed the same result of an unbalanced structure in the family and in the parental system (see Table 9.5).

The main result from the eight mothers is the low hierarchy, which leads to unbalanced family structures in all four representations (typical, ideal, and triadic representations and the representation of the family of origin). This result is contrary to the findings of Gehring (1993), where 60 per cent of non-clinical probands showed balanced family structures and only 14 per cent unbalanced ones. The grade of balance in a representation is connected to the two dimensions of cohesion and hierarchy and is deeply dependent on extreme values of these dimensions. All the unbalanced structures in the mothers' representations can be explained by the low hierarchy or hierarchy inversions. Low hierarchy corresponds to the wish of the mothers for an equal relationship. This was supported by the findings of the ideal representation and even of the family of origin, which showed low hierarchies. Compared with the findings of Gehring (1993), 77 per cent gave a medium hierarchy. The transgenerational aspect is vividly visible and this finding highlighted the loss of generational boundaries that are necessary for a family to function well. Regarding the representation of the typical family and the family of origin, similar structures are to be found, as well as some repetition of the patterns in the family of origin.

High cohesion is to be found in all the triadic representations. The figures are put very close together, without any boundaries or differentiations. All the mothers commented that this constellation is the situation they saw as most desirable, and in this situation the most comfort and happiness would be found. The triadic representation indicates in this way more of an ideal concept and wish for relationship than the lived reality.

### Comparison of the two groups

Taking into account the results of both groups (mothers and daughters), it can be seen that two daughters with divorced parents and their mothers introduced a father figure in the typical representation, and another daughter of the same group put up the father whereas her mother introduced the new partner. Mothers introduced more figures than their daughters, who concentrated on the inner family. Mothers often did introduce the whole staff of caring persons around the daughters. The mothers and the daughters of divorced families judged their family, parental and child system as more unbalanced, whereas the widows and their daughters showed more unstable–balanced family structures but unbalanced structures in the child system. Daughters seem to have the same view of the typical FAST representation as their mothers.

Regarding the ideal representation, six daughters and mothers out of nine included a male figure. One semiorphan and her mother introduced the father, two semiorphans and three daughters of divorced parents introduced the father, whereas their mothers introduced the new partner. Two of the daughters of the divorced mothers showed a balanced family structure in contrast to all the mothers of this group, who did not shown any balanced structure at all. Very similar results were found in the group of widows and their daughters.

Most of the correspondence in the representations was found in the triadic representations, where three daughters of divorced parents and one semiorphan showed the same family representation as their mothers. A similar convergence was found in the parental and child system of the ideal representations: daughters, like their mothers, regarded the present family situation shown in the family system of the typical representation as similar. The closeness of the several family members seemed to be to the daughters more visible and understandable than the hierarchy. This was to be seen at several values of cohesion.

## Conclusions

We found that the FAST complemented the other tests in this research but was also a valuable instrument for all the research done. Although coping with the loss of the father through death or divorce is very individual and the sample was too small to generalize from, some of the results could support the thesis of the theoretical background. Working with both mothers and daughters made it possible to show that the mothers' pictures of the father, and of men in general, strongly influenced the daughters' pictures of fathers and men. The FAST also reconfirmed and supported the results found in the projective tests, which made them more measurable. Nevertheless, the interpretation of any situation depended on the context of the question asked: questioning the triadic situation made a quantitative analysis easier than looking at a representation of a family of origin, which required more individual interpretation.

Regarding the questions and goal of our research, we want to point out the following outcomes: when the image of the father was more positive, the girls seemed more unburdened and showed a greater sense of reality and a positive relationship to the father and to men in general. Moreover, they showed a degree of development and problems corresponding to their age. The mothers reported a large and striking degree of sensitivity on the part of the children for their wellbeing. This concern for their mothers is touching and can lead to social competence and empathy, but it collides with an unburdened childhood and tasks of development. Most of the women talked of having a better relationship with their children after the separation or death of the father. That these relationships are closer could be proved very clearly by the FAST.

The instructions concerning the FAST are very simple to understand and to follow. Therefore there were no problems in explaining to the girls – the youngest was 5 years old – what was expected. We suggest that the FAST with its figures and map uses a medium closely related to children's games, well-known and familiar to all of us, e.g. in the game 'housey housey'. Its play-like structure made it easy and amusing to do the test, which is an important quality in research, where the question of burdening the people interviewed is always a sensitive issue. Visuality is another quality of the FAST. More and more, psychotherapy is accepting how much we think and learn in images and through metaphors. In our therapeutic work with families and individuals we can use the capacity of the FAST to make the family positions visible and to build pictures in the mind facilitating changes in these positions. The FAST also had the function of providing a systemic viewpoint. Through its visuality the FAST also had a positive impact on the people involved in the research; they were able to get something in return for their openness and commitment. One mother said that she had gained insight by seeing the FAST positions of her family of origin. So it was possible for the experimental subjects to obtain something helpful for their individual growth by contributing to the research. In summary, the FAST showed itself to be a very apposite, flexible and adaptable tool of research.

On the basis of the results of this research, two further questions arose: 'How do daughters cope with the loss of the father after a divorce?' and 'How does the loss of the father affect the relationships of grown-up girls to male and female persons?' The first question was answered in a dissertation done by the first-named author with the title of *Productive coping with divorce in childhood and youth. Results of an investigation of young women and theories* (Hunter, 1999). In this dissertation, the FAST was again used as a test in addition to the interview technique. As in the research described here, the FAST was supplemented, this time by asking the 21-year-old women who were interviewed how they wished their own families to be. The most striking result was how much the former divorce-children are willing to learn from the faults of their parents. So, predominantly, the young women interviewed wished, in their future families, to be face-to-face with their partner. Their parents, in contrast, had lost contact by not establishing common interest or as a result of frequent conflicts or great pressure. Although this came out in the interviews, it could be seen on a visual and deeper level in the FAST. Another interesting finding was that almost all of the people lending support had already been participants in the life of the divorced families before the divorce took place. Seemingly, when there is a new situation or crisis, one falls back on resources that are available and known. The known gives security and support and this is comforting in a situation in which there is already enough unknown. When no social net was established before the crisis took place, the people concerned were left without support and were in much more difficult circumstances and in a less good condition. These supporting people, in all except two cases, were also shown in the FAST representation where each subject was asked to show their future family. This support given by other people in the crisis of divorce seems to be a deep and formative experience.

The second question, concerning the effect of father loss on starting and maintaining a relationship with a male partner, is the basis of a dissertation in progress by the second author. Nevertheless, the results of this and much other research give a better background for the practical work with many affected children.

# References

Beelmann, W. and Schmidt-Denter, U. (1991) 'Kindliches Erleben sozial-emotionaler Beziehungen und Unterstützungssysteme in Ein-Elternteil-Familien', *Psychologie in Erziehung und Unterricht* 38: 180–9.

Brem-Gräser, L. (1986) *Familie in Tieren. Die Familiensituation im Spiegel der Kinderzeichnung (5. Aufl.)*, München, Basel: Reinhardt.

Buchholz, M.B. (1990a) 'Die Rotation der Triade', *Forum der Psychoanalyse* 6: 116–34.

—— (1990b) *Die unbewusste Familie*, Berlin: Springer.

—— (1991) 'Die Regression der Triade', *Forum der Psychoanalyse* 7: 47–61.

D'Andrade, R.G. (1973) 'Father absence, identification and identity', *Ethos* 1(4): 440–55.

Fassel, D. (1991) *Growing up Divorced: A Road to Healing for Adult Children of Divorce*, New York: Simon and Schuster.

Fthenakis, W.E., Niesel, R. and Kunze, H.-R. (1982) *Ehescheidung*, München: Urban and Schwarzenberg.

Gehring, T.M. (1993) *FAST Familiensystemtest. Manual*, Weinheim: Beltz.

Gill, H.S. (1991) 'Internalization of the absent father', *International Journal of Psychoanalysis* 72: 243–52.

Hetherington, E.M. (1972) 'Effects of father absence on personality development in adolescent daughters', *Developmental Psychology* 7(3): 313–26.

—— (1979) 'Divorce: A child's perspective', *American Psychologist* 34, 10: 851–8.

Hoffman, L. (1981) *Foundations of Family Therapy*, New York: Basic Books.

Hunter, R. (1999) 'Produktive Scheidungsbewältigung im Kindes- und Jugendalter. Resultate einer Befragung von jungen Frauen und Theorien', Unpublished dissertation, University of Zurich.

Kurdek, L.A., Bliks, D. and Siesky, A.E. (1981) 'Correlates of children's long-term adjustment to their parents' divorce', *Developmental Psychology* 17: 565–79.

Langeveld, M.J. (1969) *Columbus. Analyse der Entwicklung zum Erwachsensein durch Bilddeutung*, Basel: Karger.

Lichtenberg, J.D. (1983) *Psychoanalysis and Infant Research*. New Jersey: Analytic Press.

Mayring, Ph. (1993) *Qualitative Inhaltsanalyse (4. Aufl.)*, Weinheim: Studien Verlag.

Minuchin, S. (1974) *Families and Family Therapy*, Cambridge, MA: Harvard University Press.

Parish, Th.S. (1981) 'The impact of divorce on the family', *Adolescence* XVI, 63: 577–80.

—— Wigle, St.E. (1985) 'A longitudinal study of the impact of parental divorce on adolescents' evaluations of self and parents', *Adolescence* XX, 77: 239–44.

Revers, W.J. and Allesch, C.G. (1985) *Handbuch zum Thematischen Gestaltungstest (Salzburg)*, Weinheim: Beltz.

Rhode-Dachser, Ch. (1990) 'Ueber töchterliche Existenz. Offene Fragen zum weiblichen Oedipuskomplex', *Zeitschrift für Psychosomatische Medizin* 36: 303–15.

Satir, V. (1983) *Conjoint Family Therapy*, Palo Alto, CA: Science and Behaviour Books.

—— Baldwin, M. (1983) *Step by Step: A Guide to Creating Change in Families*, Palo Alto, CA: Science and Behaviour Books.

Sperling, E., Massing, A., Reich, G., Georgi, H. and Wöbbe-Mönks, E. (1982) *Die Mehrgenerationen-Familientherapie*, Göttingen: Vandenhoeck and Ruprecht.

Stern, D.N. (1986) *The Interpersonal World of the Infant.* New York: Basic Books.

Wallerstein, J. and Blakeslee, S. (1989) *Second Chances: Men, Women, and Children a Decade after Divorce*, New York: Ticknor and Fields.

# 10 Perceptions of mother–daughter relations and pubertal development[1]

### Kenneth Kim and Thanes Wongyannava

Using an evolutionary perspective on family relations and child development, Draper and Belsky (1990) and Belsky *et al.* (1991) predicted that early childhood stressors, such as emotional distance from the parents, would be associated with an early age of puberty and further autonomy from the parents in adolescence. Hence, childhood stressors and early onset of puberty could affect present relations between parents and their adolescent children. Such an outcome would be expected as an adaptive psychological, behavioural, and maturational response to scarcity or unpredictability of familial, social, and material resources in the local environment (such as father-absence, harsh or inconsistent parenting, limited or unstable family resources, etc.), which prepare children and adolescents for the environment they are most likely to encounter as adults.

Parent and adolescent relations have been of particular interest in the use of the FAST (e.g. Feldman and Gehring, 1988; Gehring and Feldman, 1988; Gehring *et al.*, 1990; Wentzel and Feldman, 1996). These studies have considered age-graded (early-, mid-, late-) adolescent groups in family relations. But from an evolutionary perspective, additional aspects of interest are puberty-linked (rather than age-graded) adolescent groups; differences between the sexes, both between and within generations, in family relations; and influence of intrafamilial sexual history in family relations. In particular, discernible patterns would be expected in the perceptions of family relations between same-sex parents and their adolescents and their mutual age of puberty and sexual history.

This study, on a small sample of British mothers and their early adolescent daughters, considers: (i) the relations between mothers' questionnaire self-reports of their age of puberty and sexual history and their daughters' self-reports of their quality of prepubertal childhood family life and age of puberty; and (ii) how these relate to their present cohesion and power representations with the FAST. It is expected that mothers' early onset of puberty and early/extensive sexual history would be associated with daughters' childhood distance to mothers, early onset of puberty, less cohesion to mothers, and less power differential with mothers. The report, then, extends the application of the FAST to include the developmental aspects of age of puberty and sexual life history, particularly in their influence from mothers to daughters.

## Method

### *Sample*

As a subsample of data designed to consider the antecedents predictive of puberty (Kim and Smith, 1998), this sample consists of eighteen biological mothers aged 33 to 52 (median = 44 years 0 months) and their nineteen pubertal (postmenarcheal) daughters aged 12 to 15 (median = 14 years 5 months; mean = 14 years 3 months, sd = 12.7 months). All but two families were Caucasian British. Fourteen had biological fathers, one had a stepfather, three were father-absent. All families were from middle-class backgrounds. Data were collected between April 1994 and June 1995, primarily from a single secondary school in a middle-class part of Sheffield. All mothers and daughters performed the FAST privately and completed their questionnaires under confidential conditions.

### *Measures*

Respondents were asked to portray their family with the FAST, using a standardized method (Gehring and Wyler, 1986). 'Cohesion' values were derived from distances between the mother–daughter pairs of figures. Figures placed on adjacent squares were scored as distance = 1, and (from Pythagoras' theorem) figures on diagonal squares were scored as distance = 1.4. The maximum possible distance between mother and daughter was 11.2. Cohesion values were determined from subtraction of distance values from 12 (i.e. 12 – distance), with increased values indicative of increased cohesion.

'Power' values were determined between the figures if elevated by a combination of 1.5 cm, 3.0 cm, and 4.5 cm blocks by comparison of their heights from mother minus daughter values, with positive values indicative of increased mother vs daughter power. Questionnaire data collected from mothers and daughters included: (i) developmental timing in years and months for their self-reported own age at menarche (first menstruation period); (ii) from mothers, their own age at first sexual intercourse and frequency of intercourse partners; and (iii) from daughters, their reported relations with their mothers and internalizing behavioural symptoms in childhood (age 7 to 11) in seven-point scales with '4' as the 'average' (midpoint) value:

'mother–self conflict' (1 = high conflict, 7 = low conflict)
'mother–self emotional distance' (1 = very distant, 7 = very close)
'anxiousness' (1 = anxious – worrying, 7 = not anxious – not worrying)
'depression' (1 = sad – depressed, 7 = happy – not depressed).

## Results

Mothers' own reported age of menarche ranged from 10 years 8 months to 16 years 6 months (median = 13 years 6 months; mean = 13 years 3 months, sd = 18.8

months). Daughters' own reported age of menarche ranged from 11 years 2 months to 13 years 11 months.

The mothers' pubertal and postpubertal measures were considered with their daughters' childhood and pubertal measures in simple ordinary least squares (OLS) multiple regressions to predict their present FAST 'cohesion' and 'power'. These measures were: mothers' age of menarche; age at first sexual intercourse (range: 13 years 6 months to 28 years 8 months; mean = 19 years 4 months, sd = 45.3 months); total frequency of intercourse partners (range: 1 to 15; mean = 3.5, sd = 3.4); and the daughters' four childhood measures and age of menarche. These results are shown in Table 10.1 (cohesion) and Table 10.2 (power).

There was one significant finding for mothers' representation of cohesion to their daughters (Table 10.1). Daughters' reported conflict with their mothers in childhood (age 7–11) was associated with less cohesion to them by their mothers. In addition, there was one significant finding for daughters' representation of cohesion to mothers (Table 10.1). Daughters' reported distance to their mothers in childhood (age 7–11) was associated with less cohesion to their mothers.

*Table 10.1* Summary of results for cohesion between mothers and daughters

| Independent | Dependent | Result |
| --- | --- | --- |
| OLS multiple regression[a] | | |
| mother's age at menarche | Mother's cohesion | ns. |
| mother's age at first sexual intercourse | Mother's cohesion | ns |
| mother's total sexual intercourse partners | Mother's cohesion | ns |
| daughter's conflict with mother age 7–11 | Mother's cohesion | $n = 19$; $F = 7.47$, beta = 0.60, $p < 0.05$ |
| daughter's distance from mother age 7–11 | Mother's cohesion | ns |
| daughter's anxiousness age 7–11 | Mother's cohesion | ns |
| daughter's depression age 7–11 | Mother's cohesion | ns |
| daughter's age at menarche | Mother's cohesion | ns |
| OLS multiple regression[b] | | |
| mother's age at menarche | Daughter's cohesion | ns |
| mother's age at first sexual intercourse | Daughter's cohesion | ns |
| mother's total sexual intercourse partners | Daughter's cohesion | ns |
| daughter's conflict with mother age 7–11 | Daughter's cohesion | ns |
| daughter's distance from mother age 7–11 | Daughter's cohesion | $n = 19$; $F = 10.96$, beta = 0.64, $p < 0.005$ |
| daughter's anxiousness age 7–11 | Daughter's cohesion | ns |
| daughter's depression age 7–11 | Daughter's cohesion | ns |
| daughter's age at menarche | Daughter's cohesion | ns |

[a] Mothers' cohesion score range: 9.80–11.00; median = 10.60; mean = 10.43, sd = 0.50; procedure: forward variable selection (child age and significant variables in first step model);
[b] daughters' cohesion score range: 7.00–11.00; median and mean = 10.00, sd = 1.06; procedure: forward variable selection (child age and significant variables in first step model).

*Table 10.2* Summary of results for power between mothers and daughters

| Independent | Dependent | Result |
|---|---|---|
| OLS multiple regression[a] | | |
| mother's age at menarche | Mother's power | $n = 19$; $F = 12.21$, beta $= 0.76$, $p = 0.005$ |
| mother's age at first sexual intercourse | Mother's power | ns |
| mother's total sexual intercourse partners | Mother's power | $n = 19$; $F = 8.57$, beta $= -1.12$, $p = 0.01$ |
| daughter's conflict with mother age 7–11 | Mother's power | $n = 19$; $F = 9.96$, beta $= 1.13$, $p < 0.01$ |
| daughter's distance from mother age 7–11 | Mother's power | $n = 19$; $F = 11.40$, beta $= -1.10$, $p < 0.01$ |
| daughter's anxiousness age 7–11 | Mother's power | ns |
| daughter's depression age 7–11 | Mother's power | $n = 19$; $F = 4.97$, beta $= 0.52$, $p < 0.05$ |
| daughter's age at menarche | Mother's power[1] | $n = 19$; $F = 14.96$, beta $= -1.76$, $p < 0.005$ |
| | | |
| OLS multiple regression[b] | | |
| mother's age at menarche | Daughter's power | $n = 19$; $F = 5.33$, beta $= 0.86$, $p < 0.05$ |
| mother's age at first sexual intercourse | Daughter's power | ns |
| mother's total sexual intercourse partners | Daughter's power[2] | $n = 19$; $F = 6.90$, beta $= -1.94$, $p < 0.05$ |
| daughter's conflict with mother age 7–11 | Daughter's power | $n = 19$; $F = 6.61$, beta $= 2.32$, $p < 0.05$ |
| daughter's distance from mother age 7–11 | Daughter's power | $n = 19$; $F = 5.21$, beta $= -1.31$, $p < 0.05$ |
| daughter's anxiousness age 7–11 | Daughter's power | ns |
| daughter's depression age 7–11 | Daughter's power | $n = 19$; $F = 5.58$, beta $= 0.91$, $p < 0.05$ |
| daughter's age at menarche | Daughter's power | $n = 19$; $F = 9.58$, beta $= 3.02$, $p = 0.01$ |

[a] Mothers' power score range: –3.00 to 3.00; median = 0.00; mean = 0.47, sd = 1.59; procedure: backward variable deletion (child age and significant variables in final step model);
[1] monotonic concave upward curve in reverse-coded menarche;
[b] daughters' power score range: 0.00–6.00; median = 3.00; mean = 2.29, sd = 1.69; procedure: backward variable deletion (child age and all variables in first step model);
[2] square root of mother's total intercourse partners.

A number of significant findings were obtained for the mother–daughter power differential, from both mothers and daughters (Table 10.2). Consistently for both mothers' and daughters' representations, less maternal power was associated with: mothers' reported earlier age of menarche and having had more intercourse partners; daughters' reported conflict with (and less distance to) their mothers; more depression in childhood (age 7–11); and earlier menarche.

# Discussion

These results show that mother–daughter cohesion and power differential are linked with (i) mothers' reported age of puberty and sexual history, and (ii) daughters' reported childhood relations with their mothers and age of puberty. These in turn suggest that mother and daughter relations during puberty are influenced, in part, by their relations in childhood prior to puberty or, alternatively, to maternal characteristics, such as age of puberty and personality characteristics, which affect mother and daughter relations and which are inherited by daughters.

In the results for cohesion (Table 10.1), mothers' lesser cohesion to their daughters could be indicative of the past conflictual relations reported by their daughters in childhood (age 7–11). Similarly, the daughters' lesser cohesion to their mothers could be indicative of prior emotional distance from their mothers in childhood (age 7–11). While mothers may have less cohesion to their daughters given their past experience, their daughters' similar less cohesion to their mothers could be an effect of childhood distance from their mother as a result of conflict with their mother in childhood (age 7–11).

In the results for power (Table 10.2), all findings were paralleled between mothers and their daughters. Mothers' reported early age of own menarche and their having had more sexual partners were consistently associated with reduced power relative to their daughters. Conceivably, mothers who had early menarche could have told of their early onset to their daughters. If these mothers demonstrated less assurance of their power to their daughters, their daughters could have recognized this and, hence, also indicate less maternal power. But it is unlikely that they would have been aware of their mothers' past sexual history. Nonetheless, when mothers reported having had more past sexual partners, both they and their daughters represented less maternal power. It could be that these mothers tended to perceive themselves as having less power over their daughters and, as a consequence, these daughters opportunistically asserted their own power over their mothers.

Less maternal power was consistently associated with daughters' reported conflict with their mothers in childhood (age 7–11). This pattern indicates that mother and daughter conflict is associated with a subsequent increase in daughters' power at puberty, at the expense of their mother. Given that any childhood conflict between mother and daughter represents a challenge to the mother's authority, the consequence may be an assertion of daughters' power in early adolescence.

Less maternal power was consistently associated with daughters' reporting less distance to their mothers in childhood (age 7–11). These results were unexpected as, according to Belsky *et al.* (1991), less maternal power should have been associated with more childhood distance to mothers (given that more childhood distance should result in more autonomy from mothers' authority or power). But this situation could conceivably represent a maladaptive type of attachment, e.g. 'enmeshment' (Gehring *et al.*, 1990), which may involve a reversal of roles in which mothers' loss of power is compensated by their daughters' 'maternal' role.

Less maternal power was consistently associated with daughters' report of depression in childhood (age 7–11). When daughters have depressive symptoms in childhood, it could be that they subsequently perceive less maternal power, while their mothers similarly perceive less power in their inability to have helped their daughters. But, given the pattern of findings, depression could be the result of a prior enmeshment with mothers; for example: (i) conflict with mothers could result in loss of maternal power; (ii) this could result in a reversal of roles; (iii) this could result in depression in daughters as they attempt to deal with the burden of a maternal role upon weakened mothers.

Less maternal power was consistently associated with daughters' reports of their early menarche. Given that mothers who themselves had early menarche felt less power over their daughters, it seems consistent that these early-matured daughters felt more power over their mothers. That is, between generations, early-matured daughters at puberty gain power at the expense of their early-matured mothers, but will subsequently lose power to their own early-matured daughters. It could be that these mothers' own adolescent experience of increased power relative to their mothers, who themselves transmitted early menarche to them, prepared them to anticipate their early-matured daughters' present assertiveness. Consistent with this interpretation, in the larger sample (Kim and Smith, 1998) from which this FAST sample is derived, mothers' early age of menarche correlated with their daughters' early age of menarche (having controlled for dual biological parentage, offspring size, and socioeconomic background). For Belsky *et al.* (1991), such a developmental outcome in adolescence and adulthood could be due to stress-dependent effects of the early childhood family environment. Hence, girls from stressful and conflictual homes could be less attached to their parents in childhood, develop internalizing symptoms (e.g. depression), have early onset of puberty, and show early autonomy (e.g. less cohesion)[2] from their parents leading toward early and extensive sexual history like that of their mothers.

Some limitations of these findings need to be considered, including:

- Socially desirable responses, particularly by mothers who represented more cohesion and less maternal power than did their daughters (e.g. mothers' median power score was 0.00 with their daughters), which suggest that they presented their families in idealized terms; further, while these adolescents' cohesion scores are comparable to those of previous reports with adolescents (Feldman and Gehring, 1988; Gehring and Feldman, 1988), their power scores accorded much more parental power.
- Childhood measures indexed by single, rather than multiple, measures.
- Small sample size.
- Limitations of cross-sectional retrospective self-report data.

Future work with the FAST, in both normal and clinical contexts, could be extended to non-Western settings (see Chapters 12 and 13) to consider the generalizability of findings across diverse cultural, social, and family environments.[3]

# Notes

1   This research was completed at the Department of Psychology, University of Sheffield, Sheffield, UK. Preliminary results were presented in poster symposium 'The Family Systems Test (FAST): varied uses for developmental psychology' at the British Psychological Society Developmental Section Conference, 11–13 September, 1996, Oxford, UK.

2   In the sample, in pair-matched representations of cohesion between mothers and their own daughters, when daughters' age of puberty was divided into an early (below median) menarche group vs late menarche group: (i) less cohesion to mothers (mean = 9.85, sd = 1.03) than mothers to daughters (mean = 10.64, sd = 0.45) was represented by the early menarche group ($n = 11$ pairs; $t (10) = -2.20$; $p = 0.05$); but (ii) cohesion did not differ between mothers and daughters in the late menarche group.

3   The authors are currently considering the association between family violence and the FAST in a survey sample of adolescents aged 14 to 19 from rural north Thailand. Preliminary results indicate that, as with Western FAST data, the girls typically represented more cohesion to their mothers than to their fathers. However, the boys also represented more cohesion to their mothers than to their fathers. These parallel the traditional pattern in Japan, where children of both sexes are closer to their mothers than to their fathers. Also relatively common is the incidence of parent-to-adolescent violence. Nonetheless, the FAST representations indicate a paradoxically close cohesion to parents, again suggestive of 'enmeshment' in family members. Given the emphasis placed on filial piety in East Asian societies, it could be that these adolescents do not have the same negativity towards such parents. Rather, their parents could be perceived as legitimated in their use of physical or corporal punishment from the point of view of the adolescents. But, consistent with Western data, there do seem to be certain familiar patterns in perceptions of family relations, such as general closeness within first-degree biological family members with less closeness to distant biological and non-biological relatives, which suggest some evidence of a persistent human nature in the family system, however transformed by society.

# References

Belsky, J., Steinberg, L. and Draper, P. (1991) 'Childhood experience, interpersonal development, and reproductive strategy: An evolutionary theory of socialization', *Child Development* 62: 647–70.

Draper, P. and Belsky, J. (1990) 'Personality development in evolutionary perspective', *Journal of Personality* 58: 141–61.

Feldman, S.S. and Gehring, T.M. (1988) 'Changing perceptions of family cohesion and power across adolescence', *Child Development* 59: 1034–45.

Gehring, T.M. and Feldman, S.S. (1988) 'Adolescents' perceptions of family cohesion and power: A methodological study of the Family System Test', *Journal of Adolescent Research* 3: 33–52.

—— and Wyler, I.L. (1986) 'Family System Test (FAST): A three dimensional approach to investigate family relationships', *Child Psychiatry and Human Development* 16: 235–48.

—— Wentzel, K.R., Feldman, S.S. and Munson, J. (1990) 'Conflict in families of adolescents: The impact on cohesion and power structures', *Journal of Family Psychology* 3: 290–309.

Kim, K. and Smith, P.K. (1998) 'Childhood stress, behavioural symptoms, and mother-daughter pubertal development', *Journal of Adolescence* 21: 231–40.

Wentzel, K.R. and Feldman, S.S. (1996) 'Relations of cohesion and power in family dyads to social and emotional adjustment during early adolescence', *Journal of Research on Adolescence* 6: 225–44.

# 11 Cohesion and relative power in family relationships and adolescent coping with a real-life stressful situation

*Ofra Mayseless and Miri Scharf*

## Introduction

The family arena in general, and relationships with parents in particular, have traditionally been regarded as a central context of development for adolescents, affecting their personality, academic achievements, and coping and adaptation (Bronfenbrenner, 1979). Specifically, close and warm relationships with parents and moderately demanding and supervising parenting were found to be associated with positive outcomes, including aspects such as self-esteem, social competence, and coping and adjustment to stressful events (see Steinberg, 1990, for a review). The overwhelming majority of the studies on parent–adolescent relationships employed self-report questionnaires, which assessed dyadic relationships in isolation (e.g. father–adolescent relationships), and were mostly administered only to the adolescent. In other cases a more general approach, looking at the family rather than at dyadic relationships in isolation, was adopted, by measurement of parenting styles (e.g. Dornbusch *et al.*, 1987; Baumrind, 1989, 1991; Steinberg *et al.*, 1989), or assessing the general atmosphere of the family (Moos, 1984). Other studies observed the family from a systems theory angle, measuring general aspects such as cohesion and adaptability of the family as a whole (e.g. Noller and Callan, 1986; Olson, 1986).

This chapter adopts a family systems viewpoint to examine the association between various family constellations and adolescent adjustment, focusing on males only. According to the family systems theory (Minuchin, 1985), the family is a dynamic organizational unit consisting of interdependent members. The structure of families can be described at different levels. In addition to the whole family system, appropriate levels of study include also dyads, such as the mother–adolescent, the father–adolescent, or the parent subsystem. By this approach, a crucial boundary exists between the generations, such that the parental dyad and the children form two separate systems. Two dimensions are usually used to describe the structure of the family: cohesion or emotional closeness between members (Boszormenyi-Nagy and Spark, 1973; Minuchin, 1974), and relative power (Minuchin, 1974). In well-functioning families, parents are recognized as having more power than their offspring, although not too much more, and the family in general is presented as cohesive, with the father–mother dyad more cohesive than the parent–adolescent dyad (Wood and Talmon, 1983; Feldman *et al.*, 1989; Gehring *et al.*, 1994).

To apply a family systems perspective, a measure is needed that can simultaneously assess dyads and the family as a whole, rather than evaluating dyadic relationships independent of the family context. This chapter reports a study that applied such an approach to measuring parent–adolescent relationships and family constellations. The Family System Test (FAST) is a clinically derived figure placement technique whereby participants symbolically portray family cohesion and power by arranging figures denoting family members on a board. Unlike questionnaires, this figure placement technique enables participants simultaneously to represent the family as a whole, as well as its dyads, and is less sensitive to self-report biases.

In addition, we extended previous research by obtaining three perspectives on the family: the adolescent's, the father's, and the mother's. Previous research indicated that each family member may have a different perception of the family, and that these perspectives are moderately unrelated, so a more complete delineation of the family may be achieved by including all perspectives (Feldman *et al.*, 1989; Gehring *et al.*, 1994). Further, studies have shown that a person's subjective perception may be a better predictor of that person's adjustment than reports by other family members, or even than reports of objective observers of the family relationships (Harold and Conger, 1997). This finding was explained by referring to the importance of subjective experience as a lens through which 'objective' events affect the individual. In this chapter, then, the association between the perceptions of the different family members is explored, as well as their differential predictions of the adolescent coping success.

Prior research with the FAST focused mainly on the relationships between perceptions of cohesion and power in the family, and other aspects of family life. Examples are the association between types of family structures and clinical status (Gehring and Marti, 1993a), or changes in family relationships across adolescence (Feldman and Gehring, 1988). In addition, several studies employed the FAST to observe and understand differences between perspectives of members in the family (Feldman *et al.*, 1989). Other work (Bowers *et al.*, 1992; Berdondini and Smith, 1996) went beyond the family arena to observe the association between family structure and the peer group, specifically bully/victim problems.

In our study, we sought to extend research beyond the interpersonal arena and to examine instrumental and functional coping in general. As well as assessing general adjustment of the adolescent (e.g. self-esteem and wellbeing), we examined coping and adjustment of adolescents with a real-life stressful situation. Specifically, we investigated young Israeli males' coping with and adjustment to basic training in mandatory military service, which constitutes the home-leaving transition for most adolescents in Israel.

## *Leaving home transition as a stressful yet normative transition*

A major normative component of the transition from adolescence to adulthood includes physical separation from one's parents to live away from home (Moore, 1987). This move usually involves only semiautonomous living arrangements, namely experiences of non-household living arrangements without all the ensuing responsibilities of an independent household (Goldscheider and Davanzo, 1986). In most Western cultures this physical separation includes a transition from high school to college, although other transitions have also been noted, such as a transition into the workplace or into compulsory military service (i.e. Germany, Switzerland, Sweden).

Research on the transition to college highlighted the importance of close and autonomous parent–adolescent relationships in fostering better adaptation and better functioning in college (e.g. Aseltine and Gore, 1993; Larose and Boivin, 1998). Several studies found that continuing parental support helps in the adjustment to college. For example, Holahan *et al.* (1994) found that initial parental support was associated with psychological adjustment 2 years later both directly and indirectly, through the young adults' sociable disposition. Larose and Boivin (1998) found perceived security with parents (especially the mother) at the end of high school to predict socioemotional adjustment across the transition. Thus relationships with parents prior to separation were found to influence adjustment and coping with a new environment.

Additionally, more general measures of family functioning, such as parenting styles, were found to predict adjustment to college (Weiss and Schwartz, 1996). For example, Strage (1998) found authoritative (demanding and responsive) parenting to predict positive adjustment to college. Adopting both an attachment and a family systems perspective, Kenny and Donaldson (1991) found emotional support from parents, and the lack of parental marital conflict, to foster social competence and lower levels of psychological symptoms among women. The study reported here expanded these results by observing leaving home for a quite stressful environment (military service). Such an environment places harsher demands on the youngster and, as such, qualifies as a stringent test of the expected association between a positive and well-functioning family system and adjustment. In particular, the question of the universal goodness of the cohesive and moderately hierarchical family structure is raised. Namely, in the rigid and structured environment of the military, adolescents from other family structures (e.g. more authoritarian ones) may be better off and may cope better.

### *Home-leaving transition in Israel*

In Israel, the great majority of the 18-year-old cohort of men (90%) leave their parents' home for a period of 3 years' mandatory service in the Israel Defence Forces. Despite some recent developments, military service, though mandatory, is highly desired and appreciated because this service is regarded as necessary to preserve Israel's independence (Lieblich, 1989; Mayseless, 1993). The timing of leave-taking from one's parents is greatly dependent on one's age (by Israeli law, 18-year-olds are conscripted) and is not affected by one's psychological readiness or the relationship with one's parents.

The army is a highly demanding, rigid, and authoritarian ecology where the young recruits, especially during the basic training period, are constantly required to obey orders and are under the very tight control of their commanders (Gal, 1986). Further, in entering military service the young recruits are required to make major changes in their life during a relatively short period of time. As they enter military service they are stripped of part of their personal identity; they have to wear uniforms, cut their hair, and perform duties even if these conflict with their personal desires. These young recruits are further exposed to considerable physical and psychological demands, such as difficult physical exercises and relatively short periods of sleep that push them to the limit of their capacities. The basic training period usually lasts 4–12 weeks, and is generally considered the most stressful period during military service by mental health authorities in the Israel Defence Forces (Gal, 1986), although it does present the young recruits, especially in combat units, with new challenges enabling them to 'test' their 'manhood' and succeed (Lieblich, 1989). Thus, although the military environment is a difficult one, it is by no means overwhelming or devastating. In fact, almost all young recruits successfully complete the basic training, adjust and cope well with its hardships, and find these experiences valuable (Mayseless, 1995).

Prior research found that close relationships with parents predicted better coping with this stressful situation (Mayseless and Hai, 1998). However, that study (Mayseless and Hai, 1998) employed only one perspective (that of the adolescent) to measure parent–adolescent relationships, and adopted a dyadic (mother–adolescent, father–adolescent) rather than a family systems approach. The major objective of the present study was to observe how perceptions of cohesion and power in the family (from the perspectives of father, mother, and adolescent) are related to general adjustment of young men in Israel, and to their coping with the hardships of basic training.

Finally, an attempt to explore a typology of familial structure in terms of cohesion and power was made, to highlight which family structure seems most conducive to better coping (in this context). Prior research suggested that a balanced, well-functioning family structure involves cohesive and moderately hierarchical structures (Gehring *et al.*, 1994). In the study reported here a cluster analytic technique was employed to derive different family structures and to observe their association with positive adolescent coping and adaptation.

## Method

### Sample and procedure

The study reported here is part of a larger longitudinal project, which examined adolescents and the parents in Israel during late adolescence and young adulthood. Eighty-five male adolescents from intact middle-class families were interviewed using the FAST approximately 1 year before the sons' conscription. The adolescents also completed questionnaires regarding their self-esteem, emotional regulation, interpersonal competence, and intimacy in close friendship. Half-way through the basic training period (approximately 5 weeks after conscription) the adolescents rated their coping and adaptation. In addition, for a subsample of adolescents ($n = 64$), two friends from their basic training unit rated their coping and adaptation. There was no difference on any of the background variables or the measures used in this study between the subsample whose friends rated their coping and the subsample for whom friends' reports were not available. Mothers were approximately 46 years old, fathers 48 years old and adolescents 17 years old at the first time of assessment. Parents had been married on average for 23 years (sd = 3.42). The number of children in these families varied between one and five, with a mean of 2.93. About one-third of the adolescents (37%) were first-born, 43% were second-born and the rest third and fourth. None of these background variables was associated with the variables assessed in this study.

## *Measures*

### *Family System Test*

Participants (fathers, mothers, and sons, separately) were asked to place figures representing father, mother and son on a $9 \times 9$-square board in a way that represented how close family members felt towards each other. Cohesion was measured by the distances between the figures on the board, where distance on adjacent squares was scored 10 and on diagonally adjacent squares 14. Next they were asked to place any number of blocks under each figure in order to represent the power of each member in the family. Power gaps were computed by subtracting the number of blocks under each family member from the number of blocks under the other family members.

### *Indicators of general adjustment*

These were completed by the adolescent.

#### ME AND MY BEST FRIEND (SHULMAN *et al.*, 1997)

This questionnaire consists of five intimacy subscales with eight items in each. In this project we used the emotional closeness scale, which included shared affect, availability, and instrumental assistance (Cronbach $\alpha = 0.85$)

#### WEINBERGER ADJUSTMENT INVENTORY (WAI; Weinberger, 1991)

The original questionnaire includes five scales, which measure several aspects of adjustment. Three scales were included in the present study: (i) self-esteem (seven items; Cronbach $\alpha = 0.72$); (ii) aggression (e.g. 'I lose my temper and let people have it when I'm angry', seven items; Cronbach $\alpha = 0.79$); and (iii) wellbeing (seven items; Cronbach $\alpha = 0.86$).

ADOLESCENT INTERPERSONAL COMPETENCE QUESTIONNAIRE
(AICQ; BUHRMESTER *et al.*, 1988)

This is a self-report questionnaire assessing important dimensions in close relationships. In the present study, one scale was included: management of inter-personal conflicts, namely the ability to know how to disagree without becoming involved in major disputes (eight items, Cronbach $\alpha = 0.75$).

## Indicators of adjustment to basic training

COGNITIVE APPRAISAL (FOLKMAN AND LAZARUS, 1985)

This is a self-report questionnaire tapping subjects' appraisal of the threats and challenges implied by the military training and their ability to cope with it. The measure includes three scales: (i) perception of challenge (three items; Cronbach $\alpha = 0.75$); (ii) perception of threat (two items; Cronbach $\alpha = 0.68$); and evaluation regarding coping effectiveness (two items; Cronbach $\alpha = 0.63$).

MENTAL HEALTH INVENTORY (MHI; VEIT AND WARE, 1983)

Level of distress during the basic training period was measured by means of nine items from the MHI questionnaire (Cronbach $\alpha = 0.76$).

WAYS OF COPING (FOLKMAN AND LAZARUS, 1980)

This measures cognitive and behavioural strategies people use in coping with stressful situations. It includes four dimensions: (i) problem-solving focused coping (seven items; Cronbach $\alpha = 0.53$); (ii) emotion-focused coping, which includes self-blaming, wishes, and self-isolation (eight items; Cronbach $\alpha = 0.75$); (iii) coping through help seeking, which includes looking for emotional and practical help (six items; Cronbach $\alpha = 0.76$); and (iv) coping through denial (five items; Cronbach $\alpha = 0.59$).

FRIENDS' EVALUATION QUESTIONNAIRE

This includes three items that tap the evaluations by friends of the new recruit regarding his coping with basic training demands in general and, more specifically, in the social and instrumental areas.

## Results

### Association between perceptions of family members

Paired *t*-tests comparing different respondents' points of view with regard to the various relationships were conducted. As can be seen in Figure 11.1, sons perceived all relationships as more distant than fathers and mothers did. Fathers perceived

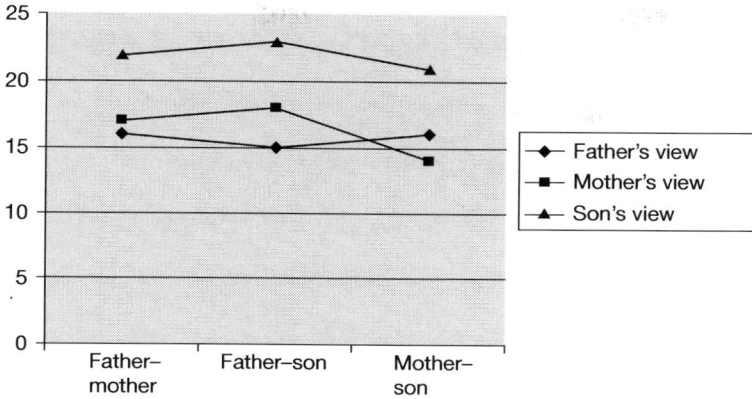

*Figure 11.1* Distances between figures on the FAST as a function of perspective.
The vertical axis refers to distance between figures measured in number of
squares, where distance on adjacent squares was scored 10 and distance on
diagonally adjacent squares 14.

themselves to be closer to their sons than sons and mothers did. Lastly, sons and
mothers perceived the mother–son relationship as closer than the father–son
relationship (all comparisons $p < 0.05$).

Similarly, we examined family members' perceptions regarding the power gaps
between themselves. As can be seen in Figure 11.2, all family members perceived
the power gap between parents as narrower than the power gap between each of the
parents and their adolescent son (all comparisons $p < 0.05$).

### Perceptions of power and cohesion and general adjustment

The associations between perceptions of cohesion and relative power (by fathers,
mothers, and sons) and the general indicators of adjustment were explored by means

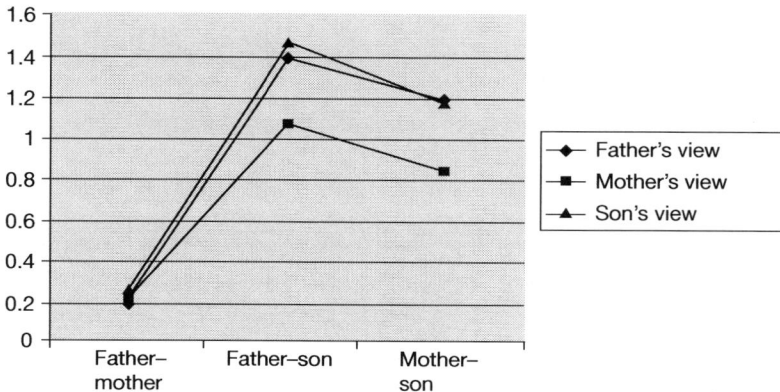

*Figure 11.2* Relative power on the FAST as a function of different perspectives.

Table 11.1 Pearson correlations between portrayals of distances on the FAST and indices of general adjustment

| | Son's point of view | | | Father's point of view | | | Mother's point of view | | |
|---|---|---|---|---|---|---|---|---|---|
| | M–S | F–S | M–F | M–S | F–S | M–F | M–S | F–S | M–F |
| Self-esteem | −0.25* | −0.27** | −0.29** | −0.12 | −0.10 | 0.06 | −0.13 | −0.14 | −0.10 |
| Wellbeing | −0.24* | −0.24* | −0.37*** | −0.25* | −0.25* | −0.16 | −0.07 | −0.11 | −0.05 |
| Aggression | 0.15 | 0.24* | 0.28** | −0.13 | 0.01 | 0.10 | 0.17 | 0.28** | −0.003 |
| Emotional closeness | −0.22* | −0.22* | −0.30** | −0.26* | −0.20 | −0.13 | −0.15 | −0.15 | 0.05 |
| Conflict management | −0.15 | −0.22* | −0.34*** | 0.14 | 0.05 | 0.15 | 0.04 | −0.30** | 0.03 |

F–S, distance between father and son; M–F, distance between mother and father; M–S, distance between mother and son.
*$p < 0.05$; **$p < 0.01$; ***$p < 0.001$.

of Pearson correlations (Table 11.1). In our study we employed the term 'cohesion', but note that the correlations were computed with distance scores. From the son's perspective, cohesion in each of the three dyads (father–son, mother–son, and mother–father) was related to higher self-esteem, better wellbeing, and greater emotional closeness to the adolescent's best friend. Cohesion in the mother–father and the father–son dyads (from the son's perspective) was also associated with less aggressiveness and better conflict management capacity. From the father's perspective, cohesion in the mother–son dyad was associated with better wellbeing and more emotional closeness between the adolescent and his best friend. Cohesion in the father–son dyad was only associated with better wellbeing. From the mother's perspective only perceived cohesion in the father–son dyad proved significant, and was associated with less aggression and better conflict management.

As can be seen in Table 11.2, when relative power was examined, fewer associations with the general indicators of adjustment were apparent. Specifically, from the son's perspective, larger power gaps in the father–son and mother–father dyads were associated with less aggression. From the mother's point of view, a larger power gap between father and son was associated with better wellbeing.

### Perceptions of cohesion and power and adjustment to basic training

The following findings were noted for adjustment to the basic training period. As can be seen in Table 11.3, from the adolescent's perspective, more cohesive father–son or mother–son relationships were associated with problem-focused coping, with less emotion-focused coping and with higher perceived effectiveness of the coping efforts. In addition, cohesion in the father–son dyad was associated with better social adjustment as evaluated by the adolescent's friends. Cohesion in the mother–father dyad, as perceived by the adolescent, was also related to his coping. Specifically, closer relationships between the parents were associated with less distress, a lower tendency to perceive the basic training period as a threat, less emotion-focused coping and higher perceived effectiveness of coping. From the father's perspective his perception of cohesion in the parental dyad was associated with better instrumental functioning of his son in basic training as evaluated by the son's friends. From the mother's perspective, cohesion in the mother–son dyad was associated with less distress, less tendency to perceive the basic training period as a threat and a higher perceived effectiveness of coping. Cohesion in the mother–son dyads (as portrayed by the mother) was also associated with the evaluations of his friends. Specifically, more cohesion was associated with better instrumental functioning and with better social adjustment. Finally, cohesion in the father–son dyad (as portrayed by the mother) was associated with less emotion-focused coping and with better instrumental functioning as evaluated by the son's friends.

In addition, discrepancies (gaps) in perceptions of cohesion between parents and sons were also related to lower levels of coping. Specifically, parent–son discrepancy regarding the cohesion in their dyadic relationships correlated with higher perception of threat ($r = 0.23$, $p < 0.05$, with the father–son gap), less use of problem-solving strategies ($r = -0.20$, $p < 0.07$ with the mother–son gap; and

Table 11.2 Correlations between FAST power gap perceptions of sons, fathers and mothers, and indices of general adjustment

|  | Son's point of view | | | Father's point of view | | | Mother's point of view | | |
| --- | --- | --- | --- | --- | --- | --- | --- | --- | --- |
|  | M–S | F–S | M–F | M–S | F–S | M–F | M–S | F–S | M–F |
| Self-esteem | −0.05 | −0.04 | 0.002 | 0.11 | 0.04 | −0.05 | 0.12 | 0.19 | 0.10 |
| Wellbeing | −0.15 | −0.09 | 0.06 | 0.07 | 0.15 | 0.08 | 0.03 | 0.22* | 0.20 |
| Aggression | −0.08 | −0.28** | −0.24* | −0.02 | 0.003 | 0.02 | −0.16 | −0.08 | 0.04 |
| Emotional closeness | −0.01 | 0.09 | 0.11 | 0.06 | −0.11 | −0.16 | 0.12 | −0.08 | −0.18 |
| Conflict management | −0.06 | 0.05 | 0.12 | −0.03 | 0.02 | 0.05 | 0.07 | 0.09 | 0.04 |

F–S, gap between father's and son's power perception; M–F, gap between mother's and father's power perception; M–S, gap between mother's and son's power perception.
*p < 0.05; **p < 0.01.

Table 11.3 Pearson correlations between portrayals of distances on the FAST and adjustment to basic training

|  | Son's point of view | | | Father's point of view | | | Mother's point of view | | |
|---|---|---|---|---|---|---|---|---|---|
|  | M–S | F–S | M–F | M–S | F–S | M–F | M–S | F–S | M–F |
| Primary appraisal of the situation | | | | | | | | | |
| challenge | 0.03 | 0.002 | 0.01 | 0.03 | 0.14 | 0.02 | 0.07 | 0.13 | 0.09 |
| threat | 0.09 | 0.18 | 0.22* | -0.05 | -0.15 | -0.16 | 0.31** | 0.22 | 0.01 |
| distress | 0.15 | 0.18 | 0.30** | -0.01 | -0.05 | -0.12 | 0.23* | 0.20 | 0.12 |
| Ways of coping | | | | | | | | | |
| problem solving | -0.24* | -0.31** | -0.21 | -0.10 | 0.05 | -0.15 | -0.13 | -0.07 | -0.12 |
| emotion-focused | 0.25* | 0.26* | 0.36*** | 0.07 | 0.02 | -0.05 | 0.10 | 0.31** | 0.14 |
| denial | 0.09 | 0.01 | 0.05 | 0.11 | 0.07 | -0.07 | 0.01 | -0.04 | 0.01 |
| support-seeking | 0.01 | -0.05 | -0.002 | -0.07 | -0.06 | -0.04 | -0.10 | -0.003 | -0.04 |
| Evaluation of coping effectiveness | -0.23* | -0.23* | -0.33* | -0.15 | -0.01 | -0.06 | -0.30** | -0.21 | -0.07 |
| Friends' report | | | | | | | | | |
| General coping | 0.03 | -0.10 | -0.17 | 0.07 | 0.12 | 0.03 | -0.23 | -0.16 | -0.17 |
| Instrumental | -0.12 | -0.24 | -0.12 | -0.16 | -0.10 | -0.30* | -0.28* | -0.32* | -0.22 |
| Social | -0.14 | -0.26* | -0.21 | 0.19 | 0.07 | -0.08 | -0.31* | -0.25 | -0.12 |

F–S, distance between father and son M–F; distance between mother and father; M–S, distance between mother and son.
*p < 0.05; **p < 0.01; ***p < 0.001.

$r = -0.30$, $p < 0.01$ with the father–son gap), more use of emotion-focused coping ($r = 0.28$, $p < 0.06$ with the mother–son gap; and $r = 0.24$, $p < 0.05$ with the father–son gap), and lower level of social functioning according to the friends' report ($r = -0.30$, $p < 0.05$ with the father–son gap).

Very few associations were found between perceptions of relative power and adjustment to the basic training period. The few significant associations were all based on the father's perspective. Specifically, larger power gaps between mother and son were associated with perception of the situation as challenging ($r = 0.25$, $p < 0.05$), and less coping through denial ($r = -0.24$, $p < 0.05$). However, a larger power gap between father and mother (father more powerful than mother) was associated with lower perception of challenge ($r = -0.24$, $p < 0.05$).

## Examination of family configurations using cluster analyses

Two typologies of family structure were explored by cluster analyses: one based on the perceptions of the whole family, the other based on the perceptions of the adolescent alone. Using the SPSS program several clustering solutions were attempted. In both cases a three-cluster solution was adopted, out of considerations of minimum number of subjects per cluster (at least seven), the theoretical inter-pretability of the clusters, and a drop in the amalgamation index (see Aldenderfer and Blashfield, 1984, for a discussion of criteria for selecting the appropriate number of clusters). The association between these family typologies and coping with basic training was examined using a series of one-way ANOVAs. Table 11.4 shows the typology that emerged by use of perceptions of cohesion and power from the three points of view (father, mother, and son).

As can be seen in Table 11.4, cluster 1 reflects a lack of fit between parents' and son's perceptions. Parents perceived the relationships as close, while the adolescent perceived them as more distant. With regard to power, the parents perceived a rather large gap between themselves and the child, while the son perceived this gap as more moderate. Cluster 2 represents lack of fit between mother's perception on the one hand, and father's and son's perceptions on the other. In these families, mothers perceived the family as close and fathers and sons portrayed a less cohesive family. Mothers', fathers', and sons' perceptions of power were also different: mothers perceived themselves as more powerful in the family than the husbands and sons perceived them. Lastly, cluster 3 reflects correspondence in family members' perceptions. Family members similarly perceived high cohesion between all dyads, and a small power gap between each parent and the adolescent. Additionally, mother and father were similar in their power according to all family members' perceptions. Thus, this cluster represents correspondence in family members' perceptions with regard to closeness as well as to power.

As can be seen in Table 11.5, cluster 3 was related to better coping, especially compared with cluster 1. Specifically, adolescents from these families perceived less cognitive threat, tended to use more problem-solving strategies, and evaluated their coping effectiveness as higher. There were no associations between these clusters and the friends' report.

*Table 11.4* Final cluster centres based on perceptions of cohesion and power by all
family members

|  | Cluster 1 (n = 21) | Cluster 2 (n = 7) | Cluster 3 (n = 49) |
|---|---|---|---|
| **Cohesion** | | | |
| mother's point of view | | | |
| mother–child distance | 18 | 15 | 12 |
| father–child distance | 24 | 13 | 15 |
| father–mother distance | 17 | 14 | 14 |
| father's point of view | | | |
| mother–child distance | 14 | 32 | 13 |
| father–child distance | 15 | 25 | 13 |
| father–mother distance | 15 | 26 | 13 |
| child's point of view | | | |
| mother–child distance | 32 | 23 | 17 |
| father–child distance | 41 | 26 | 19 |
| father–mother distance | 35 | 23 | 17 |
| **Power** | | | |
| mother's point of view | | | |
| mother–child power gap | 0.95 | 1.22 | 0.79 |
| father–child power gap | 1.29 | 0.78 | 1.04 |
| father–mother power gap | 0.33 | −0.44 | 0.25 |
| father's point of view | | | |
| mother–child power gap | 1.24 | 0.67 | 1.08 |
| father–child power gap | 1.95 | 1.89 | 1.15 |
| father–mother power gap | 0.71 | 1.22 | 0.08 |
| child's point of view | | | |
| mother–child power gap | 0.62 | 0.89 | 1.37 |
| father–child power gap | 0.90 | 1.78 | 1.48 |
| father–mother power gap | 0.29 | 0.89 | 0.12 |

Table 11.6 presents the cluster centres when only perceptions of the adolescent regarding cohesion and power were employed. Cluster 1 represents triangulated families, where cohesion in the mother–son relationships is higher than in the mother–father relationships, and there are small power gaps between each parent and the child. Cluster 2 represents good-enough families, with moderate closeness between parents and son (similar in extent to the cohesion of the families in the first cluster), and high cohesion between parents. In these families the mother–son power gap is higher than the father–son and the father–mother gaps. Lastly, cluster 3 represents balanced families, with high cohesion between all family members, a moderate power gap between each parent and the son, and a small power gap between father and mother.

Table 11.7 shows that the cluster of family structure associated with the least successful coping was the triangulated cluster where cohesion in the mother–son relationships was higher than in the mother–father relationships. Adolescents from these families experienced more cognitive threat and more distress; they used fewer problem-solving strategies, and their coping effectiveness was the worst.

*Table 11.5* Adjustment to basic training of adolescents from various family structures (clusters based on the perspectives of all family members)

| | Cluster 1 (n = 21) | | Cluster 2 (n = 7) | | Cluster 3 (n = 49) | | | Duncan post-hoc tests[a] |
|---|---|---|---|---|---|---|---|---|
| | Mean | sd | Mean | sd | Mean | sd | F | |
| **Primary appraisal of the situation** | | | | | | | | |
| challenge | 3.50 | 0.86 | 3.71 | 0.71 | 3.39 | 0.87 | 0.50 | |
| threat | 2.69 | 0.72 | 2.32 | 0.45 | 2.22 | 0.70 | 3.33* | 1>3 |
| distress | 2.32 | 0.61 | 2.18 | 0.69 | 2.23 | 0.57 | 0.22 | |
| **Ways of coping** | | | | | | | | |
| problem solving | 2.98 | 0.36 | 3.05 | 0.35 | 3.20 | 0.36 | 2.83+ | 1<3 |
| emotional coping | 2.01 | 0.57 | 1.78 | 0.37 | 1.91 | 0.59 | 0.47 | |
| denial | 2.26 | 0.37 | 2.24 | 0.52 | 2.32 | 0.53 | 0.16 | |
| support seeking | 2.52 | 0.70 | 2.34 | 0.46 | 2.67 | 0.61 | 1.06 | |
| **Evaluation of coping** | | | | | | | | |
| effectiveness | 3.95 | 0.61 | 3.86 | 0.38 | 4.34 | 0.51 | 5.31** | 1,2<3 |

[a] Duncan post-hoc tests ($p<0.05$) were conducted when the ANOVA was significant: 1 refers to Cluster 1, 2 to Cluster 2, and 3 to Cluster 3.
*$p < 0.05$; **$p < 0.01$; +$p < 0.10$.

*Table 11.6* Cluster centres based on perceptions of cohesion and power by the adolescent

| | Cluster 1 (n = 16) | Cluster 2 (n = 18) | Cluster 3 (n = 48) |
|---|---|---|---|
| Mother–child distance | 27 | 32 | 15 |
| Father–child distance | 36 | 34 | 16 |
| Father–mother distance | 42 | 17 | 17 |
| Mother–child power gap | 0.83 | 1.79 | 1.46 |
| Father–child power gap | 0.83 | 0.84 | 1.34 |
| Father–mother power gap | 0.00 | 0.95 | 0.13 |

Furthermore, their social functioning (as perceived by their friends) was the lowest (means 3.77, 4.50, and 4.22, respectively, $F(2,54) = 3.14$, $p = 0.05$). Note that in the two clustering solutions that we employed, the larger clusters generally included well-functioning families, while the smaller clusters included less well-adjusted families. This probably reflects the nature of our non-clinical sample, which comprised middle-class, intact families.

*Table 11.7* Adjustment to basic training of adolescents from various family structures (based on clusters derived from the adolescent's perspective)

| | Cluster 1 (n =16) | | Cluster 2 (n = 18) | | Cluster 3 (n = 48) | | | Duncan post-hoc tests[a] |
|---|---|---|---|---|---|---|---|---|
| | Mean | sd | Mean | sd | Mean | sd | F | |
| Primary appraisal of the situation | | | | | | | | |
| cognitive challenge | 3.51 | 1.03 | 3.28 | 0.78 | 3.60 | 0.83 | 0.92 | |
| cognitive threat | 2.78 | 0.79 | 2.23 | 0.57 | 2.30 | 0.67 | 3.61* | 1>2,3 |
| distress | 2.60 | 0.61 | 2.15 | 0.50 | 2.15 | 0.58 | 3.94* | 1>2,3 |
| Ways of coping | | | | | | | | |
| problem solving | 2.96 | 0.35 | 3.08 | 0.36 | 3.19 | 0.37 | 2.75+ | 1<3 |
| emotional coping | 2.10 | 0.54 | 1.86 | 0.49 | 1.82 | 0.59 | 1.29 | |
| denial | 2.27 | 0.39 | 2.27 | 0.52 | 2.26 | 0.54 | 0.001 | |
| support seeking | 2.36 | 0.72 | 2.63 | 0.49 | 2.67 | 0.65 | 1.48 | |
| Evaluation of coping effectiveness | 3.84 | 0.60 | 4.22 | 0.55 | 4.27 | 0.49 | 4.02* | 1<2,3 |

[a] Duncan post-hoc tests ($p<0.05$) were conducted when the ANOVA was significant: 1 refers to Cluster 1, 2 to Cluster 2, and 3 to Cluster 3.
* $p < 0.05$; + $p < 0.10$.

## Discussion

### Association between perceptions of family members

In general, several distinctions were apparent in the way the three family members depicted cohesion and power in their family. First, the adolescent sons portrayed the dyadic family relationships as more distant, and in general portrayed a less cohesive family than fathers and mothers did. This replicates prior research with American families (Feldman *et al.*, 1989) and may reflect adolescents' sense of individuation and separateness, which may be age-appropriate. Similar differential perceptions by mothers and adolescents were reported regarding conflict, whereby mothers underestimated the extent of conflict in the relationship compared with adolescents' reports (Smetana and Asquith, 1994). Second, both mothers and sons perceived the mother–son dyad as more cohesive than the father–son dyad, although this view was not shared by the fathers. This pattern of results attests to the special role of mothers in providing closeness and support for their children (Youniss and Smollar, 1985; Apter, 1990). Alternatively, it may indicate a distinct phenomenon of cohesive relationships between mothers and sons that is specific to our Israeli sample. Similar findings regarding closer relationships with mothers than with fathers in another 18-year-old cohort of men was reported previously in Israel (Mayseless and Hai, 1998). It might be that in the Israeli communal culture (Katriel, 1991), and on the eve of their sons' entering stressful and tough military service, mothers are more protective of them than mothers in other cultures. Third, contrary to our expectations, none of the family members portrayed the parental dyad as more cohesive than the parent–son dyads. If anything, the three dyads were depicted as having similar levels of cohesiveness. This indication of no distinction between the parental dyad and the parent–son dyads in terms of cohesion is surprising, and may again be related to specific cultural aspects.

In terms of perceptions of relative power, the picture is more similar to the expected pattern. On average, all three family members perceived the mother and the father as more powerful than their son, and the power gap between the parents and the adolescent son was portrayed as larger than the quite small power gap between the parents.

### *Perceptions of cohesion and adjustment*

In general, perceptions of cohesion were associated to a moderate degree with better general adjustment (e.g. higher self-esteem, higher intimacy with best friend), and better coping with the basic training hardships according to either self-report or friends' reports. Cohesion in the three dyads was important, and the cohesion in the parental dyad was almost as strongly associated with the son's adjustment as was cohesion in the father–son or the mother–son dyads. These results highlight the importance of family cohesiveness in promoting better adjustment and coping even within the military – a highly rigid, restrictive, and authoritarian context. Adolescents from cohesive families may be better equipped to cope with the hardships of the basic training period, having higher self-esteem and wellbeing, and better conflict management strategies, and being less aggressive (as indicated by our findings). These findings highlight the universal goodness of cohesive family relationships, a position mostly advocated by attachment researchers (e.g. Kenny and Donaldson, 1991).

However, our findings also highlight the usefulness of the family systems viewpoint. As indicated by our cluster analyses, an adolescent from a moderately cohesive family, where the mother–son relationships are closer than the father–son relationships, copes less successfully with the rigours of basic training than an adolescent from a moderately cohesive family where there is no triangulation. Thus, the extent of cohesiveness is not sufficient to understand the son's coping success; structural considerations are also important.

As expected, the son's perspective was more related to his coping and adjustment than his parents'. Interestingly, again from the son's perspective, perception of cohesion in the father–mother dyad was especially revealing and positively associated with markers of adjustment. Thus, our results attest to the importance of the subjective perception of the whole family in understanding one's functioning. However, again, substantiating the systemic approach, our findings indicated that the associations among the different perceptions are also important. Specifically, regardless of the extent of cohesion, inconsistencies between family members (i.e. gaps among their perceptions) were associated with lower levels of the son's adjustment. This was apparent when we used discrepancy scores as well as when we looked at the clusters resulting from the perceptions by all family members.

Regardless of level of cohesion, similar perceptions by family members seem to be conducive to better adjustment.

### *Perceptions of relative power and adjustment*

The dimension of cohesion was more predictive of adjustment than perceptions of relative power (from any perspective – of mother, father, or son). In general, very few associations were found with the power dimension. Indeed, had we used the type I error adjustment suggested by Bonferroni (dividing the alpha level 0.05 by the number of statistical tests), none of the associations with the power dimension would have been significant. Note, however, that for the few significant associations that we found, that a clear direction emerged, in that all associations showed better adjustment as a function of larger power gaps between parents (fathers and mothers) and sons. One of the reasons why the power dimension was not strongly associated with indicators of adjustment may be related to the fact that larger power gaps may not be universally good or bad. Thus, moderate levels of power gaps may be better than no power gap or large power gaps between parents and sons. Use of the power gap score as a unidirectional dimension by computing correlation may have obscured the non-linear nature of this family aspect. In line with this interpretation, the family constellation related to better coping involved both perceptions of high cohesion and portrayals of moderate hierarchy between parents and sons.

This interpretation notwithstanding, our results accord with findings of other studies that have demonstrated that while family cohesion is linearly related to individual and social wellbeing, hierarchy is not (Gehring and Marti, 1993b). The accumulation of these findings should not be dismissed, given the strong emphasis in adolescence literature on the need of parents to adjust their relative power, and the argument of researchers and clinicians that one of the developmental tasks of adolescence relates to transformation of the relationship from one of unilateral authority to one of co-operative negotiation (Youniss and Smollar, 1985; Steinberg, 1990). Our results may imply a different theoretical perspective. For example, hierarchy as depicted in the FAST may be different from granting autonomy, and the main developmental task at that age may not be to minimize the hierarchical relationships but to grant more autonomy and to decrease the extent of overt and direct supervision. In such a case, parents may still be viewed and may still act as important authority figures, yet they may exercise their authority less often and in fewer domains. It is the task for future research to explore this possibility.

Our results, especially with the clustering method, accord with clinical observations and findings (Brody *et al.*, 1998; Gehring *et al.*, 1994) that: (i) a well-functioning family is one with high cohesion and moderate hierarchy; and (ii) a triangulated family structure whereby the mother is closer to her son than to her husband may entail problematic adjustment for the son. Our findings demonstrated the usefulness of employing an empirically derived typology to substantiate theoretical claims.

The findings regarding an association between well-functioning families and better adjustment were obtained when the adjustment was to a harsh and difficult environment (military service) that does not allow much personal freedom. Indeed, the basic training period and the military service are not very conducive to the major developmental tasks of late adolescence such as self-assertion, autonomy, and individuation. One might have expected that the more authoritarian a family is (i.e. low cohesiveness, large parent–son power gaps), the easier it would be for the adolescent to adjust to a military service whose ecology is similar to the one experienced in the family. This, however, was not the case. Our findings indicated that even in this milieu (the military one), adolescents from cohesive, moderately hierarchical and balanced families, cope and adjust better than others. These family attributes are usually considered advantageous and functional in other contexts (Dornbusch *et al.*, 1987; Baumrind, 1989). The fact that they were also associated with adjustment to the unique context of the military, at least in its initial phase, may attest to their universal goodness. The association between these attributes and adaptation to military service in the long run should await future research.

In closing, our work demonstrated the universal aspects of family relations and their contribution to children's adjustment, as well as the unique culture-specific aspects of these relationships. In our study, similarity in levels of cohesiveness among the three dyads was found to be related to better adjustment. This might reflect unique ecological conditions, such as communal cultural values or a stressful environment which promote more closeness among family members. Future work could shed more light on the conditions and processes that encourage different configurations of optimal family relationships.

## References

Aldenderfer, M.S. and Blashfield, R.K. (1984) *Cluster Analysis*, Beverly Hills, CA: Sage.

Apter, T. (1990) *Altered Loves: Mothers and Daughters During Adolescence*, New York: St. Martin's Press.

Aseltine, Jr., R.H. and Gore, S. (1993) 'Mental health and social adaptation following the transition from high school', *Journal of Research on Adolescence* 3: 247–70.

Baumrind, D. (1989) 'Rearing competent children', in W. Damon (ed.), *Child Development Today and Tomorrow*, San Francisco, CA: Jossey-Bass.

—— (1991) 'The influence of parenting style on adolescent competence and substance use', *Journal of Early Adolescence* 11: 56–95.

Berdondini, L. and Smith, P.K. (1996) 'Cohesion and power in the families of children involved in bully/victim problems at school: An Italian replication', *Journal of Family Therapy* 18: 99–102.

Boszormenyi-Nagy, I. and Spark, G. (1973) *Invisible Loyalties: Reciprocity in Inter-generational Family Therapy*, New York: Harper & Row.

Bowers, L., Smith, P.K. and Binney, V. (1992) 'Cohesion and power in the families of children involved in bully/victim problems at school', *Journal of Family Therapy* 14: 371–87.

Brody, L.R., Copeland, A.P., Sutton, L.S., Richardson, D.R. and Guyer, M. (1998) 'Mommy and daddy like you best: Perceived family favoritism in relation to affect, adjustment and family process', *Journal of Family Therapy* 20: 269–91.

Bronfenbrenner, U. (1979) *The Ecology of Human Development: Experiments by Nature and Design*, Cambridge, MA: Harvard University Press.

Buhrmester, D., Furman, W., Wittenberg, M.T. and Reis, H.T. (1988) 'Five domains of interpersonal competence in peer relationships', *Journal of Personality and Social Psychology* 55: 991–1008.

Dornbusch, S.M., Ritter, L.P., Leiderman, P.H., Roberts, D.F. and Fraleigh, M.J. (1987) 'The relation of parenting style to adolescent school performance', *Child Development* 58: 1244–57.

Feldman, S.S. and Gehring, T.M. (1988) 'Changing perceptions of family cohesion and power across adolescence', *Child Development* 59: 1034–45.

—— Wentzel, K.R. and Gehring, T.M. (1989) 'A comparison of the views of mothers, fathers and preadolescents about family cohesion and power', *Journal of Family Psychology* 3: 39–60.

Folkman, S. and Lazarus, R.S. (1980) 'An analysis of coping in a middle-aged community sample', *Journal of Health and Social Behavior* 21: 219–39.

—— and Lazarus, R. S. (1985) 'If it changes it must be a process: Study of emotion and coping during three stages of a college examination', *Journal of Personality and Social Psychology* 48: 150–70.

Gal, R. (1986) *A Portrait of the Israeli Soldier*, New York: Greenwood Press.

Gehring, T.M. and Marti, D. (1993a) 'The Family System Test: Differences in perception of family structures between nonclinical and clinical children', *Journal of Child Psychology and Psychiatry and Allied Disciplines* 34: 363–377.

—— and Marti, D. (1993b) 'The architecture of family structures: Toward a spatial concept for measuring cohesion and hierarchy', *Family Process* 32: 135–9.

—— Marti, D. and Sidler, A. (1994) 'Family System Test (FAST): Are parents' and children's family constructs either different or similar, or both?', *Child Psychiatry and Human Development* 25: 125–38.

Goldscheider, F.K. and Davanzo, J. (1986) 'Semiautonomy and leaving home in early adulthood', *Social Forces* 65: 187–201.

Harold, G.T. and Conger, R.D. (1997) 'Marital conflict and adolescent distress: The role of adolescent awareness', *Child Development* 68: 333–50.

Holahan, C.J., Valentier, D.P. and Moos, R.H. (1994) 'Parental support and psychological adjustment during transition to young adulthood in a college sample', *Journal of Family Psychology* 8: 215–23.

Katriel, T. (1991) *Communal Webs, Communication and Culture in Contemporary Israel*, New York: State University of New York Press.

Kenny, M.E. and Donaldson, G. (1991) 'Contributions of parental attachment and family structure to the social and psychological functioning of first-year college students', *Journal of Counseling Psychology* 38: 479–86.

Larose, S. and Boivin, M. (1998) 'Attachment to parents, social support expectations and socioemotional adjustment during the high school-college transition', *Journal of Research on Adolescence* 8: 1–27.

Lieblich, A. (1989) *Transition to Adulthood During Military Service: The Israeli Case*, Albany, NY: State University of New York Press.

Mayseless, O. (1993) 'Attitudes toward military service among Israeli youth', in D. Ashkenazy (ed.), *The Military in the Service of Society and Democracy*, Westport, CT: Greenwood Press.

—— (1995) 'Towards military service', in H. Flum (ed.) *Adolescents in Israel: Personal, Familial and Social Aspects*, Even-Yehuda, Israel: Reches (in Hebrew).

—— and Hai, I. (1998) 'Leaving-home transition in Israel: Changes in parents–adolescents relationships and adaptation to military service', *International Journal of Behavioral Development* 22: 589–609.

Minuchin, P. (1985) 'Families and individual development: Provocations from the field of family therapy', *Child Development* 56: 289–302.

Minuchin, S. (1974) *Families and Family Therapy*, Cambridge, MA: Harvard University Press.

Moore, D. (1987) 'Parent–adolescent separation: The construction of adulthood by late adolescents', *Developmental Psychology* 23: 298–307.

Moos, R.H. (1984) 'Context and coping: Toward a unifying conceptual framework', *American Journal of Community Psychology* 12: 5–25.

Noller, P. and Callan, V.J. (1986) 'Adolescent and parent perception of family cohesion and adaptability', *Journal of Adolescence* 9: 97–106.

Olson, D.H. (1986) 'Circumplex model VII: Validation studies and FACES III', *Family Process* 25: 337–51.

—— (1990) 'Separation–individuation and adjustment to college: A longitudinal study', *Journal of Counseling Psychology* 39: 203–13.

Shulman, S., Laursen, B., Kalman, Z. and Karpovsky, S. (1997) 'Adolescent intimacy: Revisited', *Journal of Youth and Adolescence* 26: 597–617.

Smetana, J.G. and Asquith, P. (1994) 'Adolescents' and parents' conceptions of parental authority and personal autonomy', *Child Development* 65: 1147–62.

Strage, A.A. (1998) 'Family context variables and the development of self-regulation in college students', *Adolescence* 33: 17–31.

Steinberg, L. (1990) 'Autonomy, conflict, and harmony in the family relationship', in S. Feldman and G. Elliot (eds) *At the Threshold: The Developing Adolescent*, Cambridge, MA: Harvard University Press.

—— Elmen, J. and Mounts, N. (1989) 'Authoritative parenting, psychosocial maturity, and academic success among adolescents', *Child Development* 60: 1424–36.

Veit, C.T. and Ware, J.E. (1983) 'The structure of psychological stress and well-being in general population', *Journal of Consulting and Clinical Psychology* 51: 730–42.

Weinberger, D.A. (1991) 'Social–emotional adjustment in older children and adults: Validation of the Weinberger Adjustment Inventory', unpublished manuscript, Case Western Reserve University, Cleveland, OH.

Weiss, L.H. and Schwarz, J.C. (1996) 'The relationship between parenting types and older adolescents' personality, academic achievement, adjustment, and substance use', *Child Development* 67: 2101–14.

Wood, B. and Talmon, M. (1983) 'Family boundaries in transition: A search for alternatives', *Family Process* 22: 347–57.

Youniss, J. and Smollar, J. (1985) *Adolescent Relations with Mothers, Fathers, and Friends*, Chicago, IL: University of Chicago Press.

# Part III
# The FAST in Asian cultures

# 12 Perceptions of family structures by Japanese students

*Kazuo Ikeda and Takeshi Hatta*

## Introduction

Dynamism must be one of the most salient characteristics of a family structure. The factors that contribute to this dynamism are two-fold: culture and time. There are many kinds of family structure around the world (e.g. monogamy, polygamy, nuclear family, extended family). The variety in family structure indicates that family structure strongly depends upon the type of culture. At the same time, family structure also depends upon the historical time course (Hatta *et al.*, 1993; Hatta, 1994; Hasumi and Yamauchi, 1999). Even in the same culture, the influence of time (so-called zeitgeist) on family structure is crucial. For example, the most popular family structure type in Japan before the second world war was the three-generation family; however, statistics from 1997 show that 58 per cent of the Japanese population now live in a nuclear family and that 25 per cent of people live alone. Three-generation families now account for only 11.2 per cent of the population (Japan Statistics Bureau, 1999).

Japan has fostered various unique cultural characteristics. This uniqueness may be the result of Japan's geopolitical position – small islands, located in the Far East, that have never been invaded and that resisted the influence of different cultures until the nineteenth century. This being said, the Japanese adopted many things (Confucianism, Buddhism, medicine, the Chinese script, etc.) from China and Korea between the 4th and 7th centuries and, after the failure of the Mongolian invasions of 1274 and 1281, Japan continued to trade with foreign nations (China, Korea, Portugal, Holland). However, the Tokugawa shogunate government adopted a national isolation policy from 1639 to 1854. This long-term exclusion of foreigners cultivated a unique Japanese culture. Since the Meiji restoration in 1868, Japan has opened the door to Western countries, and therefore ways of thinking and lifestyles have gradually become westernized in various ways.

This unique geopolitical history doubtless generated special characteristics of family structure. One of the most influential factors affecting the family structure of Japan must be Confucian ideas. The most salient characteristic of Confucian ideas – the patriarchy in family systems – was the prototype of the Japanese family. The primary characteristics of the Japanese family and the strong influences of Confucian ideas were not quick to change, even after the Meiji restoration. Until very recently the three-generation family was the most typical Japanese family structure. This structure is based on two factors: one is the idea of seniority, which comes from Confucianism (the younger generation has to look after and pay respect to their parents), the other is economic reasons (i.e. the cost of living is cheaper in three-generation families than in a nuclear family).

However, Japanese society has experienced drastic changes since the second world war, both in economic conditions and in lifestyle. It is believed that Japanese ways of thinking have also changed drastically (Hasegawa, 1989). Recent statistics suggest that changes to the structure of Japanese families have meant a decrease in the number of family members; a decrease in the number of people getting married; an increase in the number of couples getting divorced; an increase in the number of elderly people living alone and living with their old spouses; and an increase in the number of women workers (Japan Statistics Bureau, 1999). These characteristics of the modern Japanese family are more prominent in city areas than in the countryside.

The parents of today's youngsters were born after the second world war. These modern parents faced a lot of competition during their years at school and also during their working life. They experienced poor living conditions during their childhood and rapid changes in lifestyle after adolescence, e.g. the increase in the nuclear family and the change from few to abundant material possessions.

Though it is not easy to understand Japanese families because of the complicated historical background of Japanese societies, as mentioned above, we need to consider the structural characteristics of the present Japanese familes. For this purpose, it is worth conducting a cross-cultural comparison of family structures between Japan and other countries.

There are various methods of investigating family structures. It is difficult to assess real family structures and psychodynamics using methods such as questionnaires, direct questions or observation. Projective techniques can sometimes be useful in such situations but prototypical projective techniques, such as the Rorschach test, Thematic Apperception Test (TAT), Sentence Completion Test (SCT), have shortcomings in expressing the standardized objective manner (for example, expression with numerical magnitudes).

Symbol Figure Placement Techniques (SFPTs), which were originally developed to describe family structures, seem to overcome the shortcomings of the prototypical projective techniques. SFPTs provide spatial representations of family relations and allows combined analyses of them on the basis of the perceptions of one or more family members, while at the same time allowing standardized observation of interactions (Hatta, 1977, 1994; Gehring and Wyler, 1986; Gehring, 1993).

The Doll Location Test (DLT), which was developed in Japan by Hatta (1977), is a type of SFPT used to evaluate structures of human relations not only in family situations but also in other kinds of situations. Although most SFPTs aim to investigate family structures only, the DLT can be applied for the better understanding of various interpersonal situations, mainly on the basis of cohesion, but not power, in human relations. In the DLT, the subject is asked to pin down dolls representing certain persons. The physical distance and the direction of the doll's face are taken to be an indicator of cohesion or emotional closeness and confidence. This test enables the assessment of relative distances between any given person in different social networks.

Using the DLT, Hatta (1994) and Hatta and Tsukiji (1993) examined family structures among normal Japanese college students. In these studies, students represented their parents, and parents also represented their children (students); the dyadic distances between male students and each parent were found to be largely similar. However, in the case of female students, dyadic distances between the self and mother were closer than between the self and father. The dyadic distance between spouses varied, depending on who represented the father and mother, and there was no generational boundary (i.e. there was the same amount of cohesion between the parents as between the parents and the offspring). This must be a characteristic of the modern Japanese family structure.

The FAST, developed by Gehring (1993), is another type of SFPT. In the FAST, family structures are assessed by cohesion and hierarchy and are classified into three types according to the combination of cohesion and hierarchy. In addition, the analysis of subsystems within the family (e.g. parents or siblings) is possible with the FAST.

Gehring and his colleagues performed the FAST with Swiss and Californian children and adolescents in order to investigate the family structures perceived by them, and found similar patterns in the results from the two samples (Gehring and Wyler, 1986; Feldman and Gehring, 1988; Gehring and Feldman, 1988; Marti and Gehring, 1992; Gehring, 1993; Gehring and Marti, 1993). On the basis of other studies, they concluded that clear generational boundaries are indicative of good family functioning.

Previous studies using two types of SFPT suggest some difference in family structures, and especially in generational boundaries, between Japan and Western countries. As no study had ever tried the FAST in Japan, we conducted it with Japanese students. In this chapter, we show the results of our Japanese study and the comparison with Swiss studies at both family and subsystem levels. In the first study, we present the data on Japanese undergraduate student perceptions of family structures, including two- and three-generation families. In the second study, we compare the family constructs experienced by the Japanese and Swiss subjects. We involved only students from two-generation families.

## STUDY I: JAPANESE FAMILY STRUCTURES

## Method

### Subjects

Subjects were 102 Japanese undergraduate students (76 female and 26 male) who lived with their parents in Kochi City or in the suburbs.[1] The mean age of the students was 20.7 years (range 18–23).[2] All subjects were from middle-class families, and none of the respondents and other family members had ever been treated for a psychological disorder. The samples consisted of sixty-seven nuclear families,[3] thirty-four three-generation families and one four-generation family. The mean family size was 4.4 and ranged from 3 to 8.

## Procedure

The respondents completed typical, ideal and conflict representations with FAST according to the test manual (Gehring, 1998a). The tests were administered individually in the laboratory between January 1995 and November 1998. In Study I, we used both the categorical scoring procedure (types of family structures) and the arithmetical procedure as based on Pythagoras' theorem (dyadic analyses).

## Results

### Classification of family structure with all Japanese samples

First, cohesion and hierarchy at the family level were scored according to the criteria of the FAST manual. Table 12.1 shows the results of the evaluation of all the Japanese samples in the typical, ideal and conflict situations, respectively.

Next, family structures were classified into balanced, labile–balanced, and unbalanced on the basis of the combination of the previous estimate of cohesion and hierarchy. This classification was also done according to the criteria of the FAST manual.

Figure 12.1 indicates the distribution of three types of family structures in the typical, ideal and conflict representations. In the typical representation, the largest category of cases (38.2 per cent) was classified not as balanced but as labile–balanced family structures. In addition, a substantial number of cases (27.5 per cent) were classified as having unbalanced structures. The low cohesion and relatively low hierarchy in the representation accounted for these results. The largest category of the ideal representations (42.2 per cent) were categorized as balanced,

*Table 12.1* Perceptions of cohesion and hierarchy by all Japanese samples ($n = 102$)

| Representation | Cohesion (%) | | | Hierarchy (%) | | | HR |
|---|---|---|---|---|---|---|---|
| | Low | Medium | High | Low | Medium | High | |
| Typical | 47.1 | 29.4 | 23.5 | 37.3 | 62.7 | 0.0 | 17.6 |
| Ideal | 23.5 | 35.3 | 41.2 | 47.1 | 52.9 | 0.0 | 3.9 |
| Conflict | 82.4 | 12.7 | 4.9 | 53.9 | 42.2 | 3.9 | 25.5 |

HR, hierarchy reversal.

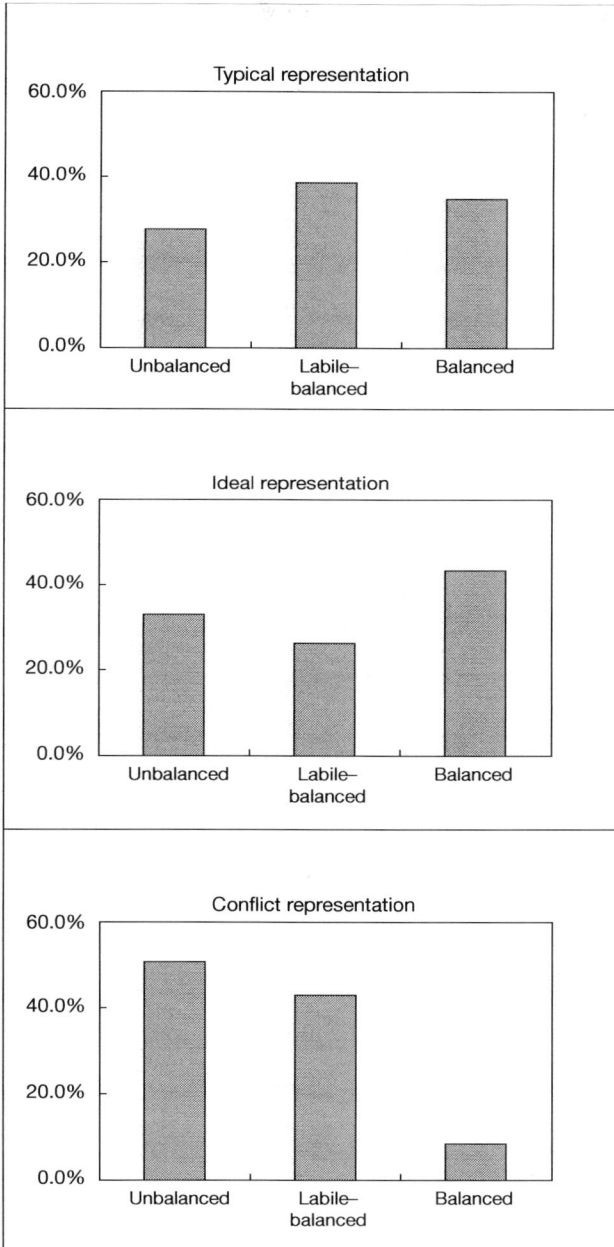

*Figure 12.1* Classification of Japanese family structures in typical, ideal and conflict representations.

but a considerable number of representations (32.4 per cent) were categorized as unbalanced. The high cohesion and relatively low hierarchy brought about this distribution in ideal representation. In conflict representation, half of all cases (50.0 per cent) were classified as unbalanced and only 7.8 per cent were classified as balanced. It is obvious that the low cohesion and low hierarchy scores in the conflict representation account for this result.

### Analysis of dyadic distances

In this analysis, we focused on the cohesion between father, mother, and subject. Cohesion was analysed by the dyadic distances, which were calculated by applying Pythagoras' theorem. Table 12.2 shows mean distances and standard deviations of all the data in the typical, ideal and conflict representations. As a whole, the mean distances were very short in the typical and ideal representations, and were long in the conflict representation.

Analyses of variance were conducted on the data from each representation to detect the differences in dyadic distance between two family members. The results show that the main factor of each representation is significant (typical: $F_{(2,202)} =$ 10.67, $p < 0.01$; ideal: $F_{(2,202)} = 17.75$, $p < 0.01$; conflict: $F_{(2,202)} = 5.33$, $p < 0.01$). Subsequent analysis by the Tukey method revealed that, in the typical and conflict representations, the distance between father and subject was significantly greater than the father–mother distance and the mother–subject distance, whereas in the ideal representation the distance between the father and mother was shorter than the father–subject and mother–subject distance. These results mean that fathers were not central in typical and conflict representations. In addition, the finding in the ideal representation indicates that respondents wish for clear generational boundaries.

*Table 12.2* Mean dyadic distances in Japanese families ($n = 102$)

| Representation | Father–mother | Father–subject | Mother–subject |
|---|---|---|---|
| Typical | | | |
| mean | 1.70 | 2.19 | 1.68 |
| sd | 1.32 | 1.30 | 0.76 |
| Ideal | | | |
| mean | 1.35 | 1.81 | 1.74 |
| sd | 0.64 | 0.91 | 0.96 |
| Conflict | | | |
| mean | 3.16 | 3.68 | 3.02 |
| sd | 2.50 | 2.19 | 2.00 |

sd, standard deviation.

## STUDY II: DIFFERENCES BETWEEN JAPANESE AND SWISS FAMILY STRUCTURES

To investigate whether Japanese respondents differ from Western ones, we compared our data from Study I with data from a Swiss study involving adolescents from the Zurich City area (Marti and Gehring, 1992; Gehring and Marti, 1993). All Swiss respondents were from middle-class families, just as the Japanese respondents were.

In the following analyses, only part of the Japanese and Swiss data was used, so that the two groups of subjects were as similar as possible. First, only Japanese nuclear families ($n = 66$, fifty female and sixteen male) were analysed because all of the Swiss sample were in two-generation families. The range in family size was from three to six (mean = 3.8) in the Japanese sample and from two to six (mean = 4.2) in the Swiss sample. Second, only Swiss respondents aged between 13 and 16 years ($n = 69$, thirty-seven female and thirty-two male) were analysed because the Japanese subjects were relatively older than the Swiss subjects.[4] The mean age of the Japanese group was 20.7 years and that of the Swiss group was 14.2 years, hence the age difference between two groups remained after this sampling. However, as previous studies using a categorical procedure have found no significant age differences between types of family structures in samples consisting of pre-, mid- and late adolescents (Gehring, 1998b; Luechinger, 1998), we used the categorical scoring for the comparison of the Japanese and Swiss samples.

### Comparison at family level

Table 12.3 shows the results of estimated cohesion and hierarchy with Japanese and Swiss samples. The distribution of the Japanese group shown in Table 12.3 is

*Table 12.3* Perceptions of cohesion and hierarchy by Japanese and Swiss respondents

| Representation and sample | Cohesion (%) | | | Hierarchy (%) | | | HR |
|---|---|---|---|---|---|---|---|
| | Low | Medium | High | Low | Medium | High | |
| **Typical** | | | | | | | |
| Japanese | 31.8 | 37.9 | 30.3 | 40.9 | 59.1 | 0.0 | 18.2 |
| Swiss | 17.4 | 49.3 | 33.3 | 21.7 | 78.3 | 0.0 | 10.1 |
| **Ideal** | | | | | | | |
| Japanese | 12.1 | 39.4 | 48.5 | 53.0 | 47.0 | 0.0 | 3.0 |
| Swiss | 1.4 | 34.8 | 63.8 | 43.5 | 55.1 | 1.4 | 11.6 |
| **Conflict** | | | | | | | |
| Japanese | 81.8 | 12.1 | 6.1 | 57.6 | 39.4 | 3.0 | 30.3 |
| Swiss | 69.1 | 25.0 | 5.9 | 45.6 | 50.0 | 4.4 | 17.6 |

HR, hierarchy reversal.

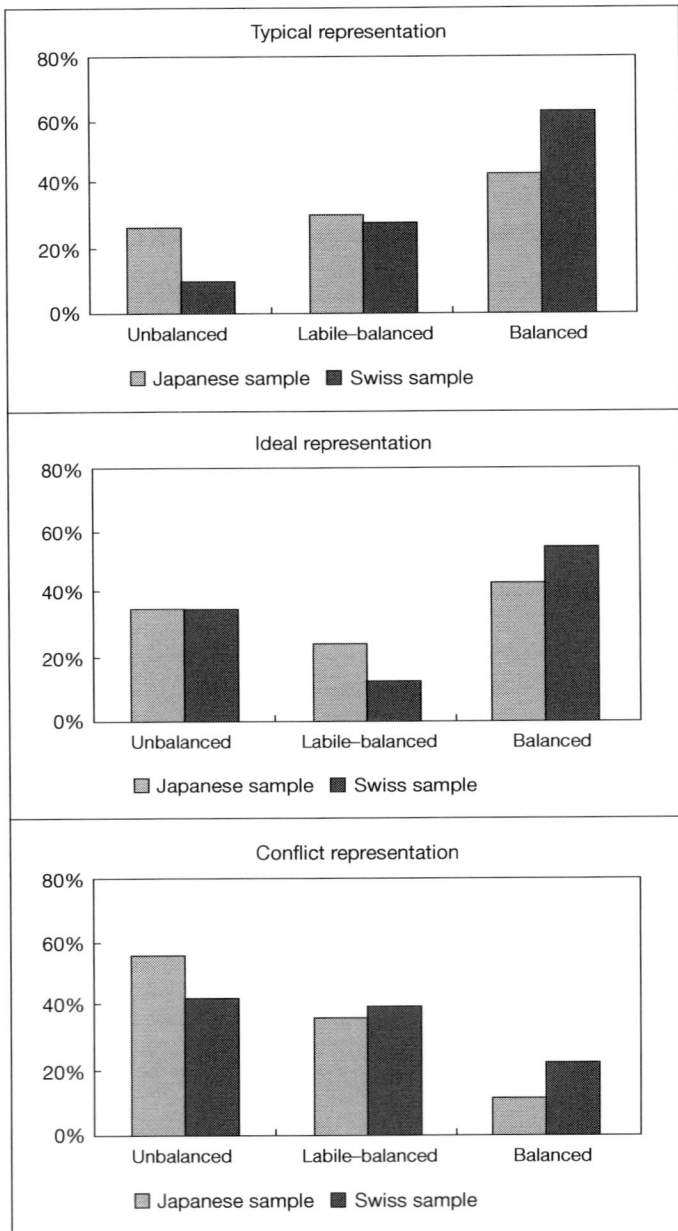

*Figure 12.2*  Classification of family structures.

broadly similar to that in Table 12.1, although the ratio of families that scored low cohesion was less with these samples than with all samples.[5]

From the estimation of cohesion and hierarchy, the distribution of the three types of family structures was calculated. Figure 12.2 shows the ratio of balanced, labile–balanced and unbalanced families in each representation by Japanese and Swiss samples. The analyses of the chi-square test revealed that the distribution in the typical representation was significantly different between Japanese and Swiss samples ($\chi^2 = 7.97$, $p < 0.05$), but that it was not significant in the ideal and conflict representations. These results indicate that the two samples did represent the conflict and ideal family structures similarly, but that they showed quite different perceptions of family structure in the typical situation.

## Comparison of subsystems

Japanese and Swiss samples were also compared at the parent and sibling subsystems. One-parent families and one-child families were excluded from the parent and sibling subsystem analyses, respectively.

Table 12.4 shows the results of cohesion in the parent subsystem with Japanese and Swiss samples. No significant difference was found by chi-square tests in any representation. Table 12.5 indicates the estimated hierarchy between parents by Japanese and Swiss subjects. Chi-square tests revealed a significant difference in the typical representation ($\chi^2 = 9.00$, $p < 0.05$) and a different tendency in the ideal representation ($\chi^2 = 5.19$, $p < 0.10$), but no significant difference in the conflict representation. This means that Japanese respondents represented the typical father–mother relation as more hierarchical than Swiss respondents. The same pattern, although not significant, was also found in the ideal representation.

The results of the analyses at sibling subsystems are shown in Table 12.6 (cohesion) and Table 12.7 (hierarchy). Chi-square tests revealed a different tendency of cohesion distribution only in the ideal representation ($\chi^2 = 4.81$, $p < 0.10$), but no differences in other distributions. These results mean that the portrayal of sibling subsystems was almost the same in the Japanese and Swiss sample.

*Table 12.4* Cohesion of parent subsystem

| Representation and sample | Low (%) | Medium (%) | High (%) |
| --- | --- | --- | --- |
| Typical | | | |
| Japanese | 36.4 | 12.1 | 51.5 |
| Swiss | 24.6 | 9.2 | 66.2 |
| Ideal | | | |
| Japanese | 18.2 | 19.7 | 62.1 |
| Swiss | 12.3 | 15.4 | 72.3 |
| Conflict | | | |
| Japanese | 71.2 | 3.0 | 25.8 |
| Swiss | 59.4 | 9.4 | 31.3 |

*Table 12.5* Hierarchy of parent subsystem

| Representation and sample | Low (%) | Medium (%) | High (%) |
|---|---|---|---|
| Typical | | | |
| Japanese | 16.7 | 65.2 | 18.2 |
| Swiss | 40.0 | 49.2 | 10.8 |
| Ideal | | | |
| Japanese | 66.7 | 30.3 | 3.0 |
| Swiss | 83.1 | 13.8 | 3.1 |
| Conflict | | | |
| Japanese | 40.9 | 27.3 | 31.8 |
| Swiss | 37.5 | 40.6 | 21.9 |

*Table 12.6* Cohesion of sibling subsystem

| Representation and sample | Low (%) | Medium (%) | High (%) |
|---|---|---|---|
| Typical | | | |
| Japanese | 35.7 | 26.2 | 38.1 |
| Swiss | 32.2 | 30.5 | 37.3 |
| Ideal | | | |
| Japanese | 23.8 | 31.0 | 45.2 |
| Swiss | 8.5 | 42.4 | 49.1 |
| Conflict | | | |
| Japanese | 64.0 | 20.0 | 16.0 |
| Swiss | 65.5 | 19.0 | 15.5 |

*Table 12.7* Hierarchy of sibling subsystem

| Representation and sample | Low (%) | Medium (%) | High (%) |
|---|---|---|---|
| Typical | | | |
| Japanese | 54.8 | 31.0 | 14.3 |
| Swiss | 54.2 | 37.3 | 8.5 |
| Ideal | | | |
| Japanese | 69.0 | 26.2 | 4.8 |
| Swiss | 62.7 | 25.4 | 11.9 |
| Conflict | | | |
| Japanese | 69.0 | 26.2 | 4.8 |
| Swiss | 51.7 | 34.5 | 13.8 |

## DISCUSSION

The present research was the first attempt to investigate Japanese family structures using the FAST. The purpose of this study was to reveal the characteristics of Japanese family structures as perceived by Japanese college students. For this purpose, the data from a Japanese sample were compared with those of Swiss samples. Before discussing the results of the comparison, we should note several points about the validity of the present study. First, although we analysed the data from the older group of Swiss respondents, a difference in age between Japanese and Swiss samples did exist. As mentioned earlier, previous researchers have shown no change in the perception of family structures throughout adolescence, but we cannot deny the possibility that the unmatched sampling in the age caused, to a certain extent, the differences between groups found in the study. Second, the family structures analysed in this research were only those represented by the students from their point of view as offspring. At this point, we cannot say for certain whether their parents perceive their family structure similarly to the students or not. An earlier study by DLT suggests that Japanese mothers of female students represented their family structure similarly to female students but that fathers did not (Hatta, 1994). We would therefore need to perform further investigations before concluding that our findings from Japanese students are also valid for their parents. Third, the comparisons drawn from this study could be regarded as a comparison between Japanese family structures and those of Western countries because, as described before, Gehring and his colleagues got very similar results with both Californian and Swiss samples (see Gehring, 1993).

From the comparative analyses in Study II, we could find not only similar aspects between the two countries but also different aspects of Japanese family structures. The similarities between Japanese and Swiss subjects were found mainly in the ideal and conflict representations. In the ideal representation, the largest group in both samples was classified as balanced, although a substantial number in each were also classified as unbalanced. The latter is because the respondents wish their ideal family relations to display high cohesion and little hierarchy between parents and children. The analyses of the parent subsystem suggest that subjects think that their parents should be highly cohesive and equally influential for their family. It is especially worth noting that more than 80 per cent of the Swiss respondents represented their parents as egalitarian, and thus had a tendency to differ from their counterparts. In general, the image of ideal states, described above, might be more consentient in Swiss children than Japanese children.

No significant differences were found between the two groups in the conflict representations. As expected, Japanese and Swiss adolescents represented their family structures in conflict predominantly as labile–balanced or unbalanced. Decreased cohesion and hierarchy of family structure account for this. This kind of structural change was also found in the Californian research (Gehring *et al.*, 1990) and may be common internationally. The decrease of cohesion was also found at the subsystem level in both countries, but the change in hierarchy was more complicated. In this study, we did not analyse the type of conflict because of the relatively small size. Further studies are needed, with more data.

The greatest difference between the Japanese and Swiss samples was found in the typical representation. The distribution of family structures by classification was significantly different only in this representation. While most Swiss families were classified as balanced, and fewer cases were classified as unbalanced, Japanese families divided almost equally into balanced, labile–balanced, and unbalanced structures. This was the result of relatively low cohesion and low hierarchy in Japanese representations. It is true that further placement of grandfather and grandmother brought about the low cohesion in three-generation families, but even in the results from nuclear families, cohesion at a family level was low. Ad hoc analyses of who caused the low cohesion revealed that the father was placed out of a $3 \times 3$ grid in twelve cases of low cohesive representation (out of a total of twenty-one cases); in only one case was the mother the cause. This means that the isolated father brought about the low cohesion in the typical representations at family level. In contrast, most of the mothers were placed near the centre of the family members, and mother and children were relatively cohesive.

A similar pattern was also found by using the arithmetical scoring procedure for Japanese family structures on the dyadic level. We found a significant difference between father–subject distance and mother–subject distance in typical and conflict representations, whereas father–mother distance was shortest in the ideal representation. The latter finding indicates that Japanese respondents wish for clear generational boundaries in terms of cohesion. The results of the present study are consistent with those of preceding findings by the DLT (Hatta and Tsukiji, 1993; Hatta, 1994). These are unique characteristics of family perception by Japanese adolescents; that is, they regard it as ideal that their father and mother are cohesive, and that they themselves have some distance from their parents, but in the real family (in the typical or the conflict situations), they perceive that their mother is close to them and that their father is somewhat isolated. Needless to say, additional developmental studies with younger subjects and the comparison of sex differences will be needed to generalize these findings.

The low hierarchy in the typical presentation of Japanese families is suggestive. We found a significant difference between Japanese and Swiss parent subsystems in the typical representation. The results showed that Japanese adolescents perceive their parents as more hierarchical than Swiss adolescents. Ad hoc analysis revealed that the father was represented as higher than the mother in thirty-nine cases (59.1 per cent), and that the reverse was true in sixteen cases (24.2 per cent). These results suggest that Japanese students perceive some difference in power between their parents and less difference between the less powerful parent (i.e. the mother in most cases) and children. This was supported by substantial cases of hierarchy reversal in the typical representation.

From the discussion above, it could be concluded that the typical Japanese family, at least as perceived by the children, has no clear generational boundaries (as suggested by Hatta (1994) and Hatta and Tsukiji (1993)). At the same time, many Western researchers (Gehring, 1985. Gehring and Wyler, 1986; Leigh, 1986) have asserted that clear generational boundaries, both in cohesion and in hierarchy, should exist in a normal or sound family. This was the background theory on which the classification criteria of the FAST were developed. According to this point of view, a highly cohesive and egalitarian relationship between mother and child in Japanese families might be abnormal. However, such relationships are common in Japanese families without any serious problems. Therefore, we could regard them as a kind of cultural characteristic of families in Japan.

These characteristics of Japanese family structure probably developed in the period after the second world war. In the latter half of the twentieth century, Japanese men worked hard to help the restoration effort immediately after the war and to support the subsequent economic growth. They gave a higher priority to their business than to their own families. Traditionally in Japan, it has been considered natural and desirable to do so. In such social conditions, most fathers could not afford to spend enough time with other family members. As a result, mothers could not help dealing with family matters and, in a sense, the mother has played the part of a 'hinge' to co-ordinate family members. It seems reasonable to suppose that the historical circumstances of the time are at least partly responsible for the absence of the father and the intimate ties between mother and children in modern Japanese families.

Of course, Japanese family structures keep on changing, too. The fact that Japanese respondents reported a desire for a cohesive parental relationship in their ideal representations provides further evidence of an ongoing change in family structures (i.e. a more inward-directed family orientation of fathers). Recent studies have shown that some young fathers were active in childcare and that such paternal involvement was associated with a positive feeling towards the children (Kashiwagi and Wakamatsu, 1994). It is also worth investigating such ongoing changes in Japanese families.

Cross-cultural research with the FAST is currently just at the beginning. The present study suggests some cross-cultural differences between Japanese and Western family structures. However, the conclusion might be controversial because there were some discrepancies regarding age and the sex ratio between the two samples. As it is possible that these factors have affected the representations, we need better-matched data before a final conclusion can be drawn.

SFPTs are very useful techniques to investigate cultural differences in the perception of family structures. Needless to say, the comparative studies of characteristics in various cultures are significant not only for the consideration of one's own culture but also for mutual understanding. Further research with SFPTs to compare family structures at large and in more detail is needed.

## Acknowledgements

We would like to thank to Drs Thomas M. Gehring and Daniel Marti for providing us with the data from the Swiss samples and for permitting us to analyse and quote them in this chapter.

This research was supported partly by a grant-in-aid for Scientific Research (# 09044006) from the Ministry of Education, Japan.

## Notes

1. Kochi City is the provincial capital of Kochi prefecture, which is located in the southwest of Japan. It is a typical provincial city with a population of about 300,000. The city centre is rather urbanized but there are fields and orchards in the suburbs.
2. Some parts of these data were analysed and reported by Ikeda (1996, 1997).
3. One case of a nuclear family was excluded from the analysis as the subject included her grandmother in the conflict representation.
4. One conflict representation of a Swiss subject could not be analysed because of missing data.
5. This is because grandfathers and grandmothers in Japanese families tended to be placed relatively farther from other family members. These results suggest that the validity of scoring criteria in the FAST should be reconsidered when applied to three- or more generation families.

## References

Feldman, S.S. and Gehring, T.M. (1988) 'Changing perceptions of family cohesion and power across adolescence', *Child Development*, 59: 1034–45.

Gehring, T.M. (1985) 'Socio-psychosomatic dysfunctions: A case study', *Child Psychiatry and Human Development*, 15: 269–80.

—— (1993) *Familiensystemtest (FAST) Manual*, Weinheim: Beltz Verlag.

—— (1998a) *The Family System Test*, Seattle, WA: Hogrefe and Huber Publishers.

—— (1998b) *The Family System Test (FAST): A Clinical and Research Tool for the Planning and Evaluation of Family Investigations*, Basle: University of Basle, Department of Psychology.

—— and Feldman, S.S. (1988) 'Adolescents' perceptions of family cohesion and power: A methodological study of the Family System Test', *Journal of Adolescent Research*, 3: 33–52.

—— and Marti, D. (1993) 'The Family System Test: Differences in perception of family structures between nonclinical and clinical children', *Journal of Child Psychology and Psychiatry and Allied Disciplines*, 34: 363–77.

—— and Wyler, I.L. (1986) 'Family System Test (FAST): A three-dimensional approach to investigate family relationships', *Child Psychiatry and Human Development*, 16: 235–48.

——, Wentzel, K.R., Feldman, S.S. and Munson, J. (1990) 'Conflict in families of adolescents: The impact on cohesion and power structures', *Journal of Family Psychology*, 3: 290–309.

Hasegawa, H. (1989) 'Human development and mental health', in T. Hayasaka (ed.) *Mental Health*, Tokyo: Igaku-syoin.

Hasumi, S. and Yamauchi, M. (1999) *Farewell Address to 20th Centuries*, Tokyo: Iwanami-shoten.

Hatta, T. (1977) 'Doll Location Test: Application to the patients of psychoneuroses', *Tekisei Kenkyu*, 10: 1–6.

—— (1994) 'Projected family structure by modern Japanese adolescents', *Social Behavior and Personality*, 22: 399–408.

—— and Tsukiji, N. (1993) 'Characteristics of Japanese family: Evidence from the results of the Doll Location Test by university students', *Psychologia*, 36(4): 235–40.

—— Tsukiji, N. and Ayetani, N. (1993) 'Structure of the modern Japanese family', *Journal of Psychology*, 126: 683–6.

Ikeda, K. (1996) 'International comparison of the Family System Test: Results of research on the cognition of family structures by Japanese university students', *Research Reports of Department of Humanity, Kochi University*, 4: 11–20.

Ikeda, K. (1997) 'Practical examples of the FAST with Japanese subjects: A research on Japanese normal students', in T.M. Gehring and T. Hatta (eds) *Family System Test (Japanese Manual)*, Osaka: Union Services.

Japan Statistics Bureau (1999) *Statistics of Movement of Population*, Tokyo: Japan Statistics Bureau.

Kashiwagi, K. and Wakamatsu, M. (1994) 'Becoming a parent and Personality Development: A lifespan developmental view', *Japanese Journal of Developmental Psychology*, 5: 72–83.

Leigh, G.K. (1986) 'Adolescent involvement in family systems', in G.K. Leigh and G.W. Peterson (eds) *Adolescents in Families*, Cincinnati, OH: South-Western.

Luechinger, D. (1998) 'Family constructs of female undergraduate students', unpublished M.Phil. thesis, University of Zurich.

Marti, D. and Gehring, T. M. (1992) 'Is there a relationship between children's mental disorders and their ideal family constructs?', *Journal of the American Academy of Child and Adolescent Psychiatry*, 31: 490–4.

# 13 Characteristics of three-generation Chinese families

*Shu Shu and Peter K. Smith*

## Introduction

In China, many families still live in three-generation households: grandparents with parents, with usually only one child as a result of the government's one-child policy, which has operated since 1979 to control the increase of population. This family situation provides an interesting opportunity to use the FAST test to examine three-generation households in a situation where number of grandchildren (sibling size) is not a confounding factor. In this chapter, we report data from the FAST with families in mainland China, to examine:

- the relative cohesion of grandparents, parents and children
- the existence of cross-generational coalitions
- the relative hierarchy of grandparents, parents, and children
- the differences between maternal grandparents and paternal grandparents, and between grandmothers and grandfathers, regarding intergenerational relationships
- the effects of education and occupation of the parental generation on family cohesion and hierarchy
- the distribution or frequency of balanced, labile–balanced and unbalanced family structures.

Finally, we compare the main characteristics of the data with those from Japanese and Western families and comment on the use of the FAST in studying three-generation relationships.

## Background

### The Chinese family configuration

Traditionally, owing to old family values and socioeconomic conditions, three-generation families in the same household were very common in China. Today, although the rate has obviously decreased, three-generation families still play an important part in Chinese family structure. Statistics show that, in 1994, 48.8 per cent of households in urban areas had three or more generations; the corresponding figure was 46.3 per cent in rural areas.

By and large, Chinese family relationships are close but hierarchical, compared with Western societies. As a guiding principle that has dominated Chinese philosophy of life for over 2,000 years, Confucian ideas urge strict hierarchy and obedience at home, putting a strong emphasis on filial piety. Grandparents are respected and influential. Even in 1996, 15.5 per cent of an urban sample revealed that the major reason for them to have a child was to please the previous generation, i.e. the grandparents (Zhao, 1997).

In recent decades, there have been some changes in this power pattern; authoritativeness is being related more to social and financial status, or individual character. Women's power within the family has increased significantly since the country put the focus on the economy, especially in urban areas where the gap in work conditions and pay between male and female employees has been getting narrower. The influence of generation and gender is generally supposed to have lessened.

Relationships across three generations can be difficult. As it is usual for both the mother and father to have a full-time job, and as public services are still at a rather low level in China, many grandparents face a dilemma as to whether to take up the responsibility of looking after grandchildren. Also, the relationships among grown-up siblings may be intense or indifferent, as a result of what they see as their parents' 'unequal' investment in themselves and their own children.

### The one-child policy and its effects

Chinese families generally want to give birth to a male child, as this would extend the family bloodline and carry on the family surname. However, family planning has been having an influence on people's views. In general, families are allowed to have only one child (urban areas) or two children (rural areas) or three children (national minorities). However, in rural China the restraint is often broken because the sex of a child is the central concern of peasants' childbearing. 'To have a boy' is the most fundamental value, and having more than one boy is also preferred. In urban areas there are fewer biases now in childrearing practices, even if this change has come passively: the family has no choice, their girl child is unique as they are very unlikely to be able to have another child. A recent survey by Zhao (1997) in the northern city of Harbin found that people's reproductive preference for boy children was no stronger than for girl children.

The one-child policy is viewed in an ambivalent fashion by the Chinese people. Hardly anything else has had so profound and wide an influence on modern Chinese family structure and everyday life. The usual worries are that too much care may lead to overinterference with the children's lives and activities and lead to the '4–2–1 syndrome' in which the four grandparents and two parents may overindulge the one (grand)child (Chen, 1996).

But Falbo's findings (1991) did not support the popular 4–2–1 theory. On the contrary, he found that Chinese grandparents have a positive impact on their grandchildren: the child with more contact with better educated grandparents does better at school; the one with a better educated grandfather has more positive personality attributes. The effect on children's outcomes of the difference between living in a nuclear or three-generational household on children's outcomes was not significant. Later, Falbo and Poston (1993) conducted a very large survey, involving four provinces, 200 schools and 4,000 schoolchildren, to compare the outcomes of only children to those of non-only children. The overall findings did not suggest any differences between only children and non-onlies, except that only children had an advantage in verbal skills. Falbo concluded that China's one-child policy did not mean the appearance of spoiled children.

### Chinese childrearing practices

Parents, including grandparents, sometimes put a lot of pressure on children to perform well at school because they want the child to be successful when they grow up, and to 'have face' is very important for Chinese people. Maybe it is something to do with numerous long-standing feudal principles, but the Chinese parenting style often impresses people as strict and mechanical. Chiu (1987) reported that Chinese mothers were most restrictive compared to their Chinese-American and American counterparts. Findings from Lin and Fu (1990) also revealed high ratings in controlling children and valuing children's academic performance for both Chinese and immigrant Chinese parents.

The role of Chinese fathers in childrearing is a bit more difficult to define. As Ho (1987) indicated, traditionally the Chinese father 'was not expected to have much to do with the care of infants or young children; that was within the province of the mother and other women'. The importance of fatherhood may emerge 'only when the child was considered old enough to be instructed and disciplined' (Ho, 1987, p. 230). Jankowiak (1992) gave an account of fatherhood in a very traditional sample from Inner Mongolia. Consistent with the traditional pattern of Chinese fathering, fathers were observed and described as incapable in infant care and showing little emotional expression to their children. However, urbanization had changed this pattern to some extent so that fathers increasingly wanted to see a closer connection between them and their children and were more involved in childrearing practices.

### Relations between family background and children's outcome

A study of Shanghai pupils and their parents by Chen and Rubin (1994) found some effects of parental educational and occupational levels on childrearing. Although levels of education and occupation did not relate significantly to family financial conditions (mainly family income and housing), higher levels of education and occupation did correlate positively with family psychological conditions, including marital relationship and social support, and parental acceptance; parental acceptance in turn predicted more prosocial–competent behaviour in their children, and less aggressive behaviour. Another study, by Chen *et al.* (1997) in Beijing, found that parents of better educational and occupational levels were more inclined to an authoritative parenting style, and less inclined to authoritarianism towards children; such an attitude was associated with children's positive outcome in school.

### The present study

Old traditions as well as new developments such as the one-child policy seem to be the major influences on Chinese childrearing practices and general family values. Despite the prevalence of three-generation families, with the exception of Falbo's 1991 study, little to no research has apparently been done into grandparent–parent–grandchild relationships in China.

There has been no previous research using the FAST in China, either. A few studies have been done in Japan using similar figure placement techniques (e.g. Hatta and Tsukiji, 1993; Hatta, 1994); these revealed some differences in family portrayals from Western samples. Gehring had proposed three categories, balanced, labile–balanced and unbalanced, to examine systematic relational perceptions among clinical and non-clinical families. In Western samples he found that cohesive and moderately hierarchical patterns, i.e. a balanced structure, were usually connected with normative families; and that low cohesion allied to an extreme tendency to either low or high hierarchy (i.e. an unbalanced structure) was likely to be perceived by members in families with 'biopsychosocial distress' (Gehring *et al.*, 1990, 1996). To determine generation-specific structural differences, he also presented the constructs of 'cross-generational coalition' and 'reverse hierarchy', which were referred to as abnormal generational boundaries. However, in the Japanese studies a cross-generational coalition pattern (relationship between mother and child was perceived as closer than that between parents) was revealed as normative, contrasting with results from Western non-clinical samples.

Thus, our study is in part exploratory, although we do have clear expectations about hierarchy in Chinese families – that power will run along lines of generation (older) and sex (male). We also intend to examine the extent of cross-generational coalitions and the applicability of Gehring's balanced/labile–balanced/unbalanced criteria of family functioning in a three-generation Chinese sample.

## Method

### Procedure

This study was carried out in Hefei (population over one million), an ancient Chinese city influenced by both the free economic policy that the government introduced in the early 1980s and long-standing conservative values and lifestyle. The families of forty students from a primary school in the city centre were selected for this study. Respondents were seen at their homes in December 1995 and were interviewed individually. Each was given the FAST test, a symbolic figure placement task to show family structure: cohesion is indicated by the distance between figures; degree of familial hierarchy can be derived by placing power blocks (of three sizes: small, medium, and large) under each figure.

When one respondent was interviewed, other family members stayed in another room, to let the respondent have no misgivings that might affect the reliability of their representation. Respondents were asked to place figures showing 'how close family members feel to each other'. After the representation of cohesion the respondent was asked to add the power blocks under the figures to show 'power in the family' in the sense of influence and decision making (*quanli*), or authority (*quanwei*). Of the 184 family members available, all gave an individual FAST response to the typical family situation. Following each respondent's completion of their family portrayal, the identity, location and elevation of all figures was recorded on a standard plot. In addition, details of age, occupation (if relevant) and educational background were recorded.

### Sample

Each family had one or two grandparents living in the same household (there was no example of both paternal and maternal grandparents being residents of the same family, which is a rare phenomenon in China). The students were twenty-four girls and sixteen boys, in the age range 6 to 12 years. Their mean age was 8.75 years. Of the forty, thirty-eight were only children, in line with the 'one-child' policy of China (Falbo and Poston, 1993). For comparability across families, we omitted the FAST plots obtained from the two siblings (and also from two cousins) when scoring.

Three-generation families are difficult to describe with a consistent, easily understood terminology. In this chapter, we will use the perspective of the child (C; CB = boy child, CG = girl child), and refer to parents (P; M = mother, F = father) and grandparents (GP; GF = grandfather, GM = grandmother, PGM = paternal grandmother, PGF = paternal grandfather, MGM = maternal grandmother, MGF = maternal grandfather).

All families had a mother, and thirty-seven had a resident father (three had no father owing to divorce). FAST plots were obtained from thirty-nine mothers and thirty-five fathers. The mean age of the parents was 36 years. Twenty-six families had two resident grandparents (nineteen had both paternal grandparents, seven both maternal grandparents); fourteen had one grandparent (eight had PGM only, five had MGM only, one had MGF only). FAST plots were obtained from all sixty-six grandparents. The mean age of the grandparents was 64 years.

The educational and occupational background was quite diverse, but could be summarized as either 'low' or 'high' for education, and 'worker' or 'official' for occupation. 'Low' means junior middle school education or lower; 'high' means senior middle school education or higher. 'Worker' refers to parents who were workers, peasants, shop assistants, and housewives; 'official' refers to parents who were teachers, doctors, engineers, and officials.

The simplified educational and occupational levels of grandparents and parents are shown in Table 13.1. It is obvious that the level of education has improved significantly between these two generations; 68.9 per cent of parents (80 per cent of the fathers, 59 per cent of the mothers) had senior middle school education or higher, compared to 36.4 per cent for their previous generation (44 per cent of the

*Table 13.1*  Educational background and occupation of grandparents and parents
(*n* = 140)

|  | Educational background | | Occupation | | Total |
|  | Low | High | Worker | Official | |
|---|---|---|---|---|---|
| Grandmother | 27 | 12 | 24 | 15 | 39 |
| Grandfather | 15 | 12 | 8 | 19 | 27 |
| Mother | 16 | 23 | 29 | 10 | 39 |
| Father | 7 | 28 | 22 | 13 | 35 |
| Total | 65 | 75 | 83 | 57 | 140 |

grandfathers, 31 per cent of the grandmothers) ($\chi^2 = 14.87$, $p < 0.0001$). The improvements are also significant in both genders (for male, $\chi^2 = 8.42$, $p < 0.01$; for female, $\chi^2 = 6.27$, $p < 0.05$).

## Scoring

For each FAST plot, we scored the following.

### Cohesion scores (the distance between each dyad).

According to Pythagoras' theorem, distance scores could vary from 1 (linearly adjacent square) to 11.3 (diagonally opposite); small distance scores (close placement) means high cohesion. We scored ten types of dyads for cohesion: GM/GF, GM/M, GM/F, GF/M, GF/F, GM/C, GF/C, M/C, F/C, M/F. For some additional analyses, we looked separately at maternal and paternal grandparents, PGM/PGF and MGM/MGF.

### Cross-generational coalition

Following Gehring and Marti (1993), a cross-generational coalition was scored when the distance between a parent and child was closer than that between mother and father (for this purpose we ignored grandparents).

### Power blocks

The small-sized power block (1.5 cm high) was scored as 1; the medium-sized block (3cm high) as 2; the large-sized block (4.5 cm high) was scored as 3. The power score was the average received from each family member.

*Reverse hierarchy*

When a child was more powerful than a parent, this was coded as reverse hierarchy – we extended the definition of Gehring and Marti (1993) to include the cases when a child was more powerful than a grandparent (but not when a parent was more powerful than a grandparent).

*Family structure categories*

For these purposes, cohesion was defined as high (all figures were placed in adjacent squares); medium (not all figures were placed in adjacent squares but they were located within a $3 \times 3$ square area, or all figures were placed in a line if the family had more than three members, or one figure was placed adjacent to one of the rest of the family who were all located within a $3 \times 3$ square area if the family had more than four members); or low (one or more figures were placed outside a $3 \times 3$ square area). Hierarchy was defined as high (the power difference between the least elevated adult (parent or grandparent) and the child was a large block or more); medium (the difference was a small or middle-sized block); or low (the difference was less than a small block).

According to Gehring's patterns of family structures (Gehring and Marti, 1993), the forty families were then grouped into three types:

- balanced: a combination of medium or high cohesion and medium hierarchy
- labile–balanced: a combination of medium cohesion and low or high hierarchy, or of low cohesion and medium hierarchy
- unbalanced: a combination of extreme values in both cohesion and hierarchy.

## Results

### *The relative cohesion of grandparents, parents, and children*

Mean distance scores for each dyad (averaged across all such dyads in all families) are shown in Table 13.2. The actual minimum dyadic distance score obtained was 1, the maximum was 6.7, the average over all dyads being 1.52. This rather small average distance score indicates very cohesive plots.

*Table 13.2* Mean distance scores for each dyad as represented by all family members ($n = 180$)

|  | GM–GF | M–C | M–F | GM–C | GF–C | F–C | GF–F | GM–M | GM–F | GF–M |
|---|---|---|---|---|---|---|---|---|---|---|
| Average score | 1.34 | 1.35 | 1.46 | 1.47 | 1.52 | 1.55 | 1.69 | 1.62 | 1.69 | 1.73 |
| sd | (0.60) | (0.56) | (0.87) | (0.57) | (0.51) | (0.89) | (0.76) | (0.61) | (0.88) | (0.60) |

C, child; F, father; GF, grandfather; GM, grandmother; M, mother; sd, standard deviation.

Married couples (GM/GF, M/F) and the mother–child (M/C) relationships are seen as particularly close. Grandparents were seen generally as closer to grandchildren than to their mature offspring/in-laws; with the latter the relationship was strongly influenced by lineage. The overall one-way ANOVA is highly significant, $F_{(9,1554)} = 5.21, p < 0.0001$; post-hoc Scheffe tests show that GM/GF and M/C each differ from both GM/F and GF/M (all $p < 0.05$).

### Are there cross-generational coalitions?

Altogether 35 per cent of respondents showed such a family generational boundary pattern, the percentages of each generation being 33.3 per cent for grandparents, 18.9 per cent for parents, and 67.5 per cent for children. Adults, including both parents and grandparents, saw less cross-generational coalition in the family than did children ($\chi^2 = 23.9, p < .0001$).

### The relative hierarchy of grandparents, parents and children

The means of power blocks received by each type of family member (averaged across all such members in all families) are shown in Table 13.3. These differed considerably, and the one-way ANOVA is highly significant, $F_{(7,172)} = 12.21, p < 0.0001$. Generation and gender were both significant influences on perceptions of power of family members. Grandparents were perceived as more powerful than parents, who in turn were more powerful than children. Within each generation of a household, males tended to be perceived as more powerful than females. The most powerful figure, the paternal grandfather, gets an average of nearly 2 power blocks from family members, a clear indication of the perception of this position.

### Are there reverse hierarchies?

For each generation of respondents, an absolute majority (overall, 89 per cent) did not perceive a reverse hierarchy in their families. Percentages who did perceive reverse hierarchy were 7.6 per cent for grandparents, 12.2 per cent for parents, and 12.5 per cent for children; differences between generations for view of hierarchical structures were not significant ($\chi^2 = 1.0$, ns).

*Table 13.3* Mean number of power blocks received by each family member ($n = 180$)

|  | PGF | PGM | MGF | MGM | F | M | CB | CG |
|---|---|---|---|---|---|---|---|---|
| Average score | 1.99 | 1.39 | 1.37 | 1.20 | 0.91 | 0.79 | 0.51 | 0.24 |
| sd | (0.98) | (0.82) | (1.00) | (0.71) | (0.74) | (0.64) | (0.45) | (0.42) |

CB, child (boy); CG, child (girl); F, father; M, mother; MGF, maternal grandfather; MGM, maternal grandmother; PGF, paternal grandfather; PGM, paternal grandmother; sd, standard deviation.

### Differences between maternal and paternal grandparents, and between grandmothers and grandfathers, regarding intergenerational relationships

Overall mean distance scores were less for grandmother–grandchild, and greater for grandfather–grandchild (Table 13.2). Respectively, they were 1.36 for MGM/C, 1.44 for MGF/C, 1.51 for PGM/C, and 1.53 for PGF/C. These differences were not statistically significant ($F = 1.25$, ns) and there was a trend for grandchildren to be less distant from the maternal grandparents (1.39) than from the paternal grandparents (1.52) ($F = 3.28$, $p = 0.075$).

### The effects of education and occupation of the parental generation on family cohesion and hierarchy

*Cohesion*

The mean distance scores given to all family dyads, and the mean power scores received by each family member, were analysed separately at the level of parents' education and occupation. No significant differences were found for educational background and distance (low 1.51 vs high 1.46, $F = 0.60$, ns). However, for occupational status, 'workers' viewed their family as more distant (1.53) than did 'officials' (1.36), at a significant level ($F = 5.81$, $p < 0.05$).

*Power*

Similar analyses were done for mean number of power blocks received. No significant difference was found by occupation (worker 0.83 vs official 0.89, $F = 0.14$, ns). However, for educational background, parents who had a higher educational background were perceived as more powerful (0.96) than parents with a lower educational background (0.61) at a significant level ($F = 4.17$, $p < 0.05$).

### Distribution or frequency of balanced, labile–balanced and unbalanced family structures

Of the 180 respondents, twenty-eight portrayed their families as of balanced structure, ninety-nine as labile–balanced, fifty-three as unbalanced. The labile–balanced structure was perceived most often (55 per cent of all 180 plots).

Generally, grandparents, parents, and children differed in portraying family structure. Although the majority of adults and children were of a labile–balanced view, children were relatively more likely to represent their family as balanced and adults to represent it as unbalanced ($\chi^2 = 14.8$, $p < 0.01$; Table 13.4).

*Table 13.4* Perceptions of types of family structures by adults and children (*n* = 180)

| Respondent | Type of family structure | | |
| | Balanced (%) | Labile–balanced (%) | Unbalanced (%) |
| --- | --- | --- | --- |
| Grandparents | 19.7 | 45.5 | 34.9 |
| Parents | 5.4 | 62.2 | 32.4 |
| Child | 27.5 | 57.5 | 15.0 |

## Conclusions

In terms of a general characterization of Chinese families, the FAST plots show that these three-generation families are generally perceived as highly cohesive and clearly hierarchical. Even so, the variation between individuals and dyads is sometimes sufficiently consistent to yield highly significant differences.

Some of the patterns are explicable in terms of traditional patterns of socialization in Chinese society. In particular, there is a clear ranking of power in families, by generation and by sex. Paternal grandfathers receive the most powerful evaluation. Compared to the impression of a 'declining' filial system in contemporary China (as stated in Ho's (1996) review), our sample seems to reflect a rather 'conservative' familial model characteristic of an inland area. The high status of the grandparents exemplifies this traditional pattern, which would appear to be different from expectations in modern Western societies, where the role status of grandparents has fallen in recent years (Smith, 1994).

The grandparents in these families appear to be well integrated. Relationships between grandparents and grandchildren tend to be seen as closer than those between father and child, or grandparents and parents; the closest relationships, however, are seen as existing between married couples and between mother and child. Children especially see the mother–child relationship as close and score highly on cross-generational coalitions.

Some suggestive trends were found regarding the influence of grandparental lineage. Traditional expectations in China would be that cohesion with a grandchild will be greater for paternal grandparents than for maternal grandparents; in our sample, more families had paternal grandparent(s) (*n* = 27) than maternal grandparent(s) (*n* = 13) living in the same household, illustrating the greater societal expectation for links with paternal grandparents. However, in contrast to such expectations, paternal grandparents were not closer to their grandchild than maternal grandparents; the maternal grandmother–grandchild pair had the most cohesive score among all the four kinds of biological grandparent–grandchild dyads, and maternal grandfather–grandchild pair the second. This trend of greater closeness of maternal grandmothers to grandchildren is, however, in accordance with findings from Western studies (Eisenberg, 1988; Hoffman, 1979; Euler and Weitzel, 1996), which indicate the significant role of maternal grandparents, particularly the maternal grandmothers, with and for whom the grandchildren felt greater closeness and liking. It is also in accordance with predictions from evolutionary theory, which we explore in more detail elsewhere (Shu, 1999).

This picture of Chinese families in our sample was generally true, irrespective of educational and occupation level. However, parents who saw their family as more cohesive usually had a better profession; and those who had a higher educational background were seen to be more powerful.

In summary, the results did not exceed the ancient Chinese pattern of close family ties and familial hierarchy. Families were perceived as highly cohesive; power relationships tended to follow strict lines of generation and gender. On the whole, the old is salient, although the new fashion is starting to play its part: recent changes, for example urbanization, have been influential in the country as a whole yet the effects are not too obvious in this study.

## *Comparison with other studies using symbolic figure placement techniques (SFPTs)*

Because of the somewhat different measures used, it is difficult to compare the results of this study with findings from the Japanese studies (Hatta and Tsukiji, 1993; Hatta, 1994), even if the involvement of the grandparent generation in our study is omitted here for comparison. Hatta's Doll Location Test (DLT) (Hatta, 1977) measures the exact dyadic distances on recording sheets (scores were computed in millimetres, although he had also a 'relative distance', which was obtained on the assumption that distance between parents, or between self and parent in 'ideal' conditions, was 1), and the responder's position is limited beforehand to the centre; measurement using the FAST is rather more 'symbolic' in the sense that each figure is positioned in a separate square on the chequered board and the distance calculation is based on the unit of 1, i.e. the distance between an adjacent dyad, and scaled up diagonally according to Pythagoras' theorem. Furthermore, there is no limit regarding where the respondent's own position can be on the board, which opens up the possibility of portraying self and others at more extreme points.

Hatta's sample is also different from ours (university students rather than primary school pupils). However, the findings reveal a mostly similar pattern for Chinese and Japanese families in relation to parent–child closeness. Mother–child is seen by children as not only closer than father–child, but also closer than father–mother. In the Chinese sample, parents represented the self–child pair more cohesively than the self–spouse pair, although the differences are very small. For the Japanese sample, such a difference is found more significantly in the mothers' representations, but the trend is opposite in fathers' representations; this may be explained by the fact that the mothers bear the majority of childrearing tasks as well as housework, and the experience of parenting can place strain on the relationship between the parents themselves. The similarities may be supposed to be a consequence of the two countries being closely connected in cultural origins. But in China the role of the father appears as somewhat more integrated in the family, and certainly not as 'undesirable' (as described in Hatta (1994)) as it appears to be for its Japanese counterpart.

There are distinct differences between the findings of this study and studies using subjects who did not have an Oriental background. Converting the cohesion scores obtained by Gehring and Feldman (1988) to distance scores comparable to ours, early adolescent respondents in the US (mean age 11.4 years) scored 1.47 on father–mother and 1.68 on parent–child distance. This is compared with 1.78 for father–mother and 1.30 for parent–child in our sample. The numerical differences may not be large but the tendency is clear: Chinese children see more inter-generational closeness while the US children see more parental closeness. This may be related to differences of childrearing practice between the two cultures. On the one hand, Chinese children may have a kind of 'misunderstanding' about the relationship between their mother and father; for example, Chinese parents are usually inclined to restrain themselves from showing mutual intimacy (physical or oral expression of closeness, e.g. kissing) before a child (Wu, 1996), and indeed try to show a certain distance instead. On the other hand, China has the tradition of valuing heirs and, once a child is born, the family focus would probably move quickly from the couple to the new generation.

### Using the FAST

The FAST was easy to carry out with persons across a wide age range (children to grandparents), and enabled both a general characterization of Chinese families and some very specific comparisons within families. However, a few drawbacks of the FAST should be noted, the main one being that it provides only a two-dimensional representation of a family system involving (in our sample) some three to six persons, so that some simplification must be made in describing a series of dyadic relationships from this. There is also the possibility of some social desirability bias in the FAST results, but this possibility is present in any interview or questionnaire-based measure; it is arguably reduced here by the holistic representational nature of the FAST, and by interviewing each person separately.

Our results do throw some doubts on the cross-cultural generalizability of Gehring's distinctions between balanced and unbalanced families, and their impli-cations. Our results showed a highly cohesive picture of Chinese families. Parents, grandparents, and children respectively represented a general view of their family as 1.48, 1.54, and 1.56 in mean distance, meaning that they usually placed figures in adjacent or nearly adjacent squares. This was also consistent with the practical knowledge we acquired through the whole survey process. However, using the balanced/labile–balanced/unbalanced distinction based on 'high', 'medium' and 'low' cohesion (see page 200), we found an unstable family structure with 84 per cent of plots being unbalanced or labile–balanced. If this is true, then, according to Gehring's ideas, most of these Chinese families should be having some bio-psychosocial difficulties. This is not the case, and the families were an ordinary cross-section from a representative urban sample without particular socioeconomic problems or behavioural or clinical difficulties.

Gehring's criterion of 'low hierarchy' is that there is no power difference between any (grand)parent–child pair or there is a hierarchy reversal. As there are more adults in three-generation households, there may be a greater chance for certain adult–child power relations to fall into this pattern. In fact, 78 per cent of our family plots were scored as low in hierarchy, which was one of the most significant cornerstones that led to the surprising findings concerning 'unstable' structure. In modern urban China, families would feel proud if they had equal power relationships; it would be seen as an indication of family harmony. There is some indication of this in our sample. There were even forty-three respondents out of the 180 who made a 'plain' portrayal without power blocks elevated to any members. Although traditional order in China requires submission to one's parents and all those senior within the family, modernization has been making significant changes to Chinese beliefs, and we cannot say a certain adult–child power relation would direct the entire familial hierarchy to an abnormal level.

Thirty-seven per cent of the sixty-three plots that were found to have such an 'abnormal' generational boundary embraced mother, father, and child within the smallest triangular area (i.e. dyadic distance scores for M/C, F/C, and M/F were 1, 1, and 1.4). This is the most cohesive representation we can offer to a triad using the FAST. Therefore we doubt whether this cross-generational coalition pattern is really meaningful to this Chinese sample, and it may reflect some limitations of the placement procedure in the FAST. Hatta and Tsukiji's (1993) study of Japanese families found a pattern of closer for mother–child and less close for mother–father relationships among most of their university student subjects; consequently they inferred the abnormal generational boundary definition to be unacceptable in their case as well.

We therefore argue that there is a cultural boundary in the application of Gehring's balanced/labile–balanced/unbalanced category scheme, and in his concept of cross-generational coalition. Their presence does not seem to predict abnormal family functioning in Eastern cultures such as China and Japan. Differing social traditions and cultural values may make them useful in the West, but inappropriate to Chinese families. However, the general applicability of the FAST procedure, and its use as an analytical tool for studying Chinese families, was well borne out in our study.

## References

Chen, G. (1996) 'Intergenerational relationships and intergenerational games', *International Play Journal*, 4: 209–13.

Chen, X. and Rubin, K.H. (1994) 'Family conditions, parental acceptance, and social competence and aggression in Chinese children', *Social Development*, 3: 269–90.

—— Dong, Q. and Zhou, H. (1997) 'Authoritative and authoritarian parenting practices and social and school performance in Chinese children', *International Journal of Behavioral Development*, 21: 855–73.

Chiu, L. (1987) 'Child-rearing attitudes of Chinese, Chinese-American, and Anglo-American mothers', *International Journal of Psychology*, 22: 409–19.

Eisenberg, A.R. (1988) 'Grandchildren's perspectives on relationships with grandparents: The influence of gender across generations', *Sex Roles*, 19: 205–17.

Euler, H.A. and Weitzel, B. (1996) 'Discriminative grandparental solicitude as reproductive strategy', *Human Nature*, 7: 39–59.

Falbo, T. (1991) 'The impact of grandparents on children's outcomes in China', *Marriage and Family Review*, 16: 369–76.

—— Poston, D.L. Jr. (1993) 'The academic, personality, and physical outcomes of only children in China', *Child Development*, 64: 18–35.

Gehring, T.M. and Feldman, S.S. (1988) 'Adolescents' perceptions of family cohesion and power: A methodological study of the Family System Test', *Journal of Adolescent Research*, 3: 33–52.

—— Marti, D. (1993) 'The Family System Test: Differences in perception of family structures between nonclinical and clinical children', *Journal of Child Psychology and Psychiatry*, 34: 363–77.

—— Wentzel, K.R., Feldman, S.S. and Munson, J. (1990) 'Conflict in families of adolescents: The impact on cohesion and power structures', *Journal of Family Psychology*, 3: 290–309.

—— Candrian, M., Marti, D. and Real del Sarte, O. (1996) 'Family System Test (FAST): The relevance of parental family constructs for clinical intervention', *Child Psychiatry and Human Development*, 27: 55–65.

Hatta, T. (1977) 'Doll Location Test: Application to the patients of psychoneuroses', *Tekisei Kennkyu*, 10: 1–6.

—— (1994) 'Projected family structure by modern Japanese adolescents', *Social Behavior and Personality*, 22: 399–408.

—— Tsukiji, N. (1993) 'Characteristics of Japanese family: Evidence from the results of the Doll Location Test by university students', *Psychologia. An International Journal of Psychology in the Orient*, 36: 235–40.

Ho, D.Y.F. (1987) 'Fatherhood in Chinese culture', in M.E. Lamb (ed.), *The Father's Role: Cross-Cultural Perspectives*. Hillsdale, NJ: Erlbaum.

—— (1996) 'Filial piety and its psychological consequences', in M.H. Bond (ed.), *The Handbook of Chinese Psychology*. Hong Kong: Oxford University Press.

Hoffman, E. (1979) 'Young adults' relations with their grandparents: An exploratory study', *International Journal of Aging and Human Development*, 10: 299–310.

Jankowiak, W. (1992) 'Father–child relations in urban China', in B.S. Hewlett (ed.), *Father–child Relations: Cultural and Biosocial Contexts*, New York: de Gruyter.

Lin, C.C. and Fu, V.R. (1990) 'A comparison of child-rearing practices among Chinese, immigrant Chinese, and Caucasian-American parents', *Child Development*, 61: 429–33.

Shu, S. (1999) 'Grandparents, parents and children: A study of three-generation family structure and intergenerational relationships in contemporary China', Unpublished M.Phil. thesis, Goldsmiths College, University of London, UK.

Smith, P.K. (1994) 'Grandparenting', in M. Bornstein (ed.), *Handbook of Parenting*, Vol. 3. Hillsdale, NJ: Erlbaum.

Wu, D.Y.H. (1996) 'Chinese childhood socialization', In M.H. Bond (ed.), *The Handbook of Chinese Psychology*. Hong Kong: Oxford University Press.

Zhao, J. (1997) 'Fertility intentions of the urban population in China', *Population Research*, 21: 42–5 (in Chinese).

# Part IV

# Clinical issues: diagnosis, intervention and evaluation

# 14 The FAST: A therapeutic tool for interactive assessment and treatment in family psychotherapy

*Sandra A. Rigazio-DiGilio*

Psychotherapy assessment is most often associated with the traditional diagnostic procedures and nomenclature proscribed by the DSM IV (American Psychiatric Association, 1994) and the ICD 10 (World Health Organisation, 1992). However, it is generally recognized that this is only a first step in completing a comprehensive assessment. The therapist commonly requires additional information about the client[1] or client system in order to construct an extensive diagnosis that can be used to design, implement and evaluate treatment (American Psychiatric Association, 1994: xxv). While often presented as an interesting method for obtaining alternative clinical data, standardized assessment tools are rarely used to extend an initial diagnosis or to monitor and evaluate the ongoing work and progress of therapy.

The FAST (Gehring, 1984) is a standardized figure placement technique that can add a relational assessment to the initial DSM IV multiaxial diagnosis. This combination offers a more holistic view of human and systemic development. Further, using the FAST at different points throughout therapy ensures that the therapist moves beyond the initial diagnosis and towards a dynamic view of change that more immediately informs and monitors the continuing course of treatment.

Because the FAST draws from a theoretical structure and language system generally recognized across disciplines, the information generated provides practical and accessible interpretations of clinical data. Using commonly accepted constructs and language encourages communication and collaboration with other agents and systems working with the family, such as schools, medical clinics and social workers. The FAST is based on salutogenic principles, offering clinical information to the therapist and client system, facilitating the identification of systemic strengths and resources that can be used to construct solution-focused treatment plans. Given its accessibility to client systems, therapists, and involved professionals, the FAST permits all the voices that are participating in the therapeutic alliance to be accounted for.

The psychometric properties of the FAST are among the highest for figure placement techniques. Therapists can have confidence in this instrument to evaluate different components of their own work, and to translate empirical research related to the FAST into their clinical arena. By combining this instrument with therapy, therapists reduce the gap between theory and practice, and simultaneously engage the family in designing, implementing, and evaluating treatment goals. This interactive approach to relational therapy increases the family's participation and collaboration as members of the therapeutic alliance. These latter two variables, consistent with the concepts of active client engagement, are significant predictors of positive therapeutic outcome (Pinsof, 1988; Weissmark and Giacomo, 1995).

The intent of this chapter is to demonstrate how using the FAST can alter the traditional dynamics inherent in therapist-controlled assessment, treatment planning, intervention, and evaluation. Historically, these remained within the purview of the mental health professional, while the client was subjugated to the role of passive recipient. Contemporary family therapy models are based on a more collaborative system of communication and participation, where the importance of the client's language and interpretations is paramount (Anderson and Goolishian, 1988; Hoffman, 1988; White and Epston, 1990; Nichols and Schwartz, 1995). When therapy includes a psychometrically sound instrument that can be interpreted by both professionals and clients, the therapeutic language system is respected and the nature of treatment planning shifts from the primary responsibility of the therapist to the shared responsibility of both client and therapist. A case study illustrates the inclusive nature of the FAST as an assessment tool and creative intervention strategy that activates change, stimulates collaborative reflection, and initiates therapeutic narratives within a client-centred language system.

## Defining interactive assessment and treatment

Interactive assessments invite clients to participate with therapists in co-constructing multiple perspectives regarding the issues that prompted treatment, and the probable solutions. These types of assessment give clients a choice in the selection of important data and encourage them to design how these data will be presented for further dialogue and interpretation.

According to Flowers (1990), specific benefits are derived when using interactive assessment procedures in the therapeutic environment. First, interactive assessments promote hope. These assessments provide opportunities for the clients to reframe their issues and realize unrecognized or underutilized resources. Additionally, by engaging in an interactive process, myths and misperceptions are challenged, and productive discussions generated. These dialogues orient clients to the therapeutic process and actually accelerate the exploration of solutions. Finally, interactive assessments provide concrete evidence of the changes made by the family and particular subsystems within it, thus reinforcing the belief that change is possible and that progress is being made.

By introducing interactive assessments to therapy, the therapist offers alternative ways to discuss and organize important data and experiences. Gehring (1998) refers to this as 'participative planning and evaluation'. This style of interaction makes room for members to draw from immediate experience as it unfolds in the session and to use this experience to generate options and solutions. Members of the therapeutic system are often able to realize hidden patterns of meaning and behaviour over time and in relation to particular situations, persons, and relationships. Often, clients are surprised at learning how similar or different their own perceptions are from those of other family members, a first step in extending client voices to include multiple perspectives and entry points.

### Criteria for selecting interactive assessment and treatment

An examination of the literature points to five criteria that help identify the types of systemic instruments best used as interactive assessment tools. These criteria are not intended to locate instruments for empirical investigation, but rather to build a library of clinical tools that can offer sound, albeit partial, assessments while also engaging client systems in less familiar experiences that promote participation, engender competence, and encourage dialogue.

- First, instruments that call for families to engage in an interactional task provide a rich source of information that serves as a point of departure for therapeutic conversation. These methods might include live, taped, or simulated scenarios that are conducted in naturalistic or clinical settings. Portions of recorded materials are highlighted and discussed. Many of these instruments are flexible enough to attend to both internal and external factors, allowing for a closer look at a broader terrain of inquiry.
- The second criterion directs us to those methods of inquiry that generate information for mutual interpretation by both the family and the therapist. These types of interactive assessments, geared towards social constructivism, become the vehicle for sharing power in the therapy sessions by stimulating collaboration, reflexivity, and a multiplicity of ideas and possibilities (Laird, 1995).
- The third criterion calls for instruments that can be used throughout the therapeutic process. Utility is the main concern here. For example, labour-intensive assessment methods may prove useful during the initiation of therapy and as part of the termination process, but would be considered intrusive at other points. Additionally, instruments targeted for repeated use need to be sensitive enough to uncover slight variations that register change while still providing continuity over the long term. Repeated exposure to such instruments should not be seen as burdensome. Instruments that meet this criterion are used to tailor treatment across particular contexts or situations, to assist a client system's ongoing evaluation of progress, and to capture changes in family dynamics over time.
- The fourth criterion suggests the need for instruments that equalize the playing field by inviting all members to participate. Assessments based on a certain level of language ability, conceptual complexity, and/or physical ability may limit the range of family members able to participate, and therefore distort a collective voice and perhaps silence a peripheral one.
- The fifth criterion addresses the need for psychometric rigour. Ideally, interactive assessment methods should render usable clinical data that can be quantifiably and/or qualitatively analysed and shared. This ensures that others

will be able to trace the movement of therapy when necessary. Such assessment will strengthen the connection of theory to practice, and offer a sense of credibility to the discourse generated by the findings.

While not suggested as criteria, there are a few additional considerations to keep in mind when choosing interactive assessment tools. One is to determine how the instrument can enhance your own clinical competence. For example, assessment instruments that focus on particular components of assessment that may be new or difficult for you can offer a breadth of knowledge not previously available. On the other hand, instruments that capture variables well known to you, but from a different vantage point or perspective, may give more depth to your knowledge base. Another source of information is gathered from instruments that direct you and the family to engage in activities not usually afforded space in the therapy room. There may be other family variables you would like to consider. Is there an instrument that would benefit a particular population you serve? Are there a range of instruments that could meet various styles of learning?

The FAST meets the five criteria mentioned above. It has a wide range of application and assists therapists to co-construct therapeutic environments built on trust, openness, reflection, and family empowerment. Additionally, because the FAST is a visual representation of family dynamics, even young children and those with limited language skills can communicate their perceptions of family functioning. The concrete nature of placing figures on the board helps move therapy away from its heavy reliance on verbal exchange and provides clients with new ways to explore family dynamics. Finally, it offers a broad-based assessment framework that is easily integrated into differing conceptualizations of human and systemic development, adaptation, and change.

### The FAST as an interactive assessment and treatment tool

The FAST is designed to access clinically relevant quantitative and qualitative data regarding how individuals, subsystems, and the collective family perceive the structures governing family organization and functioning over time and across situations. The end products of every completed FAST provide the therapist with a wealth of data to analyse how a family perceives the emotional bonds and hierarchical structures governing closeness, authority, and influence. Additionally, how clients actually do the work of the FAST offers a first-hand lens into family interaction that can be captured by the SPRINT (systemic performance roles in interaction). The SPRINT is a behavioural observation framework that is used to choose criteria for observation. The therapeutic issues, for any given family and at any given point in the therapy, inform the criteria of observation. As the task unfolds, both therapist and client take on the role of participant–observer, using the task as their focal point, similar to White's (1993) externalization process.

The self-reporting format of the FAST allows family members – individually and in various combinations – to represent their family's emotional distance and influential relationships within three settings: typical functioning, ideal interactions, and conflict situations. The three-dimensional design of the FAST elicits qualitative data through interviews about the family representations and observations. Additionally, five quantitative evaluations can be conducted using data from the various structural arrangements family members construct: relational structures, types of relational structures, differences in perception, flexibility and generational boundaries. The FAST spatializes the metaphorical boundaries that differentiate and influence interactions within generational subsystems (marital or sibling) and cross-generation subsystems (parent–child dyads) and adds another lens on the interpretations of family functioning.

A therapist capable of integrating quantitative and qualitative forms of analyses and trained in interactive assessment may want to include the FAST in their formal assessment library. Basic clinical training is sufficient to administer and quanti- tatively score the FAST. It should be noted, however, that developing systemic hypotheses requires the therapist to interpret quantitative and qualitative data. The therapist should also be aware of the fact that some of the quantitative scoring procedures equating proximity with cohesion and height with hierarchy, while logical, are open to question. For example, there is no rationale for classifying adjacently placed figures as highly cohesive and diagonally adjoined figures as moderately cohesive, or for using 1.5 cm as a distinguishing feature of hierarchy. This means that the therapist needs to address issues of consensus either in the introduction of the FAST or during administration. There are various ways of doing this, including the therapist offering a measuring stick of sorts, or asking the family to come to a consensus.

The FAST is versatile. It can be administered to children as young as 6 years and has demonstrated effectiveness in cross-cultural studies. Because of its ease of administration and interpretation (Gehring, 1998), its wide range of applications, its psychometric and therapeutic powers of discrimination (Gehring and Feldman, 1988; Marti and Gehring, 1992) and its clarity of illuminating structural properties within a family (Gehring and Marti, 1993), the FAST is an ideal instrument to use as an interactive assessment device at all stages of the treatment process. To illustrate the interactivity of the FAST a case study format is used throughout the rest of this chapter.

## Using the FAST in family psychotherapy: a case study

Assessment is the cornerstone of effective treatment. A comprehensive assessment is based on the integration of data from multiple sources to ensure an understanding of the family that is robust enough to guide treatment planning and intervention. By measuring qualitative–situative and contextual family phenomena, as well as quantitative–structural evaluation data, the FAST provides the therapist and the family with a broad range of clinically relevant information. Beginning with an initial assessment as a baseline, progress can be ascertained and, using the FAST at critical points of transition over the course of treatment, can shift the therapeutic focus. The flexible framework of the SPRINT guides therapists to tailor the observations they will track to match the specific aim of treatment. Just as valuable, the FAST is used to ensure that the family remains central in the therapeutic process by eliciting the voices of silent members, and promoting structural and perceptual change. The application of the FAST represents both an assessment tool and a therapeutic intervention. The following case demonstrates these two properties of the FAST.

### Intake information

Assessment begins at the point of first contact. Family members and therapists generate initial assumptions based on calls, conversations with others, and their own previous experience. These anticipatory hypotheses serve as filters that inform the initial assessment interview. Introducing an interactive assessment tool early on in therapy accelerates movement away from these idiosyncratic and perhaps less accessible filters. As these tools provide a common point of reference, the therapeutic system can construct a shared experience, one that all members participate in and develop meanings about. This collective experience can serve as a point of departure to initiate therapeutic conversations, and as a reference point for later evaluation. The early use of interactive assessments can facilitate the substitution of initial impressions with mutually agreed-upon goals. Incongruent goals between therapist and family are associated with ineffective treatment and early termination (Pinsof and Catherall, 1986; Coleman, 1987).

### Referral information

Maria Contro was referred for therapy by her primary care physician for depression, complicated by a sudden withdrawal of support from her extended family.

### Demographic information

The Contro family consists of Frank (52) and Maria (49), their children Mia (15) and Frankie Jr (14), and the maternal grandmother, Rosa (75), whom the family refers to as Nonni. Frank worked as a truck driver for 25 years until his early retirement, 1 year ago, owing to progressive lung cancer, just recently diagnosed as terminal. Owing to an exacerbation of Paget's disease, Maria has decreased her hours as an office manager. Although Mia was having academic and social difficulties in the tenth grade, her history was unremarkable. Frankie, a socially active child, has a history of poor academic performance. Nonni came to live with them 7 months ago, after the death of her mother. She helps with household functions.

### Forming and consolidating the therapeutic alliance

Family assessment is inseparable from joining and intervention (Colapinto, 1988). Respectful joining allows the therapist and all members of the family to engage in non-pathological, solution-focused dialogue. As this alliance evolves, members can challenge perceptions and generate alternative views and options. Throughout this process, therapist and client continually evaluate the capacity of the therapeutic alliance to stimulate and manage change. Research indicates that a therapeutic process lacking in respectful joining and ongoing collaborative engagement and evaluation contributes to poor outcomes (Green and Herget, 1991).

Solution-focused dialogue extends the search for resources beyond the family to include others participating with the current definition of the problem. Capturing this wider context depends on how well the therapeutic environment uncovers for discussion the way the family's perceptions and structure are affecting and affected by internal and external factors. These examinations de-emphasize the family as the problem and instead invite members to join as participants in defining solutions. This increases the likelihood that members will help define, and therefore be committed to, a core set of goals. Research suggests that both client satisfaction and positive treatment outcomes are associated with the degree to which families accept the issues and goals of treatment as their own (Horvath and Symonds, 1991).

In forming and consolidating therapeutic alliances, clinicians aim to provide a trusting environment to initiate inclusive and collaborative dialogue and to surface the focal points of that dialogue. Introducing an interactive tool like the FAST to the assessment process can enhance the dialogue. Asking all family members, either individually or collectively, to participate in arranging figures on the FAST board and then analysing the results in both a qualitative and quantitative fashion, helps establish three major themes of treatment. First, the family's issues will set the stage for goal setting; outside professional 'prescriptions' will not be imposed. Second, a careful analysis of the process will be conducted throughout treatment to monitor what types of gains the family is making. Third, the field of inquiry can be expanded to include significant others beyond the family boundary.

As noted previously, because the FAST is a visual representation of family dynamics, even young children and individuals with limited language skills can communicate their perceptions. Thus the matter of inclusivity is attended to. Further, the concrete nature of placing figures on the board helps move therapy away from its heavy reliance on verbal exchange and reflection and offers clients alternative ways to explore family dynamics.

Qualitative interpretations of the FAST can be a point of departure for the therapeutic dialogue. These interpretations form a starting point from which everyone can see and begin talking. The quantitative analysis helps demystify the therapeutic process. Because quantitative findings are being used, the family knows that formal measures will also be used to guide its progress. The subjective–qualitative and standardized–quantitative focal points provided by the FAST speak right to the heart of tailoring treatment by accessing the central characteristics of each role in the therapeutic process. The professional worldview of the therapist is primarily supported by the quantitative measurements, while the worldview of the client is primarily supported by the qualitative interpretations. As both paths are accessed in the therapeutic dialogue, what emerges is a respectful, inclusive, and extended co-construction of the problem and proposed solutions.

*The first session*

The nuclear family attended the first session. The initial therapeutic conversation was controlled by Maria's monologic description, not repudiated by any other voice, making hers the dominant story. She noted the point of origin as related to Frank's diagnoses, but primarily emphasized Nonni's entry into the family as the core root of the current disintegration. She did not broaden her scope of inquiry beyond her nuclear family and her mother. The conviction of her story, coupled with the lack of response from others, left no room for the exploration of alternative stressors.

Other members were reticent, even when the therapist encouraged dialogue. When dominant or silent voices exist in a family, one can hypothesize that preconceived stories, publicly or tacitly supported, have reified, sacrificing the possibility of other options. While this can occur for many reasons, the pattern can be interrupted by the introduction of interactive assessment tools that provide a point of conversation more easily regulated by family members.

The FAST was introduced at this time. In this way, the therapist set the stage for all members to work together and make a representation of their typical family relationships. As the family worked on the task, the mere notion of moving away from the reason they were there, or perhaps needing to respond to mother's dialogue, immediately relieved the situation, as each member became a bit more animated and willing to participate.

*Behavioural/SPRINT observations*

Using the SPRINT, the therapist observed several pertinent interactions. Father and mother could not agree on the placement of Nonni, even so far as whether or not she should be placed on the board. Mia watched and Frankie's head was down, while mother was loud and father listened. Mia's activity shifted the dynamics. She suggested a place on the board for Nonni. This animated the father and quieted the mother. Frankie, who had been looking away, became quite alert at the loss of the mother's voice in the room. While the shift was only momentary, the family did not return to baseline. Frankie remained alert and Mia became the one to move the figures, while mother and father discussed figure placement with less reactivity but giving conflicting directions to Mia. Both parents did come to an agreement that one figure would represent all of Maria's brothers and sisters, instead of placing one figure for each person. Figure 14.1 illustrates the final placement of figures for the typical family representation.

*Structured follow-up interview*

Once the session was complete, the therapist modified the structured follow-up questions to initiate the therapeutic discourse. The following illustrative segments demonstrate the clinical value of the structured interview.

**Intertypical representation**

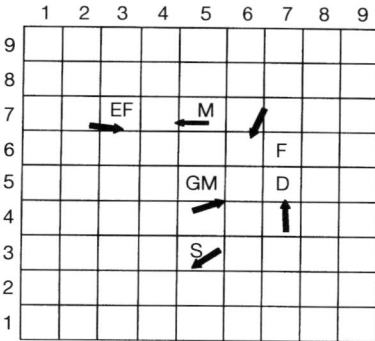

| | F | M | D | S | GM | EF |
|---|---|---|---|---|---|---|
| H | 1 | 2 | 0 | 0 | 3 | 2 |

**BO/SPRINT** M in conflict with F and D re: GM. M peripheralized and S withdraws.

**Cohesion**
Family level — Low
Parent level — Medium
Sibling level — Medium

Cross-generational coalition noted in the F/D dyad

**Hierarchy**
Family level — Medium
Parent level — Medium
Sibling level — Low

Hierarchy reversal noted between GM and M, GM and parents, and EF and parents

**Relational types**
Family level — Labile–balanced
Parent level — Balanced
Sibling level — Labile–balanced

**Interideal representation**

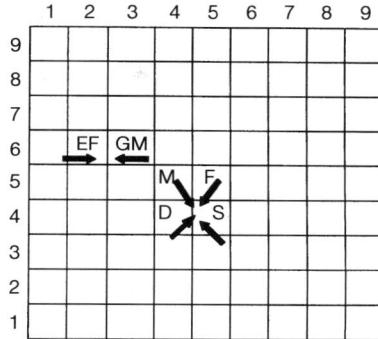

| | F | M | D | S | GM | EF |
|---|---|---|---|---|---|---|
| H | 3 | 3 | 2 | 1 | 0 | 0 |

**BO/SPRINT** M cries. F directs and D complies. S peripheral, watchful.

**Cohesion**
Family level — Medium
Parent level — High
Sibling level — High

No cross-generational coalition noted

**Hierarchy**
Family level — Medium
Parent level — Low
Sibling level — Medium

No hierarchy reversals noted

**Relational types**
Family level — Balanced
Parent level — Unbalanced
Sibling level — Balanced

| Level | Flexibility Cohesion | Hierarchy |
|---|---|---|
| Family | −1 | 0 |
| Parent | −1 | +1 |
| Sibling | −1 | −1 |

*Figure 14.1* Session one – intertypical and interideal representations. D, daughter; EF, extended family; F, father; GM, grandmother; H, hierarchy; M, mother; S, son.

*Segment one:*

*Therapist*:   (to the family) During the task, each of you seemed to think about different situations to help you make the map . . .

*Mother*:   Yes. That's because, no matter what we are doing, the same thing happens. We always seem to feel bad in these conversations, and we don't know how to fix it.

*Therapist*:   (to father) Is that what all the discussion was about . . . when you were talking about where to put Nonni?

*Father*:   Yes. See how we don't come together (pointing at the board). We don't see eye to eye. Maria feels bad because she can't stand up for herself without hurting Nonni. She used to go to her brothers and sisters, but everyone is fighting now.

*Segment two:*

*Therapist*:   How long would you say it has been this way?

*Father*:   Well, we've been hit with all sorts of things this last year, and getting Nonni settled in is just one.

*Mother*:   And a big one. It's been hard.

*Therapist*:   So the way you describe it . . . this way has been going on since Nonni came. And the way you did the task and are talking now, it seems like this happens a lot . . . when was the last time?

*Son*:   Every time it's time to eat. [laughs]

*Mother*:   Well, he's right. Before Nonni moved in we actually ate meals together. Now, Nonni cooks all day, so people eat any time they want. Don't get me wrong, I'm not complaining because she does a lot of work for me so I can do my job, but I wish we could eat together sometimes.

*Father*:   Well, I think all you have to do is tell her that, Maria. She is just trying to be helpful.

*Therapist*:   So it happens, you feel bad like this a lot, like it is happening right now in here.

*Daughter*:   YES! Just like this. Did you hear us talking about those eyes?

*Therapist*:   A little bit, but what do you mean?

*Daughter*:   (pointing at the board) Well, everyone was fighting, and Frankie didn't even help. He just looks out the window, just like here. And mom goes out to her sisters. And now, dad and Nonni are together, not with me.

*Father*:   (to therapist). It's hard for Mia. She thinks we shouldn't argue. And I can see now, she feels alone, and does not have anyone to turn to.

*Mother*:   Mia, I am sorry. All I was trying to show you is how you should use the eyes to show the therapist that people are mad or sad.

*Segment three:*

*Therapist*: How could this map you made be different, so you all were a bit happier?

*Father*: I think Maria needs to make friends with Nonni.

*Mother*: Don't do that. This is not just my problem. Do you like everything she has done here? You complain to me, and then want me to fix it.

*Father*: Maria, I do not complain about how Nonni treats me. I just worry about how you feel. I want you to feel better.

*Mother*: If you were so worried about me, you would talk to her. You get along. She listens to you.

*Father*: I do tell your mother what I want when we are here and all of you are gone, and there is no problem. The kids don't seem to have any complaints about all she does for them.

[The family becomes quiet].

The family history of chronic and terminal illness was quite significant, and visibly evident, yet this family focused narrowly on whether or not to blame Nonni or to blame Frank or Maria for not talking to Nonni directly. To determine if the family could access a broader definition of the problem and solution, the therapist reintroduced the ideal version of the FAST as a problem-solving instrument. The therapist was interested in seeing if other unexpressed issues could emerge, if the primary focus on Nonni was dissipated (i.e. the unexpressed issues of illness, conflict with children and the extended family, parental conflict and economic loss). Figure 14.1 depicts the family rendition of the ideal situation.

### Behavioural/SPRINT observations

Maria was quieter through this task, and Frank more a leader. Mia moved the figures and father seemed more the director, asking questions to prompt dialogue but clearly communicating a very particular relational style that he viewed as ideal. Frankie was again quiet and watched his father.

### Structured follow-up interview

Up to this point, the family had a narrow view of the problem and limited solutions. The therapist hoped to use the two arrangements and what he heard in dialogue to co-construct with the family a broader definition of the problem and more options for change. Up to this point, the therapist facilitated interaction with minimal interference so he could observe family interaction in a purer form. During this part of the session, he could now solicit input from the quieter members as well, being sure all voices were heard before entering into a dialogue about treatment goals. The following abbreviated exchange demonstrates how follow-up questions can be modified in a clinical setting to accelerate the treatment process.

*Therapist*:   Does this new arrangement represent a situation that has occurred at some point?

*Father*:   Yes, if you remove Nonni, this arrangement reminds me of a few years back when I left my second job, and me and the family did a lot more together.

*Therapist*:   So, it reminds you of how your family looked a few years back? How long did this time last?

*Father*:   Not long, really . . . about 6 months. We worked hard to get there, and didn't get to enjoy it . . . but it can happen to the best of us. Can't have ideal too long, might get spoiled (laughs).

*Therapist*:   Maybe that is true. But maybe not. [Talking now to the whole family] What would it take – given life as it is today – to change this typical map to be more like the ideal one?

*Mother*:   What would it take? Well, if we remembered we had a goal, something that pulled us together, and we respected it, we could be there again. See, here [points to arrangement 1] we forgot . . . and here [points to arrangement 2] we remembered what we worked for. We are both still strong. [Long pause] And the kids should respect it too. But now the outside is all they care about. I think Nonni is also complicating things, she doesn't realize that we have our ways of doing things, and we shouldn't have to totally accept her ways. She has too much time on her hands . . . that's why she does so much for the kids and Frank. If we are going to get back to this place we need to find some things for Nonni to do, Frank will have to stop letting his emphysema get him down, and get the kids more interested in the family. We are losing enough here.

*Father*:   I think it would require me to perk up a bit. She's right. I am spoiled with Nonni around. But it is not good for me. See, [pointing to arrangement 2] here they got me involved instead of moping on the couch. I know I could. It just seems hard when it's time, and then I say, 'What the hell'. And I guess Nonni sees that as me being really out of it and needing her here all the time. I like company. She's a sweetheart, but I could do more, and maybe she would feel like she could visit the other family members a little. That's why Maria smiled when Mia snuck her over there. [Winks at Mia] Thought I didn't catch that, eh?

*Mother*:   Well, we always discuss this, but then you get lazy. I feel like I will not have any of the family time we hoped for unless you let Nonni know that you're well enough.

*Daughter*:   That will make Nonni feel bad . . . if she doesn't know how to help.

*Son*:   I liked it when dad came home. We did stuff. Then it just went back to . . . like . . . when he was working . . . and then . . . now . . . it just got all tense.

On the basis of these conversations, the family generated two goals that would serve as a foundation for future work (e.g. dad's illness). The first, returning to a developmental phase where the family's image of itself was one of closeness, respect, and commitment, seemed more attainable for several reasons. The FAST activity provided a way for the family to refer to previously unmentionable events, to connect emotionally with an image of themselves as a close and happy family, and to begin etching out steps to achieve this lost identity. The second goal was to decrease their dependency on Nonni and help her expand her social network. Frank saw his part as letting her know when he needs her and when he could be alone. Maria saw her part as getting her siblings to take some responsibility in socially integrating Nonni into their lives. The children agreed that if they were more responsible at home, and less dependent on Nonni, she would feel free enough to spend time with the other families.

As the session was ending, the therapist stated that he would be able to package all the information in a way that would be interesting to examine, and he hoped the family would do the same. He also wondered who else might be invited to come. The parents both agreed, albeit with some trepidation, that Nonni should join the group, but were not sure if she would come. The therapist replied 'Her comfort level will be important, so I hope all of you will think about how to explain what we have done and perhaps we can illustrate for her somehow?'

The use of the FAST in both assessment and treatment is clear, even in the opening of the therapeutic encounter. In this session, it was used to engage the family's interest, form the therapeutic alliance, broadly define the problem using their full range of experiences, and construct treatment goals that went beyond remediation of the presenting problem. Further, by providing an environment that invited the family's perceptions and interpretations of their experience to take centre stage, a reassurance emerged that therapy would unfold at their own pace. Such reassurance allows families the freedom to interact in less familiar ways which helps to broaden the view of problems promoting treatment.

### Surfacing problem definitions with the FAST

Interpretations garnered using the FAST dimensions organize a mass of clinical information in a way that can be discussed in subsequent sessions. The irrefutable nature of figures placed on a board (i) increases the probability that members will come to some consensual notions rather than fight about accuracy; (ii) serves as a reminder of past sessions, reducing ambiguity and forgetfulness; (iii) establishes a common focal point constructed by all those in the session; (iv) helps externalize their problems; and (v) provides a relational focus to the treatment process. Additionally, having the family participate in and observe different representations by different individuals or subsystems reinforces the idea of multiple voices and perspectives. This challenges the insurmountable nature of the presenting problem by opening up different pathways to alternative solution sets.

## Standard interpretation of the FAST

The therapist completed a standard analysis of the FAST representations (see Figure 14.1). The typical representation indicates that the family perceives itself to work from a labile–balanced structure, meaning they constructed a map with low cohesion and medium hierarchy. While the parental subsystem on its own is perceived as balanced (medium cohesion and hierarchy), the placement of Nonni reveals a cross-generational coalition between father and grandmother with mother on the periphery. The family perceives several power reversals in the adult subsystem, including Nonni and Maria, Nonni and the parents, and the extended family and Frank.

In the ideal representation, the figures are placed in such a way as to reveal the wish for a very different arrangement. The family type is perceived as balanced, with medium cohesion and medium hierarchy. This time the parental subsystem is considered unbalanced (high cohesion and low hierarchy) and the sibling subsystem is balanced (high cohesion and medium hierarchy). Even when Nonni is included, there are no power reversals or cross-generational coalitions noted.

A comparison of the two representations indicated that the family demonstrated moderate flexibility in the differences between the two administrations. This offers an optimistic prognosis that can be seen by all members.

## Interweaving family and professional 'realities'

The FAST was used as an intervention to assist the nuclear family's work to integrate Nonni, as a baseline for the therapist to assess the degree to which the typical representation reified in the presence of Nonni, and as a point of departure for the therapist to begin to coach the parents' return to their position in the hierarchy. Referring to the homework assignment, the therapist asked the family to explain to Nonni what the FAST was and how they found it useful.

This intervention placed Nonni in a learner position and provided an opportunity for all members to participate actively. The Contros joined in this educational process; Frankie even explained what the blocks were for. With the family's basic understanding of the FAST reinforced through this dialogue, the therapist asked Frank to construct a rendition of the ideal relationships by asking 'What do you now perceive as the ideal situation, given what your family has learned about how it wants to be?' The therapist used this as his baseline for assessment, as an intervention to reassert the father's position in the family, and as a point of departure to set the stage for the family and Nonni to negotiate a modified structure.

During the task, father's confidence wavered as he tried to place Nonni. He seemed to relive the conflict of the previous session and would speak only partially to the goal. What was different in this section was that, when his words became confused, Maria would join him and help him present clear ideas to Nonni in a non-confrontational manner. To the therapist, this looked like movement towards a unified executive position and set the stage for structural reorganization. In subsequent sessions, the therapist would call upon this team to solidify change and set direction, especially through the critical period of anticipating the future.

**Father's ideal representation**

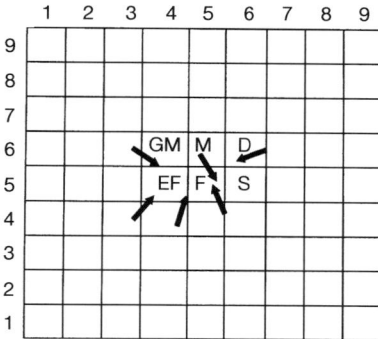

|   | 1 | 2 | 3 | 4 | 5 | 6 | 7 | 8 | 9 |
|---|---|---|---|---|---|---|---|---|---|
| 9 |   |   |   |   |   |   |   |   |   |
| 8 |   |   |   |   |   |   |   |   |   |
| 7 |   |   |   |   |   |   |   |   |   |
| 6 |   |   |   | GM | M | D |   |   |   |
| 5 |   |   |   | EF | F | S |   |   |   |
| 4 |   |   |   |   |   |   |   |   |   |
| 3 |   |   |   |   |   |   |   |   |   |
| 2 |   |   |   |   |   |   |   |   |   |
| 1 |   |   |   |   |   |   |   |   |   |

|   | F | M | D | S | GM | EF |
|---|---|---|---|---|----|----|
| H | 3 | 3 | 2 | 1 | 3  | 0  |

**BO/SPRINT**

**Cohesion**

| Family level | High |
|---|---|
| Parent level | High |
| Sibling level | High |

No cross-generational coalitions noted

**Hierarchy**

| Family level | Medium |
|---|---|
| Parent level | Low |
| Sibling level | Medium |

Hierarchy conflict between GM and parents

**Relational types**

| Family level | Balanced |
|---|---|
| Parent level | Labile–balanced |
| Sibling level | Balanced |

**Differences in perception**
**(Family and father's ideal representations)**

| Level | Cohesion | Hierarchy |
|---|---|---|
| Family | +1 | 0 |
| Parent | 0 | 0 |
| Sibling | 0 | 0 |

*Figure 14.2* Session two – father's ideal representation.
D, daughter; EF, extended family; F, father; GM, grandmother;
H, hierarchy; M, mother; S, son.

### Blending therapist and family realities: establishing a treatment plan

The therapist noted the difference found between the family's and the father's rendition of ideal relationships. As indicated in the quantitative analysis presented in Figure 14.2, the only difference in perception between the two representations was noted by a +1 change in cohesion. But closing this gap became a significant theme throughout the therapeutic process.

The therapist added this new information to his analysis of the Contros' typical and ideal representations (see Figure 14.1), which suggested that the family had not yet shifted its identity to incorporate the normative and non-normative stressors associated with chronic progressive and life-shortening illnesses. Thus, many stressors were mismanaged and left the family depleted. Nonni's entrance allowed for a slight respite, but enacted an ineffective structure. At this point, then, an alternative structure was necessary. If it was developed successfully, the sense of accomplishment and identity gained would permit the family to better deal with life tasks under a realistic understanding of itself.

Synthesizing past and present data, the Contros and the therapist refined the goals of the treatment. It seemed the first order of business would be to reorganize to a more viable family structure, and the second goal would be to look at the stressors requiring management under this new structure. To accomplish the first, the centrifugal forces operating on the family needed to be slowed down in order to integrate the meaning of Frank's (and later Maria's) diagnosis, so that his wisdom could be passed on to his family. The parents had to re-enter the hierarchy of the nuclear family and a place for Nonni to be 'helper' versus 'manager' needed to be constructed. Family and therapist needed to remain alert as to how anticipatory fears might interrupt the process. Once the reorganization took hold, the family would be able to review the management of stressors and to anticipate the future.

The FAST was used effectively to assess current family functioning, to help redefine the problem: from Maria's depression, to Nonni's entry, to reorganizing executive functions and facilitating a family to transform their identity to meet the needs of their present circumstance. Finding a solution to this problem and identifying resources inside and outside the family became the therapeutic focus for the remainder of treatment. The therapist used the qualitative and quantitative data from the FAST to help tailor interventions to the specific ways the Contros made meaning of their situation.

### Modifying the course of treatment

The next phase of treatment helped the family establish its new identity. While the content topic changed several times (i.e. the children's academic and social difficulties, Maria's relationship with her extended family, Nonni's role in the wider system, the delegation of household responsibilities), the work remained focused on restructuring the family. After a series of sessions aimed at forming and consolidating a new structure, the therapist met with the adults to examine changes and set the direction for the next phase of treatment. The focus of this transitional session was to explore how the adults hold the new structure, even in the face of conflict. Here, the FAST was used as a source of feedback and catalyst for therapy. It provoked the family to recreate interactional patterns in treatment and provided a concrete measure to gauge their progress.

To get a quick picture of the issues, the family members present were asked to do a typical representation and then Frank was asked to demonstrate how the family looked in conflict (Figure 14.3). The collective representation of typical relationships was similar to the first map of the ideal family created by Frank, Maria, Mia,

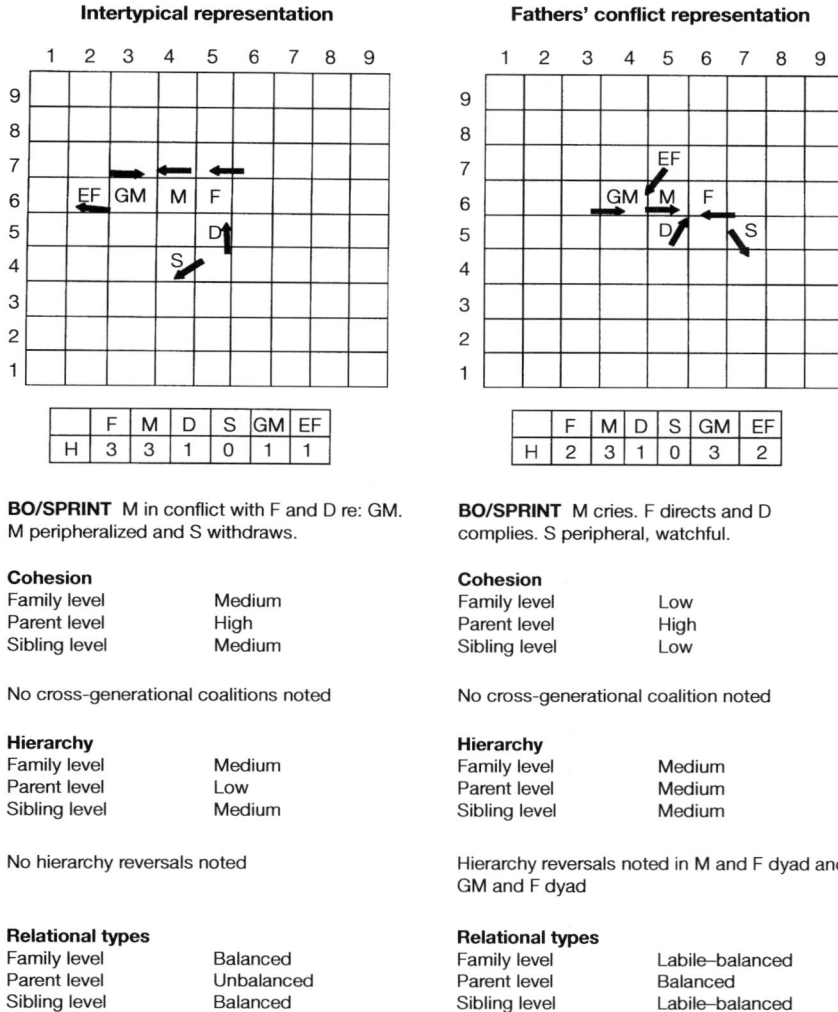

**Intertypical representation**

**Fathers' conflict representation**

|   | F | M | D | S | GM | EF |
|---|---|---|---|---|----|----|
| H | 3 | 3 | 1 | 0 | 1  | 1  |

|   | F | M | D | S | GM | EF |
|---|---|---|---|---|----|----|
| H | 2 | 3 | 1 | 0 | 3  | 2  |

**BO/SPRINT** M in conflict with F and D re: GM. M peripheralized and S withdraws.

**BO/SPRINT** M cries. F directs and D complies. S peripheral, watchful.

**Cohesion**

| Family level | Medium |
|---|---|
| Parent level | High |
| Sibling level | Medium |

No cross-generational coalitions noted

**Cohesion**

| Family level | Low |
|---|---|
| Parent level | High |
| Sibling level | Low |

No cross-generational coalition noted

**Hierarchy**

| Family level | Medium |
|---|---|
| Parent level | Low |
| Sibling level | Medium |

No hierarchy reversals noted

**Hierarchy**

| Family level | Medium |
|---|---|
| Parent level | Medium |
| Sibling level | Medium |

Hierarchy reversals noted in M and F dyad and GM and F dyad

**Relational types**

| Family level | Balanced |
|---|---|
| Parent level | Unbalanced |
| Sibling level | Balanced |

**Relational types**

| Family level | Labile–balanced |
|---|---|
| Parent level | Balanced |
| Sibling level | Labile–balanced |

*Figure 14.3* Mid-therapy session – intertypical and father conflict representations.
D, daughter; EF, extended family; F, father; GM, grandmother;
H, hierarchy; M, mother; S, son.

and Frankie (see Figure 14.1). This concrete comparison of desired versus real change, one of the benefits of interactive assessment, helped validate the family's progress.

Frank's depiction of the conflict scenario (Figure 14.3) indicated that he did not feel his voice was fully being heard. He placed Maria and Nonni in a cross-generational coalition and isolated himself with the kids. This stimulated further discussion regarding the need to attend to Frank's voice. As this discussion unfolded, Maria and Nonni began to discount Frank's perception, proffering possible explanations for 'why it really isn't as bad as Frank makes it out to be'. The therapist pointed out how this discussion was occurring as Frank's hypothesis would suggest. The adults were able to see that while under non-stressful conditions they were working more as a balanced family, under conflict they did not do as well. This clarified the next phase of treatment, working on decision making during times of conflict. This would ready the family for the eventual discussions to come regarding the eventuality of death, reorganization, and other lifephase issues more difficult to manage owing to the circumstances of chronic and terminal illness.

### *Setting a course for the future*

Subsequent sessions helped the family determine the best lines of communication between Frank and Maria and the degree to which Nonni should be involved in decisions concerning her. As the intensity of restructuring and consolidating drew to a close, the therapist invited just Frank and Marie to a session to evaluate the entire process and to determine the place of therapy in the next milestone they would face. It should be noted that, while Frank and Maria's physical conditions were often discussed, treatment would only now move in that direction. This family had lost a capacity to master life's tasks long ago, and needed to reaffirm a position and identity that would serve as a solid base for the more difficult milestones ahead. Too often, therapists working with families facing a terminal illness move too quickly to an anticipatory grief phase, and do not deal sufficiently with the root issues, which may be masked by the illness. This premature emphasis on grieving and pending loss interferes with the living process that comes with dying. In the Contro case, the therapist demonstrated respect for Frank and Maria by listening to their thoughts about therapy's place in the process, and offering both support and alternative perspectives to simply consider.

One purpose of an evaluation session is to work with the family to examine and incorporate prior change. To accomplish this, the FAST was used to bring closure to a phase of therapy. As was familiar to them now, Frank and Maria completed a representation of typical family relationships (Figure 14.4). It was used as a backdrop to validate the family's work to solidify positive changes in their cohesion and hierarchy and to help Nonni connect to others in the extended family system.

To set the stage, Frank and Maria were asked to look forward and identify potential obstacles that might set back the gains of therapy. In this session, the FAST was again used to bring closure to a phase of therapy. The family had been

## Parents' typical representation

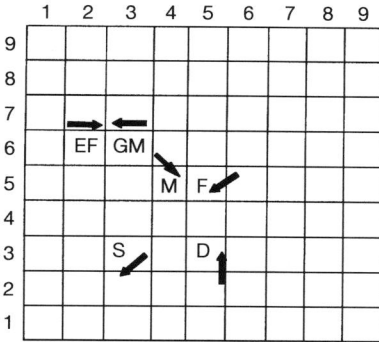

| | F | M | D | S | GM | EF |
|---|---|---|---|---|---|---|
| H | 3 | 3 | 1 | 1 | 1 | 1 |

## Parents' future representation

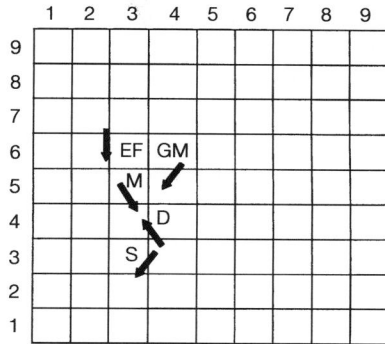

| | M | D | S | GM | EF |
|---|---|---|---|---|---|
| H | 3 | 2 | 2 | 1 | 2 |

**BO/SPRINT**

**Cohesion**
| | |
|---|---|
| Family level | Medium |
| Parent level | High |
| Sibling level | Low |

No cross-generational coalitions noted

**Hierarchy**
| | |
|---|---|
| Family level | Medium |
| Parent level | Low |
| Sibling level | Low |

No hierarchy reversals noted

**Relational types**
| | |
|---|---|
| Family level | Balanced |
| Parent level | Unbalanced |
| Sibling level | Unbalanced |

**BO/SPRINT**

**Cohesion**
| | |
|---|---|
| Family level | Medium |
| Sibling level | Medium |

No cross-generational coalition noted

**Hierarchy**
| | |
|---|---|
| Family level | Medium |
| Sibling level | Medium |

Hierarchy reversal noted in M and F dyad and GM and F dyad

**Relational types**
| | |
|---|---|
| Family level | Balanced |
| Sibling level | Balanced |

| Level | Flexibility Cohesion | Hierarchy |
|---|---|---|
| Family | 0 | 0 |
| Sibling | −1 | −1 |

*Figure 14.4* Final therapy session – parents' typical and future typical representations.
D, daughter; EF, extended family; F, father; GM, grandmother;
H, hierarchy; M, mother; S, son.

doing quite well in solidifying positive changes in their cohesion and hierarchy and in helping Nonni connect to others in the extended family system, and it was time to determine the direction for therapy.

During this reflection, the parents began to open up further conversation about Frank's illness, his increasing need for care, and his eventual leaving. Now that a stable and supportive equilibrium had been re-established for the Contros, the adults were ready to broach the topic of the future. This was a tearful moment, the family realizing that again their dream would be short-lived. But differently to before, they spoke with some modicum of confidence that they could navigate this territory. Both Frank and Maria began talking about the next 9 months and what needed to happen for the children, for Maria, for Frank, and for the extended family, including Nonni. The therapist noted that they had successfully used therapy to regain control over their family and to help integrate Nonni, and they could count on this ground to go forward.

After some careful discussion about his caretaking needs and the needs of other family members, they tried to look at the future for Maria and the children without Frank. Somewhere in this discussion, Frank laughed and pointed at the figures: 'Let's draw it out here so you know exactly what to do and [pointing at the therapist] they are going to need your help at the beginning. Can you help them make this map happen?' (see Figure 14.4).

One can see in this map that the adults, including the extended family, would take the helm during this crisis, and beyond. Their future typical representation rendered in their last session was used by the couple to begin mapping ways Maria could maintain the family's identity after Frank's death and ensure a sense of Frank's immortality within the Contro family identity. In fact, in subsequent sessions, central members of the extended family were involved to assist in constructing supportive management schedules, or to offer emotional support. As on the map, the children were held enough to grieve, but given sufficient space to continue on their developmental journey. The mother found her support with the children and with her extended family.

## Conclusion

The FAST offers an assessment procedure that measures both cohesion and power, assesses several family levels, allows for interpretation and comparison of individual and collective perceptions, and yields a more complex view of family dynamics by providing information regarding family organization across situations. Further, the FAST allows clinicians to hypothesize about treatment prognosis, plan systemic interventions, and monitor structural transformations that occur during therapy. As structural and developmental theories seem to be two of the more commonly recognized perspectives across disciplines (as evidenced by the types of relational additions in DSM IV), the FAST has the potential to become an interdisciplinary diagnostic link.

Family assessment measures are often intrusive, time-consuming, and require professional expertise to analyse and interpret. These assessments can take time away from therapy and, in an era of cost-containment, might not be considered economically viable by third-party payers, therapists, or client systems. The FAST has demonstrated its utility as a quick, easily interpreted, interactive assessment instrument (Gehring, 1998), which assists therapists to set an atmosphere of trust, consensuality, and family empowerment. In this chapter, the FAST was explored not as a complement to assessment but as an integral treatment strategy as well.

The convenience of administration, the clarity of making abstract family dynamics visible, and the effectiveness in bringing to the surface differences of opinions, make the FAST an instrument useful at all stages of the therapeutic process. Clients quickly understand what the placements represent, stimulating ideas and thoughts about the goals and direction of treatment. For many clients, putting into words their feelings and thoughts about family life can be very difficult. Often, the 'talking cure' can be misled by the person who does the most talking. Non-verbal representations minimize reliance on verbal descriptions and permit graphic and pictorial modes of communication to enter the therapeutic discourse. For these reasons, clinicians should consider adding the FAST to their professional repertoire. It is a versatile tool that can be used across generations and cultures. It propels families to be equal participants in their own development and to promote consensus building and a sense of equity and direction within the therapeutic alliance. In a time when we must deliver therapy as efficiently and effectively as possible, the FAST gives therapists a tool that can both accelerate and evaluate the therapeutic process.

## Note

1. The term 'client' refers to individuals, partnerships, family constellations and networks of wider social systems seeking or involved in treatment.

## References

American Psychiatric Association (1994) *Diagnostic and Statistical Manual of Mental Disorders* (4th ed.), Washington, DC: American Psychiatric Association.

Anderson, H. and Goolishian, H. (1988) 'Human systems as linguistic systems: Preliminary and evolving ideas about the implications for clinical theory', *Family Process*, 27: 371–94.

Colapinto, J. (1988) 'Teaching the structural way.' In H. Liddle, D. Breunlin, and R. Schwartz (eds) *Handbook of Family Therapy Training and Supervision*, New York: Guilford Press.

Coleman, L. (1987) 'Milan in Bucks County', *The Family Therapy Networker*, 11, 42–7.

Flowers, B.J. (1990) 'An interactional approach to standardised marital assessment: A literature review', *Family Relations*, 39: 368–77.

Gehring, T.M. (1984) *Der Familiensystemtest (FAST)*. Projekt für eine Pilotstudie. Universität Zürich: Psychiatrische Poliklinik für Kinder und Jugendliche (NAPS-3).

—— (1998) *Family System Test*, Seattle, WA: Hogrefe and Huber.

—— and Feldman, S.S. (1988) 'Adolescents' perceptions of family cohesion and power: A methodological study of the Family System Test', *Journal of Adolescent Research*, 3: 33–52.

—— and Marti, D. (1993) 'The Family System Test: Differences in perception of family structures between nonclinical and clinical children', *Journal of Child Psychology and Psychiatry and Allied Disciplines*, 35: 551–3.

Green, R.J. and Herget, M. (1991) 'Outcomes of systemic/strategic team consultation. III. The importance of therapist warmth and active structuring', *Family Process*, 30: 321–36.

Hoffman, L. (1988) 'A constructivist position for family therapy', *Irish Journal of Psychology*, 9(1): 110–29.

Horvath, A.O. and Symonds, B.D. (1991) 'Relations between working alliance and outcome in psychotherapy: A meta-analysis', *Journal of Counselling Psychology*, 38: 139–49.

Laird, J. (1995) 'Family-centered practice in the post-modern era: Families in Society', *Journal of Contemporary Human Services* 76(3): 150–62.

Marti, D. and Gehring, T.M. (1992) 'Is there a relationship between children's mental disorders and their ideal family constructs?', *Journal of the American Academy of Child and Adolescent Psychiatry*, 31, 490–4.

Nichols, M. and Schwartz, R. (1995) *Family Therapy: Concepts and Methods*, Boston, MA: Allyn and Bacon.

Pinsof, W. (1988) 'The therapist–client relationship: An integrative systems perspective', *Journal of Integrative and Eclective Psychotherapy*, 7, 303–13.

—— Catherall, D.R. (1986) 'The integrative psychotherapy alliance: Family couple, and individual therapy scales', *Journal of Marital and Family Therapy*, 12, 137–51.

Weissmark, M.S. and Giacomo, D.A. (1995) 'Measuring therapeutic interactions: Research and clinical applications', *Psychiatry*, 58: 173–88.

White, M. (1993) 'The histories of the present', in S. Gilligan (ed.) *Therapeutic Conversations*, New York: W.W. Norton.

—— Epston, D. (1990) *Narrative Means to Therapeutic Ends*, New York: W.W. Norton.

World Health Organisation (1992) *International Statistical Classification of Diseases and Related Health Problems* (10th ed.), Geneva: World Health Organisation.

# 15 Conceptualization of parental interventions in child psychiatry

*Thomas M. Gehring, Julie Page and Daniel Marti*

## Introduction

Family-oriented interventions have come to be increasingly recognized as an effective approach for the treatment of biopsychosocial disorders (Lebow and Gurman, 1995; Pinsof and Wynne, 1995). This fact must not, however, be over-estimated because of a number of methodological and conceptual issues have not been solved satisfactorily. Although family therapists claim to have introduced a new paradigm into mental health and health care, the status of research in this area is marginal because of many unresolved problems. For instance, therapists often still fail to achieve sufficient integration of empirically based research findings into their daily work, and the effectiveness of their interventions is often not evaluated systematically (Liddle, 1991; L'Abate, 1994). If therapists, on the one hand, could be encouraged to take more account of the complex findings of research and to formulate questions that are of special interest to their line of work, significant progress could be made in clinical practice as we know it. Researchers, on the other hand, must put more effort into studying therapies from a practical perspective and into clearly formulating the relevance of their findings to clinical work. In other words, increased co-operation between research and practice is a fundamental prerequisite for professional standards of clinical quality management (Pinsof and Wynne, 2000). In addition, the family therapeutic approach must be linked to and supported by other human and social sciences. It can be assumed that the movement of family therapy will only become widely accepted and academically integrated when it concerns itself with the knowledge and research standards established in related disciplines in the field of mental health (Shields and Wynne, 1994).

Systemic theories, well-validated diagnostic tools and systematic problem-solving strategies have a substantial potential to enable the design and implementation of effective psychological interventions (Beutler and Clarkin, 1990; Beutler *et al.*, 1995; Nutbeam and Harris, 1998). Linking theory to treatment planning can not only assist in creating interventions and predicting outcomes, but also help to explain difficulties in the realization of the problem-solving process. Comprehensive health-related or therapeutic models and guidelines should follow a structured sequence, including planning, implementation and evaluation stages. References to different theories and the use of standardized diagnostic instruments can guide practitioners at each of these stages and help them to identify key elements that are considered as the focus for good clinical performance.

In this chapter we present a concept for the participative planning and evaluation of the treatment of children's mental disorders at the parent level. The systemic approach used includes a family intake interview, typical and ideal FAST representations of the parents, and a semistructured questionnaire to discover their subjective theories about the presented problem and attempted changes.

## The relevance of parenting

According to structural family theory, a differentiated insight into the quality of parental childrearing behaviour is an important issue for a comprehensive under-standing of the development of the family and its members (Luster and Okagaki, 1993; Havas and Bonnar, 1999). Unfortunately, for many decades, research on the interdependence between parenting and health-related outcomes in children has focused primarily on the role of the mother. Recent studies have used a more differentiated approach by explicitly including the parental relationship, and fathers as respondents, to explain how the development of the child is influenced by the family environment. This enables the analysis of factors assumed to contribute to the difference between fathers' and mothers' way of coping with their children. In particular, it has demonstrated that the treatment of their children by fathers and mothers differs according to whether their partner is present or absent. For example, mothers have been shown to become more emotionally involved with their offspring when the father is present (Emery and Tuer, 1993). Given the importance of the parenting behaviour of mothers and fathers, clinicians and researchers have become increasingly aware of the necessity to include both parents when studying the influence of parental rearing behaviour on children's wellbeing.

Children are significantly affected not only by the parenting style of mothers and fathers but also by the relationship between their parents (Minuchin, 1974; Beavers, 1985; Feldman *et al.*, 1990; Wentzel and Feldman, 1996). In other words, the parental alliance has important implications for the success of the parents in meeting the demands of raising children. It is well documented that, in healthy families, mothers and fathers offer each other feedback and support on the basis of their distinct views. The influence of the parental relationship becomes even more evident in cases of distress, such as marital conflict and separation or divorce. Even when children are not directly involved in parental conflict, the emotional remoteness between parents often places the children in a severe loyalty dilemma and, as a consequence, it is difficult for them to maintain a positive relationship with both parents, a fact that hinders the development of clear generational boundaries (Haley, 1973; Gehring, 1985; Gehring *et al.*, 1990).

Just as the parental relationship affects children, so children affect the parental and marital relationship (Wright *et al.*, 1986). This has been shown by research on the changes of marital satisfaction during the transition into parenthood, as well as by studies of the effect of disturbed children on marital satisfaction and divorce (Cowan and Cowan, 1992). Nevertheless, the study of the interdependence between parenting and child development remains a challenge for the family systems approach. As suggested by systemic theory, one of the most crucial aspects is the need to focus on the dyadic and triadic relations and the consideration of the family as an organizational unit consisting of interdependent members (Ackerman, 1985; Gehring and Schultheiss, 1987). A suitable operationalization of this perspective, including additional variables such as cultural background and socioeconomic status, is an important prerequisite for a comprehensive understanding of the reciprocal relation between parent, child, and family development.

On the basis of the current state of the art in research, it can be concluded that the roles of spouse and parent become intertwined when children are born, and that the parents' relationship is an important parameter for various levels of family functioning. Partners assume different roles as parents and as spouses but, in healthy families, the boundaries of these distinct roles are blurred and flexible. In contrast, troubled families are often characterized by rigid and disengaged marital and parental relations, a situation that is closely associated with negative health-related outcomes for the family and its members.

## Dysfunctional child development

Psychosocial maladjustment in childhood and adolescence is a significant problem confronting today's society. It has been reported that almost one-quarter of children in the US suffer from mental health problems severe enough to warrant treatment (Panichelli and Kendall, 1995). While it is widely recognized that many children and adolescents have considerable personal and family-related problems, this field has been neglected until recently, when researchers began to emphasize the necessity of stringent methodological studies on its systematic prevention and treatment.

Children's developmental or behavioural problems and related distress can be a cause as well as a consequence of problematic interpersonal structures in the family. Therefore, effective treatment in child and adolescent psychiatry requires an explicit consideration of the context in which stressful patterns arise. There is substantiating evidence that parenting style and marital wellbeing do significantly correlate with various patient and family outcomes. Accordingly, parents' perceptions of family relationships provide valuable information on how to design clinical interventions.

There is a convergence among professionals from various fields that a disruption in the development of a child severely tries each family member and, as a consequence, may interfere with family functioning (see Chapter 1). Accordingly, the onset and course of a child's problem and the organizational path of the family are interrelated, but it is also well known that family members are affected differently, depending on factors such as role, personality and lifecycle (Luster and Okagaki, 1993; Gehring *et al.*, 1994; Lee and Gotlib, 1994; Perris, 1994). Therefore, as has been emphasized, the results of clinical problem-solving processes are more effective if the interventions are geared to the specific needs and social environment of the clients (Prochaska *et al.*, 1992). In other words, when evaluating maladjusted children and planning therapeutic interventions, it is essential not to focus exclusively on the patient's symptomatology or psychiatric classification of mental disorder, but to also consider patterns of family structures and the parents' attempted changes (Gehring *et al.*, 1996). However, there is still a relatively small number of empirically based clinical models and tools that account for interpersonal and contextual aspects in the conceptualization of dysfunctional child development. This paucity highlights the need for systemic research designs that reveal the reciprocal relation between individual and family variables (Kaslow *et al.*, 1996).

Of the different therapeutic approaches available, parent management training and behavioural–cognitive techniques are the best researched and have been proved by empirical studies to be efficacious methods for the psychological treatment of dysfunctional child development and psychopathology (Weisz and Weiss, 1993; Panichelli and Kendall, 1995). Furthermore, there is strong evidence that structural family therapy is a promising treatment procedure for youngsters suffering from various psychiatric disorders (Lebow and Gurman, 1995; Grawe *et al.*, 1998). According to Lee and Gotlib (1994), research on family factors involved in the origin and course of mental disorders in childhood focus as on the following three main aspects: (i) the role that family members play in the aetiology of the patient's disturbance; (ii) the effect of the patient's symptomatology on other family members and their interpersonal structures; and (iii) the relevance of family members as change agents in the context of therapy.

## Parents' attempted changes to family structures at the onset of therapy

Using the FAST (Gehring, 1998a) it has been demonstrated that parents of psychiatric patients, who in general perceive the family relationships as characterized by low cohesion and unclear hierarchical boundaries, attempt to change their family structures towards more functional patterns. Table 15.1 shows significant differences between current and ideal representations on the family level, as well as on various subsystem levels, as reported by parents of mentally disturbed offspring at the onset of therapy. Evaluation of shift patterns towards the ideal representation revealed that, both individually and jointly, parents wanted to change family cohesion and hierarchy towards balanced structures. Analysis on the dyadic level showed that both parents wished for increased cohesion in their relationship but to make no changes in the mother–child relations. However, while mothers reported that father–patient and father–sibling dyads should be more cohesive, fathers indicated more cohesion in the sibling subsystem, but no changes in their own relation to their children. Analysis of triadic relationships indicated that the parents individually and jointly wished for a significant decrease of cross-generational coalitions. As to hierarchy, the magnitude of attempted changes was relatively small. In particular, fathers and the parents together wished for a significant decrease in the patients' power and, thus, stressed the relevance of clear hierarchical boundaries. In sum, these results clearly suggest that mothers and fathers, albeit in different ways, are motivated for interventions focusing on

Table 15.1 Parents' attempted changes as assessed by differences between typical and ideal FAST representations in individual and group settings at the onset of child psychiatric treatment (n = 20)

| Respondent | Shift towards balanced structures (family level)[1] | Increase in cohesion[2] | | | | Decrease in power (patient)[3] |
|---|---|---|---|---|---|---|
| | | Father–mother | Father–patient | Father–sibling | Patient–sibling | |
| Mother | ** | ** | ** | ** | ns | ns |
| Father | ** | ** | ns | ns | ** | ** |
| Group | ** | ** | ** | ** | ns | ** |

** significant difference between typical and ideal representation; ns, not significant; [1] combined cohesion and hierarchy dimensions, [2] no differences were found for cohesion in mother–child dyads; [3] no differences were found for the power of parents and siblings.

transformations of family relationships and that patterns of attempted changes vary as a function of the setting used. Notably, the group portrayals manifested the most distinct desire for a change in family structures.

### *Changing mothers' family constructs across therapy*

In a recent study, Steinebach (1995) investigated whether family constructs of mothers with a developmentally retarded preschooler change across therapy. At the onset of treatment, mothers completed FAST representations and questionnaires about patient development and family stress. In accordance with their responses in the questionnaires, they portrayed the current family structures predominantly as unbalanced and indicated a wish for changes towards balanced patterns. While all patients had cognitive–behavioural training, mothers who indicated increased levels of family stress received additional counselling. A year later, after the completion of clinical interventions, the assessment procedure was repeated with both groups. Results showed that mothers generally displayed family structures as balanced, a result that correlated with the patients' outcome. However, those mothers who had received additional child guidance sessions were even more likely to report balanced patterns in their typical representations and also showed less discrepancy between their current and ideal family constructs. This finding substantiates the systemic hypothesis that suggests a relationship between family constructs of mothers and their involvement in treatment.

## Planning and evaluation of parental interventions

If interventions on the parent level are to be used as a treatment of children's psychosocial disorders, a consensus-oriented discourse on the problem constructs of both parents and the hypotheses of the therapist are important prerequisites of the treatment (Silberschatz *et al.*, 1989). Accordingly, the evaluation of the clinical process should consider the views of all participants involved in the therapeutic system. In the following sections we present a new model for the participative–discoursive conceptualization of interventions with parents of mentally disturbed children, which was developed at the Department of Child and Adolescent Psychiatry, University of Zurich (Gehring, 1989, 1998b). This systemic–structural approach is resource oriented and aims at improving the parenting competence of both fathers and mothers. On the basis of a systematic analysis of parental constructs regarding the presented problem and their family relations, the problem-solving process includes a discussion with parents about their attempted changes. The therapy plan is worked out jointly, and its implementation is monitored continuously, reflected upon and, if necessary, modified. After completion of treatment, the utility of the approach and the quality of the collaboration between the parents and therapists are evaluated retrospectively. In the following sections each step of this standardized procedure is described, including the test instruments used; preliminary results of a study aiming to validate this problem-solving model are outlined.

### Assessment of problem and family constructs

The conceptualization of the problem-solving process is based on the System-oriented Family Analysis (SOFA; Gehring, 1989) and on the FAST. These two instruments assess parental problem and family constructs and are applied at the onset and after completion of therapy as well as in the follow-up, and facilitate both the planning and the evaluation of the clinical procedure.

#### SOFA questionnaire

This semistructured questionnaire asks parents to give their views of the presented problem, attempted changes, goal attainment and the quality of the therapy. Mothers and fathers are asked individually to respond to the respective items. Table 15.2 shows the questions and indicates when data collection occurs in the course of treatment and follow-up. The degree of stress that the problem evokes in the different members of the family, and the parents' degree of satisfaction with the therapy, are indicated on a scale ranging from 1 to 7, with 1 signifying low and 7 high levels of stress or satisfaction. For items that are not rated on a scale, the number of statements made on each particular topic is determined. In addition, a distinction is made between self- and patient-related information given by the parents. The frequency of problem constructs is defined as the sum total of statements regarding the two categories 'problem definition' and 'problem hypothesis'.

#### FAST

Parents are asked first individually and then together to represent their current and ideal family structures. They are then interviewed to explore the subjective meaning of the representations. The quantitative evaluation is based on a determination of

*Table 15.2* Items and time of data collection by the SOFA questionnaire

| | Item | Time[1] |
|---|---|---|
| **Problem** | | |
| definition | Which relevant problems do you currently have to deal with? | $T_{1,2,3}$ |
| hypothesis | What do you think causes these problems? | $T_{1,2,3}$ |
| stress | How great is the stress the problems produce in your family?[2] | $T_{1,2,3}$ |
| coping | What is your approach to solving the problems? | $T_{1,3}$ |
| **Target changes** | | |
| definition | What kind of changes do you want to achieve? | $T_1$ |
| therapy-related | What expectations do you place in the therapy? | $T_1$ |
| **Attainment** | | |
| definition | What kind of changes have occurred since the last consultation? | $T_{2,3}$ |
| hypothesis | What do you think brought about these changes? | $T_{2,3}$ |
| **Therapy** | | |
| satisfaction | How satisfied are you with the therapy?[2] | $T_{2,3}$ |
| positive aspects | Which aspects of our collaboration do you find were positive? | $T_{2,3}$ |
| negative aspects | Which aspects of our collaboration do you find were negative? | $T_{2,3}$ |

[1] $T_1$, before therapy, $T_2$, after therapy, $T_3$, follow-up; [2] scale from 1 to 7.

two types of family functioning, namely balanced and unbalanced structures. A family configuration is scored as balanced if the figures are placed within a $3 \times 3$ square area and the parental figures receive higher power scores than those representing their offspring; all other structures are scored as unbalanced. The changes the parents are attempting are examined in light of the divergence of the typical from the ideal family representations.

### *Clinical procedure*

The problem-solving process with the parents is planned, carried out, and evaluated in a systemic setting and includes a participative–discoursive proceeding. Co-therapists observe and record the therapeutic process on video from behind a one-way mirror. The therapeutic process is monitored continuously and reflected upon in supervision. Evaluation of the treatment thus consists of a self-evaluation by the members of the therapeutic system and of a formative evaluation by an external supervisor. After completion of the therapy, and in a follow-up consultation, parents' constructs are assessed again by SOFA and FAST, and the development of both the patient and the family is discussed with the therapist. To enable summative evaluation of the therapy, a quantitative analysis of the parental construct differentiation over the three assessments is made.

The clinical procedure, which progresses in three steps (planning, problem solving, and evaluation), will now be described in chronological order, from the patient's referral to the follow-up. Figure 15.1 supplies a synopsis of the approach used.

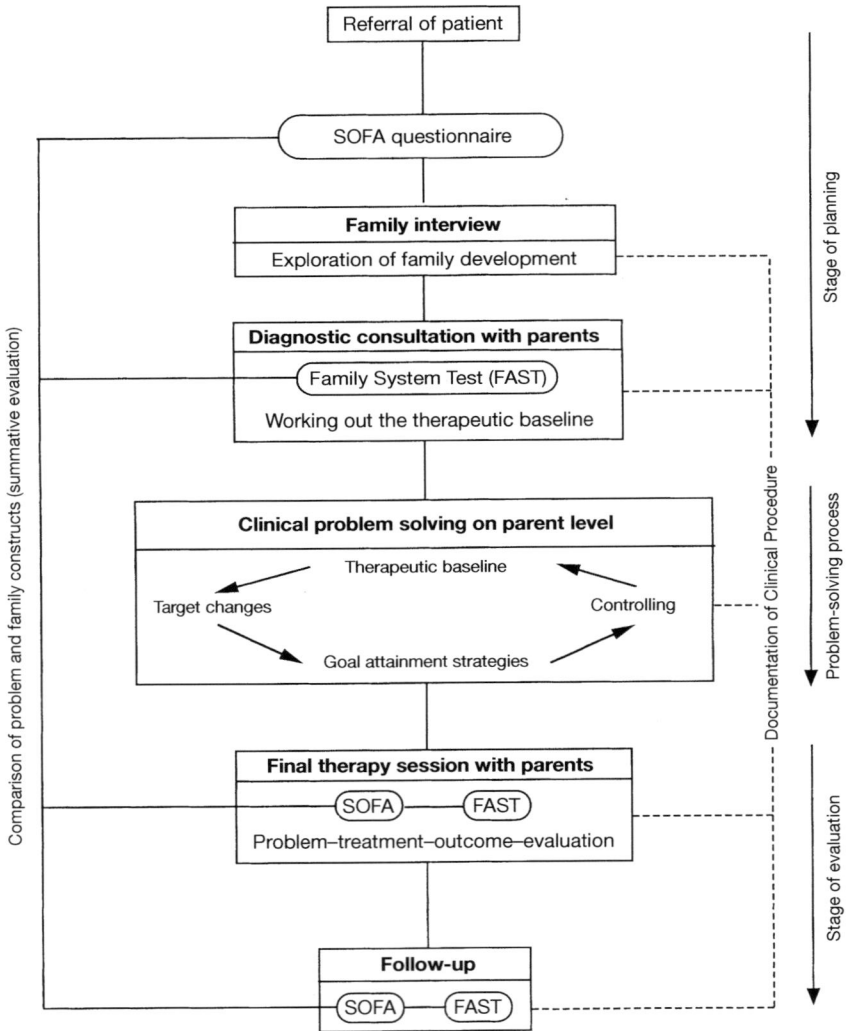

*Figure 15.1* Planning and evaluation of parent-oriented problem-solving processes.

*Planning*

The planning stage includes a consultation with the entire family and one with the parents; both of these take place within 1 month. After referral of the patient, the parents receive the SOFA, as agreed in advance by telephone. The questionnaires have to be returned before the family intake interview. Starting out from the problem constructs supplied by the mother and father in the SOFA, the first session focuses on the biopsychosocial status of the family members and the structure of their relationships, and explores desired changes. This procedure enables us to clarify whether an exclusive problem-solving focus on the parent level is indicated. This, in turn, necessitates that parents are motivated and have the resources for a collaboration, and that the patient does not need additional clinical measures. If these criteria are met, the FAST will be carried out individually and jointly with the father and the mother during the next consultation. On the basis of the represented interpersonal structures and a resource-oriented, systemic interpretation of them, parents and therapist specify together how the presented problem could be solved at the parent level. If a therapeutic baseline can be established (i.e. consensus about the relevance of the family for a solution of the presented problem and the role of a modified parenting behaviour), a therapy contract with a time limit is concluded, and the parents are informed that the counselling process will be evaluated during the final session.

*Problem solving*

The stage of problem solving, which includes exploratory as well as evaluative elements, lasts 1 year at the most. Five to eight sessions initially take place at intervals of 2–4 weeks, and at greater intervals later on. Concrete goals as to the attempted changes are discussed with the parents, including hypotheses on the effects of a modification of parenting strategies and on family roles and rules required to implement them. Individual and family-related changes that have been achieved are evaluated in the therapeutic sessions, and therapist and parents decide together whether the procedure followed so far is suitable or whether it should be modified (i.e. self-evaluation of the therapeutic process). The problem-solving process is further optimized by systematic video analyses completed by the clinical team and in supervision (i.e. formative evaluation).

*Evaluation*

The evaluation stage comprises a concluding discussion with the parents in the last therapy session and a follow-up 6 months later. During both consultations, SOFA and FAST are again completed and patient- and family-related outcomes, as well as the quality of the clinical collaboration, are reflected on together. The summative therapy evaluation is based on the quantitative determination of the changes derived from SOFA and FAST that have occurred over the period of the three assessment points. The interpretation of the results takes the clinical process into account as rated by the therapists and the supervisor.

## Differentiation of parental constructs across therapy and in the follow-up

We now present preliminary results of a pilot study that involved twenty parents who were treated according to Figure 15.1 because of mental health problems of their offspring. The aim of this research was to determine the clinical viability of the presented model and to analyse the relationship between changes of parental problem and family constructs, as well as related clinical outcomes in the context of the participative–discoursive approach used. The evaluation was based on consensus-oriented ratings by the clinicians and parents and included additional data as derived from SOFA and FAST and other standardized clinical measures.

Families were middle-class and had two parents with traditional role allocation (i.e. all fathers were employed full-time and three mothers had part-time jobs). The referred patients were boys (mean age 8.7 years) who had one sibling (mean age 6.8 years). According to ICD 10 (WHO, 1989), patients had at least one psychiatric disorder and they were not within the normal range of the GAF scale (American Psychiatric Association, 1987) and of the Child Behavior Checklist (CBCL; Achenbach, 1993). Six families had sought therapeutic aid in individual and/or family settings prior to this treatment because of psychosocial or psychiatric problems. The average number of therapeutic consultations with parents was 6.5, with the number of sessions ranging from four to eight.

The parents and the clinical team generally evaluated the therapeutic approach used and the outcome as positive. In terms of psychiatric significance, the target symptoms were improved in the case of eight patients, and a decreased number of disorders were diagnosed after completion of the therapy and in the follow-up 6 months later. Convergently, the majority of the parents judged their offspring as being in the normal range of the CBCL, a finding that also correlated with the clinicians' ratings of the patients according to the GAF scale. A telephone interview 18 months after the completion of therapy showed that two families required further therapeutic support (i.e. mediation because of divorce conflict and cognitive training because of problems of the index patient at school).

Table 15.3 shows data based on parents' reports of problem constructs as supplied by the SOFA and by their individual FAST representations of the family structures at the different stages of therapy. Results of the SOFA indicated that, at the onset of treatment, parents focused mainly on the problems of the patient. In the course of therapy, the patient-related problem constructs decreased considerably. As a consequence, there was a smaller discrepancy between patient- and self-related perception of the problem at the end of therapy. The degree of stress that the problem caused the parents, who judged this to be about the same as the stress that it caused the patient, also decreased in the course of therapy, although the magnitude of change was relatively small (data not shown). The results of the follow-up showed that the amount of reported problem constructs and the degree of perceived stress underwent only a little change after completion of the therapy. Parents' satisfaction with the therapy was stable from the end of treatment to the follow-up.

*Table 15.3* Changing constructs of parents across therapy and in the follow-up as assessed by SOFA and FAST (*n* = 20)

| Point of assessment | Problem constructs (SOFA)[1] | | Family constructs (FAST)[2] | |
|---|---|---|---|---|
| | Patient-related | Self-related | Balanced | Unbalanced |
| Therapy onset | 5.1 | 0.9 | 20 | 80 |
| Completion of therapy | 1.7 | 0.8 | 90 | 10 |
| Follow-up | 1.6 | 0.4 | 70 | 30 |

[1] Average number of reported problem constructs; [2] data in percentages.

As expected, findings on the FAST indicated that, at the onset of therapy, both individually and jointly, parents considered their family structure to be mostly unbalanced and with unclear generational boundaries. After completion of the problem-solving process, parents represented the relationships predominantly as being balanced and manifested a significant decrease of cross-generational coalitions and of reverse hierarchies, as had been their wish at therapy onset. In the follow-up, as in non-clinical families, fathers were somewhat more likely than mothers to display balanced patterns (80 per cent vs 60 per cent).

In sum, the changes that occurred across the three points of assessment tended to confirm the predictions of structural family therapy and correlated with the other clinical outcomes measures.

## Conclusions

The therapeutic model presented focused on the role of parents in the context of child psychiatric problem-solving processes. The participative–discursive approach used, which included SOFA and FAST for the planning and evaluation of the therapeutic interventions, may be assumed to have had a beneficial influence on patient- and family-related outcomes. It showed great clinical viability and flexibility and was judged positively by both mothers and fathers, as well as by the clinicians involved. The fact that almost all parents responded positively to the way the setting and time of the collaboration were structured, and that none of the therapies was broken off, provides further support for the clinical utility of this concept. This substantiates the claim that a transparent conceptualization of the clinical procedure is likely to succeed in turning parents into partners for empirically derived semi-standardized treatment.

Parents evaluated the clinical outcome beneficially for themselves as well as for the target child and the family as a unit. In particular, they reported a significant decrease in patient problems and related stress, as well as marked shifts towards functional family structures, a fact that was also reflected in their satisfaction with the therapy. Additional clinical ratings such as CBCL, GAF scale and ICD 10 demonstrated that the patients' symptoms decreased considerably in the course of treatment. These findings suggest that co-operative counselling styles and the involvement of both mothers and fathers have the potential to increase parental autonomy and problem-solving competence and, as a consequence, have a positive influence on the patient as well as enabling family development in an effective and economic way. On the basis of our experience we are convinced that SOFA and FAST are promising tools that can contribute to systematic process and outcome evaluation in the context of participative–discoursive treatment approaches.

In the follow-up, fathers were more likely than mothers to represent balanced family structures with the FAST. This finding could be interpreted as being the result of traditional, gender-specific role allocation. It can be assumed that, after completion of therapy, it will again be the mothers who are mostly responsible for child-related matters and that they are more likely to be exposed to family hassles. Accordingly, mothers also reported more patient-related problems than fathers in the SOFA at the onset of therapy and at the follow-up. Therefore, we think that although interventions at the parent level are suitable for the treatment of psychiatric disorders, they might not suffice when it comes to preventing societal risk factors for the development of individual and family problems.

Even though our time-limited therapeutic concept proved to be efficient for the treatment of mentally disturbed children, four aspects deserve critical discussion.

- First, our sample was limited to two-parent, middle-class families who were interested working in a research-oriented clinical setting.
- Second, the use of a participative–discoursive approach requires a certain level of parental motivation for a co-operative problem-solving process and calls for appropriate resources in their relationship.
- Third, some mental disorders require additional patient-oriented support and medical interventions such as pharmacotherapy.
- Finally, despite the restricted number of consultations, the clinical workload that planning and evaluation of the sessions involves, i.e. extended data collection and documentation, video analysis and reflection in the clinical team, is time-consuming and requires a great many staff and a high degree of professional commitment.

In summary, FAST and SOFA proved to be useful and economical tools for the planning and formative and summative evaluation of clinical intervention with parents. However, a comprehensive validation of the model presented necessitates further studies that take self- and family-related constructs of the patient and their siblings into account and also include an external evaluation of the treatment process by independent raters. Undoubtedly, future research on single-parent, divorced, and blended families with various ethnic and socioeconomic backgrounds, as well as on the study of client–therapist relations in distinct clinical settings, is necessary to broaden our perspective on individual and interpersonal development and to enable the systematic improvement of family-oriented treatment approaches in child and adolescent psychiatry.

# References

Achenbach, T.M. (1993) 'Child Behavior Checklist (CBCL)', authorized German version, Zurich: University of Zurich, Department of Child and Adolescent Psychiatry.

Ackerman, N. (1985) *A Theory of Family Systems*, New York: Gardner.

American Psychiatric Association (APA) (1987) *Diagnostic and Statistical Manual of Mental Disorders, DSM-III-R*, Washington, DC: American Psychiatric Association.

Beavers, R.W. (1985) *Successful Marriage*, New York: W.W. Norton.

Beutler, L.E. and Clarkin, J.F. (1990) *Systematic Treatment Selection*, New York: Brunner/ Mazel.

——Consoli, A.J. and Williams, R.E. (1995) 'Integrative and eclectic therapies in practice', in B. Bongar and L.E. Beutler (eds) *Comprehensive Textbook of Psychotherapy*, Oxford: Oxford University Press.

Cowan, C.P. and Cowan, P.A. (1992) *When Partners Become Parents*, New York: Basic Books.

Emery, R.E. and Tuer, M. (1993) 'Parenting and the marital relationship', in T. Luster and L. Okagaki (eds) *Parenting: An Ecological Perspective*, Hillsdale, NJ: Lawrence Erlbaum Associates Inc.

Feldman, S.S., Wentzel, K.R., Weinberger, D.A. and Munson, J.A. (1990) 'Marital satisfaction of parents of preadolescent boys and its relationship to family and child functioning', *Journal of Family Psychology* 4: 213–34.

Gehring, T.M. (1985) 'Socio-psychosomatic dysfunctions: A case study', *Child Psychiatry and Human Development* 15: 269–80.

—— (1989) 'Systemorientierte Familienanalyse (SOFA): Leitfaden für die Anwendung und Evaluation systemischer Kurztherapien in der ambulanten Kinder- und Jugendpsychiatrie' (Manual for the Planning and Evaluation of Systemic Brief Therapies in Outpatient Child and Adolescent Psychiatry), Zurich: University of Zurich, Department of Psychiatry.

—— (1998a) *The Family System Test*, Seattle, WA: Hogrefe and Huber Publishers.

—— (1998b) 'The Family System Test (FAST): A clinical and research tool for the planning and evaluation of family interventions', Basle: University of Basle, Department of Psychology.

—— Schultheiss, R.B. (1987) 'Spatial representations and assessment of family relationship', *American Journal of Family Therapy* 5: 261–4.

—— Wentzel, K.R., Feldman, S.S. and Munson, J. (1990) 'Conflict in families of adolescents: The impact on cohesion and power structures', *Journal of Family Psychology* 3: 290–309.

—— Marti, D. and Sidler, A. (1994) 'Family System Test (FAST): Are parents' and children's family constructs either different or similar, or both?', *Child Psychiatry and Human Development* 25: 125–38.

—— Candrian, M., Marti, D. and Real del Sartre, O. (1996) 'Family System Test (FAST): The relevance of parental family constructs for clinical intervention', *Child Psychiatry and Human Development* 27: 55–65.

Grawe, K., Donati, R. and Bernauer, F. (1998) *Psychotherapy in Transition: From Speculation to Science*, Seattle, WA: Hogrefe and Huber Publishers.

Haley, J. (1973) 'Strategic therapy when a child is presented as the problem', *Journal of the American Academy of Child and Adolescent Psychiatry* 12: 641–59.

Havas, E. and Bonnar, D. (1999) 'Therapy with adolescents and families: The limits of parenting', *American Journal of Family Therapy* 27: 121–35.

Kaslow, N.J., Gray Deering, C. and Ash, P. (1996) 'Relational diagnosis of child and adolescent depression', in F.W. Kaslow (ed.) *Handbook of Relational Diagnosis and Dysfunctional Family Patterns*, New York: Wiley.

L'Abate, L. (1994) *Family Evaluation*, London: Sage.

Lebow, J.L. and Gurman, A.S. (1995) 'Research assessing couple and family therapy', *Annual Review of Psychology* 46: 27–57.

Lee, C.M. and Gotlib, I.H. (1994) 'Mental illness and the family', in L. L'Abate (ed.) *Handbook of Developmental Psychology and Psychopathology*, New York: Wiley.

Liddle, H.A. (1991) 'Empirical values and the culture of family therapy', *Journal of Marital and Family Therapy* 17: 327–48.

Luster, T. and Okagaki, L. (ed.) (1993) *Parenting: An Ecological Perspective*, Hillsdale, NJ: Erlbaum.

Minuchin, S. (1974) *Families and Family Therapy*, Cambridge, MA: Harvard University Press.

Nutbeam, D. and Harris, E. (1998) *Theory in a Nutshell: A Practitioner's Guide to Commonly Used Theories and Models in Health Promotion*, Sydney: University of Sydney, Department of Public Health and Community Medicine.

Panichelli, S.S. and Kendall, P.C. (1995) 'Therapy with children and adolescents', in B. Bongar and L.E. Beutler (eds) *Comprehensive Textbook of Psychotherapy*, Oxford: Oxford University Press.

Perris, C. (1994) 'Linking the experience of dysfunctional parenting rearing with manifest psychopathology', in C. Perris, W.A. Arrindell and M. Eisemann (eds) *Parenting and Psychopathology*, New York: Wiley.

Pinsof, W.M. and Wynne, L.C. (1995) 'The efficacy of marital and family therapy: An empirical overview, conclusions, and recommendations', *Journal of Marital and Family Therapy* 21: 585–613.

—— Wynne, L.C. (2000) 'Toward progress research: Closing the gap between family therapy practice and research', *Journal of Marital and Family Therapy* 26: 1–8.

Prochaska, J.O., DiClemente, C.C. and Norcross, J.C. (1992) 'In search of how people change', *American Psychologist* 47: 1102–14.

Shields, C.G. and Wynne, L.C. (1994) 'The marginalization of family therapy: A historical and continuing problem', *Journal of Marital and Family Therapy* 20: 117–38.

Silberschatz, G., Curtis, J.T. and Nathans, S. (1989) 'Using the patients' plan to assess progress in psychotherapy', *Psychotherapy* 26: 40–6.

Steinebach, C. (1995) *Familienentwicklung in der Frühförderung. Die Sicht der Mütter* (Family development and children's mental retardation: The mothers' point of view), Freiburg: Lambertus.

Weisz, J.R. and Weiss, B. (eds) (1993) *Effects of Psychotherapy with Children and Adolescents*, London: Sage.

Wentzel, K.R. and Feldman, S.S. (1996) 'Relations of cohesion and power in family dyads to social and emotional adjustment during early adolescence', *Journal of Research on Adolescence* 6: 225–44.

World Health Organisation (WHO), Division of Mental Health (1989) *Mental and Behavioural Disorders, ICD-10*, Geneva: World Health Organisation.

Wright, P.J., Henggeler, S.W. and Craight, L. (1986) 'Problems in paradise? A longitudinal examination of the transition to parenthood', *Journal of Applied Developmental Psychology* 7: 277–91.

# 16 Supervision: Reflecting clinical practice and team development

*Christoph Steinebach*

## Introduction

Supervision is a special form of professional counselling. Supervision enables clinicians to:

- prepare for professional practice
- deal with difficult situations
- reflect on professional actions.

Clinical supervision, which is the topic of this chapter, aims to further the professional and personal development of the supervisee.

Supervision increasingly takes into account the rules and interactions between members of various systems (e.g. client, family, clinical team or therapeutic institutions). The expansion in its theoretical perspectives is reflected in the multitude of methods and their integration in the counselling process (Holloway, 1995; Turner and Fine, 1998). The methods refer to diverse system levels such as the family system (e.g. the dynamics in the relationship between clients/patients and their families), the therapy system (therapist–family relations), the supervisee system (relationship dynamics of the supervision group) or to the organization as a unit (relationship dynamics between clinical teams and other groups in the organization). Supervision means describing the relationship dynamics on the different levels of the system, explaining and predicting developments, and enabling durable changes to relationship structures. The complexity of the topic, the multiple methods and the many layers of relationship dynamics in the supervisee system have led to people talking about a 'special art'. Although the supervisee generally operates with research-based methods and techniques, there remains the untold area of 'artistry' in practice (Holloway, 1995). Reconstructing the field of action that has supervision as its topic is therefore a substantial and differentiated task. How can this complexity be reduced appropriately? It has been suggested that this can be done by referring to the concepts of cohesion and hierarchy. In this chapter this point is elaborated and the potential of the use of the FAST as a method in reflecting supervision and team development is discussed.

## Basic principles of a comprehensive theory of supervision

Investigations of individual development in social groups show the special importance of cohesion and power as features of families, extrafamilial groups, or organizations (Table 16.1). If we want to know the potential of the FAST as a method to show cohesion and power in the field of supervision and team development, we should explore whether the findings on these dimensions regarding well-functioning and troubled family structures are also applicable to therapy systems and team systems.

Cohesion and power are seen as multidimensional constructs (Cota *et al.*, 1995; Farmer *et al.*, 1997; Phillips, 1997) and can therefore make allowances for the particularities of any social system. Thus it becomes possible, for example, to distinguish between power and leadership. Power is a trait of a leader as well as of other group members and, when looking at mutual influences, one notices that 'upward influences' (Phillips, 1997) also enter the picture, independent of which type of power is shown (Kudisch *et al.*, 1995).

The complexity of the supervisory process can be reduced to the concepts of 'cohesion' and 'power' as described by Olson and Lavee (1989) and Gehring (1998). Cohesion means a bond between members of a group that is experienced emotionally and is connected with expectations of oneself and of others (e.g. family members, professional colleagues), the social environment or other systems of reference (e.g. healthcare institutions). Power means the influence of a member of the group or organization on other members, with the objective of achieving a common target. The degree to which someone can have a possible influence is determined by the relative position of that person to the other members of the group within a system or organization. We base our work on the following hypothesis: cohesion and power have proved to be important structural features in social systems. In the supervision process, they are of central importance for the evaluation of the client, therapy, team, and supervisee systems.

*Table 16.1* Psychological aspects of cohesion and power on various system levels

|  | *Individual* | *Family* | *Extrafamilial group* | *Organization* |
|---|---|---|---|---|
| Cohesion | Definition of self and identity | Intimate distance-regulation across lifespan | Time-limited interactions in formal and informal groups | Self-directed activity and team work in goal-oriented organizational structures |
| Power | Perception of freedom and responsibility | Independence and obedience | Situation-dependent leadership style, participation | Information policy, leadership scope |

## Individual development in the family system

Investigations that refer to developmental family psychology, family stress theory, and structural family therapy research show a strong relation between various biopsychosocial problems and the patterning of cohesion and hierarchy structures. Rigid insistence on extremes of both cohesion and hierarchy goes hand in hand with complex adapting problems in life, limited competencies in solving problems, and low communicative competencies. In general, clinical samples show a strong interweaving or detachment, a deficient role structure or rigid hierarchy (Olson and Lavee, 1989). Accordingly, past studies using the FAST demonstrated that there is a close connection between family members' subjective perception of their relationships and various individual, interpersonal, and developmental outcomes (Gehring *et al.*, 1995, 1996).

Using a sample of mothers who referred their preschool children to an out-patient clinic because of developmental problems, we investigated the connection between perceived family structures and problem-related stressors and resources (Steinebach, 1995). At the onset of the therapy with the FAST and a semistructured interview, mothers' perceptions of current family structures, their global ratings of patient development, their evaluation of their own resources and the support they received from their partners were analysed. Table 16.2 shows that those mothers who evaluated the development of their child positively and indicated high personal resources and support from partner were more likely to represent balanced (i.e. functional) family structures than their counterparts. This suggests that besides mothers' subjective ratings of patient characteristics, their perception of individual resources and social support is related to the quality of interpersonal structures in family systems.

On the basis of the construct of identity, the following discussion will consider whether these results can be transferred to the relational structures between therapist and client family (therapy system) and to those between therapist and his/her colleagues (clinical system), as well as to the dynamics in the supervisee system.

*Table 16.2* Types of family structure as a function of personal resources and partner and patient characteristics from the mothers' perspective ($n = 28$)

| Type of family structure | Personal resources | | Support from partner | | Child development | |
|---|---|---|---|---|---|---|
| | Low (%) | High (%) | Low (%) | High (%) | Negative (%) | Positive (%) |
| Unbalanced | 39 | 22 | 35 | 9 | 39 | 18 |
| Balanced | 4 | 35 | 17 | 39 | 4 | 39 |
| Chi$^2$ (df = 1) | 6.9* | | 5.8* | | 12.5** | |

*$p < 0.05$, **$p < 0.01$.

### Psychological aspects in the development of identity

Identity is the sum of attitudes to the self, of which biographical and social experiences, demands, and expectations become part (Hausser, 1989). The person who wants to develop an identity therefore has to look not only at what is stable in their life, but also at what changes. In this context, not only changes, but also stability, prove to be problematic. The assessment of one's own identity depends on how someone sees him/herself, but also on how that person believes others see him/her. People are different, and different people see each other in different ways. This means that a person has not one but several identities. In addition, other people's perception changes constantly. The idea of a positive, stable identity is therefore just a myth. A stable professional identity is neither possible nor desirable. Identity undergoes constant change, and whether this change is successful depends not only on individual competencies but also on traits of the groups that are deemed to be important (cf. the term of contextualized identity; Willke, 1995).

From the perspective of developmental psychology (Steinebach, 2000), two positions are worth emphasizing:

- Development – and this includes the development of an identity – is a process, shaped by people (Oerter, 1995; Brandtstädter, 1998), which aims at a positive concept of the self, feeling of self-worth, and an appropriate degree of internal and external locus of control (Krampen, 1987; Hausser, 1989).
- People influence the development of their partners, who develop with them, by assessing the environment with respect to its possible contributions to a positive development, or by pondering developmental aims and means, and putting these into practice (Brandtstädter, 1998; Brandtstädter *et al.*, 1986).

Diverse empirical proofs and pointers exist for these two basic positions. If we are looking for the lowest common denominator from these very different areas, we could say: development in intimate partner relationships, groups, and organizations will be positive where the existing social relationships provide a high measure of support, particularly in situations of stress; where responsibility is divided appropriately, i.e. fairly in the eyes of the participants; and where existing agreements can be revised if current conditions result in the need to do so. In short: cohesion, individual responsibility and flexibility seem of particular importance for optimal development within groups.

### Professional identity and team development

Professionals and their teams are continually confronted with high expectations from clients and the organizational unit. The central functions of teams are to inform, lend emotional support, take the weight off, and to motivate members; they are meant to qualify and optimize (Mullins *et al.*, 1994; Vinokur-Kaplan, 1995). In short, they are expected to provide developmental protection as well as gain. Teams are apparently more and more being given the same importance as primary groups, such as intimate partner relationships and families. This leads to the assumption that there is a connection between the subjective identity and the subjective perception of current team conflicts (Diener *et al.*, 1999; van Horn and Schaufeli, 1999). This assumption is backed by findings from developmental psychology, organizational psychology, and social psychology. The development and maintenance of a personal identity demands an active shaping process in order to integrate the continuity and change in the process of life into the self-image. Investigations based on organizational psychology show that professional identity is interwoven with the group processes that occur in the workplace. This holds especially true for colleagues of interdisciplinary teams (Nightingale and Scott, 1994). Studies from the field of social psychology indicate that the perception and shaping of cohesion and hierarchy are influenced by a personal need for positive identity (Harré and Lamb, 1986).

## *Team conflict and organizational psychology*

Working under increasing economic and social pressures, team members will frequently experience a conflict between organizational or team-related needs and their own interests. This is documented by psychological contributions about supervision in the caring professions (Watkins, 1995) or analyses of an organizational-psychological nature (Yank *et al.*, 1994; Guzzo and Dickson, 1996). With the perspective on the organization, the task is to overcome the dilemma between increasingly economized social work and the original psychology of the professional helper. Even if this dilemma is not resolved, life might be made more bearable for individuals if the team provides support, and as long as no other private, personal problems add to the conflict. It is still important to ask what makes conflicts bearable – between organization and team, organization and individual, or team and individual. What can an organization contribute to help resolve individual conflict? Which team traits are a gain for individual team members and a help for the organization?

Research into organizational psychology has gained a lot of ground over the past few years but answers to this question are still few and far between. This deficiency is the result of: (i) the failure to recognize groups as distinct parts of an organization; and (ii), where groups were taken into consideration, the focus of research and interventions was mainly on project groups (and there are many other different groups in organizations; French and Bell, 1994). As project groups are very different from teams in counselling centres, the findings from such research cannot be transferred without closer consideration.

Cohesion (i.e. coherence, a feeling of togetherness vs distance) and power (i.e. influence and leadership vs partnership and individual responsibility) seem of particular importance for a comprehensive description of structural features of organizations, groups, and individuals (McGrath *et al.*, 1996). Cohesion is based on open, trusting communication, but also on interpersonal attraction. These characteristics seem most obvious in informal groups. Here, a positive work atmosphere can develop that brings better results (Yoon *et al.*, 1994). The group has to leave

enough space for individual responsibility and creativity. Cohesion is thus ambivalent. The same is true for leadership. Too much leadership has a negative impact
on the motivation and co-operation of colleagues, too little leadership leaves
responsibilities unclear and thus leads to confusion and the unnecessary expenditure
of energy (Fodor and Riordan, 1995).

*Social aspects of personal identity in teams*

We have seen that groups can support the development of individuals as long as they
have certain characteristics. These characteristics we have called coherence and
individual responsibility, combined with a sufficient degree of flexibility. Similarly,
cohesion and leadership are of particular importance for communication and the
success of an organization. The construct of 'group' as introduced by organizational
psychology has some deficiencies for the teams under consideration here. Some
results and theories from cognitive social psychology therefore need to be discussed,
with a particular focus on two questions:

- First, what importance does the group have for the development of identity?
- Second, which group characteristics are beneficial and which detrimental to the
  development of identity?

Three particularities have to be taken into account: (i) everyone has his/her
own point of view in the power field between self and group; (ii) this subjective view
is distorted, particularly with respect to assessing achievements; (iii) the subjective
assessment of identity, groups, and achievement influences an individual's
behaviour in the group.

When discussing groups, close attention should be paid to the perception
of individuals. Following the theory of social categorization (Tajfel, 1981), one
can distinguish between one's own groups and other groups. It can be assumed
that in general we derive our social identity predominantly from belonging to our
own group. However, comparisons are continually made between one's own group
and the other group; the aim is to better oneself (Brewer, 1996). This leads to a
tendency to discriminate negatively against the other group; this tendency has been
found by many investigators (e.g. Pettigrew, 1997, 1998). Social categorization
and devaluation of the other group also take place when the team talks negatively
about 'the administration' or 'those in private practice'. It can be assumed that
people, as group members, sometimes pursue identity-related issues and sometimes
group-related ones (Schiffmann, 1993). If the issue is a group success, a person
has an identity gain if they think that their contribution was crucial and they define
him/herself through their job. As Schiffmann further shows, such an identity gain
is especially possible in groups with less cohesion, as otherwise the other group
members would participate in the success.

The objectives of personal identity and the group can be conflicting. With a view
to the theory of symbolic self-completion it seems possible that individuals commit
an act symbolizing the self, and thereby ignore the situations of the other group

members. With actions symbolizing the self, people endeavour (Wicklund and Gollwitzer, 1982) to compensate for a lack of success in an area that is subjectively important by displaying alternative symbols of having achieved their goal. This lack occurs normally quite frequently in view of the high personality and development ideals. Whether, how, and what identity objectives are aimed at also depends on the social environment of individual people.

### Perception of cohesion and power in therapeutic systems and clinical teams

Previous research with the FAST showed that perception of family cohesion and hierarchy is connected with important characteristics of individual and family development (Gehring, 1998). Furthermore, it has been reported that balanced cohesion and hierarchy in the patient–clinician relationship is correlated with positive clinical outcomes in chronic patients (Gehring *et al.*, 1995). The relevance of the FAST for the reflection of the relationships between therapist and family members, and between therapist and his/her clinical colleagues, will now be investigated. The following sections present preliminary results of two FAST studies that explored interpersonal structures in therapeutic systems and team systems.

### Therapy system

To gain more insight into structural patterns of the therapeutic system, Paneff (1997) investigated whether where is a correlation between the representation of family relationships (i.e. the family system) and those between the family members and the therapist (i.e. the therapy system). In this preliminary study, at the onset of treatment mothers of preschoolers with behavioural disorders were asked to portray their typical family relationships and then to depict their expected and desired relationships between the therapist and the family. Accordingly, the latter two portrayals included all family members (i.e. parents, patient, and siblings) and a figure representing the therapist. Scoring of the FAST representations was based on the arithmetical procedure. Data analysis included comparisons of the structure of family relations with those in the expected and desired therapeutic system on the system and dyadic levels. Results revealed a multitude of correlations between family structure and relational characteristics of the therapeutic system (see Table 16.3). For example, mothers' representation of expected cohesion and hierarchy in the therapist–family system was correlated with the respective dimensions in their typical family representations. Furthermore, parental and parent–child cohesion was represented similarly in the typical family representation and in the portrayal of the desired therapeutic system.

What do these findings mean for the conceptualization of supervision strategies? It can be assumed that family members' desires and expectations concerning the therapeutic relationship as assessed with the FAST are important for the further course of therapy. Our findings are important not only for the planning and assessment of family-related interventions but also for the reflection of the relationship

Table 16.3 Correlations between mothers' representations of typical family relations and their expected and desired relations in the therapeutic system with the FAST (n = 19)

| | Typical family relations | | | | | | |
| --- | --- | --- | --- | --- | --- | --- | --- |
| | Parent–child | Father–mother | Mother–child | Therapist–mother | Therapist–father | Therapist–child | Therapist–family |
| Expected relations in the therapeutic system | | | | | | | |
| hierarchy | 0.29 | 0.16 | 0.35 | −0.61** | −0.53* | −0.41 | −0.60** |
| cohesion | 0.73*** | 0.62** | 0.20 | 0.24 | 0.45 | 0.23 | 0.64** |
| Desired relations in the therapeutic system | | | | | | | |
| hierarchy | 0.43 | 0.12 | 0.41 | −0.32 | −0.23 | 0.18 | −0.34 |
| cohesion | 0.69** | 0.64** | 0.29 | −0.11 | −0.01 | −0.06 | 0.16 |

*$p < 0.05$, **$p < 0.01$, ***$p < 0.001$.

between therapist and family. In other words, we are inclined to think that reflection and evaluation of clinical interventions should exceed a purely family-related use of the FAST. However, because of the lack of empirical examination, the description of the therapist–family relationship using the FAST can as yet only generate hypotheses, and further research in this area is necessary.

*Team system*

The relationships between members of professional teams will now be considered. One major question is, 'Do similar patterns regarding the association between interpersonal structures and individual outcomes in clinical teams and family systems exist?' If we transfer our findings from family research (see Table 16.2) into this area we can assume that the clinicians' perceptions of the relational structures in their teams are connected with their personal experience of resources and support from other team members, as well as their attitudes towards difficult colleagues.

A recent explorative pilot study interviewed staff members (i.e. clinical psychologists, family therapists, child therapists, social workers, and pedagogical experts) from different child guidance clinics in the Freiburg City area (Germany). Half of the respondents ($n = 15$) worked in comparatively homogeneous 'mono-disciplinary' teams with no more than two different types of professional group. The remaining participants were working in interdisciplinary teams with people from more than two different types of professional group. There were no significant differences between these two groups with respect to age, gender, and the duration of professional experience of the respondents, or the number of regular team meetings. A relational structure analysis similar to the FAST was used to assess the perception of cohesion and hierarchy between team members. Cohesion was represented by using sticky dots that were placed on a grid system. The influence of the individual team members was indicated with number values, analogous to the blocks in the FAST. Apart from the individual representation of the typical, ideal, and conflict structures in the team, respondents completed a questionnaire about the support received from team colleagues and perceived personal resources for professional development (Brandtstädter *et al.*, 1986), as well as an adjective list for the evaluation of the 'most difficult colleague'. These measures were used as quality indicators of the current work situation.

First, we examined whether members from monodisciplinary teams perceive their relations differently from those working in interdisciplinary teams. Table 16.4 shows the average degree of cohesion (values indicated as distance) and respondents' influence over colleagues (individual power) in the two groups. Analysis revealed significant differences in the perception of ideal cohesion and typical power. Members of monodisciplinary teams wanted more cohesive relationships and rated their own influence in everyday situations as higher than did those from interdisciplinary teams. However, if the respondents' influence was assessed relative to the leadership of their colleagues, these differences evened themselves out.

*Table 16.4* Comparison of cohesion and power in mono- and interdisciplinary teams in typical, ideal and conflict representations (*n* = 31)

| Dimension and representation | Monodisciplinary team (*n* = 15) | | Interdisciplinary team (*n* = 16) | | Effect | |
|---|---|---|---|---|---|---|
| | Mean | sd | Mean | sd | *t*-test | *p* |
| Cohesion[1] | | | | | | |
| typical | 58.6 | 38.8 | 46.6 | 29.9 | −0.97 | ns |
| ideal | 17.5 | 7.9 | 31.4 | 14.2 | 3.32 | < 0.01 |
| conflict | 57.9 | 36.3 | 61.6 | 36.3 | 0.28 | ns |
| Power[2] | | | | | | |
| typical | 2.5 | 0.9 | 1.8 | 0.8 | −2.18 | < 0.05 |
| ideal | 2.4 | 1.1 | 1.9 | 0.6 | −1.46 | ns |
| conflict | 2.3 | 1.0 | 1.8 | 0.8 | −1.65 | ns |

[1] Values indicated as distance scores; [2] elevation of figure representing the respondent; ns, not significant.

Another important question was whether hints at a possible connection between an individual's perception of a typical team structure and their subjective assessment of their own situation at work can be found. Table 16.5 shows that the portrayal of the team structure was related to resources of the respondents and their perception of colleagues. In particular, balanced cohesion and hierarchy structures corresponded with high personal resources for professional development, support from team colleagues, and a relatively positive evaluation of difficult team members. Therefore, it can be assumed that there are similar patterns regarding the relationship between interpersonal structures and individual outcomes in professional teams and family systems.

Our findings show that team constellations in everyday life (i.e. the typical representation) and in conflict situations are apparently perceived similarly. The degree of cohesion between the group's members was moderate in both representations. The interpersonal structure in the ideal team, however, was perceived

*Table 16.5* Types of typical team structure as a function of personal resources for professional development and perception of colleagues (*n* = 31)

| Type of team structure | Personal resources | | Support from team colleagues | | Evaluation of most difficult colleague | |
|---|---|---|---|---|---|---|
| | Low (%) | High (%) | Low (%) | High (%) | Negative (%) | Positive (%) |
| Unbalanced | 35 | 10 | 32 | 13 | 32 | 13 |
| Balanced | 23 | 32 | 20 | 35 | 16 | 39 |
| Chi[2] (df = 1) | 4.4* | | 4.0* | | 5.4* | |

*p < 0.05.

differently. As far as cohesion is concerned, respondents at least subjectively wished for increased levels of connectedness. It is noteworthy that members of monodisciplinary teams had higher expectations of group cohesion than their counterparts. The subjectively higher influence of the professionals in monodisciplinary teams could stand for higher expectations regarding themselves and their success in team development. However, the combination of expectations of closeness and the perception of relatively high individual power (personal responsibility) is not unproblematic. It can be assumed that, in interdisciplinary teams, the heterogeneity of the group can be used to ease the burden on the individual. If these findings on closeness or distance and influencing the team are linked with the respondents' assessments of their resources for personal development, it becomes obvious that subjective ratings of individual development are likely to influence the group's processes. The objectives 'difficult members', 'developmental resources', and 'support from others' are indeed particularly important with respect to professional teams, but also to other human systems. Those who perceive developmental aspects as positive and at the same time know that they are supported by other members of the system will experience their context as harmonious and resource-oriented.

It can be assumed that the quality of team communication is important, particularly with regard to the assessment of personal influence. It is therefore likely that those who experience themselves as influential will be deeply affected by relationship problems in the workplace. Although it seems as if different aspects play a part in judging cohesion and influence, the interrelationship between these two crucial dimensions is obvious. According to prominent family stress models, the simultaneous presence of extremes in hierarchy and cohesion is problematic. Therefore, it can be assumed that those members who perceive their team structures to be caught between these extremes are likely to see the further development of the team and themselves as rather problematic.

## The FAST as a tool for supervison and team development

Cohesion and hierarchy are central features that determine the structural organization of social systems. If supervision is to do justice to its educational and counselling objectives, it has to develop certain personal and systemic competencies in the supervisees, including factors such as:

- recognition and change of cohesion and hierarchy in the client system
- the shaping of a relationship with the client and their family that is characterized by appropriate closeness–distance regulation and power
- recognition of the relational structures in the clinical team and the supervisors' group
- continual learning about the connections between environmental factors and interpersonal development in these systems.

Different strategies and methods can be used to build the necessary personal competencies or achieve changes of cohesion and power structures in these systems, (Table 16.6).

*Table 16.6* Changing cohesion and hierarchy in therapy and supervision using the FAST

| System level | Topic/problem | Objective of intervention | Measure/ intervention | Outcome |
|---|---|---|---|---|
| Family system (Index patient and members of his/her family) | Relational structures | Balanced cohesion and hierarchy | FAST in individual and group settings Observation, reflection and participative– discoursive analysis of family structures and dynamics | Greater clarity in individual perspectives Increased communicative competence Transformation of family roles and rules |
| Therapy system (therapist and family members) | Relationships between family members and clinicians or therapists | Appropriate degree of cohesion and hierarchy between therapist and family members (i.e. therapeutic alliance) | FAST as a method to visualize the therapeutic system Expectations, desires and fears regarding the relational dynamic between therapist and family members | Establishing a co-operative therapeutic relationship at the onset of treatment Decreasing therapeutic power in the course of the therapy process Decreasing cohesion between family and therapist towards the end of therapy Balanced family cohesion and hierarchy in the case of a positive therapy process |
| Clinical team system (therapist and his/her professional colleagues) | Personal interests and requirements of the team are irreconcilable Staff members do not feel part of the team | Recognition of possible common objectives and interests Compatibility between distinct value systems and team-related roles | Topic-related work on the FAST Evaluation of aims and means Planning joint activities including work and leisure time Assessment of team dynamics on the personal and system level with the FAST (e.g. reflection of individual desires and expectations of others) | Increased cohesion Functional hierarchies (i.e. competence-related decision-making processes) Increased transparency of systemic rules |

*Table 16.6 continued*

| | | | | |
|---|---|---|---|---|
| Supervisee system | The group is perceived as overly homogenous (i.e. undifferentiated ego mass) Unfair attribution of causes for failures and problems between groups | More differentiated perceptions in relation to specific problem areas More differentiated perception of situational and problem-related aspects | Planning of communication training The FAST can be used to reflect team relations on various subsystem levels and to determine personal and common objectives and values as well as the members' contribution to the problem-solving process | Expectations regarding interpersonal structures can be clarified and/or modified Differentiation of professional roles, rules and competencies |
| Organization system (e.g. therapeutic, research and administrative sections of the institution) | Conflict of identity and objectives between individuals, teams and the entire organization | Reconciliation of individual aims, team rules and organizational culture | Circular exploration of relational structures within and between groups (joint reflection of group processes) Joint case and team discussions Use of FAST in different settings with members from various teams Providing information about the organizational structure and policy (e.g. promoting and decision-making strategies) Shaping organizational needs and perspectives through colleagues | Cohesion decreases initially but increases later on without being idealized or at the expense of other groups More differentiated constructs about own and others' problem-solving strategies and actions Cohesion and hierarchy initially decrease Greater transparency regarding cohesion and hierarchy structures Reduced possibilities for unfair attributions High corporate identity Improved atmosphere (e.g. tolerance) |

What possibilities are there for effective interventions? The theoretical foundations and empirical findings point at important topics and ways of team counselling oriented towards development. These should relate to individual and team development from a multitude of perspectives. Next to reflecting case-related clinical work we should focus on the question of individual growth and its impact on personal and professional competence, as well as on the development of the team and its members (Valsiner, 1999). Team conflicts and processes can be viewed against a background of individual and joint development. They have to be assessed in respect of personal, group, and organizational aims; personal potential; team contributions; and organizational means. In the counselling dialogue, the observer's perspective oscillates between the views of individual participants and the super-ordinate team or organizational level. Such counselling or supervision will do justice to personal and team needs and is therefore experienced as real help. On the group level, ways of intervening can be pointed out that exceed traditional team supervision. Committee work above group level, participation in sessions with other colleagues, permanent joint training activities, and case seminars lead to the assumption that intergroup conflicts and inadequate attributions that stabilize the feeling of self-worth will be less determining for the supervision and team process. Cohesion and power can be determined, for example, in the framework of a 'theory of clinical leadership' (Yank *et al.*, 1994). As a consequence, the traditional wealth of methods of clinical supervision will be broadened by intervention strategies that are derived from theoretical and practical knowledge of organizational psychology. On the basis of our preliminary research and clinical experience it can be assumed that the FAST, originally designed for patient- and family-related assessment, has the potential to be a suitable tool for promoting and evaluating interventions in the context of supervision and team resource development.

## Outlook

The assumption that cohesion and power are fundamental dimensions for the description of family systems and the relational structure of professional teams in the healthcare system proved to be plausible. However, this must not substitute for further empirical research. Additional studies are necessary to clarify which characteristics of cohesion and power are of importance, so that a more comprehensive insight into the complex organization of the different social systems of distinct therapeutic teams and families with different backgrounds and developmental needs can be gained (Brown and Landrum-Brown, 1995; Cota *et al.*, 1995). In particular, patterns of transformation of these dimensions through the supervision process on various systems levels should be explored in a more detailed manner. This requires cross-sectional and longitudinal studies of interpersonal processes in various settings. Furthermore, it is necessary to point out the cultural specificity and relativity of current theories and empirical research in this field. It is well recognized not only that familial systems and their characteristics vary across different cultures, but that organizational features and communication styles vary in professional teams. Thus, patterns of cohesion and power, as well as related clinical problem-solving approaches and supervisiory strategies, should be evaluated according to specific psychosocial and environmental requirements (Triandis, 1996). At this point, the representation of subjectively important systems and collective representations of human relations in public health and social welfare organizations do clearly overlap and, therefore, both perspectives should be considered (Moscovici, 1990; Pervin, 1999). Research at the interface of developmental, social, clinical, organizational and cross-cultural psychology, and accompanying systematic work with the FAST, including clinical and non-clinical groups, could enhance the creation of innovative models for systemic supervision and organizational counselling in various contexts.

## References

Brandtstädter, J. (1998) 'Action perspectives on human development', in R.M. Lerner (ed.) *Theoretical Models of Human Development*, New York: Wiley.

—— Krampen, G. and Heil, F.E. (1986) 'Personal control and emotional evaluation of development in partnership relations during adulthood', in M.M. Baltes and P.B. Baltes (eds) *The Psychology of Aging and Control*, Hillsdale, NJ: Erlbaum.

—— Baltes-Götz, B. and Heil, F.E. (1990) 'Entwicklung in Partnerschaften: Analysen zur Partnerschaftsqualität bei Ehepaaren im mittleren Erwachsenenalter' (Development in Intimate Relationships), *Zeitschrift für Entwicklungspsychologie und Pädagogische Psychologie* 22: 183–206.

Brewer, M.B. (1996) 'Managing diversity: The role of social identities', in S.E. Jackson and M.N. Ruderman (eds) *Diversity in Work Teams*, Washington, DC: American Psychological Association.

Brown, M.T. and Landrum-Brown, J. (1995) 'Counselor supervision', in J.G. Ponteretto, J.M. Casas, L.A. Suzuki and C.M. Alexander (eds.) *Handbook of Multicultural Counseling*, Thousand Oaks, CA: Sage.

Cota, A.A., Evans, C.R., Dion, K.L., Kilik, L. and Longman, R.S. (1995) 'The structure of group cohesion', *Personality and Social Psychology Bulletin* 53: 572–80.

Diener, E., Suh, E.M., Lucas, R.E. and Smith, H.L. (1999) 'Subjective well-being: Three decades of progress', *Psychological Bulletin* 125: 276–302.

Farmer, S.M., Maslyn, J.M., Fedor, D.B. and Goodman, J.S. (1997) 'Putting upward influence strategies in context', *Journal of Organizational Behavior* 18: 17–42.

Fodor, E.M. and Riordan, J.M. (1995) 'Leader power and group conflict as influences on leader behavior and group member self-affect', *Journal of Research in Personality* 29: 418–31.

French, W.L. and Bell, C.H. (1994) *Organisationsentwicklung* (Development of Organizations), Bern: Haupt.

Gehring, T.M. (1998) *The Family System Test*, Seattle, WA: Hogrefe and Huber Publishers.

—— Brägger, F., Steinebach, Ch. and Wössmer Buntschu, B. (1995) 'Family System Test (FAST): A systemic approach to the analysis of social relationships in the clinical context', in B. Boothe, R. Hirsig, A. Helminger, B. Meier, and R. Volkart (eds) *Perception – Evaluation – Interpretation*, Göttingen: Hogrefe and Huber Publishers.

—— Candrian, M., Marti, D. and Real del Sartre, O. (1996) 'Family System Test (FAST): The relevance of parental family constructs for clinical intervention', *Child Psychiatry and Human Development* 27: 55–65.

Guzzo, R.A. and Dickson, M.W. (1996) 'Teams in organizations: Recent research on performance and effectiveness', *Annual Review of Psychology* 47: 307–38.

Harré, R. and Lamb, R. (1986) *The Dictionary of Personality and Social Psychology*, Cambridge, MA: MIT Press.

Hausser, K. (1989) 'Identität', in G. Endruweit and G. Trommsdorff (eds) *Wörterbuch der Soziologie* (Handbook of Sociology), Stuttgart: dtv.

Holloway, E. (1995) *Clinical Supervision: A Systems Approach*, Thousand Oaks, CA: Sage.

Krampen, G. (1987) *Handlungstheoretische Persönlichkeitspsychologie* (Action-oriented Personality Psychology), Göttingen: Hogrefe and Huber Publishers.

Kudisch, J.D., Poteet, M.L., Dobbins, G.H., Rush, M.C. and Russell, J.E.A. (1995) 'Expert power, referent power, and charisma: Toward the resolution of a theoretical debate', *Journal of Business and Psychology* 10: 177–95.

McGrath, J.E., Berdahl, J.L. and Arrow, H. (1996) 'Traits, expectations, culture, and clout: The dynamics of diversity in work groups', in S.E. Jackson and M.N. Ruderman (eds) *Diversity in Work Teams*, Washington, DC: American Psychological Association.

Moscovici, S. (1990) 'Social psychology and developmental psychology: Extending the conversation', in G. Duveen and B. Lloyd (eds) *Social Representations and the Development of Knowledge*, Cambridge: Cambridge University Press.

Mullins, L.L., Keller, J.R. and Chaney, J.M. (1994) 'A systems and social cognitive approach to team functioning in physical rehabilitation settings', *Rehabilitation Psychology* 39: 161–78.

Nightingale, A. and Scott, D. (1994) 'Problems of identity in multi-disciplinary teams: The self and systems in change', *British Journal of Psychotherapy* 11: 267–78.

Oerter, R. (1995) 'Kultur, Ökologie und Entwicklung', in R. Oerter and L. Montada (eds) *Entwicklungspsychologie* (Developmental Psychology), Weinheim: Beltz.

Olson, D.H. and Lavee, Y. (1989) 'Family system and family stress: A family life cycle perspective', in K. Kreppner and R.M. Lerner (eds) *Family System and Life-span Development*, Hillsdale, NJ: Erlbaum.

—— McCubbin, H.I. (1982) 'Circumplex model of marital and family systems V: Application to family stress and crisis intervention', in H.I. McCubbin, A.E. Cauble and J.M. Patterson (eds) *Family Stress, Coping and Social Support*, Springfield, IL: Thomas.

Paneff, J. (1997) 'Beziehungsdynamik in der Kindertherapie. Subjektive Familienstruktur und Beziehung in der Frühförderung' (Relational Dynamics in Child Therapy), unpublished M.Phil. thesis, Universität Freiburg.

Pervin, L.A. (1999) 'The cross-cultural challenge to personality', in Y.T. Lee, C.R. McCauley and J.G. Draguns (eds) *Personality and Person Perception Across Cultures*, Mahwah, NJ: Erlbaum.

Pettigrew, T.F. (1997). 'Generalized intergroup contact effects on prejudice', *Personality and Social Psychology Bulletin* 23: 173–85.

—— (1998) 'Intergroup contact theory', *Annual Review of Psychology* 49: 65–85.

Phillips, N. (1997) 'Bringing the organization back in: A comment on conceptualizations of power in upward influence research', *Journal of Organizational Behavior* 18: 43–7.

Schiffmann, R. (1993) 'Die Wahrnehmung der eigenen Tätigkeit in Arbeitsgruppen als Ergebnis von Selbstverpflichtung, Gruppenkohärenz und Gruppenerfolg' (Subjective Perception of Activities as a Function of Group Cohesion), *Arbeit* 2: 223–41.

Steinebach, C. (1995) *Familienentwicklung in der Frühförderung. Die Sicht der Mütter*

(Family Development and Children's Mental Retardation: The Mothers' Point of View), Freiburg: Lambertus.

Steinebach, C. (2000) *Entwicklungspychologie [Developmental Psychology]*, Stuttgart: Klett-Cotta.

Tajfel, H. (1981) *Human Groups and Social Categories*, Cambridge: Cambridge University Press.

Triandis, H.C. (1996) 'The importance of contexts in studies of diversity', in S.E. Jackson and M.N. Ruderman (eds) *Diversity in Work Teams*, Washington, DC: American Psychological Association.

Turner, J. and Fine, M. (1998) 'Postmodern evaluation in family therapy supervision', *Journal of Systemic Therapies* 14: 57–69.

Valsiner, J. (1999) 'I create you to control me: A glimpse into basic progresses of semiotic mediation', *Human Development* 42: 26–30.

van Horn, J.E. and Schaufeli, W.B. (1999) 'Teacher burnout and lack of reciprocity', *Journal of Applied Psychology* 29: 91–108.

Vinokur-Kaplan, D. (1995) 'Treatment teams that work (and those that don't): An application of Hackman's group effectiveness model to interdisciplinary teams in psychiatric hospitals', *Journal of Applied Behavioral Science* 25: 303–27.

Watkins, E. (1995) 'Psychotherapy supervisor and supervisee: Developmental models and research nine years later', *Clinical Psychology Review* 15: 647–80.

Wicklund, R.A. and Gollwitzer, P.M. (1982) *Symbolic Self-completion*, Hillsdale, NJ: Erlbaum.

Willke, H. (1995) 'Das intelligente Unternehmen – Wissensmanagement der Organisation', in Beratergruppe Neuwaldegg (ed.) *Intelligente Unternehmen – Herausforderung Wissensmanagement* (The Intelligent Enterprise – Management of Knowledge in Organizations), Vienna: Service Fachverlag.

Yank, G.R., Barber, J.W. and Spradlin, W.W. (1994) 'Mental health treatment teams and leadership: A systems model', *Behavioral Science* 39: 293–310.

Yoon, J., Baker, M.R. and Ko, J.W. (1994) 'Interpersonal attachment and organizational commitment: Subgroup hypothesis revisited', *Human Relations* 47: 329–51.

# Part V

# Conclusions and recommendations

# 17 Future directions for FAST and family evaluation

*Marianne Debry, Peter K. Smith and Thomas M. Gehring*

## Family evaluation: much remains to be done

There is a delay in the field of family evaluation with regard to individual assessment. Snyder *et al.* (1995) highlight the broad range of assessment techniques addressed to individuals and dyads, in contrast to the relative paucity measures at the extended family or community levels.

L'Abate and Snyder (Chapter 3) emphasize the inadequacies of family assessment techniques. A large number of these are not theory driven. Some present poor psychometric properties: standardization and sampling, internal consistency and temporal stability, discriminant and construct validity do not meet the expected standards. Nevertheless, there are some well-known exceptions: for example, the tests of Olson, Beavers, Epstein or Moos (Lebow, Chapter 4).

Almost all the existing measures are verbal. Most of them are self-report questionnaires, with all their inherent drawbacks and lack of suitability for young children and people with limited language skills. They are more appropriate for research than for clinical practice. On the other hand, some measures are highly qualitative and emotional (e.g. sculptures): applying them needs experienced therapists (Gehring and Marti, Chapter 1) and they are often not compatible with the usual requirements of research.

L'Abate and Snyder (Chapter 3) deplore the fact that 'family evaluation is not yet in the mainstream of clinical practice'. Family therapists are not prone to use standardized measures. In a survey of 598 marital and family therapists, Boughner *et al.* (1994) found that only 33 per cent regularly used assessment instruments. In family therapy, only 13 per cent of the respondents reported using at least one instrument; all the instruments used were questionnaires. Many of them evaluated personality instead of dyads or systems. A large number of respondents (70 per cent) held standardized assessment to be 'not at all' or 'not very' important. It is obvious that, in the field of family therapy, practitioners fail to plan and to evaluate their treatment with the help of standardized assessments.

The status of research in family therapy still remains marginal (Gehring *et al.*, Chapter 15). Research findings still have a modest impact upon clinical practice but it must be admitted that few of them are clinically meaningful or provide relevant information for the therapeutic process (Shields and Wynne, 1994; Pinsof and Wynne, 2000).

Hence, there is a gap between family theory and evaluation, between assessment and therapy, and between researchers and clinicians. L'Abate and Snyder (Chapter 3) and Gehring *et al.* (Chapter 15) plead for a more comprehensive approach to family therapy, integrating research and clinical practice. They advocate a more scientific approach to therapy, including systematic family assessment and appraisal of the treatment outcomes.

Family psychology can be defined as a science as well as a profession (Pinsof, 1992). Shields and Wynne (1994) claim that family therapy is at a turning point in its development. The discipline risks becoming marginalized in the field of health-care if research on the process and efficacy of family therapy is not strengthened. This book is an attempt to institute a dialogue and a co-operation between researchers and therapists around a common technique, the FAST. It is designed to begin to address these deficiencies.

## What family evaluation should be

Family appraisal is necessarily multidimensional and highly complex. Snyder *et al.* (1995) suggest a multifaceted, multilevel approach to appraisal to ensure that the following features are present:

- Theory-driven and empirically grounded: constructs need to have theoretical relevance, and techniques must give guarantees of excellent psychometric properties.
- Multiple levels: the interactions of individuals, dyads, triads, and the nuclear family are worth evaluating and articulating with extended and community systems.
- Multiple dimensions: relevant dimensions like intimacy, power, communication, problem-solving, support, and adaptability are to be appraised (Seywert, 1990).
- Multiple methods: assessment strategies address a wide range of means of expression. The aim is to propose to family members many media in which to represent, and to express themselves about, their family: words, drawings, postures, figurines, so that everyone can find their own language.
- Multiple contexts: the family must be observed across several settings.
- Assessment leads to a product but is also an interactive process that is as instructive as the result. Assessment techniques should allow comparisons between family members, between stages of lifecycles, between different types of family configurations, and across cultural backgrounds. It is important that they are as culture-free as possible and free from stereotypes. They must be open to a large diversity of cases and settings.

## The FAST, a breakthrough in family evaluation

The FAST is theory driven: it is clearly in line with Minuchin's theory of structural therapy (Debry, Chapter 2). The FAST is also empirically grounded (Gehring and Marti, Chapter 1). It assesses different dimensions like cohesion, hierarchy, and flexibility, which have been proved to be relevant in family studies (Fontaine, 1985). These dimensions can be determined simultaneously but are independent (Gehring and Marti, Chapter 1; Debry, Chapter 2). The FAST also addresses multiple levels of the system: the whole nuclear system, parents, siblings, and every dyad.

The FAST is a task: people are asked to do something, alone or together. It is a figure placement test requiring visual, motor, and verbal activities. It looks like a game and is easily understandable.

It is also a semiprojective technique. Participants are asked to represent family relations with a symbolism shared by them and the psychologist: distance on the square board for emotional proximity, relative height for hierarchy. Figures are identified as men and women. Coloured figures can be used in the way the respondents want.

Three representations are commonly used. The first (typical family representation) awakens the defences and is usually the representation where boundaries are clearest. The second (ideal representation) is characterized by an increase of cohesion, and by either a decrease or a status quo of hierarchy. The plots for both these representations can be influenced by desirability. In this respect, the third (conflict) representation is perhaps the most interesting because it leads the participant to spread out the figures and show more extreme positions in the family (Gehring and Debry, 1995). We can thus compare the family representation in three different settings and appraise the flexibility of the representations through different contexts.

As a product, the FAST provides quantitative and qualitative results. 'Cohesion and hierarchy scores can be calculated for the family as a unit, as well as for its subsystems, on the basis of either an arithmetical or a categorical procedure' (Gehring and Marti, Chapter 1). A relational structure is determined according to the degree of cohesion and hierarchy. The disturbances of boundaries are qualified: excessive intergenerational proximity by coalitions and deficient parental authority by hierarchy reversals.

As a process, the FAST lets the therapist observe the interactions between the members of the family when they are making the joint representation. This representation provides a lot of information on the relational patterns, which may or may not be in accordance with the FAST plot. For Rigazio-DiGilio (Chapter 14), 'the application of the FAST represents both an assessment tool and a therapeutic intervention'.

## The FAST, a technique in full development

Since the publication of the FAST, clinicians and researchers have contributed to help broaden its scope. The contributors to this book demonstrate how versatile and flexible it can be.

Some of them have created new instructions. In Chapter 7 (Berdondini and Genta), strangers have been added: two hypothetical neighbours, one of whom is a drug addict. Hunter and von Balmoos (Chapter 9) asked for a representation of the mother's family of origin and a representation showing a triad. Smith *et al.* (Chapter

8) asked the child, after he or she had completed the FAST, to imagine how they thought their parents would represent the family; the parent was invited to imagine how their child had represented their family.

New scorings are proposed. Some spatial configurations are characterized (no separation of figures, on a continuous line, one or two corner(s)) by Berdondini and Genta (Chapter 7); symbiosis/amalgamation for enmeshed figures by Meyer (Chapter 6).

The research reported in this book is summarized in Table 17.1. It covers many areas of psychology:

- Developmental psychology: attachment (Morley-Williams and Cowie, Chapter 5), theory of mind ability during middle childhood (Smith *et al.*, Chapter 8), preadolescence (Debry, Chapter 2), puberty (Kim and Wongyannava, Chapter 10), transition to adulthood (Mayseless and Scharf, Chapter 11).
- Family psychology: single-parent families (Hunter and von Balmoos, Chapter 9).
- School psychology: bullying at school (Berdondini and Genta, Chapter 7).
- Work psychology: supervision and team development (Steinebach, Chapter 16).
- Cross-cultural psychology: comparison between Japanese and Swiss families (Ikeda and Hatta, Chapter 12); three-generation Chinese families (Shu and Smith, Chapter 13).
- Family therapy: interactive assessment and treatment in family psychotherapy (Rigazio-DiGilio, Chapter 14), parental interventions in child psychiatry (Gehring *et al.*, Chapter 15).

A promising development of the FAST lies in its application to systems other than the family. For instance, Steinebach (Chapter 16) used it to investigate the therapeutic relationship. Individual and family outcomes can be measured, predicted, and evaluated. The FAST can also be used to portray the structure and dynamics of professional teams (Steinebach, Chapter 16), with perhaps a revised scoring procedure and interpretation frame. The relation between behavioural patterns in teams and in family of origin is worth studying by this means.

The samples used in the researches are more often clinical ones (seven samples with twenty to thirty participants, mean = 23) than large samples (four large samples: from 102 to 265 participants, mean = 177). One reason for this could be that application of the FAST is relatively time-consuming, being given on an individual basis to a participant or members of a family. However, it is less time-consuming than many clinical measures, so large samples are feasible.

Of the twelve empirical studies reported in this book (see Table 17.1), five include young children under 7 years of age; five are with children aged between 8 and 12 years; three are with adolescents, and seven include adults. Children or adolescents alone do the FAST in five studies, children and mothers in three studies, both parents in two studies, and grandparents in one study. One study included representations of team structures by health professionals.

Table 17.1 Characteristics of empirical studies with the FAST represented in this book

| Authors | Chapter | Sample | Age of children | Country | Family status | FAST |
|---|---|---|---|---|---|---|
| Debry | 2 | 167 children (83 girls, 84 boys) | 10–12 (age range) | Belgium | Intact, 2 children | T, I, C |
| Morley-Williams & Cowie | 5 | 24 children (12 girls, 12 boys) | 4–6 (age range) | UK | Working-class/lower-middle-class | T |
| Meyer | 6 | 31 children (21 girls, 10 boys) | 5.5–8.7 (age range) | Switzerland | Middle- and upper-class Mean size: 4.3 | T, I |
| Berdondini & Genta | 7 | 87 children (bullies, victims and control group) | 8–11 (age range) | Italy | | T, V |
| Smith, Myron-Wilson & Sutton | 8 | 11 girls, 11 boys, 20 mothers, 2 fathers | 7–10 (age range) | UK | Working-class, ethnically mixed | T, V |
| Hunter & von Balmoos | 9 | 9 girls and their mothers | 5.8–10.5 (age range) | Switzerland | Single-parent families (5 after divorce and 4 after father's death) | T, I, V |
| Kim & Wongyannava | 10 | 18 daughters and their mothers | Median 14.5 | UK | Middle-class, Caucasian | T |
| Mayseless & Scharf | 11 | 85 sons and their parents | 17–18 (age range) | Israel | Intact, middle-class | T |
| Ikeda & Hatta | 12 | 102 undergraduate students (76 females and 26 males) | Mean 20.7 | Japan | 67 nuclear, 34 three-generation families, middle-class Mean size: 4.4 | T, I, C |
| Shu & Smith | 13 | 24 girls, 16 boys, 36 parents and 64 grandparents | 6–12 (age range); Mean 8.7 | China | Mainly intact families, 'workers' and 'officials' with 1 child | T |
| Gehring, Page & Marti | 15 | 20 parents of child psychiatric patients | Mean 8.7 | Switzerland | Intact, middle-class Mean size: 4 | T, I |
| Steinebach | 16 | 20 mothers of developmentally retarded children; 20 members of clinical teams | | Germany | | T, I |

T, typical, I, ideal, C, conflict; V, variant.

Among the three types of representation, the typical one is most often required from the participants, and the conflict one least often. The typical representation is used in all the reported research, the ideal representation in five of the twelve studies and the conflict representation in only two of them. However, a variant procedure (see Chapters 7 to 9) is used in three of the studies.

This overview demonstrates that the FAST can be used in many contexts of research, with different generations and cultural backgrounds. The standardized test instructions and scoring procedures can be modified according to specific needs and types of relational systems (various family constellations, therapeutic relationships, professional teams, groups).

## Some limitations

As Gehring and Marti (Chapter 1) wrote, 'any test reduces the complexity of human systems to a few parameters, a simplification required by working models'. The working models reflect the zeitgeist of the period. In the case of the FAST, its concepts originate with structural therapy, and some limitations are ascribable to this framework. For instance, it captures the family map at a given moment and does not shed light on the family history. The FAST should not be the only measure in a comprehensive family evaluation; it should be complemented by others, and by counselling with family members.

Nevertheless, the family history could easily be integrated with modification of the test instructions. For example, it is possible to reconstruct important stages of the family development by asking the family members about the relationships when some important life events occurred (birth of one of the children, death of a grandparent, etc.). Future aspects of the family development can also be anticipated. For example, one can ask how the family thinks it will look when the children leave home.

The concept of 'hierarchy' is not as clear as the concept of 'cohesion'. It encompasses many aspects such as: who makes the decision? who sets the limits? who has influence? The real meaning that 'hierarchy' has for the respondent is not always mastered and necessitates further research (Kahn and Meier, 1999).

The material itself (square board, figures) presents limitations. Some positions are impossible because of the number of figures (Shu and Smith, Chapter 13). There is more freedom and more position opportunities for the figures placed first than for those placed last. But geometric constraints force respondents to make decisions about who is closer to whom. Respondents very often do not want to differentiate between various degrees of closeness (for social desirability reasons), when they are not pushed to do it systematically.

## Convergence and divergence

Are family representations similar when realized by members of the same family? or by respondents whose ages or cultures are different? The contributions to this book make some comparisons possible.

## Different members of the same family

Family representations tend to vary according to the members. Smith *et al.* (Chapter 8) found 73 per cent of the eligible measures to be different between an English child's representation of the family and his/her mother's representation. Chinese children represent more balanced relational structures and more coalitions than their parents and grandparents (Shu and Smith, Chapter 13). In comparison with their parents, Israeli adolescents represent patterns with less cohesion (Mayseless and Scharf, Chapter 11). English adolescent daughters reported less cohesion and more maternal power than did their mothers (Kim and Wongyannava, Chapter 10).

Other studies report similar findings for children and parents. In single-parent families, mothers and daughters both represent unbalanced relational structures with low hierarchy (Hunter and von Balmoos, Chapter 9). In the same way, at the onset of the therapy, unbalanced structures and unclear generational boundaries were represented by parents, individually and jointly (Gehring *et al.*, Chapter 15).

Gehring and Marti report that there is no correlation between individual FAST representations by members from the same family. Nevertheless, two-thirds of the fathers portrayed the same pattern as the family jointly (Chapter 1). These findings suggest that family members perceive their relationships differently and that it is necessary to gather family plots made by each of them.

There is no unique answer to the question of similarity between family constructs of family members. Results of Western studies suggest that in families with severe psychological problems all members tend to agree that their relationships are conflictual and thus unbalanced and rigid (no changes between typical and conflict representations). However, the category 'unbalanced' includes different patterns of cohesion and hierarchy.

In non-clinical families, the members have distinct views of their relationships, but they generally agree that the structure is balanced. Nevetherless, mothers have a less positive view than fathers, who represent the family most often as balanced. The representations tend to be more balanced if performed jointly by the family as a group than individually by their members (except fathers). This can be explained as an effect of social desirability.

## Participants of different ages

Completing the FAST seems easy and suitable for children. Hunter and von Balmoos (Chapter 9) stress that the FAST looks, to children, like a play activity. Studies with boys and girls in middle childhood show that they understand the instructions. Non-clinical samples differentiate cohesion and hierarchy well. They represent clear generational boundaries (Debry, Chapter 2). The boundary with the external environment seems permeable (Berdondini and Genta, Chapter 7). Nevertheless, the task does require some ability of decentration. One has to represent the family relationships from one's own viewpoint but also to take account of the relationships between others. Some degree of social cognition must be attained (Smith *et al.*, Chapter 8). Morley-Williams and Cowie tried to use the FAST with preschool children (Chapter 5). They concluded that 'the FAST lacked meaning and relevance' for many of them. Children below 6 years may have some difficulties in understanding the instructions. The concept 'hierarchy' is often interpreted in terms of age or height.

With this proviso concerning preschool children below 6 years, the studies in this book and elsewhere demonstrate that the FAST is appropriate for children and adolescents of different ages, as well as for family members of different generations (Feldman and Gehring, 1988). A convincing example is Shu and Smith's research applying the FAST to respondents from three generations in China (Chapter 13). It is relatively seldom that a technique can be used with so wide a range of ages (and with illiterate persons – some of the older participants in this study could not read). This generalizability over age gave Smith *et al.* (Chapter 8) the idea of trying out the FAST as a 'theory of mind measure'. They explored whether children and their mothers could have an insight into what the other's family representations might be.

### *Participants from different cultures*

Results from different continents are available and make comparisons possible between family structures in the US and in Europe (Gehring and Marti, Chapter 1) and between Western and Eastern cultures (Ikeda and Hatta, Chapter 12; Shu and Smith, Chapter 13).

There are some common trends. Cohesion is higher in the ideal representation and lower in the conflict representation (Gehring and Marti, Chapter 1). Conflict representations generate more enmeshed boundaries (especially coalitions) than typical and ideal ones. The mother generally seems to be closer to the children than does the father (Mayseless and Scharf, Chapter 11; Ikeda and Hatta, Chapter 12) and is more frequently involved in coalitions (Debry, Chapter 2).

However, some findings look quite different according to the culture. Eastern families seem to be more cohesive, with less clear generational boundaries. In Japan, the relationship between mothers and children is very close and egalitarian. Fathers, who seem to be less integrated into the family, are given more power than mothers (Ikeda and Hatta, Chapter 12). In three-generation Chinese families, hierarchy tends 'to run along lines of generation and sex', with paternal grandfathers receiving the most powerful status. Chinese parents and children seem closer than do spouses (Shu and Smith, Chapter 13).

Japanese and Chinese cultures are grounded in Confucian philosophy. Respect and obedience to the eldest are required. Priority to the eldest and economic reasons result in a pattern of patriarchal three-generation families. In China, the one-child policy and the three-generation family can sometimes result in the '4–2–1 syndrome', a family where six adults (four grandparents and two parents) care for one child. Although these countries have different economic and political systems, they have undergone many changes in family life and they share this common historical background.

## The issue of relational structure

The FAST is underlined by two assumptions in line with the structural theory:

- parents are supposed to be closer to each other than to their children
- parents are supposed to have more power than their children.

If this is not the case, boundaries might be seen as problematic and families could be dysfunctional. Clinical families display unclear generational boundaries (cross-generational coalitions and hierarchy reversals). Balanced relational structures with moderate cohesion and moderate or strong hierarchy are expected to be optimal. Very high or very low cohesion or hierarchy lead to 'unbalanced structures', suggesting that these families might be dysfunctional.

One can wonder if balanced structures necessarily mean healthy family functioning. Conversely, are particular boundaries (coalitions, hierarchy reversals) and unbalanced structures more associated with pathology? The results presented in this book suggest that they are frequently found in non-clinical samples.

The high prevalence of unbalanced structures in non-clinical samples is associated with variables such as:

- Period of development: (puberty): 57 per cent of unbalanced structures versus 9 per cent of balanced ones were identified in a sample of non-clinical preadolescents (Debry, Chapter 2).
- Type of representation: in comparison with the typical FAST, the conflict FAST generates significantly more unbalanced relational structures, coalitions, and hierarchy reversals. Unbalanced structures can be more reactional than structural.
- Family configuration: girls from divorced families showed more unbalanced family structures than semiorphans; single mothers portrayed their families as unbalanced: high cohesion, low hierarchy, hierarchy inversions (Hunter and von Balmoos, Chapter 9).
- Cultural background: typical structures of Japanese adolescents are more unbalanced than those of Swiss ones. Low cohesion is due to the father's isolation and low hierarchy due to weak maternal power (Ikeda and Hatta, Chapter 12). In three-generation Chinese families, Shu and Smith found only 16 per cent of balanced structures (Chapter 13). In this case, high cohesion and low hierarchy (present in 78 per cent of the plots) are associated. Cross-generational coalitions are present in 37 per cent of the plots. In comparison with US children, who portray high parental cohesion, Chinese children see more intergenerational closeness. In Israel, none of the family members depicted the parental dyad as closer than the parent–son dyads. The bond of adolescent with mother is perceived as stronger than that with father, at least from the mother's and adolescent's perspective (Mayseless and Scharf, Chapter 11).

These findings suggest that extreme scores in cohesion and hierarchy can be associated in some contexts with wellbeing. High cohesion and low hierarchy are especially frequent in family representations by non-clinical Western and Eastern samples. Cross-generational coalitions and hierarchy reversals can be understood as close and egalitarian relations, frequently between mother and child, and are not necessarily to be considered as dysfunctional patterns.

The link between relational structures and normality for clinical and non-clinical families in Eastern and Western cultures is very complex. The literature shows that families with psychological problems are more likely to show unclear generational boundaries. However, further study is needed to determine the implications of dysfunctional families showing clear boundaries, and of 'healthy' family members showing unbalanced patterns. Furthermore, we need to find out whether the FAST also shows clinical discriminant validity for Asian families, and how stressed and non-stressed families differ in these cultures.

## Future prospects

During recent decades, great changes have occurred in family configurations, in sexual roles, and in childrearing practices. Family psychology and therapy have to take this paradigmatic revolution into account. Family evaluation has proved to be an important field for research and for clinical practice, a field that deserves to be developed to a larger degree. Some challenges are to be taken up.

### The challenge of relational diagnosis

For a long time clinicians saw the origin of psychological disorders exclusively within the individual – in his or her genes, mind, or psyche. Diagnosis and treatment were focused on the individual. Since the 1960s, the systemic movement has introduced the idea that systems can be dysfunctional and produce symptoms both in persons and in their relationships. Analysis of the interpersonal and contextual factors results in a relational diagnosis complementary to the appraisal of an individual's personality (Lebow, Chapter 4).

Individual disorders are not correlated with specific relational dysfunctions. We have to come to terms with the lack of this kind of linear causality. Gehring and Marti, for instance, found that the type of disorder experienced by a child is unrelated to the portrayal of family structures through the FAST representations of parents, patients and their siblings (Chapter 1). As Denton puts it:

> The ultimate problem in such reconciliation between relational and individual disorders is that they describe different and unique levels of organisation of nature. There exist interactions between these levels, but the levels also function independently to each other. We should continue to try to understand these connective links but appreciate at the same time that it is unlikely that we will find simple, 'linear' linkages between what goes on within and between people.
>
> (Denton, 1995: 35)

## The challenge of interactive assessment and therapy

Historically, the therapist was placed in the position of expert. Following the medical model, he or she labelled the disorders and led a passive patient towards healing. Current therapy models are predicated on more collaborative methods. Placement techniques like the FAST can be used as assessment tools, which can be interpreted both by therapist and by client. 'These types of interactive assessments, geared towards social constructivism, become the vehicle for sharing power in the therapy sessions by stimulating collaboration, reflexivity, and a multiplicity of ideas and possibilities' (Rigazio-DiGilio, Chapter 14).

Gehring and Rigazio-DiGilio have both proposed a model for participative–discoursive intervention, seen as a solution-focused dialogue. The aim is to empower individuals and systems. Family members (parents) define the problem and explain their family constructs and their attempted changes. The clinical procedure includes three steps: planning, problem-solving, and evaluation. 'A transparent conceptualization of the clinical procedure is likely to succeed in turning parents into partners for empirically-derived semistandardized treatment' (Gehring *et al.*, Chapter 15).

## The challenge of families' diversity

The metaframeworks perspective (Breunlin *et al.*, 1992) emphasizes the importance of culture, gender, and development in family psychology. There are so many ways to live in a family, depending on the context of time and space (Milewski-Hertlein, 2001). Family measures should cope with the paradox of considering normative aspects and addressing the singularity of each family system.

The worst thing to wish the FAST for the future is that it becomes a test that indicates what a normal family is, a kind of universal model of sane family relationships. It is much better suited for describing family relationships in their detail and in their variety, for helping families to put their intimate experience of family life into words. For this reason, relational structures and specific boundaries might be seen more as dimensions than discrete categories.

Being more descriptive than prescriptive, the FAST can fit the extreme diversity of current family configurations. This does not preclude statistical analyses on larger samples, describing this diversity. Further research is needed on, for example, nuclear and extended families, families in transition (single-parent, divorced, and blended families), adoption, transgenerational patterns, and cross-social and cross-cultural comparisons. Future research using longitudinal designs can provide more insight into the meaning of structural patterns and their transformation across time.

The concepts of structure and boundary must remain independent of pathology, as recommended by Minuchin. Unbalanced structures or disturbed boundaries are not necessarily synonymous with disorders, even if dysfunctional families are more likely to show them.

Family issues are to be considered more in relative terms than in absolute ones. 'The point at which family patterns become pathogenic depends heavily on context (cultural background, family style, community support system), on timing (when they occur in the family cycle), and how long transitional patterns last' (Wood and Talmon, 1983: 356). This suggests the relevance of contextual and qualitative information, the interest of longitudinal studies capturing family development. For family clinicians and for researchers alike, the way to the future should necessarily be paved with relativism and complexity.

## References

Boughner, S.R., Hayes, S.F., Bubenzer, D.L. and West, J.D. (1994) 'Use of standardized assessment instruments by marital and family therapists: A survey', *Journal of Marital and Family Therapy* 20: 69–75.

Breunlin, D., Schwartz, R., and Mackune-Karrer, B. (1992) *Metaframeworks: Transcending the Models of Family Therapy*, San Francisco, CA: Jossey-Bass.

Denton, W.H. (1995) 'Problems encountered in reconciling individual and relational diagnoses', in F.W. Kaslow (ed.) *Handbook of Relational Diagnosis and Dysfunctional Family Patterns*, New York: Wiley.

Feldman, S.S. and Gehring, T.M. (1988) 'Changing perceptions of family cohesion and power across adolescence', *Child Development*, 59: 1034–45.

Fontaine, P. (1985) 'Familles saines 1. Esquisse conceptuelle générale', *Thérapie Familiale* 6: 267–82.

Gehring, T.M. and Debry, M. (1995) *L'Évaluation du système familial: le FAST*, Braine-le-Château: ATM.

Kahn, J.S. and Meier, S.T. (1999) 'Level of measurement and the Family System Test: The relationship between participants' measurement constructs and interpretations score', *Constructivism in the Human Sciences*, 4: 103–15.

Milewski-Hertlein, K.A. (2001) 'The use of a socially constructed genogram in clinical practice', *The American Journal of Family Therapy*, 29: 23–38.

Minuchin, S., (1974) *Families and Family Therapy*, Cambridge University Press.

Pinsof, W.M. (1992) 'Toward a scientific paradigm for family psychology: The integrative process systems perspective', *Journal of Family Psychology* 3–4: 432–47.

—— Wynne, L.C. (2000) 'Toward progress research: Closing the gap between family therapy practice and research', *Journal of Marital and Family Therapy* 26: 1–8.

Seywert, F. (1990) *L'Évaluation systémique de la famille*, Paris: PUF.

Shields, C.G. and Wynne, L.C. (1994) 'The marginalisation of family therapy: A historical and continuing problem', *Journal of Marital and Family Therapy* 20: 117–38.

Snyder, D.K., Cavell, T.A., Heffer, R.W. and Mangrum, L.F. (1995) 'Marital and family assessment: A multifaceted, multilevel approach', in R.H. Mikesell, D.D. Lusterman and S.H. McDaniel (eds) *Integrating Family Therapy: Handbook of Family Psychology and Systems Theory*, Washington, DC: American Psychological Association.

Wood, B. and Talmon, M. (1983) 'Family boundaries in transition: A search for alternatives', *Family Process* 22: 347–57.

# Author index

Achenbach, T.M.  14, 242
Ackerman, N.  4, 235
Ainsworth, M.D.S.  72, 73
Aldenderfer, M.S.  168
Alexander, J.F.  3
Allesch, C.G.  138
American Psychiatric Association  211, 242
Anastasi, A.  51
Anderson, H.  212
Anderson, S.A.  xv, xvi, 5
Apter, T.  171
Arend, R.A.  73, 75
Arrow, H.  251
Aseltine, R.H., Jr  159
Ash, P.  236
Ashkenazy, D.  175
Asquith, P.  171
Ayetani, N.  179

Bagarozzi, D.A.  xv, xvi, 46
Baker, M.R.  251
Baldwin, L.M.  66
Baldwin, M.  136
Baltes-Götz, B.  250
Barber, J.W.  251, 260
Barnes, H.  20
Barnes, H.L.  14
Baron-Cohen, S.  120
Bartsch, K.  71
Bates, J.E.  107–8
Bauer, J.  14
Baumrind, D.  157, 174
Beach, S.R.H.  45
Beattie, K.  88
Beaujean, J.  43
Beavers, R.W.  4, 6, 28, 35, 65, 234, 267
Beck, A.T.  14
Beelmann, W.  134

Bell, C.H.  251
Belsky, J.  73, 149, 153, 154
Benoit, D.  73
Benoit, J.C.  43
Berdahl, J.L.  251
Berdondini, L.  107, 109, 114, 158, 270, 273
Berger, M.  47
Berlin, L.J.  75
Bernauer, F.  236
Berti, C.  108
Berts, M.  107
Beutler, L.E.  233, 245
Binney, V.  71, 75, 76, 88, 109, 110, 114, 158
Bishop, D.  28, 35
Bishop, D.S.  66
Bjorkqvist, K.  107
Blakeslee, S.  134, 135
Blashfield, R.K.  168
Blehar, M.C.  72
Bliks, D.  135
Bloom, B.L.  46
Boivin, M.  159
Bongar, B.  245
Bonnar, D.  234
Boothe, B.  19, 261
Boszormenyi-Nagy, I.  42, 157
Boughner, S.R.  46, 267
Boulton, M.J.  107
Bowen, M.  4, 35
Bowers, L.  71, 75, 76, 88, 109, 110, 114, 158
Bowlby, J.  72
Bradbury, T.N.  68
Brägger, F.  249, 253
Brandtstädter, J.  250, 255
Brem-Gräser, L.  138
Bretherton, I.  71

Breunlin, D.  277
Brewer, M.B.  252
Brighi, A.  108
Brody, L.R.  173
Bronfenbrenner, U.  157
Brown, M.T.  260
Brownell, H.  119, 130
Bryant, C.  120
Bubenzer, D.L.  46, 267
Buchholz, M.B.  135, 136, 137
Buhrmester, D.  162
Burchinal, M.  71
Burns, R.C.  92
Burr, W.R.  35
Buzas, H.  46

Cairns, B.D.  107
Cairns, R.B.  107
Callan, V.J.  157
Cambier, A.  93
Campbell, D.T.  61
Candrian, M.  13, 14, 48, 50, 197, 236, 249
Carlson, C.I.  46
Carlson, E.A.  87
Cassidy, J.  73, 75
Catherall, D.R.  216
Cavell, T.A.  48, 267, 268
Cerreto, M.C.  62
Chaney, J.M.  250
Chapin, F.S.  5
Chen, G.  195
Chen, X.  196
Chiu, L.  196
Cicchetti, D.  17, 90
Ciucci, E.  108
Clarkin, J.F.  233
Cohen, J.  47
Cohn, D.A.  73
Coie, J.D.  107, 108
Colapinto, J.  216
Colas, Y.  43
Coleman, L.  216
Conger, R.D.  158
Consoli, A.J.  233
Copeland, A.P.  173
Coppotelli, H.  107
Corman, L.  92
Costabile, A.  107
Cota, A.A.  248, 260
Cowan, C.P.  73, 234
Cowan, P.A.  73, 234
Cowie, H.  71, 107, 270, 273
Cox, M.V.  71
Craig, W.M.  107

Craight, L.  234
Crittenden, P.M.  72, 74, 76, 77
Crnic, K.  73
Cronbach, L.J.  47, 161
Cross, P.  120
Crowell, J.A.  73, 74, 75
Curtis, J.T.  237
Cusinato, M.  54

D'Andrade, R.G.  134
Davanzo, J.  159
Day, R.D.  35
Debry, M.  28, 29, 36, 92, 94, 103, 267, 268, 269, 270, 273, 274, 275
Dell, P.F.  46, 52
Denton, W.H.  276
Dickson, M.W.  251
DiClemente, C.C.  235
Diener, E.  251
Dion, K.L.  248, 260
Dobbins, G.H.  248
Dodge, K.A.  107, 107–8, 108
Donaldson, G.  159, 172
Donati, R.  236
Dong, Q.  196
Dornbusch, S.M.  157, 174
Draper, P.  149, 153, 154
Duhl, B.  5
Duhl, F.  5
Dukes, J.  6, 16
Dunn, J.  71, 73
Duveen, G.  262

Edelbrock, C.  14
Eichberg, C.  73
Eisenberg, A.R.  203
Ekman, K.  107
Eldan, Z.  4
Elliot, G.  176
Elmen, J.  157
Emery, R.E.  234
Epstein, N.B.  28, 35, 63, 66, 267
Epston, D.  212
Erbaugh, J.  14
Esterling, B.A.  53
Euler, H.A.  203
Evans, C.R.  248, 260

Fagot, B.I.  72
Falbo, T.  195, 196, 197
Farmer, S.M.  248
Fassel, D.  134, 135, 136
Fedor, D.B.  248
Feldman, G.  13

Feldman, S.S. 5, 14, 32, 50, 73, 74, 75, 110, 118, 149, 154, 158, 171, 176, 181, 189, 197, 205, 215, 234, 274
Ferreira, A. xvi
Ferring, D. 17
Filipp, S.H. 17
Fincham, F.D. 45, 62, 68
Fine, M. 247
Finnegan, R.A. 108, 109
Fisher, L. 47
Fishman, H.C. 5
Fiske, D.W. 61
Fleming, B. 63
Flowers, B.J. 212
Fodor, E.M. 252
Folkman, S. 162
Fonagy, P. 73
Fontaine, P. 34, 269
Fonzi, A. 107, 108
Forte, J.A. 5
Foster, M. 47
Fraleigh, M.J. 157, 174
Freeman, N.H. 71
Fremmer-Bombik, E. 73
French, D. 120
French, W.L. 251
Friedman, A.S. 5
Fthenakis, W.E. 133, 134, 135
Fu, V.R. 196
Fukushima, M. 120
Furman, W. 162
Fury, G. 87

Gal, R. 160
Gariepy, J. 107
Gavazzi, S.M. 5
Gehring, T.M. 3, 5, 6, 12, 13, 14, 29, 32, 36, 45, 48, 50, 66, 76, 92, 94, 110, 111, 118, 120, 136, 138, 144, 149, 150, 153, 154, 158, 160, 171, 173, 180, 181, 185, 189, 190, 197, 199, 200, 205, 206, 211, 212, 215, 231, 233, 234, 235, 236, 238, 248, 249, 253, 267, 268, 269, 270, 272, 273, 274, 276, 277
Genta, M.L. 107, 270, 273
George, C. 73, 75
Georgi, H. 136
Gergen, K.J. 53
Gest, S.D. 107
Giacomo, D.A. 212
Gibson, E. 46
Gilbert, K.R. 35
Gill, H.S. 133
Goldscheider, F.K. 159

Gollwitzer, P.M. 253
Goodman, J.S. 248
Goolishian, H. 212
Gore, S. 159
Gotlib, I.H. 235, 236
Gottman, J.M 60, 63–4
Grawe, K. 236
Gray Deering, C. 236
Green, R.J. 5, 217
Greenberg, M.T. 72, 90
Grossmann, K. 73
Grossmann, K.E. 73, 74
Grotevant, H.D. 46
Guex, P. 14
Gurman, A.S. 4, 233, 236
Guyer, M. 173
Guzzo, R.A. 251

Haas, S.D. 64
Hadwin, J. 120
Hai, I. 160, 171
Haley, J. 5, 30, 234
Happé, F.G.E. 119, 120, 130
Harbin, H. 6, 16
Harold, G.T. 158
Harré, R. 251
Harris, E. 233
Harris, P.L. 71
Harris, R.N. 5
Hasegawa, H. 180
Hasumi, S. 179
Hatta, T. 179, 180, 181, 189, 190, 197, 204, 205, 206, 270, 274, 275
Hausser, K. 250
Havas, E. 234
Hayes, S.C. 48
Hayes, S.F. 46, 267
Heffer, R.W. 48, 267, 268
Heil, F.E. 250, 255
Helminger, A. 19, 261
Henggeler, S.W. 234
Herget, M. 217
Hetherington, E.M. 134
Heyman, R.E. 65
Higgitt, A. 73
Hirsig, R. 19, 261
Ho, D.Y.F. 196, 203
Hodges, E.V.E. 108, 109
Hoffman, E. 203
Hoffman, L. 136, 212
Holahan, C.J. 159
Holloway, E. 247
Holman, A. 46
Hops, H. 63

Horvath, A.O.  217
Hulse, W.C.  92
Hunter, R.  133, 146, 269, 270, 273, 275

Ikeda, K.  179, 270, 274, 275

Jacob, T.  46
Jameson, P.B.  3
Jankowiak, W.  196
Japan Statistics Bureau  179, 180
Jarrett, R.B.  48
Jenkins, H.  17
Jolliffe, T.  120
Jones, R.  120

Kahn, J.S.  272
Kalman, Z.  161
Kannas, S.  43
Kantor, D.  5, 35
Kaplan, N.  73, 87
Karpel, M.A.  46
Karpovsky, S.  161
Kashiwagi, K.  191
Kaslow, F.W.  4, 59, 278
Kaslow, N.J.  236
Katriel, T.  171
Kaufman, S.H.  92
Kaukiainen, A.  107
Keitner, D.  28, 35
Keller, J.R.  250
Kemp-Fincham, S.I.  45
Kendall, P.C.  235, 236
Kenny, M.E.  159, 172
Kilik, L.  248, 260
Kim, K.  149, 150, 154, 270, 273
King, E.  107
Kirsh, S.J.  73
Ko, J.W.  251
Kochalka, J.  46
Kokes, R.F.  47
Kolevzon, M.S.  5
Krampen, G.  250, 255
Kranichfeld, M.L.  4
Krokoff, L.J.  64
Kudisch, J.D.  248
Kunze, H.-R.  133, 134, 135
Kurdek, L.A.  135
Kusel, S.J.  107, 108

L'Abate, L.  3, 20, 45, 46, 48, 52, 53, 54,
    233, 267, 268
Lagerspetz, K.M.J.  107
Laird, J.  213
Lamb, R.  251

Landau-Hurtig, A.  17
Landesman Ramey, S.  71
Landrum-Brown, J.  260
Langeveld, M.J.  138
Larose, S.  159
Larsen, A.  20
Laursen, B.  161
Lavee, Y.  13, 248, 249
Lazarus, R.S.  162
Lebow, J.L.  4, 53, 58, 233, 236, 267, 276
Lee, C.M.  235, 236
Lehr, W.  35
Leiderman, P.H.  157, 174
Leigh, G.K.  190
Levenson, R.W.  64
Levine, L.V.  73
Lewis, C.  88
Leyvraz, S.  14
Lichtenberg, J.D.  136
Liddle, H.A.  233
Lieberman, A.L.  73
Lieblich, A.  159, 160
Lin, C.C.  196
Linfield, K.J.  62
Lloyd, B.  262
Locke, H.  14, 62
Longman, R.S.  248, 260
Lucas, R.E.  251
Luechinger, D.  185
Luster, T.  234, 235, 245

Mackune-Karrer, B.  277
Madanes, C.  6, 16
Main, M.  73, 87
Maino, E.  54
Malarewicz, J.A.  43
Mangrum, L.F.  48, 267, 268
Marris, P.  88, 90
Marti, D.  3, 6, 14, 36, 48, 50, 118, 158,
    160, 173, 181, 185, 197, 199, 200, 215,
    233, 235, 236, 249, 267, 268, 269, 270,
    272, 273, 274, 276, 277
Marvin, R.S.  73
Maslyn, J.M.  248
Massing, A.  136
Matas, L.  73, 75
Mayring, Ph.  138
Mayseless, O.  157, 159, 160, 171, 270,
    273, 274, 275
McCubbin, H.I.  20, 28, 35
McGrath, J.E.  251
McHenry, S.  46
Medlock, A.  53
Meehl, P.E.  47

Meier, B. 19, 261
Meier, S.T. 272
Meins, E. 75
Melchert, T.P. 52
Mendelson, M. 14
Menesini, E. 107
Meyer, F. 92, 103, 269
Milewski-Hertlein, K.A. 277
Miller, I. 28, 35
Miller, J.K. 53
Minuchin, P. 4, 5, 157
Minuchin, S. 4, 5, 28, 29, 30, 35, 136, 157, 234, 277
Mitchell, P. 88, 119
Mock, J. 14
Moore, D. 159
Moos, B.S. 13, 45, 50, 53, 66, 267
Moos, R.H. 13, 45, 50, 53, 66, 157, 159
Morley-Williams, L. 71, 270, 273
Morrissey, M.R. 5
Mortimore, C. 120
Morval, M. 95
Moscovici, S. 261
Mounts, N. 157
Mullins, L.L. 250
Munn, P. 73
Munson, J.A. 32, 149, 153, 189, 197, 234
Murray, E. 53
Murray Parkes, C. 88, 90
Muxen, M. 20
Myron-Wilson, R. 108, 118, 269, 270, 273, 274

Nathans, S. 237
Neckerman, H.J. 107
Nelson, R.O. 48
Nichols, M. 212
Niesel, R. 133, 134
Nightingale, A. 251
Noller, P. 157
Norcross, J.C. 235
Nutbeam, D. 233

Oark, K. 73
Odell, M. 53
Oerter, R. 250
Okagaki, L. 234, 235, 245
Oliveri, M.E. 5
Olson, D.H. 4, 13, 14, 20, 28, 35, 45, 66, 157, 248, 249, 267
Olweus, D. 107
O'Riordan, M. 120
Osborne, A. 88
Osterman, K. 107

O'Sullivan, S. 47

Page, J. 12, 233, 270, 273, 277
Paneff, J. 253
Panichelli, S.S. 235, 236
Pape Cowan, C. 73
Parish, Th. S. 135
Park, K.A. 73
Parke, K.D. 73
Parker, K.C.H. 73
Patterson, G.R. 63
Pears, K.L. 72
Pearson, J.L. 73
Pennebaker, J. 53
Pepler, D. 107, 116
Perlmutter, B.F. 46, 92
Perner, J. 120
Perris, C. 235
Perry, D.G. 107, 108, 109
Perry, L.C. 107, 108
Pervin, L.A. 261
Pettigrew, T.F. 252
Pettit, G.S. 107–8
Pham Hoang Quoc Vu 93
Phillips, N. 248
Phillips, S.L. 47
Pierce, S. 108
Pinsof, W. 212, 216
Pinsof, W.M 233, 267, 268
Plaisted, K. 120
Porot, M. 92
Portner, J. 13
Poston, D.L., Jr 196
Poteet, M.L. 248
Preli, R. 5, 16
Premack, D. 119
Prentiss, C. 71
Pretzer, J. 63
Price, S.J. 3
Prochaska, J.O. 235
Protinsky, H. 5, 16
Pulkkinen, L.R.H. 107

Rabinowitz, A. 4
Real del Sartre, O. 13, 14, 48, 50, 197, 236, 249
Reich, G. 136
Reid, M. 71
Reis, H.T. 162
Reiss, D. 5, 17, 72, 73, 114
Revers, W.J. 138
Reznikoff, H.R. 92
Reznikoff, M. 92
Rhode-Dachser, Ch. 137

Rice, J.L.  47
Richardson, D.R.  173
Ridgeway, D.  71
Rigazio-DiGilio, S.A.  6, 49, 51, 211, 269, 270, 277
Rigby, K.  107, 108
Riordan, J.M.  252
Ritter, L.P.  157, 174
Riviere, A.  120
Roberts, D.F.  157, 174
Robertson, M.  120
Robinson, M.  5
Royer, J.  94
Rubin, K.H.  116, 196
Rudd, P.  47
Rudolf, J.  73
Rush, M.C.  248
Russell, C.S.  6, 45, 66
Russell, J.E.A.  248
Ryan, C.  28, 35

Salmivalli, C.  107
Satir, V.  5, 136
Scarlett, G.  71
Schaefer, C.E.  71
Scharf, M.  157, 270, 273, 274, 275
Schaufeli, W.B.  251
Schiffmann, R.  252
Schindler Zimmerman, T.  3
Schmidt-Denter, U.  134
Schneider-Rosen, K.  72
Schultheiss, R.B.  6, 235
Schwartz, D.  107–8, 108
Schwartz, R.  212, 277
Schwarz, J.C.  159
Scolton, K.L.  73
Scott, D.  251
Selvini-Palazzoli, M.  5
Settles, B.H.  35
Seywert, F.  268
Shields, C.G.  233, 267, 268
Shouldice, A.  72, 82, 87
Shu, S.  118, 194, 204, 270, 272, 274
Shulman, S.  161
Sidler, A.  36, 50, 118, 158, 160, 173, 235
Siegal, M.  88
Siesky, A.E.  135
Silberschatz, G.  237
Simon, R.M.  5
Sjolund, M.  71
Slade, A.  73
Slee, P.T.  107
Slough, N.M.  72
Smetana, J.G.  171

Smith, D.  107
Smith, H.L.  251
Smith, P.K.  71, 75, 76, 88, 107, 108, 109, 110, 114, 118, 120, 129, 150, 154, 158, 194, 203, 267, 269, 270, 272, 273, 274
Smollar, J.  171, 173
Snyder, D.K.  45, 47, 48, 53, 62, 267, 268
Solomon, J.  75
Sotillo, M.  120
Spangler, G.  74
Spanier, G.B.  62
Spark, G.  42, 157
Sperling, E.  136
Spielberger, C.  14
Spradlin, W.W.  251, 260
Sprenkle, D.H.  45, 57, 66
Spritz, B.  73
Sroufe, A.L.  87
Sroufe, L.A.  73, 75
Steele, H.  73
Steele, M.  73
Steinberg, L.  149, 153, 154, 157, 173
Steinebach, C.  237, 247, 249, 250, 253, 270
Stephenson, P.  107
Stern, D.N.  136
Stevenson-Hinde, J.  72, 82, 87, 90
Stevenson-Hinde, P.  88, 90
Stewart, R.B.  73
Stiefel, F.  14
Stierlin, H.  4, 35
Stone, V.  120
Strage, A.A.  159
Straus, M.A.  46, 92
Strauss, E.S.  46
Strauss, M.A.  63
Suh, E.M.  251
Summers, K.J.  65
Sutton, J.  107, 118, 120, 129, 269, 270, 273, 274
Sutton, L.S.  173
Swettenham, J.  120, 129
Symonds, B.D.  217

Tajfel, H.  252
Talmon, M.  5, 158, 278
Target, M.  73
Tennenbaum, D.L.  46
Tomm, K.  49
Torem, M.S.  53
Touliatos, J.  46, 92
Tremblay, R.E.  107
Triandis, H.C.  261
Tsukiji, N.  179, 181, 190, 197, 204, 206

Tuber, S.B. 73
Tuer, M. 234
Turner, J. 247

Urbina, S. 51
Utada, A. 5

Valentier, D.P. 159
Valsiner, J. 260
van Horn, J.E. 251
Veit, C.T. 162
Vinokur-Kaplan, D. 250
Voeller, M.N. 5
Volkart, R. 19, 261
von Ballmoos, I. 133, 269, 270, 273, 275
Vosler, N.R. 5

Wagner, V. 54
Wakamatsu, M. 191
Wall, S. 72
Wallace, K.M. 14, 62
Wallerstein, J. 134, 135
Ward, C.H. 14
Ward, J. 73
Ware, J.E. 162
Waters, E. 72, 73
Watkins, E. 251
Weinberger, D.A. 161, 234
Weiss, B. 236
Weiss, L.H. 159
Weiss, R.L. 62, 63, 65
Weissmark, M.S. 212
Weisz, J.R. 236
Weitzel, B. 203
Wellman, H. 71

Wentzel, K.R. 13, 32, 118, 149, 153, 158, 171, 189, 197, 234
Werner-Wilson, R.J. 3
West, J.D. 46, 267
White, M. 212, 214
Wicklund, R.A. 253
Wigle, St. E. 135
Wilkinson, I. 3
Williams, R.E. 233
Willke, H. 250
Wilson, M. 20
Wimmer, H. 120
Winner, E. 91, 119, 130
Wittenberg, M.T. 162
Wöbbe-Mönks, E. 136
Wolf, D. 71
Wongyannava, T. 149, 270, 273
Wood, B. 4, 5, 158, 278
Woodruff, G. 119
World Health Organisation 15, 211, 242
Wössmer Buntschu, B. 249, 253
Wright, P.J. 234
Wu, D.Y.H. 205
Wyler, I.L. 49, 76, 110, 120, 150, 180, 181, 190
Wynne, L.C. 46, 52, 233, 267, 268

Yamauchi, M. 179
Yank, G.R. 251, 260
Yoon, J. 251
Youngblade, L.M. 73
Youniss, J. 171, 173

Zhao, J. 195
Zhou, H. 196

# Subject index

abbreviations 26–7
adaptations of FAST 269–72
   representation of family 118, 121,
     129–30
   strangers 109, 114, 115
   triad/family of origin 136–46
adolescence
   adjustment 157, 159, 160–8, 172–4
   dynamic perspective 39–41
   early 30, 31, 33
   family violence 155
   late 157–74
   puberty (menarche) 149–55
   stressful situations 157–74
Adolescent Interpersonal Competence
   questionnaire 162
adoptive families 54
Adult Attachment Interview (AAI) 73
aggression
   adolescent adjustment 164, 165,
     166
   attachment relationships 79
   bullying 107, 109
   marital 63
   towards adolescents 155
alcohol abuse 16
amalgamations 94, 101, 270
anorexia 15
anxiety 72, 150, 151, 152
Areas of Change Questionnaire 63
Asian cultures
   Chinese families 194–206
   family violence 155
   Japanese family structure 179–91
assessment
   *see also* interactive assessment
   family evaluation 45, 46, 47, 48, 51,
     52, 216
   initial 215–16

relational diagnosis 58, 60–7
   techniques xix, xx, 28, 92, 267
attachment
   *see also* cohesion
   leaving home 159
   measures 72–3
   strategies 72, 73–9, 86–8

balanced attachment relationship 72, 74,
    75, 77–8, 79–80, 82, 84, 85
Beavers Scales 65
behaviour
   checklist 242, 243
   disorders 15, 253
   introverted 134
   observation 214, 215, 218
behavioural-cognitive techniques 236,
    237, 241
Belgian study 30–3, 271
bias xvi, 51, 59, 60, 118, 205
bullies 71, 107, 109, 110, 112, 113, 114
bullying 107–15

cancer 15, 16–17, 50
case studies
   boundary restructuring 33–4
   cross-generational conflict 39–41
   family psychotherapy 215–30
Child Behaviour Checklist (CBCL) 242,
    243
childrearing, China 196, 197, 204
children
   assessment techniques xx, 6, 51
   development 145, 149, 150, 154,
     173–4, 234–9
   divorce impact 134–5
   egocentrism xvi
   family evaluation 50
   father relationship 136–7, 191, 204

first graders 92–104
gender preferences 195
grandparents relationship 203–4
mother relationship 190–1, 201, 203,
   204
one-child policy 194, 195–6, 197
parental interventions 233–44
as part of triad 136–7
preschool 71–88, 253, 274
understanding other's views 107,
   119–21, 125, 128–9
China 118, 195–206, 271, 274, 275
Circumplex Measures 66
client
   clinician relationship 254, 257, 270
   engagement 212, 233
clinical discriminant validity 14–16
clinical interventions
   conceptualization and evaluation 7
   family evaluation 47–8, 50, 52–4
   interactive assessment and treatment
      211–31
   parental role 233, 236
   planning and evaluation 214–16,
      237–41
clinicians, personal development 247–61,
   270
cluster analyses 168–71, 172, 173
coercive attachment relationship 73, 74,
   75, 78–9, 82, 83, 85, 86, 87
Cognitive Appraisal questionnaire 162
cohesion
   adolescents 155, 157
   bullying study 112, 113, 114
   definition xix, 4, 272
   evaluation 8, 49
   family structure 12, 17, 205, 236,
      275–6
   FDT/FAST comparison 94, 97–8,
      100, 101, 105
   hierarchy relationship 35
   interactive assessment 219, 225, 227,
      229
   Japanese families 182, 184, 185,
      187–8, 189
   mother-daughter relations 149–55
   portrayal 7–8
   respondent's perceptions xv
   scoring 6, 11
   stressful situations 157–74
   supervisory process 248, 249, 251–2,
      253–60
   three-generational families 194, 197,
      199, 200, 202, 203, 205

triad 144
college
   Japanese students 181–91
   leaving home 159
Columbus pictures 138
computer-assisted interventions 53
conflict
   adolescents 164, 165, 166, 171, 172
   mother-daughter 149–54
   within family 15, 17, 41, 227–8, 234
   within team 251–3, 260
Conflict Tactics Scale 63
consensus sensitive family 115
coping
   adolescents and stress 157–74
   loss of father 146
   questionnaire 162
counselling, professional 247, 260
couples
   cohesion 201, 203
   new partners 143, 144
   relational measures 62–5
coyness 74, 78, 79
cross-cultural comparison
   attachment relationships 76
   family structure xxi, 6, 180, 185–91,
      197, 204–5
   family violence 155
   FAST as tool 215, 231
cross-cultural psychology 261, 270
cross-generational boundaries
   development 29, 42
   early adolescents 31, 32
   relational structures 38–9, 42
   stress 5
   troubled families 16
cross-generational coalition
   cohesion 8, 11
   FDT/FAST comparison 94, 101, 106
   structural perspective 30, 31, 33, 34
   three-generational families 194, 197,
      199, 201, 203, 206
culture
   *see also* cross-cultural
   Asian 191, 206
   bias 28
   FAST advantages 48, 51, 272, 274
   relational structure 174, 179, 275
   team development 260–1

daughter
   father image 133–46
   father relationship 39–41
   pubertal development 149–54

death of father  133, 134, 138, 140, 141,
   143, 145
defended attachment relationship  72,
   73–4, 74–5, 79, 81–4, 86, 87
depression  54, 150–4, 216, 226
developmental changes  35, 42, 71, 214
developmental psychology  8, 133–4, 236,
   250, 251, 270
diagnosis
   interactive assessment  211, 230
   relational  58–67, 211, 276
disengagement
   attachment relationships  71, 74, 86
   concept  29, 35
   family relationships  36, 60
distance
   *see also* cohesion
   Chinese values  205
   dyadic  6, 171–2, 181, 184, 190, 204
   emotional  150–3, 161, 164–6, 205
   FAST representations  124, 141, 164
   treatment  53
divorce
   child development  234
   daughter impact  133, 134–5, 137,
      138–46
   family structure  275
Doll Location Test (DLT)  180–1, 204
Draw a Person Test  94
drug addict  109, 114, 269
DSM IV  58, 59, 211, 230
dyad, family unit  137, 157–8, 160, 171–2
Dyadic Adjustment Scale  62
dyadic distances  6, 171–2, 181, 184, 190,
   204
dynamic perspective  29, 34–41, 214

education
   Chinese children  195–6
   parents  194, 196, 198–9, 202, 204
emotional bonds *see* cohesion
emotional distance  150–3, 161, 164–6,
   205
emotions, regulation  161, 205
enmeshment
   attachment relationships  71, 75, 153–4
   cohesion  155
   concept  29, 35
   family relationships  34, 36
environment sensitive family  115
evaluation
   family  6, 45–55, 267–9
   family functioning  3, 28, 45, 49, 50, 65
   family structure  xix, 180–1

FAST concept  12
   hierarchy  6, 8–9, 11, 49, 50
   parental interventions  237–41, 243
   qualitative  9, 141, 217
   quantitative  8–9, 217
   test procedures  3, 92
   treatment goals  212
evolutionary perspective  149, 204
extended families  51, 100, 106, 216,
   218, 230
external boundaries  4, 107, 112, 114,
   115

FACES III  13, 45, 66
FACES IV  66
false belief  88, 119–20
family
   diversity  277
   empowerment  214, 231
   evaluation  6, 45–55, 65, 92, 267–9
   healthy  49
   interventions  55, 233–44
   map  30, 41
   myth  xvi
   overprotective  114
   perception of  118
   planning  195
   psychology  8, 268, 270
   psychotherapy study  211–31
   relational measures  65–7
   stress  4–5, 33, 35, 154, 157–74, 257
   theory  8, 45–7, 234, 268
family boundaries
   definition  xix, 4
   external  4, 107, 112, 114, 115
   FDT/FAST comparison  94, 99, 101,
      106
   internal  4, 107, 114, 137
   structural perspective  29–34, 41
family constructs
   Belgian preadolescents  30
   first graders  92–104
   mother  237
   parental interventions  238, 242
family development
   family evaluation  51, 235, 240
   FAST benefit  18, 272
   systemic approach  6, 15, 42, 211
family drawings
   attachment relationships  71, 75,
      79–82, 83, 87
   FDT/FAST comparison  93, 99–104
   imaginary  93–7
   test (FDT)  92–104

Family Environment Scale (FES) 13, 45,
    50, 53, 66
family functioning
    adolescent adjustment 159
    bullying 108
    child development 235
    conceptualizations 34
    evaluation 3, 28, 45, 49, 50, 65
    interactive assessment 226
    social cognition 119
    stress 5
    systemic theory 42
family interaction 51, 75, 221
family interactive task 49, 65–6, 93–4, 97,
    100, 102–3
family of origin 136, 141, 144, 145, 146,
    269, 270
family relations
    *see also* family drawings
    child's viewpoint xvi, 73, 87–8
    mother-daughter 149–55
    spatial representations 5–6, 97, 101–2,
        112–13, 124
    stressful situations 157–74
family structure
    *see also* representation
    bullying 108, 109, 114–15
    description 3–4
    divorce 141–3, 145
    evaluation xix, 180–1
    flexibility 94, 99, 106
    Japan xxi, 179–91, 204
    one-child policy 195–6, 274
    parent-sibling subsystems 187–8
    parental interventions 234–5, 236–7
    restructuring 226–8
    stress 4–5, 158, 160, 168–71
    three-generational families 194, 200,
        202–3, 205
    triangulated 169, 170, 173
    troubled families 14–15, 16
family systems
    adolescent adjustment 157–8, 172
    analysis 3
    assessment methods 61
    evaluation xix, 49
    extended 51, 100, 106, 216, 218, 230
    individual development 249
    representation 34, 51, 71–2, 87–8, 273
family therapy
    collaborative system 212
    family evaluation 52, 92
    family of origin 136
    parental interventions 233–44

participative-discursive approach 238,
    239, 242, 243, 244, 277
relational viewpoint 58
research 267, 270
FAST
    adaptations 269–72
    adolescent adjustment 158, 161, 167
    application 8, 16, 17–18, 88
    bullying study 109, 110–13
    clinical discriminant validity 14–16
    concept xx–xxi, 3–7, 8
    development 269–72
    family evaluation 48–51, 268–9
    as family interactive task 93–4, 97,
        100, 102–3
    FDT comparison 93, 99–104
    future uses 276–8
    interactive assessment and treatment
        211–31
    interpretation 11–12, 215, 217, 224,
        230
    limitations 87–8, 272
    mother-daughter relations 149
    parental interventions 238–9, 242–3,
        244
    participant differences 273–4
    procedure 7–12
    protocol 7, 10
    psychometric properties 12–14, 16,
        28, 35, 211
    scoring 11, 94, 112, 215, 270
    social cognition/theory of mind
        118–31
    supervision tool 248, 257–60
    therapy closure 228–30
    three-generational families 194,
        197–200, 205–6
father
    adolescent relationship 158, 160
    child relationship 136–7, 191, 204
    China 196, 204
    daughter relationship 39–41, 133–4
    family representations 50, 109, 136,
        225, 227
    image 133–4, 138–46
    as part of triad 136–7
    son relationship 33–4, 157,
        162–74
FES (Family Environment Scale) 13, 45,
    50, 53, 66
figure placement techniques
    concept xvi, xx, 3, 6
    preschool children 71
    SFPT 180, 181, 191, 204–5

flexibility, family structures 94, 99, 106, 224
follow-up interview
    content 9, 12, 26
    interactive treatment 218, 220–1, 221–3
    parental interventions 241, 242–3, 244
foster families 54, 143
Freudian model 29
Friend's Evaluation questionnaire 162, 167

GAF scale 242, 243
gender, Chinese families 195, 203–4
generational boundaries
    *see also* cross-generational boundaries
    adolescents 157
    China 197, 201, 206
    cohesion and hierarchy 4, 8, 14
    depiction 13–14, 273
    divorce 144, 234
    dysfunctional child 243
    FDT/FAST comparison 94, 101, 106
    ideal representations 17
    Japan 181, 184, 190–1
    relational structures 275
    troubled families 16
Germany 253, 255, 271
Global Assessment of Relationship
    Functioning (GARF) 65
grandparents 118, 141, 143, 190, 194–206

health-related outcomes 14–16, 17, 221, 226, 230, 234
hierarchy
    adolescents 173
    Chinese families 194, 195, 197, 200, 201, 202, 203
    client system 254, 257–60
    cohesion relationship 35
    definition xix, 4, 272
    divorce 141, 144
    evaluation 6, 8–9, 11, 49, 50
    family structure 12, 236, 275–6
    FDT/FAST comparison 94, 98, 100–1, 105
    individual development 249
    interactive assessment 219, 225, 227, 229
    Japanese families 180, 185, 187–8, 189–90
    portrayal 7–8
    respondent's perceptions xv
    structural perspective 31

three-generational families 194, 197, 200, 201, 202, 203, 206
hierarchy reversal
    China 200, 201
    FAST concept 9
    FDT/FAST comparison 94, 101, 106
    Japanese families 190
    structural perspective 5, 16, 29, 31, 32
    widows 141
human sculptures 5, 136

ICD-9 58
ICD-10 15, 17, 211, 242, 243
identification 134
identity 39, 160, 171, 226, 250–1, 252–3
imaginary family drawings 93–7, 99, 103
individual assessment 49, 58–9
individual development 249, 252
interactive assessment
    attachment relationships 76, 78, 87
    client engagement 212
    family constructs 93–4, 97, 100, 102–3
    figure placement techniques xx, 6, 17
    future prospects 277
    multiple perspectives 212, 213
    relational measures 58–67
    SPRINT 9
    and treatment 211–31
interdisciplinary teams 255–7
internal boundaries 4, 107, 114
internal working model 72, 73
internalization 133, 154
interpersonal distance sensitive family 115
intimacy 4, 34, 53, 74, 161
introjection 134
Israel 158–74, 271, 275
Italy 109, 110–13, 271

Japan
    cultural differences 274, 275
    family structure xxi, 179–91, 204, 271
    mother-child relationship 155

laboratory measures 60, 61
language 51, 211, 212, 213, 217
leadership 248, 251–2, 260
leaving home 158–74
lifecycle 35, 42, 54, 130–1
Locke-Wallace Adjustment Test 14, 62

Marital Attitude Scale 63
marital functioning, questionnaires 62–4
Marital Interaction Coding System 65

marital problems 33, 53, 59, 159, 234
    *see also* couples
Marital Satisfaction Inventory 53, 62
McMaster Measures 66
Me and My Best Friend questionnaire 161
menarche (puberty) 149–55
Mental Health Inventory 162
military service 158–74
Minnesota Multiphasic Personality
    Inventory-R 58
Mongolia 196
monodisciplinary teams 255–7
mother
    child relationship 190–1, 201, 203, 204
    China 194
    daughter relationship 149–55
    family constructs 237, 253–5
    father image 133, 134, 136, 138–46
    as part of triad 136–7
    sexual history 149
    son relationship 158, 162–74
    theory of mind 121–6, 128–9

naturalistic measures 61, 76
neonatological research 136
non-verbal techniques 51, 54
nuclear family
    interactive assessment 218
    Japan 179, 180, 182, 185

observational data 49, 214
occupation, parents 194, 196, 198–9, 202,
    204
organizational psychology 251–3, 260
orphans 134
outpatient studies 50

Parent-Adolescent Communication
    Questionnaire 14
parent-adolescent relationships
    puberty 149
    stressful situations 157–74
parental interventions 233–44
parenting
    bullying 108, 109
    child development impact 234–5
    China 196, 205
parents
    boundary restructuring 33–4
    education/occupation 194, 196, 198–9,
        202
    relational structure 275
    relationship relevance 234
    respect for 195, 206, 274

partners, new 143, 144
peer relationships
    attachment 71, 73, 77–9, 87
    bullying 107, 108, 109
perception 9, 118–31
personal development 247, 256, 257, 260
personal resources 249, 252, 255–7, 260
perverse triangle 30
pharmacotherapy 244
Positive and Negative Quality in Marriage
    Scale 62–3
power
    and leadership 248
    therapeutic systems 253–7, 257–60
power in families
    bullying 71, 113
    China 195, 196–7, 198, 199, 201, 202,
        203, 206
    family relationships 75, 82, 124
    gender effect 203
    mother-daughter relations 149–55
    stress 5, 157–74
preadolescents
    bullying 108
    relational structures 35–9, 118
Preschool Assessment of Attachment
    (PAA) 72, 73, 76, 86, 88
preschool children 71–88, 253, 274
preventive interventions 54
privacy 4
problem definitions 223
problem-solving process 74, 165, 233,
    238–41
professional identity 250–1, 252
programmed writing 53
projective techniques
    attachment 72
    family functioning 28
    family structure 180
    representation of family 88, 93, 102,
        138, 145
psychiatric treatment
    family evaluation 50
    parental interventions 233, 235–6
psychometric properties 12–14, 16, 28,
    35, 47, 211, 213–14
psychosocial wellbeing 7, 14, 235
psychotherapy 145
puberty 149–55, 275

questionnaires xx, 28, 62–4, 161–2, 238

relational diagnosis 58–67, 211, 276
relational measures 59–67

relational structures
    attachment theory  72, 73
    clinical status comparison  15
    cohesion and hierarchy  36–41
    divorce  141–3
    FAST  36–41, 275–6
    FDT/FAST comparison  94, 98–9,
      106
    interactive assessment  219, 225, 227,
      229
    intergenerational  194, 202
    stress  4
relational therapy  212
relational viewpoint  58–9
representations
    *see also* family drawings
    by preschool children  71–88
    dysfunctional child development
      236–7
    family of origin  136
    FAST  9, 13, 30, 41, 269
    internal  133, 134
    theory of mind  119, 121–31
    triad  136–7, 145
    variability  118–19, 272–4
Rorschach test  180

school
    bullying  107
    leaving  159
school psychology  270
self-esteem, adolescents  157, 161, 164,
    165, 166, 172
Self-Other Profile Test (SOPT)  54
self-report measures
    instruments  62–3, 65–6, 161–2
    reliability  47, 60, 267
    therapists  239, 241
semiorphans  134, 140, 141, 143, 145
Sentence Completion Test (SCT)  180
Separation Anxiety Test (SAT)  72
sexual history  149–54
shyness  134
sibling
    relationships representation  100, 103,
      106
    rivalry  54, 195
single-parent families  133–46
social cognition  118, 119–20, 131
social competence  157, 159, 161, 162,
    170, 173
social psychology  251, 252–3
socioecological factors  51
sociograms  5

SOFA questionnaire  238, 239, 240, 241,
    242–3, 244
son
    father relationship  33–4, 157, 162–74
    mother relationship  158, 162–74
spatial representations  5–6, 97, 101–2,
    112–13, 124
SPRINT (systemic performance roles in
    interaction)  9, 213, 215–16,
    218–19, 221, 225, 227, 229
strangers  100, 106, 109, 114, 115
stress
    adolescent coping  157–74
    family  4–5, 33, 35, 154, 267
    identity development  250
structural perspective  28, 29–34, 49,
    234, 238
structured interviews
    follow-up  218, 220–1, 221–3
    relational diagnosis  64, 66
subsystems  29, 31
supervision  8, 18, 239, 247–61
Switzerland  93, 138, 184–91, 238, 271,
    275
symbiosis  94, 101, 136, 270
Symbol Figure Placement Technique
    (SFPT)  180, 181, 191, 204–5
System Oriented Family Analysis
    (SOFA) questionnaire  238, 239,
    240, 241, 242–3, 244
systemic theory  xix, 15, 28–43, 49, 146,
    172, 233

team development  250–61, 270
test instructions  7–11, 21–2, 42
test instruments  47, 61–7, 92, 138,
    213–15
test materials  7, 8, 23–7, 272
test procedure  7–12
test-retest stability  13, 50
Thailand  155
Thematic Apperception Test  58, 180
Thematische Gestaltungstest Salzburg
    (TGT-S)  138
theory, family  8, 45–7, 234, 268
theory of mind  71, 88, 118–31
therapeutic alliance  211, 212, 216–18
therapeutic baseline  240, 241
therapeutic discourse  217, 218, 224
therapeutic interventions  54, 211–12, 216,
    226–8, 238
therapeutic system  248, 249, 253–7, 270
therapists
    client relationship  253–5

family evaluation  46, 47, 51, 52, 55, 211
FAST procedure  8, 9, 18
personal development  247–61, 270
standardized measures  267, 277
three-generational family
   China  194–206, 274, 275
   Japan  179, 180, 181, 182, 190
time
   family structures  4, 179
   interactive treatment  212
   for test  6, 8
   theory of mind  130, 131
timidity  134
treatment
   efficacy  48, 52
   goals  212, 216, 221, 223, 226
   plan  211, 212, 226, 231, 233, 238
triad
   FAST development  269–70
   father image  133, 136–7, 138, 141, 144–5

UK
   bullying studies  109

family evaluation  46, 92
mother-dauther relations  150
perception of family  120
preschool children  73
studies  271
understanding other's view  107, 119–21, 125–6, 128–9
USA
   family evaluation  46, 92
   family structure  189, 205

victims, bullying  71, 107, 109, 110, 111, 113, 114
visuality  145–6

Ways of Coping questionnaire  162
Weinberger Adjustment Inventory  161
Weiss-Cerreto Marital Status Inventory  62
well-adjusted children  107, 109
well-functioning families  5, 16, 18, 157, 160, 170, 173
wellbeing, adolescents  164, 165, 166, 172, 173
widows  140, 141, 143, 145
workbooks  53–4

Printed in Great Britain
by Amazon